TALES FROM THE ENDLESS SEARCH FOR SPEED

By Dan Binks and Norm DeWitt

Foreword by Tommy Kendall

Publisher:
Norman L. DeWitt
3779 Milan St.
San Diego, CA 92107
USA

Printer:
CreateSpace, an Amazon company
4900 LaCross Road
North Charleston, SC 29406
USA

Date of Publication: December 2, 2013

ISBN 978-0-9911755-0-5

Dan Binks

ACKNOWLEDGEMENT

DAN BINKS

Special Thanks To:

My wife Sherri, my son Phil and my daughter Sara.

My parents, Marge and Phil Binks.

People who helped get me started in racing: Bob Swenson, Jim Bailey, The Brengle Family, Fuzzy Stewart and everyone from West Coast SCCA.

Gary Pratt, Jim Miller, Doug Louth, Bill Delong, Tom Mikrut and Everyone at Pratt & Miller. Phil Conti, Clayton Cunningham, Dave Draper, Jack Roush, Mark Honsowetz, Jim Durbin, Brad Hand, Rich Reichenback, Randy Goss, Mark Kent, Doug Fehan, Dave King, Frank Parker, Tom Ghent, Dave Henninger, Russ O'blenes, Rick Voegelin, Fritz Kayl, Warren Frieze, Norm DeWitt

A Special Thanks to all the drivers that I have had the pleasure of working with: John Morton, Bob Lobenberg, John Paul JR, Bill Adam, Ira Young, Jeff Kline, Jack Baldwin, Tommy Kendall, Max Jones, Paul Newman, Mark Martin, Robby Gordon, Jon Gooding, Greg Biffle, Kurt Busch, Kyle Busch, Chuck Hossfeld, Ron Fellows, Johnny O'Connel, Max Papis, Jan Magnussen, Olivier Beretta, Oliver Gavin, Tommy Milner, Antonio Garcia, Jordan Taylor, PJ Jones, Parnelli Jones, Doug Louth and Max Jones

To all the guys that have beat me. You make me want to keep coming back!

Norm DeWitt

ACKNOWLEDGEMENT

NORM DEWITT

Special thanks to the many racing legends who were so generous with their time in helping me with this book and withstanding my endless questions... Sir Stirling Moss, Phil Hill, Dan Gurney, Chris Amon, Vic Elford, Bob Bondurant, Sebastian Bourdais, Geoff Brabham, Tommy Kendall, Kenny Roberts, Don Garlits, Brian Redman, Nobby Clark, Stuart Graham, Roger Penske, Dick Guldstrand, Don Devendorf, Jean Alesi, Takuma Sato, Rubens Barrichello, Parnelli Jones, Greg Biffle, Joe Leonard, Paul Gentilozzi, Jorge Lorenzo, Rod Coleman, John Morton, Bobby Unser, Simon Pagenaud, Troy Corser, Davide Tardozzi, Allan McNish, Marc Lieb, Donald Davidson, Jan Magnussen, Scott Dixon, a slew of others.

Without the help of those on the engineering and manufacturing side of racing, this book would have been impossible. Special thanks to Gian Paolo Dallara, Andrea Vecchi, Gordon Kimball, Derrick Walker, Jeremy Burgess, Jack Roush, Trevor Harris, Ken Anderson, Andrew Heard, Rick Mayer, Jim Campbell, Ron Tauranac, Bob Liebeck, Ben Bowlby, Andrew "H" Smith, Massimo Meregalli, Simon Marshall, Michael Czysz, Michael Messina and Mauro Piccoli (Brembo), Paul Butler, Craig Hampson, Ammar Bazzaz, Hisatake Murata, Al Ludington, and Ulrich Baretzky, Wolfgang Ulrich, & Martin Muehlmeier of Audi

I am humbled to have the participation of the legendary front row of the 1991 75th running of the Indianapolis 500, Rick Mears, AJ Foyt, and Mario Andretti, along with my childhood hero Sir Jackie Stewart, who helped with this book and is the reason why "FASTER" is in the title.

CONTENTS

FOREWORD

The crew chiefs that had achieved legend status by the beginning of my career were the likes of Smokey Yunick, Dale Inman, the Wood Brothers and George Bignotti. Like the hero drivers of same era, they were on a pedestal that seemed sufficiently high such that no current wrenches could ever rise to their exalted level. A funny thing happens if you are lucky enough to hang around for a while. At some point you look up and twenty five years have passed and thousands of races have been run and won, and some of the same guys always seem to end up in victory lane. The success that follows them through a series of drivers, teams, series and leaves little doubt that they have had a disproportionate amount of influence in those successes. This is the case with Dan Binks.

My career could have taken a big turn the wrong way was when I left Clayton Cunningham's team (Malibu Grand Prix RX-7). I was with Chevy, and the first race with the Beretta was without him. He was like my security blanket, the guy who was there when I had come into my own, and he was a huge part of it. I couldn't get him to come at first, and it could have turned out way differently. When he wouldn't move from California to outside of Detroit, I didn't blame him. I knew that was a tall ask.

Binks was much better off not driving and I was much better off not working on cars. At Lime Rock we went golfing and Binks was driving the golf cart. We are coming down the hill towards the clubhouse and he started swerving to fish-tail the cart. One of the fish-tails hooked and it started to flip over. It landed on top of Binks and he's basically doing the splits underneath the cart with his head on his knee.

Dan Binks and Tommy Kendall

The golf bags looked like somebody just flung them, it was a total yard sale and we just howled laughing. Then on the 1989 Cars & Concepts Chevy Beretta, I was twisting on the Watts link trying to see its range. The jack came out and pinched my finger, and I had an indentation to match the links on either side. That's how we arrived at a deal... Binks works on them and doesn't drive them. From my standpoint it was 'I'll drive them and I won't work on them'.

By the time I retired in 1997, it was clear to me that Dan Binks was well on his way to becoming one of the most successful crew chiefs in sports car history. From 1986-1997, we conspired to win 9 championships and quite a few races, but what was a nice career for me was just a start for the Binkster. What makes him so special is a lot harder to quantify. While he never stops thinking about how to make his car unbeatable, he truly relishes the battle. Dan loves to mentor guys and for somebody who is such as competitor as he is, he's got a heart. The whole paddock is populated by guys who have worked under Dan. Brian Hoye is a good example, the crew chief on the #4 car which has had a hell of a run lately. Dan really loves it, he loves to compete and he loves that more than winning. Even if things go wrong he's still got a huge smile on his face. When I was doing it, I was all about the results. If I didn't do well, I was miserable. He is absolutely at his happiest when he totally exhausted at the end of a twenty-four hour race, having given his all to persevere. He is a rare mix of competitor, warrior, artist, innovator, leader, teacher, and entertainer. His competitive fire is hard to quantify.

Tommy Kendall

CHAPTER ONE

DAN BINKS

Dan Binks – 2007 GT1 Pratt and Miller Corvette

The family roots for Dan Binks guaranteed a fascination with speed and machinery. His Father, Phil Binks, had raced for years, perhaps the highlight being the race against Jack Brabham and Stirling Moss in the production car race at the 1960 Times Grand Prix at Riverside. Being raised down the road from Elkhart Lake, Wisconsin certainly didn't hurt. Phil – "I saw my first MGTC in Chicago and decided that someday I was going to own one of those, but the first race I saw wasn't until Palm Springs in 1952, when I was in the Navy. When I went back home, I saw the last Elkhart Lake race on the streets. In 1955 they had the first Road America race when I was working across the lake at the YMCA camp. I drove around the track when it was just gravel, and then again 2 weeks later when it was new asphalt."

1952 Elkhart Lake sports car races
– Photo courtesy of Phil Binks

"I had an MGTD at that time... 100 over, the head had been milled, a different cam, with a bunch of work done. In July of 1958 I went to Hourglass field in Mira Mesa. There were no driver's schools in those days, you showed up as a novice and they let you drive. But, there was one, called the Road Race Training Association. The instructors were Sam Hanks and Ken Miles. Ken was my instructor, and was my racing hero. Years later when I got my Dolphin Formula Junior, I found out that I had the ex-Ken Miles car, which was really neat."

Phil Binks working on his hotrod MGTD – 1958

Marge Binks – "We met at Del Mar. He said to me – 'I understand you are getting a Sprite." As it turned out, Phil Binks had purchased the first Bugeye Sprite in San Diego. Phil – "There was this new car coming out and it was going to be 1500-1600 dollars. So, I went down to the Austin-Healey dealership to get my name on the list early in the spring of 1958. I went up to the owner of the local dealership, Palmer Hughes, and said 'Hi Mr. Hughes, I want to be on the list for that new Austin-Healey they are going to make.' He said 'I don't have a list.' I told him... 'You do now.' I went to Santa Barbara for the races and there were two factory Austin Sprites there, and they won H production. I took delivery in August 1958, put as many miles as possible on it, and started racing it that September. It was lighter than the MGTD and less powerful, but around Hourglass field it was 10 seconds a lap faster. It was also my 'go to work' car."

Marge – "Phil said that he had a Sprite and that started us talking... one thing led to another."

Pit Pass and Course Worker credentials – 1958

"When Phil and I started dating, he drove his car to the race track, I drove my car to the race track, and my car just became the spare parts. I had planned to go to driver's school, but my father had different ideas. Phil and I ended up getting married. Dan was born in 1963." The acorn didn't fall far from the tree. Phil – "We had a 62 Volkswagen with a seat belt I put in back for Dan. I'm thinking about the new baby (Molly), got into a corner too fast, and I lose the Volkswagen. The rear end comes around and I'm fighting to keep from doing something really stupid, and from the back seat I hear this little voice 'Go Dad Go.' He was about 15 months old."

Phil and Marge Binks

Academics weren't the strong point in these early years, much being focused around a lack of reading ability. Marge – "His teacher told me she didn't care if he was reading Playboy magazine, as long as he would read it and could tell me what he read." Dan – "There was nothing that was ever officially diagnosed, but I really struggled."

Sadly, dealing with undiagnosed learning disabilities was hardly something unique. Sir Jackie Stewart similarly struggled mightily in his grade school years. Jackie - "When you are dyslexic, and you suffer the humiliation to the level that you do by your teachers and your peers, as it moves from the classroom to the playground, you are driven to be better than anybody else at what you do, whenever possible. Even at the menial tasks... I often say that I clean windows better than anybody else, because I want to be sure there aren't any streaks left. When I was at school, if I had left the window streaked, I would have been criticized and therefore punished for it. I learned that if I was going to clean a window, I would have to clean it perfectly. The same applied to floors... I'm very good at floors (laughs). So therefore, you go about your business in a totally different way I think, than a normally educated and scholastically competent person."

For Jackie, being a then-undiagnosed dyslexic had inspired him to raise the level of his game through what became a characteristically overwhelming attention to detail. Stewart – "No question, it raises your game because one of the other things is that you failed consistently as a younger person at school... you are a failure. Therefore when you find yourself doing something where people give you recognition and praise for, I think it probably amounts to 3 or 4 times the amount of appreciation that you would receive vs. a person with no learning problems. So, you try harder. In my case, when I was serving gas, or checking the tire pressures in a customer's car, checking the radiator water level, windshield washer levels, oil on the dipstick... all these things I did with more commitment. Therefore, I got more tips. And the first car I ever bought was bought from tips earned while working at a garage serving petrol. So, you do try harder and that falls into anything else you do. When I went Olympic trap shooting, I shot for Scotland and then Great Britain. I put more into my trap shooting than probably I ever did into my own motor racing, because it was the first thing I was any good at. I won the Scottish, the English, the Welsh, the Irish, the British, the European and Mediterranean Coupe des Nations... I won all of those through real determination, commitment, and dedication. I probably put more into it, than the more skilled individuals."

That same quality applied to Stewart's car racing. Jackie - "By the time I got into driving racing cars, and keep in mind at that time there were no sponsors in it, I therefore went about the business of making sure that my car was well prepared for each event that I took part in. Even when I started to drive for other people who were inviting me to drive their cars, I would make a stronger effort perhaps than other drivers, because I felt that I had to continue to prove myself. Attention to detail is one of the assets that I think people with dyslexia have over the other folk, because they are so clever that they don't need attention to detail... they don't think. In my life, I can't deal with open loops; I've got to close all the loops."

Dan Binks was to find his calling in directing his focus to taking apart whatever contraption passed his way. Marge – "The first time I can remember him taking apart something was at 8 years old. So, we had a rule at the house, that he couldn't take anything apart, or fix anything, until he could read it and show us in words how he would fix it. He could always take anything apart and fix it without looking at the instructions. We had to force him to read. He could do all the math in the world, but reading was like pulling teeth."

Dan specialty soon moved from taking apart everything in sight, to fabricating whatever met the need of the day. Marge – "Kathryn (Dan's youngest sister) had just gotten a tricycle for her birthday. Dan conned her out of it, took it apart, turned it over, and made a big wheel out of it. When Dan was in Jr. High, he made a sidecar for his bicycle. He took it to Holtville, we figured, 'how bad could it get?' Dan started giving people rides, lifting the sidecar up in the air. It wasn't long before every kid in the neighborhood had to have a sidecar, so Dan was making those."

Phil Binks- "One time I came home, and Danny was 9 or 10 at the most. The garage door was open, I happened to be in the neighborhood on a job. There were 3 kids sitting on the front lawn, and Danny is working on the lathe. Open gears, flat belt drive... an ancient very scary lathe. He had watched me work on the lathe but he had no permission to use it. He looked over at me, and keeps working... well the smoke is coming out my ears. Pretty soon he takes the part out... there was an axle for a kid's bike that was galled, he was cleaning it up to put it back together. I asked him why the kids were sitting in the yard. Dan said 'Well, when I'm working on the lathe, I make them stay in the front yard so they don't bother me and cause me to make a mistake.' It took all the wind out of my sails, what was I going to say? I told him 'for God's sake, don't tell your Mom.'"

Of course it wasn't long before Dan got his fingers caught in the lathe, coming at the worst possible moment. Marge – "It was the day that Grandma Binks had died. When we came home, Dan wasn't there, and Catherine was acting really strange. She was about 10, and Dan had been teaching her how to drive, so he wanted her to drive him to the hospital. Catherine called Nadeen Brengle, who then took him to the hospital. They've sewn his fingers back on... and now his hands are all bandaged up like a boxer. At this point, I'm ready to kill Dan, because the kid doesn't listen to anything I say to him." Phil – "It's hard to turn the lathe off, when both your hands are caught in it."

The bicycles eventually led to an off-road motorcycle. Phil – "Dan wanted to buy this motorcycle from a friend of ours, a Steen's Hodaka with the earl's forks for $250." Marge – "I told him if he could save up $250, he could buy it and I would buy all the safety equipment. I figured I was safe because this was a kid that couldn't get 4 quarters together, much less $250. Well, it didn't take him any time at all…"

Dan's first car was a Fiat. Phil – "It was a 600 sedan, but it was made to look like an Abarth with the rear deck lid open. He had all the kids at his High School convinced that it could do a wheelie, he had taken a picture of it with the front end of the car jacked up, it wasn't doing a wheelie at all… he was always screwing with people. That was the one he got caught going 100mph on Balboa Ave. with." Dan – "It was a car we got from Bill Haneline Jr. He felt bad for me and sold me this car for 5 or 600 bucks. It had an electrical problem and those Fiats had toggle switches… everything I tried was just more and more expensive, so I finally said 'screw it."

It was time for plan B. Marge – "He rewired it with that cheap TV antenna wire; it was all he could afford." Dan – "My Dad had this spool of antenna wire and I just ran that thing all around the car, I hooked up the taillights and headlights… everything onto that one wire with one regular switch. Just using the s**t that my Dad had in the garage."

Dan Binks' first car, and first race car. A Fiat 600

The next casualty was a highly modified MG Midget, with large sway bars front and rear. Dan – "My Dad was still trying to drive the MG, but it ended up being too much of a hassle. It sat in my Dad's garage for maybe 10 years, he had visions of racing it, but it never ran and he never had the money for it. We just worked on it a little bit at a time. The Midget was pretty straightforward, with an H Production motor that was 11:1. There was a big cam from Schneider, in those days you could walk in and Dave would give you a deal if you were a young kid. Those Midgets, they didn't want to get rolling from a stoplight or whatever, you had to rev them to the moon and let the clutch out, or just try to be out of everybody's way. It was fun, and I just revved the s**t out of that thing. It was a decent car, it wasn't rusted or anything. I never piled it up, other than when I rolled it over. It's one of those things that I probably shouldn't have lived through, but I did for whatever reason."

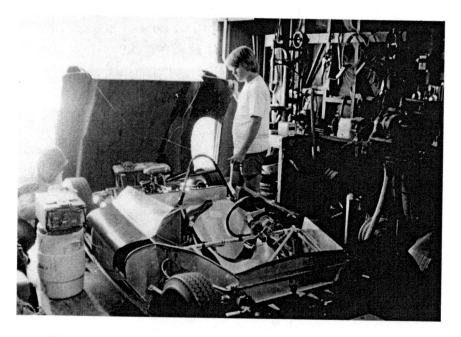

Teenage Dan Binks plotting his next escapade in the Dolphin

The Brengles had 5 boys, and then Danny was somewhere in the middle. Marge – "Dan's sisters Molly and Kathryn always said they had 6 brothers." The potential for vehicular mayhem had increased exponentially. There were also the times when Dan got into Phil's private reserve, taking the 1962 Dolphin sports racer out to the local late night car cruise meet in a local parking lot. Marge - "Danny had waited until we went to sleep, came outside, opened the garage and pushed the car down the street. They put flashlights on the top of the front fenders and I think it was David Brengle who was with Danny when they took the car to Fed-Mart to cruise. It had a phony license plate that said 'Dolphin'. Another time he took the car to high school."

Molly, Dan, and Kathryn Binks

Marge - "Officer Bob would come to the door and ask 'Mrs. Binks, whose car is he driving today?' The police would tell him his car doesn't have windshield wipers. I'd ask them, 'Was he speeding this time? Well then we are making progress!' One time the police were chasing him down Clairemont Mesa Blvd for speeding in the MG Midget. It didn't have the windshield on so he pulled under a semi and hid. He got caught once going 100+mph on Balboa, the only thing that saved him that time was the Police Officers Association sticker that belonged to Uncle Jack, on the back window. They told him 'The only reason your ass isn't going to jail today is because of Uncle Jack.' Dan was on a first name basis with every police officer in San Diego County."

Binks in Fuzzy Stewart's Datsun 1600 Roadster G Production

The racing started early for Dan Binks, racing autocross across the parking lot of the local football stadium. "I drove Fuzzy Stewart's Honda 600 in the 24 hour slalom autocross race at San Diego Stadium back in the 1970s. It had all these big lights on it, and I didn't even have my driver's license yet. He asked me at about 9 at night if I wanted to drive the car." Resolving chassis issues in those early autocross days wasn't terribly advanced. Dan – "We just drove around the problems. We thought we knew... but we didn't."

Dan lived in perpetual maniac mode driving a black VW GTI around town like he stole it. He finished up high school, and started his collegiate phase. Marge – "One day in the summer of 1983 we get a call from Jim Bailey... Bob Swenson had given him Dan's name, and he wanted to offer Dan a job in Los Angeles. Swenson told him 'you'd better call his Mom first, because she wants him to go to college.' If I said no, I'd lose a son... Dan would never forgive me. If I said yes, I'd lose a son, because he's going to move to LA. Phil said 'you know what you've got to do...' Dan was working at a garage down in Pacific Beach doing oil changes, and tune-ups, and he didn't get home until 7pm. They talked on the phone that night, and he went up the next day for the interview. He had 3 days to pack and move to LA."

Dan could finally have that chance to make his mark in auto racing, and he threw himself into that opportunity with total and complete dedication, much as Stewart had done 20 years previously. Jackie Stewart - "When I joined Ken Tyrrell, that was a big learning curve for me, as it was when I joined Ecurie Ecosse before Tyrrell, because Ecurie Ecosse had already won Le Mans twice. I joined them because of being a Scottish driver, and they were already a really professional team and I learned a lot from them as they had previously had very experienced drivers. When I went to Ken Tyrrell, I was going to another level. It was a works Formula 3 chassis and John Cooper himself was very keen that one of his cars was doing well, and I was the one at that time. And I was with Tyrrell all the way through to the end of my career. So, you do try harder and you are more dedicated. And when success comes, I don't think you get as intoxicated by it, as some folks do. Because you think 'I'm going to fail again, so I'm going to keep trying harder.'"

Dan Binks – "Bob Swenson was a family friend who had been involved with my Dad in Fiat powered Dolphins and all that. He saw that I tried and worked hard. Jim Bailey was the crew chief with Phil Conte, and he and Bob had been friends since the late 1960s. Bailey called me up and said "Swenson tells me you can turn a wrench" and got me in, so that was when I started paying attention to details... at Phil's."

The Conte Racing Lola T-600 with Dan Binks, mechanic

Dan quickly made a favorable impression, quickly progressing from team go-fer to working on the car. Marge — "Bailey was an interesting man. He said to Dan, 'don't get suckered in with all these guys and all their BS. There are only certain people in this field that you ever want to listen to, and I'll tell you who they are.' Danny respected Jim Bailey enough that he did whatever Bailey told him to do, and listen to whoever Bailey told him to listen to. I have to credit Bob Swenson for having the foresight to see what he saw in Dan, and I credit Bailey for really giving him the groundwork education in automotive preparation. He put him with the best fabricators, the best people in the field. A self-taught guy, he knew the best from the rest."

All one has to do is to review the highly publicized prosecutions that followed, to reach the obvious conclusion that many of the teams racing at the highest levels in IMSA were funded by the drug trade. Bailey was right, as in many ways the series had become a playground for folks that you didn't want anything to do with. Despite all the distractions, Dan was completely engrossed with the preparation of the cars.

As with Danny Sullivan, who used to sweep the floor at the Tyrrell factory and eventually ended up driving for the team in Formula One, Dan made the most of his first big break, willing to work crazy hours and do whatever it took for the cars to be prepared to their highest level, in particular the Lola T-600, a game changer in it's day. Dan - "They were running in IMSA GTP with a Lola T-600 for drivers Bob Lobenberg and John Morton. They ran 3 or 4 races with a Can-Am car as well, a Lola T-333 Frissbee."

John Morton — "My first 2 years with Phil Conte were my Can-Am team, running the Frissbee. I was always looking for sponsorship, and I'd already gotten the Frissbee when I first met Phil. I set up a meeting with him, and he was very enthusiastic and nice, but he said 'I couldn't put any of my own money into it. The most I could ever put in was 5000 dollars, but I'll write letters for you.' We became friends, but 5000 dollars won't get you very far. Phil Conte got that T-600 because he had traded an old Mirage to Carl Haas for the rolling chassis. It was Phil's first foray, although he had been my sponsor with the Can Am car the previous 2 years. He decided he wanted it to be his team, so we kind of switched positions, and I was the driver for him."

Lola had introduced the mid engine prototype ground effects car to the IMSA series in 1981, with the introduction of the T-600. The success of the GTP class that proved the launching point for Dan Binks' career might never have happened if it weren't for an injury suffered by Brian Redman in a Can-Am car, followed by a number of highly unlikely events. Brian – "In 1977, they changed the rules for Can-Am and made us put bodywork on our open wheel single seat F5000 cars. At the first race for the new season at St. Jovite, Canada, I saw the new car for the first time. I went out and spent 15 or 20 minutes in it, it was prepared by Jim Hall of Chaparral Cars. I came in the pits, and Jim said 'how is it?' It was good, I really didn't want anything but I wanted a bit less downforce on the front of the car, to take ¼" off the front wing. On the next lap at 170mph it took off, went about 40 feet into the air, turned upside down and then came down. That broke my neck (C-1), smashed my left shoulder, broke 3 ribs, my heart stopped, and the ambulance blew a tire on the way to the hospital."

Brian – "A year later, here I am... I've been badly injured, not earning anything, 2 children away at school... I had to sell my 917 Porsche, which I'd been keeping as a long term investment. By 1979 I was really feeling the pressure of not earning anything. I told my wife that I either had to go work for Lola Cars in Huntington or Carl Haas in Highland Park, Illinois. I'd gotten three Formula 5000 championships for Carl Haas and Jim Hall, so I rang up Carl. He told me I could come sell Lola cars for 30,000 dollars a year. I said 'including a car?' No car. Well, after I got there John Bishop brought out new rules for GTP. IMSA was trying to break Porsche domination as they had won every race for 4 years. So, I went to Carl and said 'Lola can build a car with a Chevy or Ford engine that can win this new championship. Carl said – 'Go see Eric Broadley, and while you are there see this fellow John Bright who is looking for a job'. So, I went to Lola, and Eric said 'I need an order for 2 cars for 75,000 dollars each, they won't be modified T-70s, they will be completely new cars.' So, I went back to Carl fully convinced that as the Lola importer, that he would order the cars."

First T-600 at Lola with Eric Broadley
– Photo courtesy of Lola Heritage

It didn't work out that way. Redman – "Carl said 'I'm not ordering them, but you find somebody to buy the first 2, and I'll split the profit with you on future sales.' So, I got Roy Woods and Ralph Cooke to agree to buy the cars. When they bought the cars Carl said to me, 'What are you going to do, manage it?' I told him, 'Manage it? I'm going to drive it.' John Bright started work on it in December of 1980 and I told him to have the car here in March, regardless of what Eric says. Eric is a notorious changer of things, changing everything all the time. The 2 cars came out, we tested at Sears Point and the car was pretty good. It had big tunnels, but nobody really knew how to do those things so the ground effects weren't very much. The state of the knowledge about underbody ground effects was very low. We were going to run the Riverside 6 hours, but we didn't know anything about the 350 Chevy, or the new Hewland gearbox, the VG. We didn't know anything about reliability, so we decided to enter it at Laguna Seca in a one hour race. The pressure was tremendous. The night before the race Carl Haas came up to me, took the cigar out of his mouth and said 'Brian, if this car doesn't win tomorrow, Lola Cars is going bankrupt.' We qualified 5th because the Porsche turbos could turn up the boost for a short period, to get 800 horsepower. It was ok, as we had 600hp, which we would have all the way through the race."

One can assume that given what was at stake, Carl Haas had a longer than usual conversation with the car before the race. Brian – "Early in the race I could feel a wiggle going into turn 2, and I knew it was either a loose wheel or a flat, but if I stopped in a 100 mile race, there was no way to get back. I dropped back to about 10th place but then on the 12th lap, the car was ok. I caught up John Paul Jr., the leader in the 935, and took the lead with a few laps to go. It was a great first race for a new car." As it turned out, a wheel nut had loosened and then retightened itself. "John Bright said it was his fault, he hadn't tightened the wheel nut properly before the race. It came off, broke the safety clip off, and then wound itself back on again. The next day the car was up on jack stands and I looked at the left rear wheel nut and said to Eric Broadley 'take a look at that!' Eric bent down, studied it, stood up, took his glasses off and said 'Yes, Brian. That's what's supposed to happen, but I've never seen it happen before.' The T-600 was a good basic race car, it didn't really have any faults and we had some great races with it… and at Laguna Seca, Carl sold 3 cars!"

Brian continues - "It really was a very small operation at Cooke-Woods, John Bright did a fantastic job of maintaining it through the season, as we didn't have a spare engine and had about 3 or 4 guys. We finished 2nd at the 6 Hours of Mosport, the following weekend was Road America… another 6 hour race. Following the race at Mosport, the guys took the engine out and flew it to Midland, Texas (Chaparral). We went to Chicago as fast as we could and went to Carl Haas' workshop where the car was completely stripped. Everything came off and was crack tested. The engine came back on Thursday afternoon, by Friday morning at 8AM we were at Road America ready for the first practice session." Brian Redman went on to claim the series championship. At the end of the season Brian retired from the sport, going out on top.

Thanks to Redman and the T-600, prototypes had returned to American endurance racing where they remain up through today. John Morton – "Being the first of anything it's got an advantage at first, as in 81 with Redman when it won the Championship, but there were no other GTP cars at the time and Brian was the impetus for building that car in the first place. The T-600 wasn't the best car for the time (1983) compared to the March; it didn't have as much grip."

Regardless of his increased opportunities in car preparation, nothing much changed with Dan's driving habits. John Morton – "At Daytona we were running the Lola T-600, Phil Conte and I had gone out to dinner and we were driving back to the hotel when we see a truck blast out of a gas station burning rubber, hauling ass up the road. Phil says – 'That's my truck.' It was Danny. When we got back to the hotel, I don't know what Phil said to him… it was getting caught with your pants down. He was a little on the wild side, and has come a long way from racing Fiats."

The IMSA GTP Conte Lola T-600

Dan – "When we got to the race track, we never did have enough guys so I started working on the car. One thing led to another, and they figured out that I could change an upright or bleed the brakes, getting everything ready for the mechanics. It became apparent to them that I wasn't your average kid, I'd spent a lot of time working with Fuzzy Stewart, my Dad, and Wayne Mitchell, and so I knew what needed to be done. I was rough around the edges, I'd come in late… but I didn't mind working hard and staying there late stay there and doing whatever needed to be done. It might be midnight, it might be all night, you just don't know. All the other guys went home, but I'd stay there. Jim Bailey and I worked real close together, and that is probably what paid off for me, as he got to where he'd trust me. At Conte after about 6 months I was more like the car chief. There wasn't enough people to have titles, I think there ended up being 4 of us, and we had a couple of 'fly-in' guys at the races."

With those big V8 powered Can-Am and Prototype IMSA racers, Dan had started at the highest levels of American sports car racing. Dan – "They both had Chevrolets in them and were kind of cool. We raced against the VDS guys, with the history of them… Count Van Der Straten. Morton was the development driver, Lobenberg was young, wild, and crazy… he just drove around everything."

Binks using the radar gun during a test with Conte Racing

Dan Binks – "The Lola T-600 we had was actually built for Danny Ongais, it was the very last one built and was delivered to us in black. Holbert was the target, and once in a while we could get close to him." John Morton – "It was a little obsolete, but it wasn't that far off when we first got it. It never was a horribly good car, but we did 8 races with it. It never won a race although we led Daytona and Sebring with it."

The T-600 in its 3rd season was no match for Al Holbert in the Porsche powered March 83G. Dan – "You know... Lobenberg was wild enough and crazy enough to try and keep up for a while. Morton wasn't going to drive that close to the edge, tear Phil's stuff up, and not get a ride." A common combination, the wily veteran teamed with the fearless new talent... but saddled with an elderly T-600 it was not going to work. Dan Binks – "Well, Lobenberg was fast but he had a lot of distractions. John Morton was awesome. Lobenberg could let it rip for a few laps, but 40 laps into it he didn't anymore. Morton could just do it over and over, he was consistent... just awesome." So if it was the Runoffs, you'd want Lobenberg in the car, but if it was an Enduro, you'd want Morton? Dan – "Exactly."

John Morton – "Dan was kind of a beginner in a way, he was just this chubby little kid that liked racing. He actually wanted to drive himself... he had done some driving and he was really pretty darn good, but he didn't really have the physique for it (smiles). Dan was good, but he wasn't the dead serious guy that he became later... he was just a fun loving kid who was devoted to it. He came by it naturally; his whole family was involved in racing."

Dan – "We ran part of the season in 83, and then most of 84. As it was the very last T-600, Lola was done with it and they were moving on and building new cars. In the end Chris Cord was making parts because Lola wouldn't get them to us. Joe Cavaglieri was fabricating all the suspension, rocker arms, and the stuff for the Frissbee."

Mid 1984 brought Tony Adamowicz to Conte racing alongside Morton. The two had previously teamed up for the Daytona 24 Hrs race in 1979 driving Otto Zipper's borderline ancient front engine Ferrari Daytona. The night before that race, Zipper had died and the team ran the old Ferrari with a black stripe across the hood to a near win. Tony refers to it as a Rocky Balboa effort that was robbed of victory, when the broken but winning Interscope 935 coasted dead stick across the finish line.

Adamowicz recalls his arrival at Conte Racing – "My job was not necessarily to re-design the car, my job was to drive the car. It was like the problem I'd had in my entire racing career; you got in the car and drove it. There was no practice, no tests. Had we had more time and budget to do that it would have improved our situation quite a bit. But John and I were competent drivers and paired well together, we'd already proved in 79 that we could drive together. John isn't a big complainer and neither am I, so we drove around the problems. The T-600 wasn't up to snuff, it wasn't competitive, but that all changed with the March."

Binks at Conte Racing

Binks continues – "We ran in 85 with a March-Buick powered GTP car... John Paul Jr. and Tony Adamowicz drove it. At Daytona we blew up, it was a disaster. We put 6 engines in, I think we actually put a blown up one back in, because we lost track of all the engines. They hired a new guy (in place of Jim Bailey), who I didn't see eye to eye with. When I'd go into the office to talk to him, he'd be cleaning his 45. I was 21 years old, was probably a bigger pain in the ass than I could have been, but I could have helped him and he didn't want the help. I saw the handwriting on the wall that it was falling apart, and decided to go someplace where I was wanted."

Mid 1985 was the beginning of the Malibu Grand Prix RX-7 era for Binks. Dan – "Jeff Kline called me, and I had known him a little bit through club racing, and he asked me if I would come over to work there. I went over there and had lunch with him, and he told me it paid around 500 dollars a week. I was only making $275 a week at Phil's. A career move and I was in a bad time not getting along with the guys and not making any money. I thought I had made it, man."

This was 'driver' money, for the time. Dan had only been in professional racing for a couple of years at this point, and in contrast team driver Jack Baldwin had spent 15 years trying to get such an opportunity. Jack Baldwin – "They were paying me 25 grand a year. That was my break, after years of struggling." For Baldwin it was a chance with a top team in a professional series, and by this point his racing career had already spanned 15 years.

Jack Baldwin - "The 1972 US Formula Ford Championships was held at Mid-America. It was a race where they invited past champions, current champions, the top points holders... they picked the best drivers and since I was the Southeastern division champion, I got invited. I was on the pole; it was one of those classic races where the positions swapped every lap. I ended up winning by a car length, so I was the US Formula Ford Champion. It was all about getting picked for the Formula Ford Festival over in England. Every country, depending on the size of the country, could send up to 3 drivers. I was supposed to be driving a factory Titan, but when I went over there was no factory Titan. I shipped my engine over… but the car was so bad that I wouldn't even put the engine into this piece of crap. Still, I was actually doing pretty good, but there was a big crash in the second turn on the first lap and I got nailed. When I got back I thought… I'm 23 and the US Champion, this is going to open some doors."

The doors did not open. All anyone wanted to know was how much money he could bring to a team. Trying to scratch out a living, at one time Baldwin had the merchandising rights for his good friend Evel Kneivel. Later, Baldwin spent years in the rock & roll T-shirt business. Jack – "My accounts were Aerosmith, Kiss, Boston, and Ted Nugent… in Atlanta I had the largest T-shirt store in America, across the street from the largest record store in the country. But once I realized that this wasn't going to get me to where I wanted to go in racing, I got out. My whole goal was to sponsor myself, because I was pretty frustrated. I just couldn't get any traction or find a sponsor. I drove the car, worked on the car, towed the car… that was the world we lived in. I'd get a ride here, a ride there, but never enough to make a difference."

A longtime friend from Tampa, Joe Varde had put together a Dodge Daytona, and he asked Baldwin to help him with it for the Champion Spark Plug Challenge series in 1983. At this point, Baldwin was flat broke and 34 years old. Jack – "Every time I would get to drive a car, I would take it to the front. Damn… I know I can do this! But, I decided I would give myself one more month… and if it didn't work out, I would have to find a job and move on. I got on the phone, round the clock. Ira Young asked me 'what is it about you that should make me pick you as a driver?' I told him - because I want to win… and I will win. He told me that we had a deal. I will never forget that moment."
Jack Baldwin won the 1984 IMSA GTU Championship.

Jack Baldwin leads at Watkins Glen 1985
– Photo courtesy of Jack Baldwin

Needless to say, Binks couldn't have found a hungrier driver to work with than Jack Baldwin. Also, for Dan, his previous work on the GTP prototypes was perfect training, as the team ran not only the sports car, but also had a prototype. Dan Binks – "Ira and Lori Young owned Malibu Grand Prix; I worked on both the Camel Lights car, and the RX-7. I worked with Clayton Cunningham, who did Bob Reed's stuff, and had Jack Baldwin and Jeff Kline in the Mazda GTU RX-7, and then Tommy Kendall after that. Jeff and Jack also drove the Camel Lights car. With the lights car, we actually won Mid-Ohio in 1985, with a Mazda powered Alba."

The busy schedule did nothing to slow the creativity when it came to playing jokes upon others in the team. Phil Binks – "One of the drivers for Clayton Cunningham was always complaining about the car. Well, they took his rental car and put acetylene in the headlights. You take an automatic center-punch and put a little hole in the headlight. Fill the headlight with oxygen and acetylene. Then put a piece of magic tape over the hole and wait for the driver to turn the headlights on. They didn't expect it to blow the entire front end and bumper off the car. He called the rental agency saying that all he did was turn on the headlights, and the whole front of the car blew off. Must have been a power surge… (laughs)."

For 1985, Dan Binks was also preparing a Sports 2000 car at the Runoffs, for Bill Fickling… and mentioned after the race that the car had finished "First Loser". When Dan said that, it was obvious that he was going places in the sport, with the highest of expectations. Binks was to win his first professional championship later that year with Jack Baldwin, who was the most successful driver on the Clayton Cunningham team in the mid 80s, through sheer determination and driving skill rather than finesse.

Jack Baldwin 84-85 IMSA GTU Champ
– Photo courtesy of Jack Baldwin

Dan Binks – "We won GTU in the Mazda for 85 with Jack Baldwin… he made it work for him, I won probably 10 races with Jack. He was an interesting guy to work with, as he didn't care that much about the car, he wasn't that picky. In those days, I don't think the drivers knew what the car could do… that it could be that much better. Jack had been driving the Peerless Camaro and our RX-7… those cars just weren't that good. We tried hard to work with him on setup but as a development driver it just didn't work, he'd say things like "Yeah… it might be better… might be worse…" In those eras before on-board computers and telemetry, your only guide to improving the car other than driver input, was the stopwatch.

Tommy Kendall in the Malibu Grand Prix RX-7 at Cleveland '86
– Photo courtesy of Mark Windecker

What isn't commonly known is that Dan Binks was once listed as a co-driver at the 24 Hours of Daytona. Phil Binks – "They wanted him in case the car quit out on a corner, then he could go out and work on it… but he actually drove. He called me and said, 'Dad, I'm 12 seconds slower than John Morton.' I asked him how many laps he'd had, and told him that Morton has had DAYS around that track."

For 1986, Tommy Kendall came onto the team. Dan – "Jeff Kline had moved on, and this kid comes into the shop… his Dad is with him, and had a few bucks. At the end of 85, I think his Dad gave us 100,000 dollars." So, was Dan Binks having one of those moments where he felt like Crew Chief for the rich kid of the month? "Exactly… I'm wondering what I'd gotten myself into."

Tommy Kendall – "The other side of it was that I'd been racing a little bit of Jim Russell stuff. I'd run a season of the school and a season of the Pro series. I also ran 4 races in '85 with my Dad's team in an older RX-7… an old Trinity car built by Dave Kent. I was getting ready to do the same thing again for 1986, but I overheard a call at our shop. Somebody called and our crew chief Paul Kopina picked up the phone and said 'no, I don't know of anyone' and hung up. I asked 'who was that?' Paul said 'It was Clayton Cunningham, and Jack Baldwin is leaving. Mazda is in, Firestone is in, but they are looking for a driver who had a little bit of funding to go with that.' Baldwin had won the prior 2 titles. Ira Young owned the team but was stepping back and it was Clayton's team in 1986."

This was beyond opportune, as Malibu Grand Prix team was the pinnacle of GTU, and obviously Kendall was pursuing it. Tommy – "I thought 'Oh My God', so I found out more details. Basically they needed 100,000 dollars to make up the budget shortfall. What we were going to spend to run 4 races in my Dad's car, it was about the same that they wanted to run 17 races in the factory championship winning RX-7. I went to my Dad and he said that sounds good. So, we went to Mazda and they said they don't want a young driver, they preferred older owner-operators… the Amos Johnson, Roger Mandeville, etc… that type. They were looking at Bob Reed, who was a Dentist and they were probably going to go with him if he came up with the funding. But, they said 'we need a 3rd driver for Daytona and Sebring.' So it was Reed, John Hogdal, and me, and we finished 2nd at Daytona. At Miami, I was running my Dad's RX-7. Clayton fielded it, so it was run under CCR colors, but Reed was running the Malibu car. To be honest I never thought about what it was like for their side with me coming in."

Dan Binks – "We go to Daytona with the RX-7 and the thing isn't very good but we've got great power. Tommy had run pretty good, and at Daytona we finished 2nd. The next race was Miami and it was a sprint race, he was driving by himself in a GTO/GTU race. Mark Honsowitz would change the front tires and I would change the rears. Tommy raced his ass off, and I think he finished 3rd. We walked up to the car after the race where it was parked in the pit lane, and Honsowitz walks up to him and says 'What was the matter?' Here's Kendall thinking he had the best race of his life, and it was like a lightbulb moment for Tommy that these guys expect a lot."

Kendall – "I was happy because it was the best I'd ever finished, I think it was 4th. He said 'What's wrong?' I thought, 'what do you mean what's wrong? I thought that was awesome!" Binks – "From then on Tommy figured it out, that every time we go, we plan on winning. Tommy was just devastated. You couldn't have hit him any harder in the stomach. He was thinking 'that wasn't good enough?' But that set the tone and from then on, that guy gave 110% every time, and he was awesome."

Tommy Kendall – "Then we went to Sebring and had a big lead until we basically had another engine change, same as at Daytona, and we finished 2nd. After Sebring, I was leading the points and Reed couldn't or didn't come up with the money. So we went back to Mazda and they said 'No, we really don't like the idea of young racers' which is ironic compared to what happens now with the obsession over youth where if you can even reachthe pedals, they want you. But, they agreed to 2 more races at Atlanta and Riverside, where I think I was 2nd in both of those.

I was still leading the points, but even though Reed was pretty much out of the picture, but Mazda still didn't want me in the car as I was too young. They said they still don't like it, but said ok to 2 more races, and go to Laguna Seca."

Kendall was beginning to pass the audition, although it was to result in an extremely awkward situation at Charlotte. Tommy - "We came to Laguna and I won… it was our first win, and then we went to Charlotte. It was supposed to be a 2 driver race with Reed, as he was in for the longer races at Charlotte and Elkhart. But, I'd won at Laguna and the team was kind of getting behind me now. So, I got in the car and it was either Danny or Clayton who said 'At the pit stop, Reed thinks he's getting in the car, but he's not. Just don't get out at the pit stop.' At the pit stop he's there with his helmet. I won Charlotte and after that they decided that I'm in for the year. We won the Championship." Binks - "We won 3 or 4 times that year and won the Championship in '86 with Tommy and again in 87. Tommy and I raced together until 1997."

Kendall at Mid-Ohio '86 in the Malibu Grand Prix Mazda RX-7
— Photo courtesy of Mark Windecker

Kendall, although still enjoying great success, had noted the age of the equipment. "The car was in its 5th season by then, I mean that car was tired. Downing had built it and won the championship with it. Then he ran it another year, finished 3rd, and then Baldwin won 2 championships with it in '84 and '85. Then I got into it and won the championship with it in '86 and '87. The new car wasn't finished until the last race of 1987."

The following year brought an initial split between Kendall and Binks. Dan – "I stayed at Clayton Cunningham's shop and for 1988 Tommy left, he went with the Cars & Concepts Chevrolet Beretta. Kendall called me up and said 'Hey, what do you think about moving to Michigan, I could really use your help?' I told him that I was a California guy, and don't really want to go to Michigan, although the whole factory team thing seemed like it was kind of cool. When Tommy Kendall calls you and says he needs some help, you've got to listen, because he's such an enabling driver. When I came from Clayton's, I went to Cars and Concepts, and they didn't want to pay me what I had asked for. I went there for way less money; it was kind of screwed up... I said, 'ok, pay me what you want to pay me, but if we win the championship, I get the whole thing plus some.' I made that deal with Tony Coullier and Dave Draper. When I got there they were in a heap of big trouble. It was a fast car with a whole bunch of problems. They might have won the championship without me, but I doubt it."

Tommy – "With Cars and Concepts Beretta, we won the first race at Miami right out of the box which was good. It was built by Peerless, who had built Baldwin's car in GTO. It had a transaxle with the gearbox in the back, and a carbon tunnel. It was a very important program for Chevy as it was the first time the marketing was overtly tied to the production car. Cars and Concepts were making a Limited Edition Beretta GTU for Chevrolet. It was a big program for Chevy. Before that Chevy factory racing was always back door, and this was the first time that it was above board and officially involved with racing. I wanted Dan to come with me, but he didn't want to. He switched over before Sebring, and I realized how important he was to my deal."

Kendall and Binks celebrate a Beretta victory

"General Motors was funding the Cars & Concepts GTU team, a guy named Dave Draper was the owner. It wasn't very organized; they were a business trying to race cars. It was an ok thing, it started out with the cars being fair at best, hard to work on, but they handled pretty good and they had pretty big power. The car was kind of a hybrid, they had a carbon fibre tunnel, it was right at the time when they said "you have to use a unibody" and then said "you don't have to use a unibody." Being front wheel drive, they then allowed it to be rear wheel drive... it was starting to be a real race car. But, we ran a few races, and it was a disaster. It took a while to get the car close enough, the team was disorganized and it was their first year."

Anything that happened on-track, paled in comparison to

the off-track rental car adventures. Racers are enough reason to never buy a used car from a rental car agency. It wasn't unusual to see rental cars being flogged in showroom stock classes at the local autocross, but as usual Binks took things to another level. Phil Binks – "After leaving the track, they were on the way back to the hotel, chasing each other down the road. Well, Dan loses it and goes backwards into somebody's front yard, catches a berm so that the car flies through the air and lands on a woodpile. The bottom of the car has been pushed up by landing on the woodpile, so they get the car off the wood, get in the car so that their backs are against the roof and their feet on the floor... and push. They straightened the car out, but said it didn't drive quite the same." Marge – "Another time at Daytona, they were racing rental cars backwards down the beach, sometimes in the water. One night at Del Mar they raced the rental cars around the practice track for the horses. Tommy and all the guys were here, rented vans, and did the Cloverleaf Grand Prix..." From time to time, Dan's mechanical skills were called for. Kendall – "There was a time where Binks totaled a rental car, and then got it into good enough shape to turn it in unnoticed. It was still totaled, but you couldn't tell it."

The Del Mar Grand Prix was the end of the season event, and the Beretta of Kendall was leading the manufacturer's point battle by 2 points heading into that race. Kendall – "In '88 I had clinched the driver's championship before the last race, but not the manufacturer's championship, so for the last race we ran a 3rd car that my brother Bart was in (the 2nd car was Max Jones). We were ahead for the manufacturer's championship but it was close."

It was a wild ending to the season. Dan Binks - "That was the year that they sealed the track, which was getting all over the tires." Kendall - "It was the weirdest thing. When the tires got hot, they would pull the sealer up. It was making a shell on the tires and the times would fall off by 4 seconds. I figured it out right before qualifying that it felt good when I was warming up the tires, when you are usually careful. I thought, what if we qualify on cold tires, and so we ended up on the pole by a pretty good margin. I don't remember the specifics but I got wrapped up in trying to win. I was leading the race and told them 'what do you think about changing tires?' They were saying 'no, no, you are leading.' Well, I overrode them and came into the pits for new tires with 6 laps to go. I was in the back with tires that were 4 seconds faster and I had 5 laps to pass the entire field. There was so much more grip, but then they started getting hotter. I caught Amos who was in the lead, and it wasn't very smart on my part because I didn't need to pass him to win the manufacturer's championship."

Binks – "Tommy ran into Amos (Johnson) on the last lap, it didn't quite end up in a fist fight but it was pretty close." Tommy - "To this day he (Amos) probably doesn't believe this is what happened. Coming up through the pack, I had come up on Bart and did the same exact pass on him that I was then to try on Amos. Thinking back on it, if I would have nicked my brother and taken us both out of the championship… it was centimeters from heroic to just disaster. There was a chicane with a jump on the back straightaway that would throw the car to the right. I was getting such a good shot out of there and was catching Amos too fast and misjudged him. I tried to pull out, but I was in the air and hit Amos and it shot him right into the wall. Coming up was a fast left hander and the course doubled back before the checkered flag. Now, he's damaged and decides he's going to turn left, cut through the course, cut off 2 corners and blast me before I get to the checkered. He was limping and turned left to cut the course right as this Merkur was coming at full speed in 4th and Amos T-boned him. His car was destroyed, and now he was even madder. But, he had to be a little mad at himself for cutting in front of the Merkur." Binks – "When Tommy ran into Amos, he was angry. I was yelling at Tommy… 'they're coming, they're coming' and Amos whacked the guy that was driving the Merkur. You sort of feel like that was meant for us. Really and truly we should have got it. And, by the way, I fully expected Tommy to pass him. Tommy wasn't there to follow somebody."

Kendall had won the GTU Championship for the 3rd straight year, and Chevrolet was Manufacturer's Champion. Tommy – "It was supposed to be a 2 year program in GTU, but we accomplished our goals in that first year. " It was time to move on. Kendall - "We went to Trans-Am the next year with a new car designed by Trent Jarmin, who was in-house at Cars & Concepts. A nice guy who had designed racing cars before, an older guy who was really enthusiastic… but the car wasn't very good. We spent a ton of money, I'm sure we spent more that Roush did on Dorsey's championship car. My best finish was 2nd and I finished 3rd in points. It was tough for a group of guys who had done nothing but win, and it was hard to take. We even cut the roof off at one point because it had this big greenhouse. The SCCA was trying to help us out, so they let us have a lower template, and the '89 Beretta ended up being a chop-top Beretta. The only template they had was a centerline template, so the centerline of the hood, windshield angle, the roof, back glass and rear deck had to be the same. Doug Fehan got involved because the '89 year was such a disaster, and Fehan was hired by Chevy to assess everything. He wanted to get rid of both of the drivers and the designer, and have Bob Riley design it. Chevy decided I was staying."

Kendall continues - "The next year, Chevy kind of cleaned house and brought Bob Riley in for the next Beretta in Trans-Am. Riley had sort of changed the Trans-Am game with his first car, and 1990 was his next generation car. It was a breakout year and it was a pretty wild looking piece. There were these negotiations with the SCCA, where you present your body. You didn't run new bodies every year, so you tried to get in as much as you could. He tried to tuck in the area behind the front wheels, make the top of the fenders square, you wanted some coke bottling, and to have a skirt under the door. We cleaned house, and won 6 races in the Beretta. We were the only fuel injected V6 and it was easy for them to add weight to us. When we got to Elkhart Lake, my V6 weighed the same as the V8 Mustangs, with substantially less power. So, what we did was to go back to the old 18 degree cylinder head and carburetor for R K Smith's car at Mid-Ohio. It was a spec we had never run before and where we got to take 175 pounds off the car as there were no penalties for that. At Elkhart they told me to try RK's car and I said 'I'm driving this car... no way am I going back to the fuel injected car, this was way better.' By season's end, Kendall had won his first Trans-Am Championship."

1990 Trans-Am championship winning Chevrolet Beretta

Soon the team of Binks and Kendall moved up to GTP and the impressive Pratt & Miller team of Chevrolet powered Intrepid racers. Pratt & Miller had started out with the goal of building and racing a cutting edge prototype for 1991. The Intrepid by Bob Riley was to become one of the most famous cars of the

GTP era. Binks - "We had decent budgets with the Intrepid, but nothing like what Nissan and Toyota were running at the time. We went from being a factory effort with the Trans-Am car at Cars & Concepts to a pseudo General Motors factory effort with the Intrepid at Pratt & Miller. It was a really innovative car."

Kendall – "The Intrepid…I think it altered the trajectory of sports car racing. The Europeans had smoother tracks and were thinking lower downforce. Riley had this car in his head forever and thought it would be better everywhere. Finally Jim Miller said, 'let's build it.' Miller, Binks and I, and all the Trans-Am guys who had just won the championship were part of the Chevy package. Miller's guy was Wayne Taylor, as they had been racing the Spice with no factory support."

Kendall with the Intrepid in 1991
– Photo courtesy of Jerry Howard

"I did just a few laps in the Intrepid and told them that I was pretty sure that the car was faster. Wayne got the first Intrepid, while Danny and I ran the Spice for the first 3 races. We went to West Palm Beach with the old Riley modified Spice and I sat on the pole for one of my first GTP races, I think I had 2 starts the year before. At Miami I should have won the race as I was on Boesel in the Jaguar like a cheap suit at the end. He was blocking me like nobody's business, but I didn't have the confidence yet, as I think Raul Boesel was the reigning World Sportscar champion at the time. If this would have been me 5 years later and a guy blocked me like that, he would have wrecked. So, I finished 2nd."

The car generated higher downforce than perhaps anything seen in sports car racing before or since, and in pushing the envelope to new extremes, the car broke a spindle at the end of the straight at Watkins Glen with Tom Kendall behind the wheel. The resultant grievous injuries to Kendall changed Binks' philosophy. Phil Binks – "The whole front of the car was shattered." Marge Binks – "Dan had always felt you are responsible for a man's life here, the driver's life was in your hands. That accident really hit him… that everything has got to be absolutely perfect. As good of technology as there is, as good of materials as you can get, everything has to be the best. That was when it really shifted for Dan." Dan Binks – "You get a few chances to get better… if not we need to move on!"

For 1992, the team built an updated Intrepid GTP car. The team did not compete in the long races, only the sprint races. The 2 year saga of the Intrepid saw one win, but left a distinct impression upon all who saw the cars race. Binks – "Tommy rushed back, he wasn't ready. General Motors was done with Tommy after his accident. I don't know if it was a 'damaged goods' thing, but it just went sour after the wreck." It was the end of racing prototypes for Dan Binks and Tommy Kendall.

Kendall - "We were there at first with Mike Dingman, Roush hadn't built a new car in a while and was off doing NASCAR. Mike Dingman was a Ford board member and he was kind of a wealthy guy and was funding this development. That's how I got hooked up with them originally in '92, was as a coach doing some testing for them, and doing the GTS car after we left the GTP stuff. For '93 I was at Roush in IMSA GTS with a hybrid tube frame/monocoque car. It was similar to that 88 GTU car, but thought out. It had a full independent rear end. I've thought about that car, as Ford sold it to South Africa for Sarel to run it in a South African series... I liked it."

Dan - "I left and went to Jack Roush for the GTS car in 1993. Jack approached us and said he'd like us to do this, if you want to come over here (GTS). It was really screwed up for me, as they had already hired somebody to do my job before they hired Tommy. It was really bad, hard on me. They hired this team manager, I was like a car chief on the 2 car team, and this guy was micro-managing everything I did, it was f***ing torture. I'm thinking... if you weren't Tommy Kendall, I wouldn't be here right now." Marge Binks – "That was not an easy transition at all; he wasn't welcomed with open arms, but Kendall had him up on this pedestal. It was ugly, frankly he was devastated, and it was the lowest I'd ever seen Dan."

The season opening race was the 24 hours of Daytona, a race that Jack Roush had dominated, having won from 1985-92. Kendall - "Emery Donaldson was the boss. For race duties he ran one car and we ran our car. Emery was alright, and I applaud him as there were a lot of haphazard things going on in those days. He had this military style where he was convinced there was only one way to do things, and that was his way and he was right. I was listed in both cars at the start of the race but I would get in whatever car was running better in the race, as I was the only one running for the Championship. They would hold me out long as possible as whichever car I got in first, then that would be the one I was in for points. After I was committed (Binks' car), we had an issue... I think it was a starter, and we were 2 or 3 laps down. I knew that sometime in the morning the order would come out to 'hold position' as that was just what they did. But they didn't understand how yellows work, didn't know how to get laps back from the faster class. They would say Pit, and Binks would say 'Don't Pit'. The next thing you knew, we were leading."

Dan – "For Daytona my car had Tommy, Mark Martin, Robby Gordon, and Robbie Buhl, and we're running along in 3rd at the time. First yellow and the Team Manager pits the 2nd car before they do the wave around. He tells me to pit and I told him "I'm not pitting." He said "PIT"… I said, "I'm not pitting." So, he pits the 2nd place car, and I'm staying out, we get the wave around and now we are a lap ahead of everybody. The 2 cars in front of us made that mistake, but we'd been racing GTU for years and knew what the deal was, you don't stop until they pick the leader up."

It happened again. Binks - "6 hours in, the same freaking thing happens… yellow flag and now we are in the lead by two laps. Jack is just fit to be tied, he knows at this point that he screwed up and had hired the wrong guy. Jack says- "I don't give a s**t what you do, you pit when Binks pits." We end up winning the race, and it was awesome. Jack didn't know me from Adam, he hired me because Tommy said "hire him". Jack gained a lot of respect for me after that race, knowing that we had won the race by just not being stupid. He thought he had hired the right guy, but at that point he was figuring out that maybe he didn't. Jack Roush – "Dan was always one of the brightest and most adept at all the competitive opportunities of anybody that I worked with."

It was obvious that the situation couldn't last. The result was an in-house smack-down over the proper tools to use for rebuilding a gearbox. Kendall - "Where it changed was the showdown in the shop. Emery was over-focused on process, and there wasn't enough common sense in it. There were a number of things that led to Binks being the Alpha dog. Emory told everyone, "There's too much time wasted in the shop, we're changing over to air wrenches." Binks said, "I don't think that's a good idea." Emory said that it would save a lot of time on building a transmission from a box of parts. So Binks said he would beat him while building a transmission with regular wrenches. All the team gathered around, and when Emery said he would beat Binks by 25 minutes, Binks said he wasn't going to take him 25 minutes (to build the trans). It was totally like a Rocky movie. That's a cool thing about Binks is that he operates at a different speed and intensity than most, and he does phenomenal work at double time. I was giving guys a tour of the (Roush) shop in the middle of winter time, and Binks went running by really fast. The guys asked if the building was on fire or something, but I told them that it is just the speed he works at... flat out."

What if Dan had been given the air tools and Emory given the standard hand tools? Binks - "I'd have whooped him. There was no way that Emory was going to beat me. He was a team manager... not that he couldn't have taken it apart and put it back together, but I was doing it every week. It was a no-win deal for him. He was trying to flex his muscles a little bit, and I flexed back. I was pissed off, that should have been my job. And I'm still pissed off. He was there for 7 or 8 months and they paid him for the whole year, more than I made there after 10 years. That's a little sour to take."

Miami brought additional drama. Dan – "I'm the kind of person that wants to work on my race car, and then wants to go home. If I didn't have to talk to anybody, but could just work on my race car, I'd rather do that. Personality problems, dealing with people who have their feelings hurt... I hate dealing with that kind of stuff. So, we go to the 2nd race at Miami... Jack is really starting to figure out that the other guy isn't the right guy. There was some engine problem, and Jack calls me at midnight and tells me that we have to work on the engines, and to meet him at the airport where he is bringing these parts for us to install in the morning. So, since 8AM we are at the race track thrashing on the engines, and here comes the Team Manager at lunch time... the cars all ripped apart. He wants to know what is going on, and Jack tells him that he called Binks and its getting handled. It was awkward at best. They demoted him after Miami, and then put him in charge of the Trans-Am team, so then they were going to different places and he was off my back. We won 3 or 4 races that year and won the IMSA GTS Championship, we didn't have the best car, but we won Daytona and did well at Sebring, so our bonus points were good, and we only clinched by one or two points at the end of the year over Clayton's drivers, Millen and Johnny O'Connell."

Danny worked hard to raise the discipline within the team. Marge – "They set it up to work 5 day weeks, 10 to 12 hour days, but they no longer worked weekends. Every single day is ½ hour of pit stop practice. Dan said that was the only way that they were going to get this stuff done right." Dan had moved from being a gifted mechanic and setup specialist, into a crew chief, and now was moving into an organizational position as well. That continues through today at Pratt & Miller.

Jack Roush reflects upon those years of success with Dan Binks – "I road raced for 14 or 15 years, and the best performance we had was with all the cars we took to Daytona. We went 14 times to Daytona, once with an RS car... which was before Danny. We won 2 races with the Trans-Am cars, and the ten 24 hour races that we won."

"That was the high point of our road racing... we never got beat at Daytona for all those times with our road race cars there. That was on Danny's watch."

Dan – "I was there 10 years, and did all the road racing stuff. I really liked the Trans-Am deal, because it was a 100 mile shootout, take the gloves off and punch it out for an hour, which was kind of cool compared to the long races over in IMSA. Tommy was so good compared to those other guys, we'd play games like 'how fast do you think the pole would be?' He'd go by on the start-finish line on his fast lap and just start laughing and say 'What did you think of that?'"

The IMSA GTS car was the beginning of the Binks-Roush era

Binks – "He knew it was faster than we had talked about. He was such an amazing driver that it wasn't even fair racing against those guys... they just weren't Tommy Kendall. I'd love to say it was the car, and if we hadn't done stuff… and we did good stuff… but we had the best driver every day. Every time he showed up, he brought his 'A' game. He could do whatever we needed, if we didn't hit the car absolutely perfect he could carry it. He was able to get more out of the car than anybody else we dealt with, at least in those cars (Trans-Am) for sure."

The end result was the hat trick of 3 straight championships in Trans-Am, from 1995 thru 1997 for Kendall and Roush Racing. Jack Roush – "The last year we ran Tommy Kendall in the Trans-Am series, my recollection was that it was a 12 race series and Tommy won the first 9 races of the 12 race schedule. At the 10th race, he had the 'misfortune' of having contact with a car that he was lapping, got spun out and wrecked. The guy came back the next 2 races and took Tommy out of contention… in those last 2 races. It kept us from sweeping the series." Binks – "It wasn't even fair going to a Trans-Am race with Tommy, he was so damn good."

Binks/Kendall were the most formidable team in Trans-Am since the early days of Penske/Donohue with the Sunoco Camaro

It wasn't just Kendall, as the car preparation and development was in another league. Phil Binks –"Gentilozzi would go out there and flog it, and get a good time. Tommy would go out there and knock a couple of tenths off."

Phil – "At the end of the day, Tommy would always be on the pole. I went up to Danny and asked him how much faster could you have gone? He answered, 'a second and a quarter, or so.' You only go as fast as you have to, you have to be careful." Dan Binks – "One of these days, I'd like to get that All-Sport car from Jack. I don't know how I could ever do it, but that would be really cool to have."

Does Jack Roush miss road racing with Dan Binks after all these years? "I do very much, but across 14 years we won 50% of the races that we entered. The sponsors, sanctioning bodies... everybody got tired of us, and Ford in particular told us that there was not much value, wasn't much promotional benefit from us winning the races... there was only the negative side, we'd been so dominant. So, when the sponsorship dried up, I decided not to fund it myself and we quit. It's kind of funny; I'd won a few drag races early on when I started drag racing in 1966... NHRA... IHRA... but in road racing (as a team) we won our first race with Greg Pickett's Trans-Am win in 84. My son just won our 400th race, in March of this year with an RS car, so the 400 wins began and ended with a road race."

Jack Roush Jr. tells the story about getting that 400th win for Roush Racing – "It was a huge honor. There was a lot of drama that day. We qualified with a new record at Homestead, but we got put to the back as Grand-Am and our competitors felt that we had an unfair advantage over a part that we had. Starting at the back, by the time I got out of the car, we were in the lead. Billy Johnson hopped in and did a great job for the rest of the race and we got 1st."

Was there a certain degree of satisfaction that the road racing side of the operation brought home that 400th win? Jack Roush

Jr. – "Oh yeah…. for me personally, I feel a big attachment to road racing. I grew up watching my Dad road race and I also raced go-karts. I had wanted to do full size car racing, and drove NMRA drag racing in 2004. In 2006 I got the chance to hop into the Grand-Am Mustang, and it's been a blast. It's kind of a flashback to be here driving on a lot of historic tracks, and there are a lot of familiar faces, it is definitely a small world."

For the team that today has become synonymous with Ford operations in Nascar, their road racing roots run deep and those efforts continue today. However, a road racing comeback does not appear to be in the cards for Jack Sr. – "I've got 5 Nationwide cars, 4 Cup cars, 4 more that I build the cars for… a dozen more that run my engines… and I'm past the age that most people retire."

Tommy Kendall – "The thing about Binks was that after time, he believed in me, and I believed in him like nobody's business. You don't get off on bad tangents as much. Once at Portland in the warm up, I thought I felt this weird buzz at little bit and I wasn't even sure… but I told him, so they changed the motor. Later they found there was something wrong with it, and it wouldn't have lasted. Likewise, if they wanted to change the car, whatever he wanted to do, I was game for. That was the benefit that you couldn't develop in a short period of time. Those are the intangibles that help you in avoiding wasting time and energy."

Dan and Tommy Kendall tried to move over to the NASCAR truck series for 1998, but things didn't go as planned. Jack Roush – "Tommy Kendall was all set to come to the truck series, but he ended up being reluctant to sign the contract that we prepared for him… on his terms. After we did that the third time, I took it off the table and we proceeded with Greg Biffle. Greg Biffle was about 28 years old, an extraordinarily motivated and able racer. He wanted it so bad; he wrecked and had a number of problems the first year." Greg Biffle – "The first year… the rookie year…

the thing that comes to mind was that we were all sort of learning together. I don't think the crew chief Randy Goss had any experience either; he was a snowmobile and motorcycle racer. They hadn't really competed in the truck series, it was fairly new. We were learning about the trucks, just as much as I was learning about the series, the tracks, and NASCAR. It was definitely a learning curve together."

It was an odd combination of successful racers. Dan Binks – "Randy Goss was the crew chief, because he had more oval track experience." If Goss had more oval track experience, it was probably from riding dirt ovals on his motorcycle. The team was completely new to this type of racing. Randy Goss was a 2 time AMA Grand National Champion dirt track racer had made the transition from rider to crew chief, from dirt oval to paved oval. Dan Binks had arrived in NASCAR from his roots in the carbon chassis world of IMSA. Was the concept to take a handful of talented guys and throw them together to see what happens? Biffle – "Yep, let's see what happens. It was a culture shock probably, for Dan. The stuff is so different, but I remember Danny really well because he was our best, technology-wise. He reminds me of the guy who has worked for me forever… Roger Ueltschi. Danny could build anything, tig-weld, fabricate, engineer something in his head and get it onto the truck. He could do about any task, gas pedal geometry… there's a lot of stuff we were doing to those trucks that had never been done before." Holding his fingers slightly apart Greg recounts that first season. "We were that close, I don't know how many times… just so close to winning a race. It was a lack of experience on our part. Loudon, New Hampshire – we're not going to make it, we have to pit under green. So, we take fuel only, but we needed a whole can of fuel and we didn't put tires on. We were in the pit long enough to have put tires on. Opportunity lost, and they beat us on the white flag lap." Greg Biffle won Rookie of the Year honors for the Truck series.

It was all coming together for 1999, and the highlights were many. Biffle – "The second season was a different story; we won more races than anybody ever had in the series. The first win was at Memphis, and it was so bittersweet… God, we worked so hard. Then we won our 9th race in Las Vegas, to date, nobody has ever won more… we still hold that record. We won 9 times, and it was pretty remarkable. Once we figured out what we needed to do, we were pretty much unstoppable, and we continued to get better and better."

Binks with Greg Biffle at Roush's NASCAR Craftsman Trucks

Greg continues -"Our downfall was… and I suppose I should tread lightly around this… after the Las Vegas race, they (NASCAR) decided that they didn't like our intake manifold. I'd already won 3 races with it. They penalized us 120 points and fined us 60,000 dollars. We lost the championship by 8 points."

Since the early days of NASCAR, the game between car builder and rules enforcement had led to some progressively creative rule bending with hidden fuel supplies, sometimes rumored to be stashed within the roll cage. Cars became progressively more obviously modified in profile and eventually led to the use of body templates in an attempt to maintain control over the aerodynamics. There is no doubt that internal engine modifications have played as significant a role in the search for advantage.

Greg picks up the story of the intake manifold that cost the team a championship – "The truth has to be known. Most of the time, the guys in the engine shop spend the winter working on things. Well, through that winter of 98-99, they worked on this intake manifold that made 6 or 8 more horsepower at high rpm, for the big tracks... top end tracks. We took it to the Disney World speedway, which was the first race of the series. We had the NASCAR tech inspectors check the engine, carburetor, and intake manifold... I even witnessed this, which is rare. They took the intake manifold, brought this tool over and checked it with this tool. They turned it over, looked at it, checked the part number... and said 'You're good to go'. The intake manifold was fine, so we put it on the truck and finished fifth in that race. Then, all through the season, we were winning. It wasn't until 3 races before the end of the season, that they decided it wasn't legal anymore. Their thing was 'you modified the intake manifold after we looked at it.'"

Jack Roush – "The second year, he should have won the Championship except for a penalty that NASCAR imposed, that was not right. They took points away under a circumstance that was just not right, based around an intake manifold that we had won several races with... and it had been inspected several times. They decided they didn't like it, late in the year they said the (original) inspector didn't know what he was looking at, and that it shouldn't have been approved. Biffle would have won the Championship in his second year if that had not been the case."

Greg Biffle – "The story goes... another NASCAR official was looking at this intake manifold. We'd won 9 times, and they were thinking 'these guys are doing something'. They asked the tech inspector who had approved the manifold if he had seen or approved that intake manifold... he had amnesia all of a sudden."

It would be safe to say that this outcome stuck in the craw of every member of the Roush truck team, as well as with Jack. For 2000, the team was to take no prisoners. Greg Biffle – "In 2000, I think we won 5 times that year, and won the championship by 250 points. The guy (the inspector that had originally approved that intake manifold the previous year) did come to me after I'd won the title the next year, and apologized. He knew... he knew that we had come to them and asked if it was ok, what we'd done to this intake manifold."

Dan returned to Pratt & Miller in October of 2002. One of the most dramatic championships in his career was in his first season with Corvette Racing. Dan – "In the season finale at Miami in 2003, the championship was on the line in GT1, and everything was unraveling right near the end of the race. "The deal there was that we needed to finish the race in the top 5, and we'd win the championship. Johnny got a little aggressive and broke the left front suspension. So, he pitted and came in with the tire flopping around, so I looked in there and thought, 'Oh my God, we're done.' It was just wiped out, everybody was on the radio saying 'We've got to finish, what can we do?' So, I grabbed a red tie down, and I wrapped it around the control arm about 2 or 3 times and stuffed the control arm into this pocket. Basically it had ripped the heim joint off the end. I just wedged it in the corner, and ratchet strapped it as hard as I could. I said 'Johnny, take it easy.' He leaves the pits and says 'Hey, this thing is awesome; I don't know how you guys did that.' I told him 'Johnny, you need to SLOW DOWN. You don't understand, you need to slow down'. I don't want to say on the radio that 'hey, you've got a ratchet strap holding the front suspension on', because they might stop us. We had 15 laps to go, 30 miles. I said to Johnny...'Dude, 2 seconds a lap slower, just take it easy."

"Later when he came in and looked at it, he said 'Oh My God', but that's the one that won the championship, a crazy idea like that. It's just the things that you have to do, to go to the next level, and that's what we did. I probably put him into a position that I shouldn't have, but he's a race car driver and he knows there are going to be times where he's got to do these things. Johnny was smart enough to know that when I said he had to take it easy, that he needed to take it easy."

The Pratt & Miller team celebrated a final victory with the GT-1 car at Le Mans in 2009. Dan - "The podium at Le Mans was ridiculous. We had been there so many times and had them slip away. Even with 10 minutes to go, I was worried that it would slip away because at that place, you have to make it around that last lap. You can't believe how long that 4 minute lap is at the end to make it around. I was crying like a little kid. I've won races from the Daytona 24, Sebring, a NASCAR championship... if that day at Le Mans was my last day, it would have been fulfilled. My whole life for that day, that was like Wimbledon, the Daytona 500, and the Indy 500... Le Mans."

Dan Binks has been at the Pratt & Miller Corvette team since '02

Dan - "That was it, and I was really emotional. Crying on TV... everybody gave me a bunch of s**t. In every email I opened for the next week they said 'I just saw Dan Binks cry on TV, unbelievable'. Even right now it's emotional. I saw an interview with the rapper Lil Wayne and Larry King asked him 'what do you dream about?' He said 'Larry, I can't dream this big.' That's how I felt that day."

At Le Mans 2011, it was again highly dramatic for the Corvette team. Jim Campbell, US VP for GM's Performance Vehicles & Motorsport division tells the story of that race at Le Mans – "We had the number 73 and 74 Corvettes. The 74 got out to a big lead but in the middle of the night got tangled up. So the Ferrari took over the lead by a pretty good distance. The #73 car that Danny was on, Beretta, Garcia, and Milner had a big job to do, to chip away at the Ferrari lead. You can't give up in a race like that. Danny, the drivers, and the whole crew stayed focused with that 'never give up' attitude. There were some incredible conditions on the 8-1/2 mile course at Le Mans where it was raining in one part, sprinkling in another, and sunny & dry in others. The car was running on slicks, and Danny was coaching Tommy Milner on that stint. Tommy had the stint of his life, as did Danny Binks. They kept that car on the track, on slicks, and at 2 hours and 10 minutes (remaining), took over the lead, going by the Ferrari and never looking back."

"They expanded that lead with Milner at the wheel, and Danny called for a pit stop for a driver change, fuel, and tires. Garcia got back in the car, and he finished the race off for the win. It was a serious high pressure situation with the rain, running on slicks. Dan called a great race, the crew and the drivers executed at such a high level to deliver a win for Chevrolet and the Corvette community. It was an incredible day. I have so much respect for him... it's just incredible. He is an asset to the team, and it is proven time and time again, he generates respect amongst the crew, the drivers, and the teams in the paddock. At Le Mans, one of the biggest races for Chevrolet, the Corvette community was cheering him and the Corvette team on that day from the stands at Le Mans, and through the live feed from the car sent around the world. Corvette customers, fans, and supporters were with the Corvette team that day in a major way, and I think in some small way it makes a difference."

"I watched Dan Binks work so smart under serious pressure; he quarterbacked that win at Le Mans. Making the right calls at the right time and delivering a win for the Chevrolet C6R program. It was an incredible job that he did. He's a guy that appreciates the level of the competition, especially at a race like the 24 Hours of Le Mans, and the meaning of winning that race."

Jim Campbell continues – "After we came back from Le Mans, we brought the Corvette team, the drivers, Danny Binks, Doug Fehan, and the Chevrolet engineers to Powertrain Headquarters and did a celebration. I don't think Danny had been to one of those before, and I demanded that he be there, because I know the role that he played. I was so happy to introduce him to all of our engineers, all of our group. I asked him to join the drivers in signing autographs for all the Powertrain employees. He did it gladly and I was proud to have him there."

Dan Binks has moved up from the winner podium at Le Mans to challenge a somewhat less prestigious version of same... the 24 Hours of Lemons. Dan – "I've done 3 of them, and technically I've won two of them. The 1st one, they didn't know who we were... it was the guys from Pratt & Miller, and we won that first one by 200 laps. The next time we were back again with that Toyota, but AER, the engine manufacturing guys... I had called them and asked if they'd give us a Toyota engine. They said, no... but they'd give us an American engine for Lemons. I figured I needed to do it with an American car so I built a 3rd Gen Camaro. They built me a hot rod 350 V8, super fast. They gave me a 200 lap penalty for the engine. That hurt us..."

When you bring your hot rod to the Lemons race, you sign it over. Basically they can smash your car, they can take the engine, do anything they want. Jay Lamm said "I'm taking that engine." So, I told him... 'Ok, I'm here to have fun and if you need to take my engine, let it rip. I'll help you get it out.' When they had their after-party, John came over and said 'You didn't leave?' I told him 'If I have to give you this engine to race here, it's no skin off my nose… it was free.' Everyone else who he told that he was taking their engine had left, so he told me 'Don't bring that engine back." We've got a new car now… they said 'no more V8s for me'. So I got a 4.3 litre V6 out of an S-10 in a 3rd Gen. 2650 pounds, makes good power, the engine has been on the dyno. They can take any of it apart. It's all junk parts, but it's GOOD."

Dan lives in Michigan with his wife and 2 children. His son Philip has been to Le Mans, and most of the ALMS races. While finishing high school, Philip had a position working on weekends with Robertson Racing, racing the Ford GT in ALMS. In early 2011, Philip's involvement remained dependent upon his continued presence on the honor roll at his high school, the principal excusing his absence as long as the grades remain intact. Post-graduation, Philip continued to work with endurance racing teams in the Grand-Am or ALMS for 2012/13. Dan is currently with his long time employer Pratt & Miller and is heavily involved in the preparation of the next generation Stingray for the 2014 season. Obviously Dan has found ways to achieve at the highest levels despite his early struggles.

Jackie Stewart – "Well, I think ironically all dyslexics of more mature years… in those years when they were growing up, there were no assessments to speak of. The educational authorities have a lot to answer for, because there are a great many mature dyslexics around the world who have never been properly assessed and to this day don't even know that they are dyslexic, and are still complexed because of it. I was fortunate because both of my sons were having trouble when they entered a new school, and they insisted upon an assessment being made. That assessment was carried out, and at that same time, at the age of 42, I was identified as a dyslexic."

Sir Jackie Stewart – Formula One World Champion 1969, 71, 73

"By that time, I had already won the World Championship 3 times, had won a lot of Grand Prix races, retired from racing, and was well and truly established in the business world. I guess like so many other dyslexics, I found ways around the problem. One of the assets of being a dyslexic, since you can't think like 'the clever folk', as I call them, you have to find other ways of doing business, and that means thinking out of the box."

"So, any success that I've had, including my motor racing, was from thinking slightly differently than most people think about how they go about even normal activities."

Looking across Sir Jackie Stewart's career, there has been great success not only as a driver, but as a journalist, broadcaster, F1 team owner, author, trap shooting, corporate spokesman... pretty much anything Jackie set his mind to.

Stewart - "You mentioned my role as ambassador for products, or affiliations with the Ford Motor Company or as spokesperson for a company like Rolex... I've now been with Rolex for 44 years, under contract. I'm still on board of Moet Hennessy, and I've been with them since 1969... 43 years."

"What you do, because you in so many ways continue to feel inferior to others, you try harder to do whatever responsibilities you have to a higher level, to do it better than anybody else in the company could do, or anyone else that they would consider for the job."

"Part of my job has been to bring a lot of money into auto racing, Formula One of course, but also the formative classes of the sport. I'd always had the policy that you under-promise, and you over-deliver. When I did well at anything, people were surprised that I did well. From my point of view, it's been an asset, as therefore I'm more focused, I'm more committed, I'm more dedicated.... and I deliver. And as long as you under-promise and over-deliver, you'll never get sacked." Across his many careers, Jackie Stewart truly has delivered, and despite all that success, it hasn't changed his absolute commitment to excellence in every endeavor he has pursued.

Dan Binks similarly made the most of his opportunities despite his struggles with reading, and also consistently over-delivered. Dan sees it as more being in the right place at the right time, but obviously there was more to the story. Dan - "Without being accepted at Phil Conte, and without going to Clayton's... working with incredible guys like Joey Cavaglieri, Clayton, Jim Bailey, all those guys in my life early-on when I needed somebody to say 'hey, that's not right' or 'Yeah that's good but I'd do it this way'. All those guys helping me along was the key. I was just some hyper kid from San Diego that though I knew more than I did. They recognized that I had the ability, and they helped me along which was huge. If I wouldn't have gotten out of San Diego, I'd just be working in some shop right now. I look at it like I'm one of the luckiest guys on the planet."

Dan Binks helping his Dad to sort out the ex- Ken Miles Dolphin

CHAPTER TWO

THE CHASSIS

1971 Porsche 917/10 Can-Am aluminum chassis

Without a chassis that is stiff in torsion upon which to hang the suspension and wheels, the job of race car development becomes compromised as the structure deforms under the suspension loads imposed. The racing cars from the middle of the 20th century left much to be desired in this aspect.

Stirling Moss drove a specially built Maserati for the Race of Two Worlds in 1958 at Monza, one that perhaps best sums up the experience of driving a car where the speed capability far outstripped the chassis.

The Maserati that Sir Stirling Moss drove at the 1958 Race of Two Worlds. An experience that Stirling was lucky to survive

Stirling – "A disaster, a pretty unnerving experience, really. They took a sports chassis and then put a great big V8 in the front, basically the same engine I'd been running in the Le Mans car (450S). It had about 450 horsepower or something like that." One can only imagine what a flexible chassis combined with the most powerful sports car engine of the day might be like on the bumpy Monza banking. Worse was still to come. Stirling – "The steering sheared, or there was a failure in the steering mechanism somewhere. My arms were crossed at 175mph, there was nothing I could do at all, as it had very poor brakes. We were running about 3 or 4 feet from the top (of the banking). All I could do was push back on the steering wheel, push my feet on the brakes, and hope. It shot to the top of the banking and knocked down 3 of the posts, bent back the Armco. I don't remember anything good about it, I can tell you that much."

It wasn't much better at Ferrari however Luigi Musso took pole in the Ferrari at an average speed of 174mph. Indianapolis driver Jim Rathmann was impressed – "I didn't know the guy, but after a while I knew he was the bravest sum-bitch on the race track. He was standing up in the car, up out of the seat." Phil Hill – "The 4.1 Ferrari's handling was horrible… one of the old cars, with typical horrible negative camber on the inside wheel, in the back it was a DeDion axle. It was my first race in a big powerful car, it had 400 horsepower. It was tremendously fast, going over 180mph on the straights. Dan Gurney and I went down to one of the corners and watched Musso get almost out of the car. It was the first race that ever I wore a seat belt, the only way you could stay in the car." Dan Gurney – "What I saw in Musso, was that something was driving him. I don't know if he realized it, but it looked like he was bouncing so hard, he was almost coming out of the car… but he never did lift. It was an example of courage."

Asked about running on the rough Monza banking, Rathmann recalls – "It was shaky, it was a parabolic curve… you had nothing underneath in the turns. It bottomed out all the time, A.J. Watson had to weld the car back together on the pit stops." Despite the Watson roadster literally coming apart beneath him, Rathmann dominated The Race of Two Worlds, winning all 3 heat races. A. J. Foyt was a reserve driver for Juan Fangio that day, and was to win the Indy 500 three years later with a Watson clone.

Jim Rathmann's 58 Monza Race of Two Worlds winning Watson

A.J. – I won in '61 with the Trevis. The Floyd Trevis car was a little bit heavier than the regular Watson. It was beefier in the frame than the Watson, but A.J. (Watson) built the best car. The strength of the Watson was that it was lighter, and anytime you can make something lighter, it's going to be a lot better. As for differences, that's about it. We had a Watson tank... a Watson tail on it."

Given Rathmann's experience with frame breakage in his Watson, it is small wonder that the Watson clones were often built of somewhat stronger and heavier construction. Driving the front engine Indianapolis roadsters of the day was certainly not for the meek, and as the Maserati/Ferrari efforts had showed at Monza, racing the European versions could be tantamount to suicide. Desperately needed chassis improvements were on the horizon for such high horsepower cars.

Despite the above stories, there were cars in the front engine era of F1 that were the tremendous to drive, with chassis that offered both beautiful balance and a forgiving nature. The one most often mentioned is the Maserati 250F. Phil Hill – "It was a great car. The Ferraris never handled as well as that Maserati did. It was so manageable, it wasn't really all that fast, but you could take liberties with it. With the Ferrari you could slip into over-driving it so easily, and it didn't pay off. You lost, rather than gained. With the Maserati, you could get it sideways and dirt track it, all kinds of things."

Phil Hill wasn't the only driver who felt such appreciation for the Maserati 250F's quality early in his career. Another was New Zealand's Chris Amon. Chris – "It was brilliant. I always felt that it taught me how to drive. Actually, my Father owned that car. It was a little bit unique; as it was the car that Rubery Owen bought as a development test bed for the BRM in 1954. It was modified a bit as it had Dunlop disc brakes which Stirling's car also had... the only 2 with disc brakes. The oil tank, instead of being in the tail, it was on one side of the cockpit, which didn't shorten the car much but it moved the weight around a bit."

Chris Amon's Maserati 250f – one of the greatest cars of any era

"My career all comes back to that Maserati, although I never knew it at the time. I think one of the reasons that Reg (Parnell) picked me, is that he saw me drive that car in 1962 in New Zealand, where he apparently told people that he hadn't seen a 250F going like that since Fangio. So, I guess I can put it down to the 250F for getting Reg's attention." Reg Parnell brought Chris Amon onto his F1 team soon after.

Initial developments in improving chassis rigidity during the 1950s involved using tubular space frames in lieu of the beam or ladder frames popular for so many decades. In 1954 Vittorio Jano's Lancia D50 introduced the concept of using the engine as a stressed member, a concept well ahead of that time. For the 1956 season a collaborative effort by Frank Costin (aerodynamics) and Colin Chapman (chassis) resulted in the revolutionary Vanwall F1 car, perhaps the best example of the space frame art.

1963 Lotus-Ford driven by Jim Clark in the Indianapolis 500. Note the tub extends to the rear bulkhead to cradle the engine.

By 1962, Chapman of Lotus started the next revolution with the innovative stressed monocoque Lotus 25. He had found his latest inspiration in the aircraft and aerospace industry, using sheets of formed aluminum that were riveted to bulkheads to create the hull, known as the bathtub, or later shortened to "tub". The end result was a structure with ½ the weight of the previous car with a massive improvement in torsional resistance. This type of construction, or variations on this theme, were the major design element for the following 20 seasons of Formula One.

A notable exception to this design philosophy was the continuing success of the space frame cars from Brabham, who did not resort to the then-typical aluminum tub construction until 1970. Their cars had won the 1966 and 67 World Championship with Jack Brabham and Denny Hulme. Ron Tauranac, designer of the 60s Brabham cars, recalls his philosophy behind their construction – "There were two main reasons for staying with space frames. The first was aerodynamic. There is a law of areas, from the front you start with an ellipse, the area should progressively increase to the maximum, and with the original simple monocoque it consisted of two tube sections starting between the front wheels which considerably increased the area there which then decreased. With a space frame the body sides curved in so that they tucked in to the frame at the front wheels. A second reason was the simplicity of repair in the case of accident damage when away/abroad. Another reason was probably tire development; a chassis needs to be sufficiently torsionally stiff so that making a adjustment to say the anti roll bar at one end effects the handling at the other. Improving tire design and increasing tread width gave greater grip levels; this was magnified further by ground effects. It is significant that in the junior formula, Lotus changed their car back to tube frame when they were consistently being beaten by my cars."

By 1966, designs that debuted for the new three litre F1 included the H-16 cars, the BRM P83 and Lotus 43. Each car had a shortened monocoque that now incorporated the engine as a stressed member. This design trend continued the following year with the elegant Lotus 49 and the compact Cosworth DFV.

In endurance racing, the 3 litre prototypes mandated after 1968, had met their match at Le Mans running against the 5 litre Gulf-Ford GT40, which was allowed to compete as it was considered a limited production sports car. The glaring loophole in the rulebook was soon to be exploited by Porsche and Ferrari. With 25 cars needed to meet the criteria for using 5 litre engines, Porsche built the 917 flat 12 and Ferrari introduced their V-12 powered model 512.

The revolutionary compact and elegant Lotus 49 of 1967

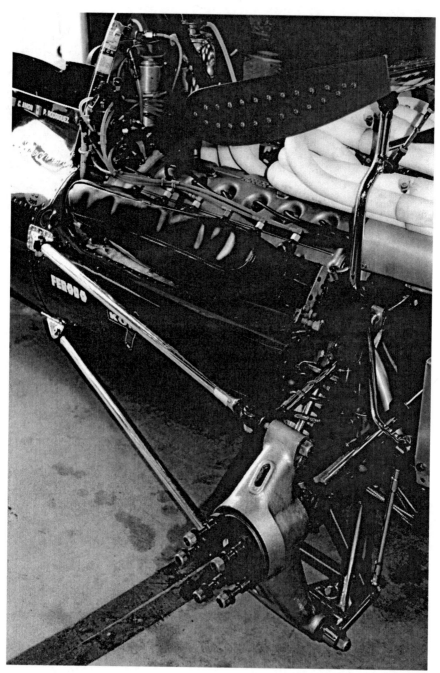

1969 Ferrari F1 – typical of the cigar monocoque era of the 60s. Note that the Ferrari chassis continues to cradle the engine.

Both designs were to find immediate success, the 917 leading much of the 1969 race before retirement, which led to a fight to the finish between the proven Porsche 908 and Ickx in the GT-40. Beaten again by John Wyer and the Gulf team at Le Mans, Porsche brought Wyer into the fold for 1970-71, the result being the legendary Gulf-Porsche 917K. The legend may have been greater than the reality, as the 917 was an evolutionary step for Porsche. It retained the tube frame construction and the air cooled flat 12 was essentially a continued upsizing of the design theme that had been present since the early 1960s, originally based upon 4 cylinders and then first moving to a flat 6, then eventually to a flat 8 with their 1962 Formula One car and later sports prototypes, all being air cooled with a single central fan.

Tony Adamowicz was amongst the very few to race both the 917K and 512 in their glory days. Tony – "The Porsche had an aluminum tube frame. One car they did with a magnesium frame which was really lightweight but of course would be a very touchy thing. Once you get a magnesium fire, you can't put it out. The Ferrari was also a tube frame car also, but it was steel. I drove the 512 for the first time in 1971 at Daytona with Ronnie Bucknum. Ultimately we finished 2nd to Rodriguez/Oliver in a Porsche 917K, on the same lap but we were having valve spring failures. If you wanted to a car to finish and do well, Pedro Rodriguez was your guy. We passed and re-passed during the night, on the banking, in the rain."

"My 512 experience was quite good, we also raced a 512M in Ecuador and won, and then finished 3rd at Le Mans in the NART car... so we had a 1st, a 2nd and a 3rd in one season... not bad. The 917 was an entirely different animal. Tony – "My first experience with the 917 was at Monza, and David Piper asked me what I thought of his 917. I said 'David, I think there is something seriously wrong with it', which is not something you want to tell someone who is offering you a ride in his car. I told him that I could feel it flex going down the straightaway, the

The 1971 Porsche 917K won Le Mans despite a flexi chassis

The Ferrari 512S – Enzo's answer to the Porsche 917

entire car was flexing. David said – 'Oh, they all do that.'

Adamowicz offers a comparison – "The Ferrari was always stiffer, and it felt like a real race car, and handled like a real race car. One thing about the Porsche that gave it the edge was that there were more Porsches. Another was the compliance the Porsche had within the suspension and tires, allowed it to be very flexible in terms of weather changes. It could be raining or dry on the same track on the same lap. You always felt like the car was kind of cushy, which helped it a lot in the rain. I think that is why Porsche won the World Manufacturer's championship with the 917... that flexibility. Also, they were on Firestone and we ran Goodyear on our 512. Goodyear never had intermediate tires; they only had rains or drys. Firestone had drys, intermediates, and rains. Now, in my opinion, the Goodyear was better in the rain, but not having intermediates tires was a big disadvantage."

As if the 917 wasn't quite enough of a flexi-flier, one can only imagine the driving impression when boosting horsepower by a factor of two, with the twin turbocharged 917/10 Can Am car of the following year. The car is variously attributed to have 1100hp in that first season, again with an aluminum tube frame, reinforced to take the additional power. Can-Am races were run without pit stops, and the 917/10 of 1973 was equipped with over 70 gallons of fuel tank capacity, placed alongside the driver. When offered a ride in the Can-Am series in late 1973 with Vasek Polak's 917/10, Jody Scheckter whose early driving style might be best described as grabbing a car by the neck and flinging it into submission... was uncharacteristically concerned. In his autobiography, Jody confided that he had serious second thoughts and felt that perhaps he should not let himself drive this car. Brian Redman was given the opportunity to drive one for Vasek as well.

Brian Redman – "Around August, Vasek (Polak) rang me and asked 'You come and test new 917/10 at Willow Springs, and then race at Laguna Seca and Riverside?' So, I go to Willow

Springs and there was Jody Scheckter's 917/10... there were 2 of them. I drove both cars and told them 'Scheckter's car feels more solid on the road.' Vasek says 'No, they are the same.' The engine broke at Laguna so we went to Riverside. On Friday in the very fast turn (9) at about 200mph I felt something move at the back of the car. I went into the pits and we had broken the right rear... not the suspension, but a tube. Then it happened again on Saturday, but with a different tube."

The Can-Am dominating Porsche 917/10

"Saturday night, I hadn't slept a wink all night, as I thought that I'm going to be killed tomorrow. On Sunday morning I said 'Vasek, I don't think the car is safe.' He told me that the guys worked all night and the car was perfect but if I don't wish to drive it is ok."

Brian was soon to discover that this particular death trap was essentially a lightly modified early 917 chassis with the turbo engine installed. "In the race I was laying 2nd to Mark Donahue in the 917/30 when it broke again... this time it broke big time in the same turn, I went sideways and missed the wall on the outside of turn 9 by nothing, and came into the pits. I got out and looked at the back of the car, and it had pulled out the bottom wishbone mounting point from the chassis. It was only then, that I'd noticed that a 917/10 didn't have a single mounting point; they had parallel links with 2 mounting points. I went to Vasek and told him that the car shouldn't have a single mounting point. He replied 'Yes, it's the Jo Siffert Can-Am car from 1969.' That was designed for 600hp instead of 1100hp. So I told him - 'You copied the bodywork off the Scheckter 917 and then put in an 1100 hp engine?' Vasek said - 'Yah… yah…' I was lucky."

In that same race, Hurley Haywood had finished 2nd in the Brumos Porsche 917/10 (a real one), taking third place in the series overall. It was just as much a leap of faith. Hurley – "My frame of reference was basically a 300hp 911, and I went straight from there to the 917." Mark Donohue helped me come up to speed; I was just stunned at the power and acknowledged what could go wrong. The aluminum frame was pressurized so that if the frame lost pressure, we knew there was a crack. We tried to make the best of what we had… use it to the best of our abilities."

In future years, the world of endurance racing followed F1 convention and reverted to aluminum monocoque construction. The Lotus 72 of 1970 fired off another design trend in F1 of wide flat monocoques, with side radiators and a shovel nose design also exemplified by the Championship winning McLaren M23.

An interesting counterpoint to from that trend came both Mike Pilbeam's BRM P201 and by Gordon Murray's Brabham BT44, which both found inspiration in the car as a compact triangulated design, or more accurately an Isosceles Trapezoid when the tub is viewed in section. The pyramid has four corner points at the base, and the beauty of that type of structure is that every side angle is by its nature, a triangle. The short wheelbase and tidy Brabham BT-44 remains amongst the most recognizable and memorable chassis from the era.

1973's McLaren M23 had success across 5 seasons of F1

Murray was to revisit this same design trend with his stunningly beautiful BT46 Alfa-Romeo of 1978, initially an even more elegant design than the BT-44. However the surface heat exchangers failed to provide the needed cooling, and a conventional nose radiators were soon installed. With the introduction of the BT-46B fan car, which provided its cooling from the rear mounted fan, the original clean design of the car returned, only to find that car banned after a single appearance when it won the Swedish Grand Prix. The following year brought the V-12 version of the Alfa and the BT-48 with sidepod tunnels that followed a now-conventional layout for aerodynamic success.

Motorcycle racing had not been oblivious to the chassis revolution going on in F1. The Spanish company Ossa with their monocoque chassis single cylinder 250 was ridden in 1968-70 by Santiago Herrero to four GP wins and nearly captured the 250 World Championship in 1969.

The 1974 BT-44 Trapezoidal monocoque was one of Gordon Murray's most beautiful and clean designs

Peter Williams found TT success with the monocoque Norton John Player Special in 1973 and even Gordon Murray got into the act with a similar chassis for the 500 Suzuki twin. These attempts notwithstanding, in motorcycle racing the engine developments were streaking ahead of the chassis and tire technology. In 1973, Suzuki stepped into the fray with their 750 water cooled 3 cylinder racers, which redefined the concept of evil. Legendary for their absolutely terrifying handling, the previous years' Daytona 200 champion Don Emde rode one at Daytona at their debut. He since has remarked that the experience played a big part in his retirement decision. In testing with the bikes at Road Atlanta, US Suzuki Team Manager Merv Wright recalled that Paul Smart found the bike impossible. Similar to the earlier GP bikes of the

60s, these bikes had been developed in Japan by their test riders and engineers, being brought to America to be campaigned. Mitsuo Ito, Suzuki's legendary development rider and racer, held great regard for these early days of computer aided design which became an experience for all concerned. Merv Wright – "Smarty pulled in and said he couldn't ride it. Mitsuo Ito told him "Impossible, it was designed by computer." Paul's response was – "Then let the f##king computer ride it."

It wasn't much better in 1974, as Yamaha raised the stakes with their 4 cylinder 700cc TZ750A. Factory Yamaha racer, Gene Romero recalls the challenge – "Those TZ750s were really a 2 wheeled hot rod. It was almost violent compared to what you had been running. The TZ700s and the early TZ750s had rubber band forks and shocks on 'em, but those things were rockets. When testing at Daytona on the main straight at about 160mph the thing would do this wobble, and begin to shake. We tried everything, but it still had that problem. It just scared the living s**t out of you. I came into the pits and said 'I do not want to do this anymore'. I was going to tell them that I was going to quit. Then a light came over me saying 'you are going to have to go work for a living'. I figured out the problem, you just had to fight your way through that vibration wobble at speed and above it the wobble would go away." As with Stirling Moss and Phil Hill at Monza in 1958, the 750cc racers of 73/74 had an insufficient chassis to deal with the recent gains in horsepower, with the possible exception of the monocoque JPS Norton.

On through the 1970s in Formula One, the speeds increased and the stress on the chassis multiplied. Fatigue was a factor, as torsional forces twisted the structures, working rivets and bonding methods loose. Eventually a honeycomb metal skin was adopted for its superior resistance to these forces in the mid 1970s.

Why the design trend to the ever lower and wider monocoques, which one would think would be terrible in axial bending? Gordon Kimball had worked with Barnard at Parnelli in 1976, and then again with the Chaparral Indycar program from 78-80. Gordon – "They were terrible in bending, but torsion is the big one. Usually bending is not the big problem, it's more in transferring the torsion and making the anti-roll bars work. If you have changes in torsion, you unload the wheels and can't make the car work. That vulnerability really affects the result. The bending load doesn't actually hurt anything, if there is bending under deflection it doesn't change things." It doesn't change things other than loosen up every rivet in the tub? Gordon - "Well, that's true…"

Ken Anderson is also a F1 designer and former Chief Engineer for Penske Racing. He is perhaps best known internationally for his F1 Ligier and Onyx designs from the late 1980s. Ken – "The low side chassis were actually pretty strong because typically the low sides were fairly large cross section to carry the fuel cells."

That was another advantage to the low/flat era of monocoque construction. Gordon Kimball - "They were carrying so much fuel, that it would lower the CG of the fuel and was probably worth it even if it weren't as structurally stiff. It was to lower the CG height, as every bit of the chassis was full of fuel… behind the seat, down both sides in those days."

With the introduction of ground effects and the "wing cars", or "tunnel cars" of the late 1970s, the amount of downforce acting upon the suspension skyrocketed, and the F1 tubs were no longer like a bathtub with a pair of tubular structures attached to hold the steering shaft, instruments, and also act as roll over protection. Similarly, by the early 1980s, the Indycars had gone from a low and wide monocoque housing the fuel, to a fuel cell directly behind the driver. Gordon Kimball – "The fuel cells had gone down enough in size that you could get it all in behind the driver. It was hard, and the fuel load was high, but you could get it in." As a result, the available space in the sidepods for downforce was changed drastically.

The Lotus 79 had raised the bar in Formula One during the 1978 season, but the high levels of downforce led to continual problems in torsion with the rivets working loose in the tub from the additional stresses and continual pounding. However, the problems of the 79 were nothing compared to where Lotus was headed with their subsequent designs.

The 1980 Lotus 81B, as with the 80, struggled with a weak tub

Mario Andretti recalls the unsuccessful Lotus 80 he tried to defend his World Championship with in 1979 – "The deal with that car was simply this... they were getting much more downforce out of it because it had more square inch area (for the underbody aero). Colin was very stubborn about a lot of things, and we were realizing that to be able to handle the downforce and eliminate the porpoising, we needed much stiffer springs. Stiffer springs than we had ever thought of before... we were somewhere in the 1200-1400# area, but before that we were only in the 600-700# range. We were testing at this dangerous and very twisty French circuit. We needed a lot of downforce, and we didn't have springs stiff enough so we started putting in packers. What was happening was that the car would work great for a couple of laps, but then it would start popping rivets on the tub. I kept saying to Colin, that we need to strengthen the tub because it's twisting. If I hit some curbs hard enough a couple of times, the car by the next corner has changed… it is crossways. The car would be twisted and he did not freaking believe that. I could not convince him. So, that's where he was going wrong. Everybody else… the competition… they had that nailed down and were building much stiffer chassis that would be able to run the proper spring rates. The Lotus 80 had great potential, but I couldn't convince him, and Colin fell behind on that. I can tell you that at Jarama, Spain, where we finished third… I think that was the best finish we had with that car… the car towards the end of the race was a disaster. I kept saying, 'Colin, this car changes dramatically during the race.' The mechanics would tell him that the chassis was coming apart. It needed to be reinforced."

For the Can-Am series of 1980, there were similar issues with the new ground effects Lola T-530. Geoff Brabham - "I'd signed up with VDS and they had that Lola. It was a difficult car because the chassis cracked almost the first time you ever got it. When we got the car and took it out for its first test, the chassis would crack straight away. It had sliding skirts…I think in those days, I don't know if they understood the loads. It was a difficult car to get right because of the strength of the chassis and how you had to get rid of all the cracks. They were tough to drive, the steering used to lock up on it and I remember at Laguna that the chassis flexed so much when you went through the corkscrew that the steering would just freeze up. You couldn't turn the steering wheel, all of a sudden."

There was so much chassis deflection that it actually seized the rack? Geoff – "Yeah, I remember by the time I finished that race at Laguna I had to ice the tendon in my elbow because the steering got so heavy at certain points that you just couldn't turn the wheel." Keke Rosberg has been known to refer to the single seat era Can-Am cars as 'S**tboxes. Geoff – "Yeah, I don't deny that. They weren't the greatest cars built in my opinion."

While Lotus was struggling with the difficult model 80, 1979 brought the ground effect tunnel car era to Indycar racing, none so comprehensively well thought out, as with the Chaparral 2K, the Yellow Submarine. Kimball had continued working with Barnard in those early days of ground effect development, now working in England for Jim Hall on the Chaparral 2K. Although his role in the car's development was significant, most importantly he had become the Sorcerer's Apprentice. Gordon - "John was working in the front room of his house in London and I was up at VS Fabrications in Luton, where the car was built. He might come up to the shop once a week, but I'd always come down to the house for Sunday dinner, and spend the afternoon going over stuff. He'd give me layouts and general schemes. I did the engineering, and all the detail drawings. Technically it was fun, because we were thinking on the same wavelength, we'd talk on the phone in the evening, once a day. It was great for me, a great way to learn. I could see a master at work, and then got to do the detail stuff when I got to understand why he did what he did. It was a really good education."

Considering the effect that the car was to have upon Indycar racing at the time, it was surprising to find that the team had no access to a wind tunnel during the design stage. Was the Lotus 79 the primary influence upon the design of the 2K? Gordon – "Actually, I think John got a lot of help from Patrick Head at Williams, as they were friends from school days. Williams were doing enough wind tunnel work in the early days to understand ground effects. The FW-07 was a good car."

In 1978 and for the first few races of 1979, Williams had run the FW-06 non-ground effect car, the best of the flat bottom cars in an era where that no longer mattered; such was the advantage of the Lotus 78/79. As always, when Williams makes the technological leap, it is a quantum one, and the FW-07 was to be the best ground effects car of its era.

The Williams FW-07B won the 1980 World Championship

It is hard to understand Al Unser walking away from Jim Hall and the soon to be dominant Chaparral at season's end, until one considers the options. Al had the opportunity to drive the Longhorn, a copy of the FW-07 built under license from Williams GP Engineering. Gordon – "I'm speculating, but I think he and Jim Hall had a falling out. He drove for Jim 2 years, and won here (at Indy in 1978) with the Lola. He won all the 500s in 3 new cars because he wrote off every one of them."

Is that what it takes to get a new car from Jim Hall? Gordon – (laughs) It probably was, but it wasn't worth it. That was the year at Michigan where he got up on top of the wall, when they still had guardrail. That car got up on top of the guardrail posts and the posts tore the bottom out of the chassis. They were all big crashes."

It was the overall package that made the Yellow Submarine a car of legend. There were no weaknesses. Gordon – "That underbody was just a good, simple straightforward underbody. The aerodynamics were good, but was just a very basic tunnel shape. The underwing was 'the thing of the moment', but you ignored basic physics at your peril. The car was really good overall, completely. Torsional strength, the stiffness of the chassis, suspension geometry, the gearbox was low drag… it had all the things that you need to do anyway, and it was a good car.

That balance can be easier said than done. Derrick Walker was the chief Engineer for Penske Racing during that early ground effects era. Derrick - "The good thing about ground effects is that you get a lot of downforce, and it can mask what a car is really doing. To actually manage the car, and make it drivable through all the speed variations, bumps, roll, cornering and all that… the ground effect masks it to some degree. But, there was no doubt that as you got the car's suspension stiffer for the downforce, the more flex you'd get and the more cracks you'd get. With those stiffer springs, the chassis had to be strong enough to support it. So, we'd have to build a stiffer chassis as the downforce levels were increasing. It really makes you think 'well, we need a different car."

1980 brought Johnny Rutherford and the Chaparral an Indy 500 win and series Championship. Gordon - "The Chaparral deal… the original plan that John thought Jim had agreed to, was setting up a Chaparral shop and side office in England for fabrication, building all the parts and stuff. The whole thing wasn't going anywhere, from what I could see. I wasn't really interested about living in Luton, it was pretty dreary."

Carbon fibre tubs were the next major innovation in racing to arrive, as John Barnard's McLaren MP4-1 had its debut in 1981. Previous to this, Gordon Murray had been using carbon structures within his Brabhams of the late 1970s, but Barnard's carbon tub built in a partnership with Hercules Aerospace was a game changer. Soon the carbon tub would end the era of riveted metal tubs in F1, but it wasn't an overnight change. The great disadvantage of the aluminum tub was that upon studying the stresses, typically the tub was made from whatever the minimum thickness of material was determined to be. With carbon tubs, and the use of computer generated finite stress analysis, there were numerous advantages. First and foremost was that the material only needed to be as thick in any given area, as was needed to satisfactorily resolve the forces involved. Also, given that carbon can be either a directional material or a multi-directional material, it gives yet more advantages in controlling the desired or undesired deflection.

Gordon Kimball arrived at McLaren in 1984. Gordon – "We built the cars in 84 because McLaren had gotten a big enough autoclave, before that Hercules had built the chassis. Now most people build chassis out of weave, but almost all of those early carbon tubs the carbon was uni-directional. We would then lay that carbon in the direction that we wanted it, and in the number of layers based upon the loads. That is the most efficient way. It gets harder to do when you are doing shapes, and that is why cloth is easier to consolidate over a female molded shape. Ours were all flat chines and stuff. That is the nice thing about carbon, as you can put it exactly where you want it, and how much you want. The chassis was a constant thickness, as the honeycomb was cut to different heights depending upon the thickness of the carbon... the number of layers. Sometimes the honeycomb looked like a beach, with steps in it. There were continuous plies that ran down the side of the chassis, and we machined the honeycomb first so where the plies were thicker, or in areas where you had to reinforce it, the honeycomb was stepped. The carbon plies were different thicknesses on the inside and the outside, so both sides of the honeycomb were machined. It is just a consolidation spacer. In some areas you'd have 4 layers of uni-directional, but in some areas there were 6 or 8. Nobody is doing that now."

However, the downside of some early carbon tubs could be horrendous, as this was the era that preceded the adoption of pre-season hammer or hydraulic ram tests, which determined the ability of a carbon monocoque to withstand impact before expecting a driver to use it. One need only peer into the remains of either Villeneuve's or Pironi's shattered 1982 carbon Ferraris to see just how dangerous being at the tip of the chassis technology sword could be. Despite the steep price paid by their drivers, the Ferraris were always fast and won the 1982 F1 Manufacturer's Championship.

As always there are two competing schools of design. One is to embrace the revolutionary concept which can equate to hitting a home run, but more often starts a struggle through the inevitable learning curve, potentially alienating sponsors and risking the real possibility of being technologically 'lost at sea'. The other path is to let the rest of the paddock learn the hard lessons while you continue to refine the proven technology of the day. The downside of that approach is obvious, as once the superior technology du jour is proven to be consistently superior, you had better been pursuing a parallel development program to eventually avoid a long stay at the wrong end of the result sheet. In 1982, Williams stayed the proven course and introduced the aluminum honeycomb tub FW08. Despite only winning one race that year, Keke Rosberg was to win the Drivers World Championship through consistent solid performances. For 1983, Williams primarily raced a revised 08C version, but the long time successful combination of normally aspirated engine in an aluminum chassis, was at the end of its long run. Ferrari with its carbon turbocars again won the Manufacturer's Championship, the pendulum had swung towards favoring the innovative side of the pitlane, with their 1.5 liter turbocars and carbon chassis. By the end of 1984, the aluminum monocoque era was over.

The chassis configuration of the typical ground effects car

of the late 1970s (F1) and early 1980s (Indycar) was to move the fuel into a cell mounted between the driver and the engine, freeing up the sidepods for aerodynamic downforce. There was a raised portion of the monocoque structure that had replaced the tubular front hoop which held the dash and steering wheel. The net result was a low monocoque in the area of the cockpit sides, with raised bulkheads in front and behind. Wasn't this a major compromise in the torsional integrity of the design, to say nothing of the side impact protection for the driver?

Gordon Kimball – "The problem was the size of the steering wheel along with the driver's hands, and nobody wanted to go wide enough with the bodywork. You didn't dare make it like we can now in carbon, you needed a big section so that it didn't fold up onto the driver. If you were responsible, you needed at least ¾" of section there, and nobody wanted to go wide enough. That era of soft aluminum sheet with honeycomb was almost criminal. The panel stiffness was great, but those cars were 'gooey'. The Chaparral (2K) had fairly high sides, but everybody was fighting section, it was the widest part of the car and nobody wanted to go wider."

One then wonders why the low side protection monocoque designs continued into the carbon tub era with the 1981 McLaren MP4-1. Kimball – "I was there in 84, 85 and 86. John had done a pretty good job on the first one (the 1981 MP4-1) so in the time I was there, there was a lot of polishing. The way we molded the early McLaren, they were internally molded onto aluminum blocks that we then had to unbolt and lift out, one at a time through the cockpit opening. Then the seat back was molded in the original, as we needed separate blocks for the fuel cell. The way we were doing it, you'd have had to split the blocks into 3 pieces, taking the middle part out if the opening at the top was smaller than the widest point of the chassis, which would have been really hard. That was what the aluminum chassis looked like in those days, and it just was what it was. It just took time, and even the bodywork was low in those days. It looked dangerous, and it was."

Derrick Walker – "I think they would be more protected (with the carbon/aluminum honeycomb cockpit sides). Not having the sides there, what's going to happen to the driver then? It's going to get him sooner. I don't think they had looked onto the safety issues as much as they should have done at that point. They were probably just thinking… there's the fuel cell and you have to get the fuel in up high, and over there is the dash that needs to be up so high to hold the steering wheel and the gauges and everything."

Ken Anderson - The last aluminum chassis in F1 was the FW09B in 1984. Williams took their usual pragmatic approach to things and hired Brian O'Rourke. The FW10 was the first chassis designed to be made from CF rather than 'fabricated' from it. The rest is history." With 2 wins for Rosberg and 2 wins for Mansell, there was little doubt that Williams was back from the technological wilderness. Much of this success was thanks to the composite expertise of O'Rourke, whose previous efforts had included developing fighter aircraft. Frank Dernie's subsequent FW11 was to become the fastest chassis for 1985/6, but with Mansell and Piquet trading wins, Prost with his usual efficiency scored yet another title for McLaren.

This approach to tub fabrication continued on into the 1990s. Kimball – "We were still doing male molds my whole time there… even later at Ferrari (1989 Ferrari 640 F1), it was male molded. The chassis were aluminum honeycomb with carbon skins. They were molded all together. You laid up the skin, and then you consolidated it, put the honeycomb on and laid up the outer skin and consolidated that. Then you cured it all together in the autoclave, and then the dashboard bulkhead went in… it was glued and screwed. I think on that one that the suspension bulkhead was aluminum, but the dash bulkhead was carbon. The carbon made it much stiffer, so there was less of a penalty."

Soon, Barnard had abandoned the male mold carbon tub design. Kimball – "The Benetton was a female molded chassis. Technically speaking the male mold was better because we got better consolidation, but in the end it just wasn't worth the work. By 89 or 90, other than at Ferrari, I think everybody was doing female molds. With a female mold, you don't have any bodywork." And now today, fully 32 years after Barnard's revolutionary MP4-1, the latest cars such as the Audi R18 are still constructed from carbon with aluminum honeycomb. Is there no acceptable alternative to using aluminum honeycomb in the carbon chassis? Kimball – "There was a nomex or paper honeycomb, but the aluminum is stronger. There have been major refinements, they just aren't obvious. Things like resins, fibers, and how you build them with the depth or strength you need in the honeycomb. Even better than that, is that it is fantastic in a crash; it absorbs so much energy."

What was the first carbon chassis in Indycar? Derrick Walker – "I had left Penske in 1988, for the Porsche team and Al Holbert. I stayed on to run the team after Al died (plane crash). For 1989 we had a conventional car, we ran a Porsche engine in a March chassis in 1989 for Teo (Fabi). But they saw Formula One going to carbon, so the rule book said that at the end of 1989 if a manufacturer wanted to build a chassis in carbon, he could. So March, who was building the car under contract for Porsche... March saw this in the rule book and said 'ok, we are going to build a carbon chassis.' March was well ahead of the game, they designed a very low chassis... the first low chassis."

Derrick – "In the old days they were higher on the sides to get the stiffness. You had to, but with carbon you could still get the stiffness and could get the driver down very low and then lower the sides. So the 1990 March-Porsche was designed as a carbon chassis. When the other team owners found out that we were building a carbon chassis, they all had a big meeting to talk about it. I was in the room with Porsche and we made out case.

We had applied to Kurt Russell that we should be able to make it based upon the rules. The owners changed the rules, right there in the room, to make it a honeycomb aluminum car. Because the car was low and had to be made out of the aluminum honeycomb, it was a flexy-flier… it was just crap. It was a disaster; they chased Porsche out of Indycar, and they were very upset. Porsche just ran to the end of the year and cancelled it. I think the owners feared Porsche. Of course at that time, Porsche had built fantastic machines like the 917, and they knew if Porsche put their mind to it there was a lot of technology they could draw from. The engine was already the best in the paddock, they had the money and the desire, and it was only a matter of time before they would get into the car. The team owners saw them as a real threat to dominate. It was a black day, and then in 1991 the other teams all made carbon chassis."

Of course, 1991 was still a full decade behind the earliest carbon tubs in Formula One. Derrick Walker on carbon chassis in Indycar – "Formula One, they don't hit the walls quite like we did, and we had to learn what that was all about.

One of the biggest problems of the Porsche was the unconventional turbocharger location. Derrick – "It was the biggest screwup known to man, in my opinion. It wasn't Porsche's design, it was March. What they did was to put the turbocharger at the front of the engine; they wanted to move that weight forward. The exhaust came up and out of the bodywork just above the fuel cell, and this thing obviously was heating the fuel. We managed to contain it, but there was a lot of mechanical work we had to do, in order to save it from melting. One side was the air intake, the other side the exhaust. When the guy was refueling the car, there was a great big exhaust belching out."

Despite all these stunning developments in open wheel racing, during the early 1980s in endurance racing the learning curve was still almost embarrassingly vertical, with the occasional radical innovation such as the carbon chassis Ford Aerospace

Mustang GTP of 1983. In comparison there was the dated technology of the T-600. Dan Binks – "The Lola T-600 was an all aluminum monocoque, pop riveted together, a sports 2000 with a top on it."

The chassis stresses changed dramatically with the arrival of the Electramotive Nissan, the next major advance in IMSA GTP. With the improvements in ground effects over the next few seasons, the spring rates went through the roof and the chassis were tasked like never before. The first high-downforce GTP car was the 1985/86 Electramotive Nissan, and one of the drivers was Tony Adamowicz. Tony - "Conte Racing with the Lola T-600 had been my introduction to GTP racing. To then go from the Lola to the March, the Jaguar, and then the GTP Nissan... that Nissan was beyond anything else I had driven, nothing had anywhere near that downforce or horsepower, it was a totally different animal. It was an animal that was unleashed. At Electramotive we had 5500# springs in the front of that car. Fifty five hundred!" With that early GTP Nissan there was probably more movement in the tires or the tub. Tony – "Oh yeah, nothing starts out perfect, especially from Lola. The tub wasn't that great, they made a whole new tub. That car accelerated and braked at about the same velocity, physically it was a very demanding car to drive."

After years of success in Trans-Am, Binks was moving back to IMSA GTP. For 1991, Binks and Kendall had combined their talents for a run at the top echelon of endurance racing. In the 6 years since Binks' previous GTP efforts with the Lola and March, the prototype world had changed. The Intrepid GTP car raised the downforce levels beyond even the Nissan.

Binks - "The Intrepid... this thing has got a carbon fiber tub made in Indianapolis and for a guy like me to go work on it; I wasn't sure how strong this thing was. We're gluing all these little bushings in to hold wing mounts and undertrays... I'm just thinking 'Oh my God, I hope this thing is tough enough.'

Working on it was a little bit eerie. The car was very expensive; basically Jim Miller paid Riley to design the car. The Intrepid chassis wasn't anywhere near stiff enough. When it wrecked at Watkins Glen, it just powdered the tub. It didn't have zones where it would absorb energy in a crash, and it folded at the seat belt mounts. For 92 we made the center section way stiffer and made crush zones with carbon cones or wedges instead of multiple bulkheads." Tommy Kendall - "The 92 car was safer, just as fast, but even if it wasn't a mechanical you could have an 'off' for any another reason at those corner speeds."

Kendall driving the much improved 1992 Intrepid
– Photo courtesy of Jerry Howard

There was an earlier carbon tub GTP car, designed by Bob Riley in conjunction with Ford Aerospace... the Mustang GTP. Bob Riley had also played a large role in the early success of the Roush road racing operation, much as he later did with the Intrepid GTP car for Pratt & Miller.

Jack Roush tells the tale of the early history of Riley's involvement with his team, and the early days of Roush road racing. "Bob Riley was a design engineer for the Ford Motor Company, working on pickup trucks. In his career on at least 2 occasions, he had been working for Ford Engineering and had taken a hiatus to go work on Indy car projects. At Ford he wasn't being as productive as he could be... wasn't being as productive as he was capable of. In 1981, Ford came on the scene with their SVO operation and Michael Kranefuss, using a Ford of Europe Capri (the Zakspeed Capri), so they brought that over and raced it as a GTX Mustang. At the end of 81 or 82, they came to me... I was involved with them doing all kinds of things at the time. They said 'Jack, we want to design a front engine GTP car. We want to use Ford Aerospace; we want to have a carbon fiber tub. We're going to put the engine up front to provide some opportunity for downforce. It's a radical new design, and we'd like for you to build the car, Ford Aerospace will help with all the components. Do you know an Engineer who could help with all this?' I told them -'As a matter of fact... I know a guy, and as far as I know he's designing rubber insulators for pickup truck body mounts, but he's a world class race car designer. He had worked on road race cars for decades as an avocation, not as a vocation. If you transfer him in here, I can work with him.' That introduced Bob Riley to SVO and he designed this GTP car, in concert with Ford Aerospace. It won its first race at Road America."

The Ford Mustang GTP raced in 1983-84, and although it never won another race, the car turned heads at every track where it competed. It also had brought Riley and Roush together, and their efforts were soon to find great success in a different series.

Jack Roush – "I was building the engines for the Trans-Am cars and the Kelly girl cars, the results were not there and I was getting some criticism about my engines from the drivers in 1983. I said that what I need is a fresh Bob Riley design on a Trans-Am car, and we'll go set the record straight on what we can do with our engines in Trans-Am. So, Bob Riley designed the car, it was under his job assignment for Ford that he designed me a car. Charlie Selix, Gary Pratt, and I ended up building the. Greg

Pickett was our driver and we took it to Road Atlanta, the first race. Pickett qualified in the top 10 and was working his way up to the front, went off while lapping a car, put a hole in the radiator and didn't finish the race. So... we go to Summit Point, which was the 2nd race. He was leading the race, and knocked the front suspension off lapping a car, but we won the next two races. We came back to the Detroit Grand Prix in 1984, and Pickett wrecked his car in the first corner of the first lap of practice, but I had built a car with the same design for Tom Gloy, and he won the race. We won the Trans-Am manufacturer's title for Ford in 1984. The only IMSA race we ran that year was the finale, which we won... and the next year was the first year we ran the 24 hours of Daytona." The Roush built, Riley designed Mustangs won 17 of the 34 races held in 1985-6.

For 1993, Kendall and Binks were re-united at Roush racing to run the GTS Mustang in IMSA. Dan – "It was one of those things where carbon was new to that kind of car, for sure. Don Hayward designed it, he was a Ford engineer... and it was Doug Louth's college project working with the Ford Motor Company. The composite shop at Jack's made most of the parts to make it happen. The Carbon GTS Mustang was pretty cool; we had a lot of quality people working on that car. And putting Tommy in anything wasn't quite fair."

For 1994, Dan Binks and Tom Kendall went Trans-Am racing with Roush. It was basically an evolution of the Riley design. Dan Binks – "Jack had several Riley cars in the early 90s, it was an evolution. We moved the suspension pick up points a little bit." Jack Roush – "They were Riley designed cars, but I constructed them. They weren't Riley cars in the sense that Riley had a chassis building operation. They were Roush built cars..."

After the Trans-Am days and then a few years in NASCAR trucks, Dan Binks was to return to Pratt & Miller. Dan – "I went to Corvette Racing at the end of 2002, and we used production steel frames, right from Bowling Green. At that time we only used the hydroformed rails, we were able to run our own shock mounts, our own upper control arms. We removed the aluminum cradle that the street car had at that time, and used chrome moly for the cradle."

The GT2 car has an aluminum frame vs. the previous ALMS car. The entire body was made of carbon fiber, which was a first for the team. Starting in 2009, the carbon fiber work was done in-house. Dan – "Our carbon shop is awesome. 2008-2009 was when we opened it. We had a small composite shop before, but we took it to the next level with the new shop, doing all that work in-house. When we switched over, we started doing Camaros, doing all that bodywork for Grand-AM."

Weight saving wasn't the key to why the team switched to aluminum frame, as under GT2 rules, the car was far heavier. Dan Binks – "It was 1145 kg for GT1vs. 1245 kg for GT2. General Motors wanted us to use the ZR-1 chassis, it was their new baby. We had never done a steel cage on an aluminum chassis before and we were all worried about it. We just did the best job that we could with all the guys at the shop, Doug Louth worked really hard on all that stuff. We did destructive testing on the connections, to learn how to do it and came up with the best way to hook the roll cage to the aluminum chassis. We machine an aluminum taper in the chassis and then there is a steel stud that has a thread on the end with the same taper. They prep the metals and then run them in and torque them along with using special glue. It actually has a thread that pulls it in onto the taper. So, it uses a taper like a valve retainer, but then we put glue on it just to make sure they don't come undone or get loose. They did such a good job, that we still use that connection today (2012)."

The basic structure has proven to be safe and strong. What changes have occurred across the 4 seasons running in GT-2? Binks - "We were really reluctant to run the aluminum frame cars, but we wanted to run the wider ZR-1 body style, and in the beginning it was only the ZR-1 that had the aluminum frame."

Laguna corkscrew 2010

"Later on, I think you could get one in the ZO-6, and the carbon edition (a trim package, not a carbon frame)." Dan summarized the durability of the GT2 Corvette chassis at Sebring in 2011 – "There are a couple of little tweaks, but basically it is the same one as in 2009. If you walked up to the 2 chassis, you wouldn't see any difference. There basically aren't any changes on the main chassis since chassis #1 from Mid-Ohio 09. That chassis was really durable, it was the chassis that got wrecked at Monterey (Laguna 2009), and that was a 54 G hit, which is ridiculous for these cars. I thought it was a write-off but the floor was intact, the tunnel was intact, it just wrinkled up the frame rails. We cut it off at the firewall and put a new front on it, it wasn't that big of a deal and we were able to save it. I would not have believed that an aluminum frame car could have held up that well, the guys that crash the production cars over and over, they do an amazing job and all that stuff pays off for us. Chassis #1 is here at Sebring."

In 2012 the revised Pratt & Miller GT Corvette had its debut at Sebring, with an increase in track allowed by the rules. Added are dive planes at the front of the car, along with a higher rear wing height. Jan Magnussen – "I'm very pleased. Everything has changed; it is a big jump from last year... 2-1/2 seconds faster than last year. The overall width of the car is 2" bigger than last year. So, it is a huge step forward with the wider car and the higher rear wing." Is it approaching the sorts of lap times from the GT1 days? "It's getting closer. It is a big jump and the improvement of the car is all over. It is just a better package. Better balance, better power... the whole thing. For everybody else, it's the same though. But, it looks like we will have more fun this year." That proved to be the case as the Pratt & Miller Corvettes were to win the ALMS GT Manufacturers Championship in 2012 and 2013, 10 of the previous 15 years.

In motorcycle racing, chassis development has gone from the flexy fliers of the early 70s, to the concept of rigidity above all. Eventually the designers recognized that some compliance is necessary for rider feel and getting the power down while at a variety of lean angles and surfaces. Is there an optimal solution on this concept, with massive beam rigidity when upright and more supple allowing deflection when leaned over? Stuart Shenton, technical director for Suzuki in Moto GP – "It is different technology from Formula One where they want the stiffest platform. Here we are on to something completely different. We look at the 3 axis. We have Yaw, Bend, and Torsion. It's a balance between those, and it is something that we do play with. If the balance isn't right, it can create a lot of problems... Bend for us, is not currently an issue, not the one we look at the most. Torsion and Yaw we look at a lot more, the idea is to get it right. You can have a chassis that is too soft or too rigid, you have to have it in the correct area to work with the tires and the suspension, and the amount of grip you have available."

If a chassis were soft and had the ability to deflect, one could see that it could react like a leaf spring, and rebound from that deflection. Stuart - "Anything like that would be un-damped. But, it does change sometimes, every 2 or 3 years. Things like tire grip improves, suspension improves... corner speeds go up, they all have an influence on it. It's a moving target and what works one year might not work the next. Tire performance, sometimes it comes down to the amount of grip you have. Construction plays a part, but it's not the only defining factor in the tire that has an influence on that. It depends upon the rider as well, a motorcycle is a very personal object, and riding techniques can be quite different from one rider to the next as well. Different riders might have different stiffness of chassis, while using the same tire. It's a whole tin of worms." The tin of worms had recently become more complicated when shifting from the somewhat supple Michelin tire designs to the more rigid Bridgestone construction. The differences have to be compensated for by the chassis and suspension... back to the drawing board.

The man with the greatest winning record in MotoGP racing is Valentino Rossi's engineer, Jeremy Burgess. Jeremy looks back upon a radical year of change for the Honda 500cc GP team. "The biggest thing that changed in 1989 was Eddie Lawson and Erv Kanemoto put 13 different chassis through the 1989 bike. They worked furiously. It clearly came from Eddie Lawson's experience on the Yamaha, and the fact that we went to a full deltabox chassis. I believe the 1990 bike at 115 kilograms was the best bike they ever made, and a few of the chassis engineers felt the same way. It was a big step into carbon fiber, and the rear subframe had gone. It was super light, and then of course when the rule went back to 128kg and we made the engine cases out of aluminum and some other things. From that point on, the chassis didn't really change until Valentino rode it in 2001, when we lifted the engine up and back 10mm to get more rear grip. Mick (Doohan) rode the same chassis as everyone else... Honda only built one chassis." It gives one appreciation for what was accomplished in that single year, that the chassis remained essentially unchanged for the following 11 seasons.

However static and predictable the equipment had become, it was still possible for Honda to get completely confused in the 2000 season. It was the classic case of changing multiple items at once, and leaving the engineers and riders struggling to solve where they had lost the setup. Burgess – "Alex Criville had asked for something, as the World Champion. All our testing was done with Valentino on the old engine, as we were going to be getting the new engine later on. We got to Philip Island for a test with the new engine, and there was nothing right in the middle where you wanted to pick the throttle up in the corner. Valentino crashed coming out of Siberia, but didn't think much about it, thinking it would just take an amount of time to get used to it. But the new engine which Criville had asked for was absolutely useless, even Valentino identified that it wasn't as good."

Keep in mind that at this point Valentino Rossi was the 250GP World Champion but was still very much the new kid on the block in 500GP. Burgess – "In South Africa, Valentino was faster than all the other Hondas, but then he crashed... same sort of thing, mid-corner picking the throttle up. The load didn't go to the back, and he lost it.

So, by the time we got back to Japan, we're moved to the back of the pecking order again, while they found old cylinders to give to Alex Criville, Okada, and Gibernau. All our engines were bitsas after that. I got all the old used cylinders that were still good enough to use. They weren't very good, but it was what we had until they manufactured some more cylinders. But, we didn't change the swingarm because we had an engine problem. They were changing swingarms, chassis. I felt clearly there was nothing wrong with the forks, nothing wrong with the chassis."

Jeremy continues – "At Jerez, there was absolute chaos in the Repsol garage next door. We'd look over the wall and there were shocks, forks, and chassis spread everywhere. For some reason, those guys weren't smart enough to work out what the problem was. They wanted last years' swingarm, last years' forks... when we got the engine, we didn't make the chaos that they made. We knew we needed the engine, and we got the engine, and got 3rd in the race. You know where the problem is, if you've got the experience. We got it sorted out and finished 2nd in the Championship. Away we went, from that point on." Away they went indeed, and the pairing of Rossi and Burgess went on to win 7 MotoGP World Championships that decade. As much as the riding talent of Valentino Rossi was on full display, so was the synergy of rider and engineer in determining how best to improve the machine.

Recent developments in motorcycle racing have carbon chassis appearing in the prototype class, MotoGP. Jeremy offered some insight as to working with carbon frames and the current technical limitations within the class. "That gives you an advantage if it works, for a short period of time because the others will catch up... or it can put you in a place where you are dealing with a whole group of people that really have no idea about it. When you are dealing with an aluminum chassis it's probably a lot quicker to work with, people can weld, people can drill holes all over... you can't just go drill a piece of carbon fiber without a certain amount of risk. The process of development appears to be a little bit slower than perhaps it would be with a deltabox frame."

The drills and grinders were in full use with the early Honda RC45. Al Ludington confirms that this was often the process in adjusting the chassis to help their bike turn during his years as team manager for the American Honda Superbike program. Al – "It's like that in the first year when you get a bike. I remember going to Laguna with the RC45, in its first year back in 1994… that first year it was a tremendous pooch. Magee was having his mechanic drill holes back behind the steering head, and connecting them with a whiz wheel (grinder) to try and get the front end a little nicer. That's what you do for a year or two, until they get something that they like." Worthy of note, is that drilling holes in the steering head of the frame is thankfully less common than in the past, as confirmed by Greg "Woody" Wood. In his years of experience with Fiat Yamaha, Tech 3, Yoshimura, and American Honda, he had never experienced that modification, perhaps because those teams hadn't quite reached such levels of desperation.

However, as Jeremy Burgess noted, there is something to be said for the ability to modify such things at the race meet rather than ordering up a new frame for next time. In contrast, Ludington is a firm believer in this new carbon technology, in a world where computer modeling has become more and more accurate. Al – "They've got finite element analysis, they've got computational fluid dynamics… these computer simulations have been around long enough that they are getting really accurate. In F1, the data is getting so freaking close, that the wind tunnel is just used for confirmation. It's way better than 'cut and try, cut and try'. With the development of the Pirelli F1 tire, they computer simulated tires and cars when neither one even existed. Ferrari and McLaren sent Cad files of the new car, and Pirelli would build computer tires to put on there and got within about 5% of actual." Theoretically, the same could be done for frame design. In practice it hasn't proven to be so easy.

At Ducati in 2011, Nicky Hayden was working with the team to try and get increased deflection in yaw. "Lateral stiffness... there's a lot of ways to get stiffness, it depends. In beam we want it to be stiff, but we want it softer on the lateral to make it turn better." Does Nicky think that the inherent flexibility of carbon with an almost infinite number of potential combinations of fiber weave with material and directional options, to say nothing of the types of resins, is an advantage? Or has this created a nightmare of confusion? Nicky – "Carbon... it's taken us a long time to do it. It's a lot more to go through than it was before."

At Indy, Valentino Rossi shared his analysis of the strengths and weaknesses of the latest carbon framed Ducati – "The bike has good stability at the rear, the gearbox is not too bad, also the engine is quite good... but we need to pick up some feeling at the front when turning. It has always been difficult to understand what is happening at the front... with the front tire when you are turning the bike." The lack of front sensitivity persisted and it was of little surprise that before long, Rossi's Ducati was equipped with an aluminum frame.

Issues of chassis ductility in yaw while under power were well on display at the 2011 French MotoGP at Le Mans. The double apex corner leading onto the back straight has a bump right at the point where one wants to feed in the power. Many of the machines tracked well over this bump under power, but the Repsol Hondas of Pedrosa and Stoner would take a big twitch as the tail stepped out when the power was applied. As it turns out in this case there wasn't a correlation between lap time and the inability of the chassis to absorb these forces. Jeremy – "But they're the fastest thing here, and that could be interesting..." Difficult and twitchy to ride, does not always equate to slow.

If there is one thing that has been the hallmark of Yamaha in GP racing, is that their bikes are consistently rideable. Lawson vs. Gardner, Rainey vs. Doohan, Rossi vs. Stoner, Lorenzo vs. Pedrosa and Marquez... the Yamaha always seems to be a more complete balanced package, whereas the Honda approach was more often a cross between a rocketship and a handful. Tom Houseworth was the crew chief for Ben Spies at Yamaha in 2011-12 – "Their (Yamaha) chassis have always been great, and we are just a little down on power."

Burgess and Rossi struggled with the carbon framed Ducati

"The other brand... their chassis aren't as good but they are FAST. It's been that way forever." A trademark of the brand, it continues across the various eras up to today. Although highly effective, it can be scary to watch the Repsol Honda.

Tom – "They've been scary to watch for a long time." As always, all the developments in the world may be lost upon an ineffective chassis.

As for now, the Honda/Yamaha wars continue their annual battle for supremacy, each in their unique and consistent way.

Valentino Rossi (Yamaha) and Marc Marquez (Honda) doing battle for second place while headed into the corkscrew section at the 2013 United States Grand Prix. Marquez won the race

CHAPTER THREE

ENGINE AND DRIVETRAIN

Matra 12 cylinder engines of every variety at the Matra Museum

There was a time, when there was no set pattern or layout for the controls of a racing car. In the 1950s, every time you got in a Ferrari Grand Prix car, the shift pattern might have been different. At times it was all the way across the gates and then back in the same direction to upshift from 1st to 2nd. One would think somebody would have tapped the designer on the shoulder and said "You know…." Phil Hill - "Don't do that…. (laughs). They (the designers) had the power. I would go back over there to see the new car, and you're not going to say, 'you can't do that.' They would do all sorts of things to get the driver lower and over to the side, to improve the car… and they would put the gearbox around you that way." Did the drivers see themselves as a necessary inconvenience, in which Ferrari wished the car would just drive itself? Phil – "We thought that was an erroneous opinion. But then we decided it was real." The desired participation from the cockpit was essentially 'shut up and drive'.

Another factor was at play, as with Ferrari it was always about the engines, even into the 1990s. John Barnard had developed the revolutionary 1989 paddle shift V12 Ferrari 640 after he previously had changed Formula One with his first carbon tub GP car, the 1981 McLaren. American motorcycle GP team owner Kenny Roberts later was later to work with John Barnard, and reflected upon the mindset at Ferrari. Kenny – "He (Barnard) said, there were the motor people and me. If the motor people wanted something that f***ed with the aerodynamics, you lost."

Clearly there has been great progress made across the past 50 seasons of racing, one of which was to make operating the controls as intuitive as possible, and another is encouraging the potential synergy of driver and engineer. It also helps when there is cooperation between the various departments tasked with developing a finished and successful package.

In racing, the state of the art is constantly in flux, an uneasy balance of evolution and revolution. In examining the progress of engine and drivetrain development, perhaps an obvious starting point would be a discussion on the variety of fuels used in racing. Since the days of Germany's Silver Arrows from 1937-39, increasingly exotic fuel blends were being used to increase power in their 2 stage supercharged engines. Their blends of different types of Alcohol, Benzene, and high octane gasoline were the result of a search for increased octane and engine output.

Rod Coleman was one of the AJS factory riders back in the day when the legendary AJS Porcupine raced in Grand Prix. He vividly recalls the effect upon those in the vicinity of a pre-war Mercedes GP car.

Rod Coleman – former AJS factory rider from the early '50s

Rod – "Talking of acrid smells from some forms of Nitro/ alcohol fuels, I think the worst I have ever smelt was with John Surtees at Goodwood a few years ago he was driving one of the 1939 original works Mercedes Benz. It was impossible to stand anywhere near the exhaust outlet." It completely took away one's breath and stung the eyes." Worse than that, there are also increased health risks as a result of exposure to the toxin Benzene, which include Leukemia.

Rod Coleman also recalls some of their fuel experiments in that immediate post-war era of 2 motorcycle Grand Prix racing. Rod – "Wood Alcohol (Methanol) has been out of date for a long time because Isopropil Alcohol is much more efficient and does not use big carburetor jets. The mixture that Mobil gave us at AJS away back in 1951 was Isopropil plus Nitro Benzene and water. I can't remember the ratio for each only that for water which was 10%. There was not only more power with an Isopropil mixture, but the only change in carburetion was one jet size larger. This was essential for the success of the seven hours endurance records because we did not have to carry a lot of weight in fuel and of course had a lot less time-consuming stops for refueling."

The use of "dope" or alcohol based fuel was more commonly used in the days when high quality gasoline was either heavily rationed or unavailable in many part of the world. There were also other factors. Rod Coleman – "Regarding the use of alcohol in New Zealand and Australian racing this was really a legacy of speedway where the Dirt Track JAPs used nothing but alcohol based fuels. Then because they outperformed any other make of engines they became the only engines used in speedway. It was then thought that because they only had cast-iron cylinders and cylinder head it must be the alcohol that was the reason for the performance. It was even thought by the pundits that a highly tuned alcohol burning cast-iron engine of any make would be able to compete on level terms with an authentic alloy engined race bike such as Manx Nortons etc."

Rod's experiences in Europe enabled him to bring back much of the acquired knowledge from the British tuning masters of the day. Rod – "When I returned from Europe at the end of 1951, I had gained a lot more knowledge about all the various alcohol blends through working with the Vacuum oil company at the AJS factory when we were preparing a 7R2 for all the world endurance records that we established. There was a considerable gain in hp if using the various Nitro blends, so consequently I built the engine of my 1951 Manx Norton with this new-found knowledge. The result was that in my first road race back in New Zealand I had an easy win almost lapping the entire field. However the fuel blend that I used left a very strong smell around the circuit. The result was that NZ ACU announced that alcohol fuels would be banned from use in road racing forthwith."

The same did not hold true with Australia. Rod – "In Australia the same sort of thinking applied so that when I first rode at Bathurst in 1953 I found I was really at a disadvantage with my AJS 7R2 and Manx Norton being on petrol because the Australians were not only into alcohol but the top riders were also up with the play on the various Nitro blends. So to make sure of winning everything in 1954, I had to rebuild my engines so that I was on an equal footing.

Ironically, the greatest American motorcycle road racer of his time, Cal Rayborn was killed in late 1973 trying to adapt an ex-Coleman Suzuki to alcohol fuel at the last minute while racing at Pukekohe, New Zealand. It remains a textbook example of how serious the consequences can be for making last minute major modifications to previously well sorted carburetion. Things started to go wrong soon after Cal arrived in New Zealand, as there wasn't one of the new TR750 Suzuki triples available for him to race. Chip Hennen – "Cal gets down there, and there is no factory TR750 for Cal, but there was for Ron (Grant)." For obvious reasons, Cal Rayborn did not wish for his debut with Suzuki to be on anything but their fastest equipment.

Rod Coleman – "It seems that Ron Grant was the motivator to get Rayborn to compete at Pukekohe but it was a very much a last-minute exercise. When Joe Lett arrived at Pukekohe on race day, he had driven up from Wanganui during the night and knew nothing about Rayborn until Ron Grant approached him and told him that he must lend his TR500 Suzuki to Rayborn to race that day."

Joe Lett's bike was the Suzuki 500 previously raced by the late Geoff Perry, recently killed in the crash of an airliner while flying to America for the National at Laguna Seca. At Daytona in 1972, Geoff Perry had found that the Coleman Suzuki air cooled TR500 twin with a works replica frame to be highly competitive. However, there was a huge difference in the speeds of these machines between early 1972 and late 1973 as it was now the 2 stroke 750cc era. Only a state of the art 500 could have been competitive as Rod Coleman showed that season with the prototype water cooled Suzuki TR500. Rod – "Suzuki had sent me a new prototype lightweight liquid cooled TR500 for which I was required to send them written reports after each race and describe modifications that we applied. They were pleased when Dale Wylie showed them that it was competitive against the TR750 and won the Championship. At the end of the season it was then flown back to the factory." Since Cal Rayborn did not have access to a TR750, and with the new liquid cooled TR500 back at the factory, the ex-Perry Suzuki was probably by far the best machine available on such short notice.

The situation rapidly deteriorated as Cal and Lou decided to roll the dice with modifications to the engine allowing the bike to run alcohol. Chip Hennen – "Cal and Lou agreed to run it on alcohol, to give it the extra horsepower to be competitive against the TR750. Running a bike on alcohol would turn a bike into a missile, but the carburetion has to be so precise... they are very prone to seizing. Joe Lett wanted to run it on standard gasoline as it was pretty quick as it was, and he was entirely blameless. Cal wanted to run it on alcohol... they called it "dope" in those days, I don't remember what the actual blend was. He wanted to beat

Ron, and it got the better of him. As fast as Cal was, he couldn't overcome that deficit."

Rod Coleman - "The whole situation was even more ridiculous when it is realized that there was only very few hours left before practice started. Why Rayborn's mechanic (Lou Kaiser) should think that he could produce some magic performance by converting the Suzuki to alcohol is beyond my belief. There was very little time to do this work and he should have taken notice of the more experienced people who were advising against what he was trying to do. Even so Joe Lett and two others did try to help but when they were ignored and could see that the basics of tuning for alcohol were being ignored they left them to it. They were horrified when they saw frantic filing to increase the carburetor slide cutaways. Increasing the carburetor slide cutaway would reduce the oil supply to the engine when closing the throttle, a known factor to cause piston seizure. I think that the action of trying to use alcohol should not have been done and if there had been an ACU official around he should have stopped it." The use of alcohol was not so common at the time in 2 stroke road racing engines. Ken McIntosh, the tuning and fabrication guru from Auckland also considered the other possibilities – "I think the trouble was the "Devcon" used to modify the ports may have lifted off with the alcohol. Alcohol was normal for all the ¼ mile speedway in NZ, but I think most of the old 4 stroke GP bikes and Yamaha TR, etc used Avgas."

Early in the race at Pukekohe, Cal Rayborn was killed when the bike seized in a high speed curve. However, in this case, it wasn't a failure of the Devcon that locked up the Rayborn modified engine, as upon disassembly, the engine was nearly perfect. Rod Coleman – "The Police made a very thorough examination of the TR 500 which Rayborn rode and in fact kept it for three months before returning it to Joe Lett. It showed that it had only a light nip on one piston." Fine can be the line between ultimate performance and disaster when mixing fuels.

Even at the lowest echelons of racing, fuels were being experimented with for improved performance. Wayne Rainey's first race bike was the recipient of Sandy Rainey's creativity in rules interpretation. Wayne – "My Dad being the innovative guy that he is, looked through the rule book on "fuel", and all it said was that you must have fuel. So, the next thing I know he's telling me "Don't tell Mom, but you're not going to school today, we're going to test something." So, we go off to Saddleback park on a Tuesday afternoon, he'd brought all the jets. We were running 95% Nitro, 5% Alcohol… and I went and rode this thing. This thing was a lethal weapon, it was so fast… I remember doing big 'ol feet on the pegs power slides, it would wheelie when I'd shift gears." Chad McQueen became the recipient of this technology when Sandy inadvertently mentioned it to one of Steve McQueen's friends. Chad – "Those were the good 'ol days man. We were running Nitro and Alcohol mixed, and we took it pretty seriously back then. Pretty soon the starting line was like, "what the f**k is that smell?""

There were downsides to the Nitro powered Honda Mini-Trails. Jeff Ward – "We had Nitro in my bikes, and we had an SL70 with a lightened flywheel, but it blew up. We blew the whole side of the motor off, and put 4 holes in my leg from the shrapnel. The mixture was a little too wrong, but there was some power… it was some pretty lethal stuff." Wayne Rainey and Jeff Ward became the masters of the Top Fuel Honda Mini-Trail, Ward a multiple MX and Supercross Champion, and Rainey a 3 time 500cc road racing World Champion.

Innovations in auto racing technology had also brought the use of previously unheard of fuels. The exotic fuel blends perhaps reached their peak in the 1500cc Turbo era of Formula One, which in the beginning were primarily limited to water injection. Mario Andretti was to experience the peak of this early turbocar era, driving the 1982 Ferrari 126C2, perhaps the most powerful F1 car of its era. Mario - "My last ride in Formula One

110

was the Ferrari turbocar, substituting for Pironi. In qualifying they had water injection to prevent detonation; they had so much blower pressure in there. For qualifying it was over 1000hp. At Monza when I put that thing on pole, it was between Piquet and I… whoever came in, had the quick time." That year of 'qualifying specials', the Brabham BMW team was closing off the pop-off valve for qualifying, and the actual output of Piquet's car was anyone's guess, although numbers in the range of 1300hp were rumored. No doubt Ferrari had also provided Andretti with that little extra as well, given Ferrari's tradition of bringing their best out for the home GP. Mario – "It was quite a duel until I did the 2nd Lesmo flat, it was 5th gear already… that was so satisfying. I tell ya what, I loved that car. I would have won the race, but I lost a blower (turbo) on the left side and finished 3rd."

It wasn't long before the water injection was supplemented (and eventually replaced) with the 80+% Tolulene based pre-heated fuels of the mid-1980s. There were voiced concerns over the potential health hazards to the teams from the fuels they were exposed to. Tolulene can cause neurological disorders, and could only be considered acceptable when compared to the Benzene based fuels of the 1930s, which were a proven carcinogen. Adding to the challenge was that Tolulene lacks the lubrication provided by gasoline, so fuel systems were problematic until new solutions were found to enhance system durability. Still, despite these issues, Tolulene fuels were the state of the art for almost a decade. Emanuele Pirro – "Initially, it was excitement. The fuel was delivering so much more power, so much more sharpness in the engine and we were all excited. But, from early on we felt there was a strange smell, with a pain in the eyes when you were following a car. Later, the safety of that fuel became an issue but in the beginning it was just a cool thing. I was using it in the normally aspirated engines of the late 80s and early 90s. It was bringing 50 to 60 more horsepower."

In the early 1990s, the era of Tolulene based fuel in Formula

One was legislated out of existence due to those safety concerns. However, Dan Binks was just getting started with similar ideas on maximizing fuel performance, and was well at work with exploring his options at the outer limits of rulebook interpretation. Dan – "I was with Roush in Trans-Am, and the SCCA said they were going to use this fuel tester and it must read between this and that range. Ok, the fuel tester was made by Klotz, and they make their own race gas. So, I call the guy at Klotz and said 'Ok, what's the deal?' He said 'Well, it has to be between here and here.' So, I say – 'Ok, how much does it cost to have the best gas that still tests between here and here.' He says he has to have an order for 7000 gallons. I told him 'Ok, we're willing to do that, will it pass?' He said ok, so we had the best gas they knew how to build in that range. They put something in it so that it looked like it was in that range, they tested it over and over again. That stuff… you could pour in 30 horsepower. It wasn't cheating as they made the machine and sold the machine to the SCCA."

Of course, the manufacturer of the testing equipment knew how to maximize performance within the limitations of their own equipment. The SCCA probably thought they had achieved an independent verifiable system of measurement. The reality was that Binks found the fatal flaw in the SCCA plans, and as always was quick to exploit it. 30 horsepower never came so cheap.

In the mid 1980's during F1's turbo era, a revolution was similarly underway in IMSA. Electramotive Nissan had brought their high downforce GTP to the game and the available power was like nothing previously seen in IMSA. Team driver Tony Adamowicz – "We could dial in, at any given time, 1000hp, which eventually Electramotive got as high as 1500hp… from a 3 litre engine. It was an amazing process that I was glad to be a part of, and I've never had an experience like that before or since. The one big advantage they had over Porsche and Bosch was the engine's electronic management system controlling fuel management and spark timing, developed by John Knepp and Don Devendorf.

112

Even with their old GTO car, with an in-line 6 cylinder non-crossflow head production engine, it was producing 850hp with 650 ft lbs of torque. It had dual fuel injectors spaced on the manifold; none of the injectors that were available could deliver enough fuel to the engine. It was a monster, and we had total reliability. We were testing at Mt. Fuji with the GTO car and Porsche was also testing there. We could pass Porsche 962s going up the front straight, waving at them as we went by. Porsche and Ford both wanted that engine management system big time, but Don's loyalty was with Nissan, and he never gave it up. Don was an absolute genius; he had also worked for Hughes aircraft and was a NASA troubleshooter."

Today, the wizardry continues. With the American Le Mans series commitment to alternate fuels and alternate technologies, it was a natural for the series to attract the new generation low-emission Diesel technology and various Ethanol blends. Initially the Pratt & Miller Corvette team went to an E10 blend, but later in the GT-1 era, that changed to E85. Reminiscent of the Tolulene fueled era of F1, there were initial problems with the fuel system, as adhesives in the fuel cell were failing in the early E85 cars, but those concerns were quickly dealt with. The Corvette team won the Green Challenge at Petit Le Mans in 2009 with their GT2 car, and by doing the most while using the least, showed that racing involvement is relevant, and it continues to improve the breed. One suspects part of the reasoning for changing from E10 to E85 may have been in response to the well publicized "fuel or food" debate in reaction to increased food prices and reduced supply, but for 2011 the Corvette team was back to running E10. Binks – "Now we are at 29.1 on the restrictor because we are using E10 now, previously we were at 28.8 with the E85. It looks like there's an advantage there, we don't really know yet. Another reason we did it is that we are already 30# heavier than the competition, 1260 vs. 1245 (kilos) and with the E85 you'd have to carry 30# more fuel to start with, so we'd be 60# heavier. It's all a trade-off, and every week you have to look at the puzzle and see if it makes sense to switch back & forth. We've tested both, and right now we think the way to go is with the E10, but if it was all up to the computers, we wouldn't have to come here on Saturdays."

The alternative fuels become yet another variable to game for the greatest advantage. Dan - "We used E10 last year at Sebring, but this year (2012) we are back to E85. So we've been going back & forth between E10 and E85. It's all in what benefit you can get. But at Le Mans, everybody is on the same gasoline over there... no Ethanol in France." Is there a separate engine development program for the gasoline based fuel? Dan - "We actually ship fuel over from Europe and all that. It's a disaster, an expensive disaster." The Green Challenge for the ALMS is a big part of their series marketing, so as a result anyone who wishes to compete at Le Mans has to create a parallel gasoline engine development program. "Yeah, but our guys are good enough that if there was an advantage from one week to the next, we would change. They know what to do."

The debut of the Corvette GT2 spec engine – Mid Ohio 2009

Do the gasoline fueled engines run to the same degree of clean burning as the Ethanol based engines? Binks - "They run better than they did, for sure. The life of the sensors and the residue in the exhaust, they are all really good now. It's running so close to optimal all the time that the sensors are like on your production car, and they just run forever now."

Of course, the challenge with any series that allows a wide range of engine designs and fuels becomes finding a fair equivalency formula. In the early 1990s, the rule makers of the Indianapolis 500 struggled with stock block formulas vs. the pure racing engines from Ilmor, Cosworth, and Honda. Tony George – "Someone is always going to be at a disadvantage. The teams that can afford it might go out and acquire all the equipment so that they have all the bases covered, all the options. Whereas teams which are not in such a financial position would be relegated to run whatever they had, on whatever type of circuit. Not being able to optimize, and have the best showing... this sport is fueled by sponsorship, and no one wants to hitch their wagon to somebody that doesn't have the possibility of contesting for the win."

Perhaps the most egregious example was the 1994 Ilmor "stock block" engine that dominated the 500 with Penske Racing. In this case, a team with substantial financial resources was able to develop an entirely separate and secret development program around the stock block formula. Tony George – "I personally didn't like equivalency formulas back then, and certainly that particular example it showed what kind of result equivalency can produce. There are still people today who talk about that... that it was an engineering challenge that was brought together to become absolutely the most insane thing allowed to happen at the Indianapolis Motor Speedway. I didn't like equivalency formulas before that. Stock Blocks and Turbochargers... it never worked. Trying to come up with a different way to make the same concept work is not where we should like to focus our energy."

As a result of this difficulty, most racing series have become more and more like a spec series. Jeremy Burgess is the most successful engineer in MotoGP history, and for him as with many others, these limitations have taken something away from motor sport. Jeremy - "At the moment everybody has the same tires, everybody has the same suspension, everybody has the same brakes, everybody has the same wheels... the only thing that's made by anybody else is the engine and the chassis. It shouldn't be that difficult to sort out. It's rather bland right now; we have those 2 components on the motorcycle that aren't in common with anybody else. In my opinion, in a prototype sport, there's not tons of excitement in MotoGP. In our sport we should be embracing more technical partners rather than driving them away. It would be great if some of the teams were here on Michelin tires. It's the Bernie Ecclestone theory, you'll always have people bitching and moaning unless they are on the same stuff. That's not what racing was ever about, it was company technology vs. company technology. Unfortunately over the generations, and with the television we have now, it becomes more of a show. 18 times a year you'll see at 2pm on your TV, motorcycle racing... an exciting show every week. And to keep it exciting you need close racing, so the bikes have to be closer to the same. I enjoy innovation, and that is something that has been taken away."

In any discussion of racing engines, the Group 7 racers of the mid 1960s provided for one of the greatest eras of endurance racing, when the prototypes from Ferrari, Maserati, Ford, Chevrolet (Chaparral), and Porsche fought for sports car racing supremacy. The 7 litre capacity limit for the big prototypes played into the hands of the American manufacturers who already had NASCAR programs for their 427 powerplants. In the endurance racing series dominated by 3.3 litre Ferrari sports cars, there was an obvious advantage to bringing in the heavy artillery with twice the displacement for a circuit with a 3 mile straight. So, in Ford's 2nd year to challenge at Le Mans, that is exactly what they did.

For 1965 at Le Mans, Chris Amon was driving the new 7 litre Ford GT, teamed with the greatest endurance driver of the day, Phil Hill. Chris – "Phil had quite an aura. In those years just before I got over into Formula One, he was winning the World Championship and winning Le Mans and sports car races on a semi-regular basis. He was almost a boyhood hero of mine, so to get to drive with him at Le Mans was very special."

The big problem was the massive torque of the engine, which just overwhelmed the car in its 1965 configuration. Amon - "I'll never forget the start of that race, as Bruce (McLaren) was starting in that yellow car he was sharing with Ken Miles. I started in our car and the known weakness of the car was the gearbox. We were told to take it very easy getting it off the line at the start. I had photos that were taken at the start of that race, showing the black lines behind Bruce's car, and black lines behind mine." Not surprisingly, the cars did not reach the finish line.

The following year, the 7 litre Mk. II Ford was to win Le Mans, driven by Chris Amon and Bruce McLaren. It was a moment of great satisfaction for Ford, as they had been left at the altar in their attempts to buy Ferrari 3 years previously, when Enzo Ferrari abruptly ended negotiations. From that perceived insult, the seeds of the entire Le Mans program had been planted. Now, it was Ferrari's turn to be obsessed with revenge.

It wasn't long before Enzo Ferrari put out the feelers to obtain the services of Ford's 1966 Le Mans winner, Amon. Chris - "I was actually approached by Keith Velocette of Shell, and I remember very clearly to this day… it was between Can-Am races and Bruce was running the Formula One car at Watkins Glen, and I'd come down to the Glen for the weekend before heading to the west coast for the next Can-Am race. Keith came up to me and said 'Mr. Ferrari would like to talk to you. Would you be available to fly over on Monday?' I was completely taken aback. I said to Bruce – 'I've been invited to see Ferrari.' He said… (laughs)… his language wasn't very good as I'd always agreed to stay with him for '67. I got into Milan 1st thing Tuesday morning and drove straight down to Modena and out to Maranello."

"When I went initially to Ferrari for the first and only meeting to sign the contract, it lasted all of about 10 minutes. It said in the contract that I was to drive for Ferrari. I had an interpreter at the time, and I was saying that it didn't say anything about Formula One. Ferrari was sitting at his desk saying 'No, it doesn't.' So I said, 'You know… I want to drive Formula One.' He was basically saying, 'do you want to drive for Ferrari, or not?' He had suggested that I was going to drive Formula One, but he wasn't going to put it in the contract. I guess I gave it about 10 seconds thought, and decided to sign it anyway. Ferrari said 'We'll have to go across the road and have lunch now' and that was it. I had to fly back to JFK that night so I sat there at lunch drinking mineral water. When we came out of the Cavallino, Ferrari said 'you don't seem to drink any wine.' I told him that I was in training. He said 'When Mike Hawthorn signed his contract he drank ½ a bottle of my best malt whiskey."

Ferrari didn't bother with entering the first Grand Prix of 1967, in South Africa. Chris Amon – "They really wanted to concentrate on the 24 hours of Daytona, and I think they felt that South Africa was going to be a distraction. Plus the fact that I don't think the new Formula One car would have been ready for South Africa, and would have had to use the car that they used at Monza in 1966. Ferrari was incensed that they had been beaten at Le Mans in 1966 and he was determined to bounce straight back. I think underneath everything, Ferrari always preferred Sports Car racing to Formula One. He saw Formula One almost as a necessary evil, whereas the Sports Car was much more aligned to the production side of things."

With Bandini/Amon leading the 1-2-3 sweep at Daytona in the 24 Hours with the new 4 litre P4, and their subsequent win at the 1000km of Monza, Ferrari had proven they had raised their game in anticipation of Le Mans. Ford, with their new 7 litre Mk4 then won the 12 Hours of Sebring, where Scuderia Ferrari was absent. It was all leading to a clash of the titans at Le Mans.

Chris – "I've got to say that we got a little bit distracted by Bandini's death at Monaco. I probably didn't help the cause by going off to Indianapolis for a month, either. Realistically, if Bandini and I had been together, we would have certainly given them (Ford) a go. But they had so much more straight line speed than we had, and I think we really would have struggled. We were certainly aware when we went there that it was going to be difficult, but we did think we could run the Ferrari flat out for the whole 24 hours, and we didn't think the Fords could. We were bargaining upon the fact that the new Mk 4s were relatively new and may not be as reliable. Of course, Dan and A.J. drove the door handles off the thing anyway. I think we were running 2nd at the time when I got that puncture and fire, but realistically we were never going to touch them."

In addition to all the engine diversity of the 60s/70s, driveline innovations were not limited to the engines. During the mid 1960s, a revolution against the world of manual transmissions was brewing at Chaparral Cars. One would think with racing the automatic transmission Chaparral, tasks involved in driving the cars would have been simplified, as one thinks there is nothing more intuitive than when a car that seamlessly performs functions that used to require driver effort. Nothing could be further from the case, as old habits can be very hard to break. Phil Hill – "The first time I raced the earlier 2D... there was an obstruction between your throttle foot and your brake foot. The steering gear and some shrouding on it... 2 foot driving, it wasn't that simple for us. At Daytona in 66, I went to dodge a Corvette who cut me off on the banking. I had to go up into the high lane, which was where all the frost was, it was so cold. I didn't have time, and had to go instinctively for the brakes, I'd managed to get my right foot around the steering column to the brake pedal, at close to 200 mph while sideways on the banking. In the 2F, they reinforced the barrier between the 2 pedals so you couldn't do that anymore."

By 1967, Hill had become a believer. Phil – "It was great, it had 3 ranges and a torque converter, which would lock up pretty early, so there was plenty of torque, depending on what gear you were in." Of course with the available grunt of the 427 Chevrolet powerplant, one did not need a large number of gears to keep within the powerband, and as a result automatic transmission developments did not spread beyond Can-Am and the 7 liter endurance prototypes of 1967.

The Chaparral 2F that won the season finale at Brands Hatch '67

In recent years, Formula One has been limited to 2.4 liter V8 engines, with much of the parameters and rev limits specified. Much of the attention seems directed upon the exhaust system and how it can be used to aerodynamic advantage. This, coming from a series that once boasted the BRM H-16 with its stacked flat 8 layout, flat 12s, V-12s, V8s, turbo V6s, turbo V8s, turbocharged in-line 4s, and turbine cars.... all running under the 3 liter normally aspirated, 1.5 liter supercharged formula. For the technically minded, that era was a technological Disneyland, vs. the tighter specification formulas that were to follow.

Ferrari had led the way with their flat 12, 1.5 litre car of 1965, but reverted to the 3 litre V-12 engine for the 1966 and 67 seasons in Formula One. The cars won a few Grand Prix, but with the advent of the Cosworth V8, the Ferarri was clearly struggling to keep pace for much of '67. Chris – "We had a horsepower problem all year, until we got the 4 valve engine for the last 2 or 3 races which didn't entirely overcome the problem, but it went a long ways towards it. In terms of being competitive, really 1968 was the year, as I really could have won the championship in 1968."

Using the V-12 wasn't a foregone conclusion for 1968 as the Tasman car seemed a match for the previously dominant Cosworth powered Lotus. Amon had a near dead-heat finish with Jim Clark's Lotus 49 in the Tasman series finale of early 1968 with the V6 Dino. Chris – "We pretty much went wheel to wheel at every race. It was the last race of the series at Sandown, near Melborne, actually the last race that Jimmy ever won. It wasn't quite a dead heat, as he beat me by a nose cone and I could have won. It was about 6 weeks before he died and I've always felt since then, thank God he won that race."

Did you ever feel like telling the team 'Give me one of these Dino engines in 3 litres'? Chris – "Yeah, that was talked about. Not so much with the V6, but there was talk of maybe doing a V8." In the end Ferrari stayed with the 4 valve V-12 for the 1968 season.

There was a long streak in the 1968 season where unpredictable weather on race day meant that Ickx would start on wets, and Amon would start on dry tires, so that Ferrari covered its bets with a split strategy which effectively killed Amon's shot at the title. Ickx was known as a rain master, so given the driver lineup, it made sense as to who got which tires with a split strategy. Chris – "Ickx was very good in the rain, and I've got to say that I hated the rain. I got pole for 3 races in a row, and in two of them it rained and messed things up."

The amazing thing looking back at the 1968 season was how many races that Chris Amon led, after starting from pole. But, it seemed there was always something going haywire with the accessories on the Amon Ferrari. Water hose splits… water pump shaft shears on the grid… one was temped to ask Chris who supplied the pumps and hoses to Ferrari to know exactly whose products one should never use. However, if Chris was in second or worse, the car would often finish. "Yes, exactly. It always seemed to keep going when we weren't able to win. I was leading by a minute or so at St. Jovite when the gearbox broke. I'd driven the whole race without the clutch, as it had packed up at the start, so it was pretty hard on the box."

What of the flat twelve 3 litre Ferrari GP engine that was in the works? Chris - "After the British Grand Prix of 1969, I said that we were wasting our time, as the thing was getting slower and slower. They kept saying with the V-12 that 'we've got "x" amount of horsepower', but in the car it never had anything like that. I thought we should miss 2 or 3 races and get the new car ready for Monza, and they agreed to that. The flat 12 was supposed to be ready for Monza. I ran the 1970 car 3 or 4 times at Modena… at the Autodrome, in August of 1969. They cylinder heads, pistons, valves, fuel injection… everything was identical to the V-12. The second time I ran it, it managed 3 or 4 laps before it broke the crankshaft. It kept breaking the crankshaft, I think it was a 4 main bearing crank, with needle roller bearings. They had developed an oil separator pump, which was the secret to the DFV

Cosworth, whereas we had terrible scavenging problems with the V-12. The second time I ran it at Monza, it was something like 15 km quicker on the straight than the V-12 car."

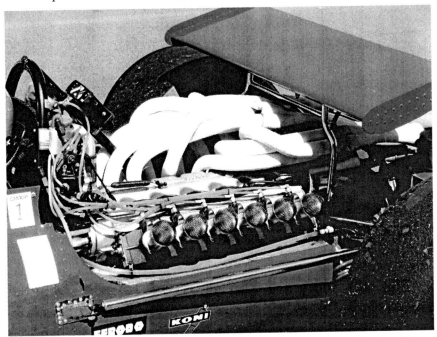

The 1969 V-12 Ferrari - final spec before reverting to the flat 12

"Also, with the V-12 car, you could come out of the pits, do one lap warming up, and go for it. The next lap your oil temp would be up to 110 or 115 degrees. With the flat 12 car, not only was it quicker on the straight, but it would take about 4 laps to get the oil temp up to 90 degrees. With the V-12 it was beating hell out of the oil, and robbing all the horsepower."

Amon – "Ultimately, they went with the boxer, the flat 12. Interestingly enough, had I stayed with Ferrari, we probably would have brought a 2 ½ litre flat 12 out here (Tasman series), which would have been a development of the 3 litre sports car engine that was well into the planning stages." As it turned out, the flat 12 Ferrari rivaled the Cosworth V8 for supremacy throughout much of the 1970s.

Niki Lauda's 1976-77 spec flat 12 Ferrari was the best car in F1

The mid 1960s was also an era of increasing drivetrain complexity in Grand Prix motorcycle racing. In 1966, Honda was dominating GP motorcycle racing with their legendary 6 cylinder 250/350cc machines. Top privateer rider Stuart Graham was soon to find himself struggling with this, the most advanced and challenging motorcycle of it's time. Stuart – "Midway through 66, by the time we got to Belgium, I was 4th in the 500cc World Championship, looking like the promising newcomer. At Spa I qualified the Matchless G50 on the second row, and after racing in horrendous conditions, I ended up 2nd to Agostini in the Grand Prix, which probably looked good on paper. A lot of experienced riders had thrown it down the road, and Jim Redman had crashed the 500 Honda and broke his arm. By the time I'd gotten to East Germany the following week, Honda had offered me the bike."

The 6 cylinder Honda RC166 is one of the icons of racing history, but Stuart's initial reaction was less than favorable. Stuart

– "I jumped into the deep end, and was stuck onto the 6 cylinder Honda and sent out to learn my way around the old Sachsenring, with none of this 'go testing first' or preparation. Looking back it was not ideal, but that's what happened in those days. The bike was set up for Jim, who was much heavier than me, on very much stiffer suspension. On a bumpy and quick circuit the thing was scary at first. I had been riding my G50, which has about 50 horsepower, 4 speed, it was a very sensible thing... well the Honda had about 65hp, 18,000 revs, 7 gears, ½ the weight... it was a completely different animal. I came in saying "Christ, this thing is just wiggling around all over the place. Hailwood looked and me and shrugged his shoulders saying, "Yeah, they do, don't they?"

Being a teammate to Hailwood could be a stiff challenge. Stuart – "He was so naturally quick, but he was relatively non-technical, he just got on and rode the thing completely naturally in his typically brilliant way. The thing had a terrible habit of having 7 gears and 7 neutrals, it would go into neutral on the downchange, then the engine stopped and you'd be freewheeling into the corner, terrified. I'd go back to Mike saying, "It does this, it does that"... and he'd say "Yeah, didn't they tell you that?" When I'd complain about something to the team, they'd look at me and say "Well you know, Mike doesn't have a problem." I'd go to Mike, and ask him if he had this problem and he'd say, "Oh yes, and it's a real bastard." He'd just get on with it, he was so quick but he probably didn't know why."

Honda team mechanic Nobby Clark - "Stuart would complain to me about all the neutrals, and I'd tell him 'the crankshaft doesn't have any flywheels, it has these little bob weights that when you shut the thing off and the revs die down, it just stops. That is normal, and you have to keep the revs at 6000 and above.'

The 6 cylinder bikes and their miniaturization caused other challenges on the diagnosis side as well. "If you had a bent valve or something, on the 6 cylinder if one valve wasn't opening, you couldn't tell by just touching the exhaust pipes, because they were getting so hot. If you took the pipe off, you could see by the flame if both valves were opening."

Everybody talks about the sonic experience of the 6 cylinder Honda, but anyone who has experienced it, knows the 5 cylinder 125 is the true chain saw from hell. Nobby – "Ohhh, it is the noisiest racing motorcycle that has ever been built. At certain Grand Prix, they would make us warm the 5's up together, in the same area. The noise was so bad that it would affect our sense of balance. To warm them up, you had to rev them, and I remember some of the guys would warm them up between 18,000 and 23,000 rpm. They were frightened that they would stall it, so they'd keep the revs way up there."

The 5 cylinder wasn't only a headache in the literal sense; it was also one in the setup challenges as well. Nobby – "The engines were good, but they were very VERY temperamental when it came to carburetor settings. If a cloud went overhead, that would upset the carb settings, and you'd have to start all over again. It was hell when you had like 5 jet settings that you could play with. With the 6 cylinders, when the carburetion was right, it would stay right in a rainstorm on a cold day, or whatever. I think one of the reasons was it was the first bike where we were using flat valve (slide) carburetors on them. We didn't have the same experience that we had with the cylindrical slide carburetor."

If the 1966 seven speed 250cc Honda had proven a challenge for Stuart Graham, it was nothing compared to the small displacement Suzuki GP racers of 1967. It was the final year for the radical multi-cylinder GP bikes, and Stuart's first year racing a 2 stroke. At Suzuki, as with Honda, their focus was also on increasing the number of cylinders to increase power.

The 1967 Suzuki 50cc twin cylinder engine

The Suzuki twin cylinder 50cc and twin 125cc racers were being out paced by the Yamahas, so an internal "race" inside the Suzuki Design Team was allowed to take place, V4 verses Square 4. The 125/250cc Design Teams furiously worked in the dyno rooms and on the test track. Stuart – "The 250cc Square 4 wasn't as powerful as they had planned and had rear cylinder cooling problems. It would seize if you looked at it wrong, but the 125cc V4 was a missile straight off the drawing board. Design worked stopped immediately on the Square 4 250cc and a V4 250cc was built. Then the FIM bombshell came to disrupt their plans, mandating a shift back to twins. Suddenly, there was no point anymore in continuing development. Stuart added that abandoning the program probably was the correct decision, as he was told in 1966/7 Suzuki had spent in excess of £2,000,000, a fortune at the time. Stuart - "Suzuki was trying to raise their game in GP racing, and had numerous engine programs under development for the 50cc, 125cc, and 250cc classes. They had square 4 and V-4 programs for the 125, and a square 4 program for the 250." Suzuki was to fall victim to the complexities of having too many engine programs under development at once.

Stuart – "With all the delays, we didn't get the thing (125-V4) until the end of the season, at the last Grand Prix. At the same time, they were working on the 3 cylinder 50, which I saw running on the test bed. With Honda's withdrawal from the 50cc class, I think they saw that the 50cc class was finished, but they had built the 50cc triple just in case. Typical Japanese, always looking at more revs, more cylinders... simply wonderful stuff, I just have an amazing admiration for these guys."

The never-raced 50cc triple was the Swiss watch of racing engines with 19 hp at 20,000 rpm (which equates to 380 per liter, one of the most powerful normally aspirated motor ever built), but it had been legislated out of existence with the rules changes for 1968 requiring single cylinder machines in the 50cc class and was never raced. The secrecy around that motor remains to this day. When asked to comment, 1960s Suzuki development rider and factory team racer Mitsuo Ito says... "That was a secret. I tested the bike in 1967. The rings and clips for the piston were so tiny." The 50cc three cylinder engine was basically a Square 4, with one cylinder removed and the magneto installed in its place. In a world where 250cc 6 cylinder engines were, and still are considered a wonder, this was the miniature and amazing equivalent of a 15 cylinder 250cc engine in terms of displacement per cylinder.

Things were of similar levels of miniaturization at Honda. How was it working in this sleep deprived world of a GP mechanic, repairing tiny marvels such as 2 cylinder 8 valve 50cc machinery? Nobby Clark – "Your fingers never get smaller, they stay the same size. But when you get parts that continually get smaller and smaller, it really is a challenge. We used to use tweezers on the

50s, with the 6 cylinders and with the 5 cylinder 125s. I think that when it comes to engine development, motorcycles were miles ahead of Formula One. The 50cc bike was producing more horsepower per litre than anything that had ever been produced. It was really big numbers."

If the Suzuki 3 cylinder 50cc engine didn't provide sufficient complexity, consider that the gearbox was a 14 speed affair. When asked what it was like trying to downshift fast enough, Mr. Ito explained – "14 speeds, I would practice downshifting (as his foot is going tap, tap, tap) as fast as I could. The bikes had a powerband of 300-350 rpm, you had to look at the tach all of the time." A 20,000 rpm motorcycle with a 350 rpm powerband would be a challenge for even the most experienced racer. Stuart – "There was a bit of a steep learning curve in going from a 4 stroke to a 2 stroke, lots of differences in technique. We first went to Montjuich Park in Barcelona, not the easiest of places to ride these peaky things with millions of gears and revs on a twisty slippery place like that!"

From 50cc 14 speed marvels, Stuart Graham moved to the polar opposite of the racing powerplant spectrum, driving a 1970 Chevrolet Z-28 Camaro, the American muscle car. Graham - "You can't beat the sound of an old Chevy, there is nothing like it. I fell for this lime green with black stripe Z28. The brakes and the road holding were agricultural, but the sheer grunt of it made my E-type feel positively anemic." In something akin to Ford's large displacement response to Ferrari at Le Mans in the previous decade, Stuart's 427 Camaro dominated the British Championships, with 2 wins in the Royal Automobile Club TT at Silverstone. Past winners of the RAC TT include such legends as Nuvolari, Caracciola, Moss, Collins, Hulme, Graham Hill, and Derek Bell, an honor roll of motorsport history. Stuart stands alone, having won the RAC TT as well the 1967 50cc Isle of Man TT for Suzuki. Having experienced it all, Stuart Graham's preference is for thunderous V8s over small displacement technological marvels. Stuart – "I took to it like a duck to water. You can keep your screaming V12s; give me a bloody good V8 any day."

Stuart Graham would have loved the IMSA Lola and Frisbee Can-Am cars that Conte raced in the early 1980s. Dan Binks – "The Lola T-600 was pretty basic. It had a big VG Hewland transmission, it was like a Formula Ford transmission times 10. The Can-Am gearbox was a DG300, the VG was made for something with about 40% more power. The Can-Am car had maybe 500hp from a 5 litre engine, while the IMSA engine had quite a bit more power. The VG gearbox was easy enough to work on. The car had a Salisbury differential, there were different ramps we could work with, but we didn't have a clue as to what we were doing. The problem with the Salisbury was that whenever you would touch the gas pedal it would lock, and the car would just want to go straight."

Later, with the IMSA March, they were using the newest innovation in differential design, the Torsen. Dan – "In 85 we ran the Torsen differential, it was quite a bit better; it would allow us to turn with the gas on, basically. Later at Roush racing they were to come to different conclusions.

After the RX-7 years at Clayton Cunningham racing (Malibu Grand Prix), Dan moved on to work with the Cars & Concepts Beretta. A vibrating nightmare of complexity, the car was a trial by fire for Binks – "It was a disaster, we had engine vibration problems with the "Oddfire V6", 3 litre. It was basically just a short 350 Chevy, so the engine fired 90 and 150 apart, and it was really screwed up. There were serious vibration problems because of the way the firing order was. It actually had a transaxle made out of a Doug Nash unit, something General Motors had worked with him on, it was held in place right in front of a Franklin Quick-change. You learn things as you go along… the vibration problems were big, a front engine with a front clutch. The driveshaft ran at engine speed with the transmission being in the back. So, in this particular instance when we'd rev the car on the jack stands, the driveshaft would be spinning 9000 rpm without being in gear. Basically, the driveshaft was the input shaft of the transmission, and it just shook the car apart. It would shake the MSD boxes apart, the alternator would fall apart... anything that wasn't safety wired."

Tommy Kendall – "The driveshaft always ran at engine speed, and we had this major vibration. We finally got it on this chassis dyno of sorts where we could spin it at speed and the guys were underneath it to observe it at speed for the first time. I was in the car and the guys all came scrambling out of the pit, as under the strobe the driveshaft was doing this big 'ol noodly thing. It was the first time they'd ever seen it in action with a strobe, and they all came firing out of there."

One would think all this rotating mass would have been a huge drag on the power of the drivetrain. Dan – "It was, and for the drivers if they put their foot on the gas pedal or the brake pedal, it would be like it was tickling them, it shook so bad. But we got the driveshaft big enough and tough enough. Originally it had pretty big u-joints we were buying from all these people, but the problem was that they just weren't big enough. I made some 4-1/2" driveshaft flanges, welded them together and we finally ended up going to 935 Porsche CV joints in the driveshaft."

The following year, 1989, Cars & Concepts switched over to the Trans-Am series, and sadly the Oddfire V6 came with as well. "It was a 4.5 liter V6 for Trans-Am, with a Weismann transmission and a 9" Ford rear end. The Weismann guys helped us out, but the thing was just gigantic, the gears were big and the thing ran really hot. For 1990 we ran a different Beretta, a Riley with a different V6 in it, and won the championship. It was a big time learning curve going from GTU to Trans-Am with an underpowered car and all that, but for 90 we got our own engine with splayed valves. A prototype cylinder head brought the power way up."

Binks working on the Intrepid in 1992

For 1991, Dan Binks and Tommy Kendall arrived at Pratt & Miller to campaign the Intrepid. Dan – "Super high downforce, with an un-restricted 400 inch Chevy V8 engine with those splayed valve cylinder heads designed by Roger Allen for General Motors, and it made 800 horsepower."

Binks – "That thing was pretty cool, for the time, but that car wasn't as slippery as the Porsche 962 and it needed all the torque and horsepower it could make. The Intrepid had really steep front angles and huge tunnels, it was a drag monster."

When returning to run the Trans-Am series with Roush for 1994, there were some developments with various differentials, none particularly satisfactory. Dan – "From the beginning it started out with Detroit lockers, and it was just horrible. They were on, or off."

With a locker "on", it will push the front of the car. With the locker "off" if the car was neutral under acceleration it will now be loose during off-throttle corner entry. As a result you have to set the car up to have some corner entry oversteer and some corner exit understeer... or suicidal amounts of one or the other if you get the car neutral on either exit or entry. Dan – "Exactly, and there is nothing you can do to help either one... it's always a band-aid. When the power was on, it was a spool, and when the power was off it was an open diff and unhooks the rear tires from each other. As soon as you touch the gas it locks the rear wheels together and wants to shove the front."

For many years the rage was the Torsen differential. Binks had experience with those in the Trans-Am series during the Roush years. Dan – "The last time we ran a Torsen was in '95. They were very smooth on the power, smooth off the power... but they were hard to adjust. If you wanted a different bias, you had to buy all new pieces. It was like getting it redesigned, and it wasn't like something you were going to get next week. The biggest downside for us was that we had to use the stock car type quick change. The Torsen wouldn't fit in a 9" Ford, and the Torsen differential itself wasn't durable enough to run a normal Trans-Am weekend. 100 miles of practice and 100 mile race... figure maybe a 200 mile weekend and we were putting in brand new stuff, running 200 miles, and throwing it all away and starting over again. I mean putting one in Brand New and it wouldn't go 200 miles. It just wasn't cost effective and it wasn't tough enough for the power and abuse that we were giving it. In the end we ran the Detroit locker because everybody did it, and they were reliable. The Torsen... at that point we just couldn't take the chance of having a failure. We could win the race with a Torsen, or we could win the race with the Locker. But if the Torsen failed, we couldn't win the race."

The Salisbury rear end, or limited slip with clutch packs, has less issues with varying chassis balance problems, other than that they tend to slip more as the temperatures rise. A bit of understeer at the start of a race, often translates into oversteer if the temp rises beyond the baseline. With more slip in the plates, the rear wheels are not as effectively tied together and increased slip equates to reduced push in front. Dan – "Absolutely, but in our cars we don't have that problem anymore because of the way that the cooling system is. In the old days, at one track the diff would be 180 degrees and the next place you'd go it would be 350 and cook the oil right out of it. Now, our stuff just runs at 175 all the time."

Binks with the Roush team in their days of Trans-Am dominance

For many years in the 70s, Porsche ran their race cars with a spool, which if nothing else ensured a lot of traction under power, along with predictable handling on corner entry and exit. Audi's published specifications for the R18 state that the car has a limited slip differential, although admittedly one wound up really tight would appear to have similar characteristics to a spool, possibly having just enough slip to reduce the chance of axle breakage. Dan - "I don't know, what Audi are going to tell us and what they actually do... who knows. But it seems like when they push those cars around, if it does have a slipper its super tight compared to what we run."

The diff that Corvette Racing currently runs doesn't drag a wheel around the paddock? Binks - "Nah, not anymore. The diffs that we have now lock when you put the power on, and unlock when we don't. It's not a locker; they are a lot more involved now compared to what we ran years ago." So, with the torque sensing fluid diff, does that eliminate the need for a very tight mechanical setup on the slipper? Dan – "Right, it seems like you don't have to (running a tight slipper)." Why didn't Roush run a spool with the Trans-Am car, was it an accelerated tire wear issue? Dan – "I don't know that... but Tommy was good enough to run the locker, and by that point it didn't matter."

In comparison, Corvette uses a viscous fluid coupling vs. a traditional clutch plate type limited slip diff, and it has given more consistent results. Still, there are challenges with the setup vs. the spool. Dan - "It's a Salisbury with ramps and clutch packs along with a viscous coupler. It's a standard Xtrac piece, and you adjust the amount of slip with the ramps. With the viscous coupler, there are different numbers that you can pick... the lower number has more slip, but you actually have to take it apart to change it. We mess with that, sometimes one car will have one, and the other car has another to try and see where we are at and which one is better than the other."

Andrew Heard is the VP of Xtrac, which has been in existence since 1984 and now makes transmission and driveline components for every level of motorsport. Andrew -"It's the sort of thing that was first developed for touring cars way back It has been very popular in sports cars. We did a version of it for Champ Car back about 10 years ago. With Pratt & Miller they.

are actually combining a torque sensing diff (the slipper) with a speed sensing diff (the viscious coupler) into one. Normally you've got compromises with one vs. the other. And with changing the ramps in the torque sensing diff, it gives you a lot more tune-ability. My rough rule is that you want it more speed sensitive when exiting a corner, but on corner entry you don't have differential wheel speed, you are just trying to get stability, and that's where the torque sensing diff is good. If you can get it in the middle of the range on the mechanical, and then add the speed sensing to it, then you are even better."

If this sounds as much 'a recipe for confusion' as a potentially better mousetrap, that's because it is. Dan – "So many times when we are running our cars… there are so many ramps in them, and viscous couplers, the driver is saying this or that… to where you are thinking 'is the diff wrecked?' Is it not doing what we are thinking? Did somebody put it together wrong? When you have a spool, that's what you've got." No doubt that in the world of an endurance racing differential, less can be more. However, if you can get that magic combination of where each type of diff is primarily actuating within its optimum range, it would be better than any low tech alternative.

What was the state of the art in Le Mans prototypes, and what kind of differential adjustment was available to the drivers of the LMP1 Peugeot? Simon Pagenaud – "None, it was something we were working on for the future, the evolution that was coming up. It is a shame that we didn't get to finish with that. The diff that we had was very reliable, very efficient, and we had been hoping for some sort of quick adjustment in pit lane, but could not do it. When the track changes in practice, maybe we would try something else… but we could only do it by taking it apart."

The heart of any car is the engine, perhaps more than most when the topic is racing American V8s with Jack Roush. Dan looks back at the early Trans-Am years with Jack - "We had a couple of issues early-on where the tuning and some stuff wasn't great."

Kendall – "In 94 we were running 8800 revs, close to 9000. We were getting horrible mileage, and we were hard on the rear tires… part of that was the 4 link. I had gone to Jack, because Gloy was running 8200 with different cams, was easier on tires, and had more mid-range. Our valve springs would barely make it 100 miles, we'd have to change them right before the race. Gloy was running valve springs for 3 races; it was just a better idea."

Kendall continues - "Other than Daytona, Jack only came to see one race in 5 years, and that was the Detroit Grand Prix. He was totally absentee, but was he was still directing the engine stuff. I couldn't get him to change it, I told him 'Jack I think we really need to change this', and he kept saying 'peak power, that's what it's about… peak power'. Well, the exhaust we were running made it sound like we were running 10,000 rpm. So I actually had put a piece of red tape on the tach at 9800, just as a mind-f**k, in case anyone ever looked in there. It happened finally at Mosport when we were all lined up waiting for a session and I think it was one of Pickett's guys that looked in there. Sure as s**t, around that time Gentilozzi started this huge campaign to get a rev limit. The irony was that we were running 8800… Gentilozzi was running 8800, Gloy was running 8200 and had the best package. So, they limited the revs to 8200."

Paul Gentilozzi - "Giant port motors was Jack's deal. Jack and I go back to way before Tommy Kendall was born, and Jack always liked big port volume and big rpm. We were drag racers, and when you come from Pro Stock, that's just what you build… that was just Jack's philosophy. I don't remember that story about the rev limits, but I'm old, and I would have bitched about anything they did because they were winning and I wasn't. So, in that circumstance you just bitch about everything the other guy does."

Kendall – "Actually, it saved us, as it forced Jack to do what I couldn't get Jack to do. The first engine we tested with, they said it wasn't even close to what we were going to have. The powerband was linear, so broad, and I told them that if it doesn't get better than this, we are in so much better shape.' We got better mileage, better tire wear, faster..."

Gentilozzi – "They used to have a claimer rule. They had an intake manifold rule in Trans-Am that the manifold could only cost 2500 bucks. So we're at Road America and they qualified on the pole. I had put my money up with SCCA tech, to claim it. Qualifying was over, they had taken the car to tech and I was 3rd, they were 1st. Their manifold was really special, as Jack would spend hours on the dyno working out the fuel distribution. He had popsicle sticks glued onto the floor, trenches and all kinds of s**t. Edgar finds out that I'd claimed the manifold, so I see him run to the pay phone and I'm sure he calls Jack. He goes back to the tent, and we're watching because we are not allowed in the SCCA tent when they are tech-ing, and I'm going to buy this manifold for 2500 bucks. Suddenly this Lincoln town car pulls up next to the SCCA tent, Edgar takes the manifold off and runs for the car, jumps in the back seat and it takes off. He'd rather be disqualified rather than give up that manifold."

So, did Paul just claim the manifold again at the next race? "Before the next race, Jack got the rules changed and the SCCA ended the claiming rule. Jack flew this plane and sometimes he would pick me up. He'd have this manifold with him... it was "the favorite manifold' and whoever in the team that was fastest that weekend would get THE manifold. I could learn from it, but I was running a Chevy and I was just trying to screw with him. They tried to give me a manifold off another engine. They were all upset, and I got my money back."

Binks – "At the end in 97 we had the power. It saved everybody money, the later engine was way better. We actually sold some of those engines to Huffaker. He called me up and said that he had dyno'd some of the other engines he had bought for Trans-Am, and at 6000rpm ours made 50 more horsepower than the other ones he had. The cylinder heads that we had... we had a bunch of guys working on it, a guy named Rick Swayne had come up with this port that flowed, and it wasn't Jack's normal port, which was gigantic. They came up with a port that flowed as much, but was 25% smaller. The thing would run off the corners big-time. Everybody thought we had traction control, but we didn't need it when we had that kind of power."

Gentilozzi – "It was great competition. We were a small time shop and didn't have nearly the resources, but we were brash competitors. We didn't have the position technically or experience-wise to really compete head to head, and they were better than us for a long time. But then we started sneaking up, and we'd get more poles, or lead more laps. The last year they ran the program, we were pretty darn competitive."

Paul Gentilozzi was champion with a Corvette program the following year. Paul - "You judge how good you are by the guys you race against. They were always really good to race against, and they'd do anything to win just like we would. When you are in that position you really don't like your competition, but I'd always respected them. I like Danny a lot, but I love his Mom. He has to be adopted. She doesn't deserve him, as bad as he is. But, the Binks family is really important to racing and I have high regard for Danny."

The technology got significantly wilder with the 2006 GT1 Pratt & Miller Corvette. Binks - "In 2006 that was the first GT-1 C6, and that car basically had a different block than the previous cars. It had the LS-1 block before that, and we went to the LS-7 block. We had already been doing the Nikasil blocks for a while, and had a pretty good history with that. Flash chrome bore, just like a motorcycle. You get it close with the aluminum and then they send it to US Chrome, just like everybody else does. The nice thing is that it is lighter than a production block with iron sleeves. The bore centers were the same with those motors, as none of that stuff could be changed. At time we were selling them to customers, people could buy them from Katech or General

139

Motors. It wasn't like hush-hush parts; it was something anybody could buy if they had a reason to. Those cars had an approved GM motorsports cylinder head, they were parts you could buy. But with the restrictors, you don't need the giant ports that some of those LS cylinder ports had at the time."

7 Litre GT1 Pratt and Miller Corvette engine – 2006 specification

The sheer grunt of the GT1 Corvette was staggering. Dan – "The torque was incredible; I think it had a little bit better than 600 ft/lbs of torque at 3000rpm. Working on them my entire life, I had a pretty good appreciation. We hooked up at Daytona and I was able to drive Bob Blaine's car. It gets your attention going 200mph on the front straight at Daytona in a Corvette. That's pretty impressive in this day and age. And coming off the line, you can't believe... the electronic ignition, traction control... all that stuff comes into play. It makes it easy for an old guy like me to mash the gas and get close enough to gain a whole new appreciation for how bitchin' those cars are. I call the guys (drivers) on the phone and ask what they are doing, and Johnny just said 'Trust me. You can just hold the throttle down there.' You do it, and wow... it's just impressive."

Dan continues – "I'm thinking in that timeframe with the 427 we had a little bit over 600hp with 32.5mm restrictors. They were a fair amount bigger than we had in the following years (2007 – 31.2mm, 2008 – 30.6mm). All of which are a fair amount bigger than what we run today. Right now we're at 29.2 (2012 GT2), for 5.5 litres. The first year GT2 engine was the GT1 engine with smaller cubic inches. It went from 7 litre to 6 litre, and then eventually down to 5.5, where the whole thing changed a fair amount, although they were LS-7s with sprayed liners. These are 5.5 litre production blocks off the assembly line, GM's division has been doing the engines. We obviously had those engine problems at Le Mans (2010). It was not what we wanted but without tough days, you don't learn the lessons you need to learn." Both cars had retired with similar engine failures at the Le Mans race. Binks continues – "...but we've had pretty good luck and they are working really hard on the engines. All we have used is the LS-1 block and the LS-7 block. There was some talk about going to an LS-3 block with iron liners, as there were some issues with the chrome stuff, but they worked all that out."

As with the previous Cars & Concepts Beretta, the driveshaft spins at engine speed.

Binks – "When we originally did the driveshaft spinning at engine speed in those Berettas, the engine was shifting at 9000 rpm, and there was all kinds of vibration problems. Nowadays with the engines turning way less rpm, in the 6000 range, the driveshaft is way safer, first of all. And the composite tube we use now has come so far. The first times that we did this, we used steel driveshafts that whipped back & forth, they were a really poor design. The carbon is way lighter, and it just helps all of

141

that, it just makes it glass smooth."

The GT1 Corvette used a sequential shift lever to operate the transmission, and soon after Dan's arrival at Pratt & Miller the team switched manufacturers. Binks - "Going from the Hewland to the Xtrac was just unbelievable. We had some issues with the Hewlands, and they didn't give us the best stuff. Xtrac attacked our problem, which was having big torque, where Hewland had just discounted it. They just wouldn't take us serious when we would say that this thing makes so much torque down low, that it busts parts. Gary Pratt finally said, 'ok, we are going to change to Xtrac.' The first one that they brought was a modified Bentley, from the prototype, which was making big power. So, they put a spacer in it and the 4th/5th/6th gears had wider gears than even the Bentley. We put them in, and from day one those things were rock solid, shifting up and down with no problems. In those days you had to have manual shift, so it had a shift cut on the handle that automatically cuts the engine on shifts, cuts it just enough to make it change directions and take the load off the dog ring and put it into the next gear. You just can't believe it could shift that fast with your hand. On the downshifts they still had to blip, and with the big gear splits like at Le Mans, you'd have to rev it up a bit when you go through neutral. Especially from 6th to 5th, you'd have to blip it pretty good, give it fuel. Still, those Xtrac gearboxes were awesome. When we changed from the Hewland to the Xtrac, it was worth something like 1.3 seconds at Le Mans... just from the transmission. It wasn't the efficiency stuff as much as it was just shifting it quicker. Plus, they were just super durable. You'd take it apart after 30 hours and they look like you just put it together."

Andrew Heard recalls those earlier years of the Pratt & Miller Corvette effort. "It was one of those things where we knew they weren't happy with what they'd got, but they were nervous about making adjustments to things, and it then maybe not being any better... kind of a case of 'the Devil you know.'"

Was a limiting factor the physical time to take a sequential shifter to select the next gear? Heard – "Yes, back then it would have been more the mechanics of the transmission, and their electronics in terms of how quickly they can bring the power back in. With the GT2 car (2009), it was a different transmission, but still a manual sequential and we did some development work with them on the fork design. A lot of the shifting is in terms of the mass of the system. I know the driver is trying to manually change from one gear to the other, but there are a lot of components in the transmission that move every time you do a shift. Reducing that mass that is moving… it's a relatively small mass, but it all comes into play and there was development all through that time. The gear width didn't change much, and the gear width doesn't really affect the shift itself as the gears don't actually move. They are all straight cut… other than that we do transmissions for street supercars, like the Bugatti Veyron where we do all the helical cut gears, where noise, vibration, and harshness are a factor. Race boxes are all straight cut."

This was all taken to the next level with the 2011 GT2 car, where the latest rules allowed paddle shift technology to be implemented into the GT cars. Binks – "It's got a Megaline paddle shift that's really cool. They have an engineering interface with Xtrac so all their parts already fit our transmission. It's just like a video game now, the shifting is unbelievable. It shifts faster than you could shift by hand, and on the downshifts it blips the throttle for you, it has matching revs. So now you just concentrate on the brake pedal, no heel and toe… that's new for this year."

Andrew Heard – "We have worked with Megaline for many years in sports cars, and then the relationship got really strong 3 years ago when we put that system on the Indycars. They are the supplier of that system, and we provide and do the integration of it into the vehicles with our transmissions. On the GT2 it was very much just an external actuator bolted on, but now it's been integrated into the transmission with the newest (2012 GT2) one.

They (Megaline) are the most experienced at providing that kind of product. I remember when we put it onto Bill Riley's Mark 11c, maybe 10 or 12 years ago before Sebring. We tested at Putnam Park, everything seemed to work but they were still quite nervous about it. I gave them an extra set of dog rings in case they needed them for Sebring, but after the race they gave them back... it had just run flawlessly."

Rob Dyson ran those Riley & Scott cars at the time. Rob – "That's right, the guys weren't so sure about this whole thing. We had plenty of backup, we could shift to a regular backup gearshift if we needed to, and we were prepared to do that. One car ran with it, the other car didn't. When we first started doing it, we needed the software and had an organization that kind of helped us. We now have incorporated that into our racing effort. The hardware was surprisingly simple in how it all worked. It wasn't anything trick. In fact, mechanically it looked like it would work better than the usual. To the greatest degree, you automate it... you take the human frailty out of it. You couple that with the hardware, and if that is beefy enough... and if you have software that doesn't allow you to downshift until the wheel speed and engine speed are equal, then that stops someone from overrevving when they downshift. We just put 2 and 2 together. It is just remarkable at how fast it all is. But, the guy that is setting up the gearbox has to do it really right. There is now much more precision required in setting a gearbox up. But I was surprised at how quickly everyone adapted paddle shifting, in all forms of racing. The reason why is that it absolutely works."

There are issues other than just embracing the technical improvement side. Dyson - "The problem I have with it, is looking at it as a purist, part of the technique of driving is in knowing how to upshift and downshift. Going into a corner and braking, double clutching and downshifting from 5th to 2nd. That was the one thing as an aficionado... it does eliminate the human element to a greater degree."

Andrew Heard - "We currently also do the BMW GT car, Audi, all the new Lolas, the Orecas, Pescarolos... " Despite the popularity of their equipment, some of Xtrac's most impressive engineering in the paddock has been from working with Pratt & Miller. Andrew – "We've done a great job of working with those guys at Pratt & Miller, where for their application they've basically taken our proven sports car technology. When we do this sort of scenario for sports car gearboxes, things might change a little bit here, or a little bit there, depending upon where your wishbone mounts. But Pratt & Miller is doing a non-stressed installation of it, so we were able to send them a Cad model of the internals of the gearbox. We said – 'you tell us how you want the case around it?' We've ended up with this gearbox for the GT2 that is this beautiful, small compact transmission; it's like the skin around the internals. In a lot of applications you have situations where the gearbox is stressed. The shape of the transmission housing comes from the shape of the car, and you end up with a transmission volume that bears no resemblance to what is inside the transmission, more about what is outside the transmission. For their application Pratt & Miller said they don't need any of that, we just want it strong enough to mount it into the chassis. For its capacity it is really very nice. We did something similar with the BMW, but theirs is far more conventional where we used our existing patterns to a large extent. With Pratt & Miller we were able to do all new pattern-work to produce this beautiful installation."

The new gearbox casing has been described as being 'shrink wrapped' around the gears. Binks - "Absolutely, they run the finite element analysis on those magnesium transmission cases and they don't put anything extra in them. They just put metal where they need it. In the old days it was a big square box."

Is it still possible to blow up the engine on downshifts, and will the Megaline system match-rev in the gear selected regardless of the consequences? Dan Binks – "There is a fudge factor, and we don't want to cut it off at a really tight tolerance because they have to downshift so often, sometimes you have to tell them to wait a while. But, if they ask for it really early, it won't shift. It won't let it downshift twice, and it won't let it downshift before the revs are close to within say 500 rpm. Say you want to downshift at 6000, it will let it downshift at 6300, but won't let it downshift at 7000… it won't let you blow it up, and we've had drivers in the past that were just brutal on the parts… you talk to them, and talk to them, but they just can't get used to waiting to downshift. It's a huge advantage."

Andrew Heard – "Straight away, what it took away was engine over-revs. In the Indycar series, there were a lot of drivers over-revving engines every weekend. The bill from Honda was huge, and now one over-rev pays for this system. We went an entire season with only one over-rev, and we've taken a lot of that responsibility from the driver." Engineer heaven? "Exactly, I do remember at one of the very first tests at Putnam, Scott Dixon was the driver that was testing it. When he jumped out of the car we asked him what he thinks of it. He said – 'It works really really good… I hate it.' He felt he had previously had an advantage over some of his rivals with the way he was doing the shifting. I imagine there were others who shared his views."

Did you have a perceived advantage with the old system? Scott Dixon – "Well, I think that especially in the longer races I think we had a good handle on it, and the style that I had worked with the gearbox fairly well. We never seemed to have problems with dog rings, where some teammates that I'd had over the years had struggled with some of that stuff. What I was more worried about was that if you miss a gear on a downshift, it creates opportunities for racing and passing."

Scott continues - "It's much more difficult to drive a car when you have to look after the gearbox. The way you brake… whether you use the clutch or not, there was a lot more management with a sequential box, or even an H pattern. Some of us are so different... Dario would brake with his right foot and clutch as he goes down all the gears. I would heel and toe with my right foot as I go down all the gears. There are so many ways of achieving the same thing."

Scott Dixon on the way to the 2013 title – 1st pit stop at Fontana

"With the paddles it does everything for you, it blips the engine, it changes it down. When it is electronically controlled it does everything it should, and it takes away opportunities."

Renault ruled the GP starts with their hand clutch system in F1 for years. What about the development of the hand clutch in Indycar? Scott Dixon – "Well, I think if the hand clutch was assembled the way it was meant to be, it would be ok. I don't know what it is at the moment... it seems to be again a moving target. Your bite points are changing constantly... I don't think it's a very high tech piece for the kind of cars that we are running. The clutch is a bit of a fundamental problem at the moment actually, especially when they are talking about standing starts coming with Edmonton. You can kind of change the way the clutch ramps in and out, and when it works like it should it works pretty well. But sometimes, especially at the start of sessions... it won't even really work. There is a fundamental issue, whether it is software or master cylinders. F1 is much more sophisticated, a very different system with dual clutches. I think the ones they have now have an even larger array of options where you have a stage one clutch that slips all the way through, and you have a stage two clutch that locks in."

There is another technology that has emerged in recent years, most prominently in Formula One, with 2 gears engaged at once to reduce the lost time between gear shifts. Honda for 2011 had also incorporated this (or similar) technology with their 'seamless shift' gearbox in MotoGP. Andrew Heard – "I think it's been in Formula One for 5 years. It's certainly new on the bikes, but it's not new technology. There are many different ways to do it, and 'seamless' is just an overall term. We have a mechanical system called IGS, for instantaneous gearshift because that's what it is. With our 'instantaneous' it is 2 gears engaged at once, it is seamless."

What is unusual about the new Xtrac seamless IGS system is that it does not rely upon hydraulic or pneumatic actuation. Andrew – "There are different ways to achieve this, and with a Formula One box for example, when they are working there is no reason that there would be any more wear than with a conventional F1 gearbox. But there are massive levels of control required. The hydraulics that they do the shifts with responds very quickly and accurately with the moving parts. You are engaging 2 gears at once, and if you don't pull out the original gear quickly enough, you get a catastrophic failure. It is very much dependent upon the speed and accuracy of the 4000 psi hydraulic system. The way Formula One does it is elegant, but absolutely not practical for anything beyond motorsport. They use the high pressure hydraulics for changing gear and for control of the differential. The externally adjustable differential allows adjustment to the preload setting in the diff, to change the characteristic in the corners. It is something we have done for many years, and has been done traditionally by a mechanical adjuster. You'd push a gear in through a port in the side of the gearbox to wind up the preload on the plates. Formula One has fully active differentials, run off the hydraulic pressure. It was like that in WRC Rally cars as well, but they've dumbed down their rules a lot."

Andrew Heard - "In general, rules changes in Formula One are good for us, as we get to do something new again. Today the gear widths are regulated, 14mm, just over ½". Before they were regulated, some of the gears were down to about ¼"... reliable for a race (as in one). That's all they have to do, there were not these 4 race transmission regulations. We had done tremendous amounts of work to optimize every gear ratio so that it could be the minimum mass that it could possibly be; it was a massive project for us. Now they are talking about 9 speed transmissions where the ratios are fixed, and where you have to run the same transmission for 4 or 5 races. At Monaco, you might only use the first 6 gears..."

Xtrac has branched out into more than gearbox components in F1. Andrew – "This year, for one of the teams we are doing the entire system, transmission casing and hydraulics as well. It was an area we weren't sure we wanted to get into, but have learned huge amounts from it. We needed a clean room, and the logistics of it..."

Have the hydraulically actuated F1 transmission designs been incorporated into Sports Car racing? Andrew - "I believe the current rules would allow them in Endurance racing, but I'm not sure if they would last for a 12 or 24 hour race. A lot of the retirements in F1 are down to hydraulic failure. If you go with lower pressure hydraulics, then everything gets more reliable, but it gets bigger and heavier. Then you've got such a weight penalty for that system that I don't think the benefits would be worth the negatives, especially when there are other ways to do it."

Has the 4000psi impact pressure of the F1 hydraulic actuated gearbox been an issue simply due to the impact loads on the gearbox internals? Andrew – "That can be an issue with hydraulic. That's one of the reasons we use pneumatic 100-150psi in

Indycar. It gives that cushion, that compressibility that you don't have with hydraulic fluid. It's a very similar system; the reliability of the system is just fantastic." Is the shift time significantly compromised between the 4000psi hydraulic actuation vs. the 150psi pneumatic?

The 2012 spec Xtrac Indycar gearbox and differential assembly

Andrew – "You have to be careful in how you quantify the shift time. In reality it should be from when torque reduction starts, and when you are back to full torque. Sometimes that torque reduction can take a while before the torque comes off efficiently to release the dogs. It really is more an engine management characteristic, and the same applies for the time it takes to put the power back on. Some engine manufacturers can do it quicker than others. The actual mechanical part of the shift tends to take somewhere between 15 and 18... maybe 20 milliseconds. And that is with the air (pneumatic) one. But the time between when the torque reduction starts, and back to full power, that can take 60 milliseconds. If we make a 10 percent improvement, it's a very small portion of the 60. The engine management is where you are going to see a lot of people starting to play with that in this (Indycar) series... and they will probably be coming to our trailer for spare parts because of it."

Heard continues - "Then when you've got an entirely mechanical system like our IGS, you get exactly the same result without any need for that high level of control. Also, it is purely a manual shift, and is absolutely relevant. Regulations-wise, where you are not allowed assisted gear changes, then that is still legal. The IGS is not standard fitment in any of our transmissions yet, it is still in development. But now, there are starting to be regulations... I think the 2014 Sports Car regulations say that instantaneous gear shifting will not be allowed, although we are not sure yet what the limitations may be. But as the rules are now, I'm sure it is legal."

How does the 150 psi Indycar pneumatic system compare to the 4000 psi F1 hydraulic for shift operation? Rubens Barrichello - "Yes, there is a difference, but they (Indycar vs. Formula One) really aren't comparable. The Indycar revs up to 12,000 and you generate a lot more friction, whereas at 18,000rpm the shift is that much stronger. I think they've done a really good job putting the gears up to here (paddle shifters), as you have your hands on the steering wheel and that's the way it should be."

The 2012 Xtrac Indycar differential system is not adjustable on the fly, so it requires some compromise on setup. Andrew - "For the new Indycar gearbox, we've done a new one that actually uses nitrogen pressure. The guys have already got nitrogen in the pit lane (tire pressure), and that sets the pressure on the preload in the diff. They have a regulator in the pit lane, so they can adjust the pressure on the plates, instead of with a mechanical adjuster. It is cheaper, lighter, and easier to adjust... but it is only adjustable in the pit lane. It is not driver adjustable and there is still compromise. There isn't much wear on the plates, but what changes the diff requirements is more from as the track changes, or the tires go away. The ideal differential setting now, vs. at some point in the race is not necessarily the same. But, in Indycar the driver can adjust the sway bars or the cross weights, making the weight jacker adjustment while on the track." Indycar drivers have other methods to find a balance, to compensate for their inability to achieve differential adjustment while on-track.

Rubens Barrichello brought his vast F1 experience to Indycar

Do you miss that having that little knob on the steering wheel to hydraulically adjust the differential? Rubens – "When you've had something electronic you've driven with in the car that can compensate for balance… it's a lovely thing to have. To be honest, Formula One had excessive stuff on the steering wheel. In Indycar there are a lot of spaces in the steering wheel to have something like that. But if you ask me 'do I miss it?' No, I don't, because here it's more pure. You go back to the pits where they can operate on it. But, it you ask a driver… any driver… if you could get a different setting from corner to corner by changing a little knob, he would say 'Yes, I need this.' In Formula One, there was a time when you could have different diffs for every corner, when it was done electronically. In the past few years it was more manual, and if you wanted change, you had to actually do the clicks yourself... for the balance. Here (in Indycar) you have to get out of the car, talk to the engineer... go through the process. It is a different world, and you are back to proper racing."

Takuma Sato was another recent veteran of both F1 and Indycar. What is his perception of the evolution of the F1 differential system? Takuma – "It could adjust corner by corner. Going back to 2002, it was advanced using a tracking system with the GPS and corner by corner you could change the setup completely automatically. In my F1 days, the most involved year was 2004. Technically you had to drive it really well, and you had to understand all the systems. You feel the car corner by corner and then build up the confidence for the next lap. The feel for the car is very important, if you can't feel the car you wouldn't go faster. Then after 2004/05 you had to do it manually, which is more fun for the driver. You weren't adjusting for every corner, as that would be too much. It was used from new tires to old tires when the balance keeps changing. It is nice for the driver to be able to adjust the thing, but now all you have to adjust is your driving, which is ok."

One wonders if an ever changing diff setting, being electronically revised from corner to corner would have raised the 'spooky factor', making predictability and consistency with the car's handling a constantly moving target. Takuma – "It is the opposite to what you say. Low speed to high speed, it makes it connected really well. In terms of the feeling, almost every corner you feel the same thing."

So with compromises in setup removed, it feels really good everywhere? Takuma – "In terms of the balance... yes. You are getting less understeer, and less oversteer."

"When you have a mechanical diff in a manual car, you might have to deal with massive low speed understeer and high speed oversteer... or whatever."

Takuma Sato had a stellar drive in the Super Aguri at Spa 2007

By 2007, driving the Super Aguri, what was the state of the differential art in F1? Takuma – "There was not much left for the driver in aid systems from the technical side. They were very simple cars... not much electronics in those days." Now driving in Indycar where they lack the ability for the driver to adjust the diff while on-track, is that function missed? Takuma - "I don't necessarily miss the thing, but I wish that it had it."

What has the Launch control sequence for pit stops been for the GT1 Corvette? Binks - "The launch control was straightforward as long as it was in first gear, had pit road speed selected, and as long as the air jacks were on for more than 10 seconds and it would say 'ok, I'm ready to launch'. The driver would hold the starter button down and as soon as the air jacks sensed a 25# decrease, it started the engine. With only a 25# decrease, the car hasn't even moved, it's still on the jacks and it's crankin'. So, on the way down it would start the engine to go... pretty bitchin' stuff."

This all sounds more than a bit like the 'Mike Andretti rule' from CART racing, when they outlawed drivers spinning up power to the rear wheels while the car was still in the air. Dan – "It's about as close to that as you can make it. When I pull the air jack handle, the driver is in control then, and if he's pushed the button it's ready to rock and roll."

What is the current (2012) sequence of events when the car comes onto pit road? "Basically the driver hits the 'pitlane speed' button. It turns on all the fuel pumps so it doesn't have any air bubbles. Our car (the #3 car) has the lower headlights flashing, the #4 car has the higher headlights flashing, so you can tell which car is coming, because they look the same, especially at night when you can't see the orange banner on the window of the 3 car. They come to a stop, and you fill it up with gas. As soon as the gas tank is full, it has a 'full' light, so that tells all the mechanics that it's time to change tires. Once the air jacks are activated, the driver is holding the starter button and when we are done with the tires, I pull the air jack hose and as soon as the pressure drops at the air jacks it says 'ok, I'm allowed to start now.'"

The starter would obviously be key for a successful pit stop. Dan - "In 2002, they had one starter in it, and it failed. They lost the championship when the car wouldn't start on the track. From then on, Gary decided we would have the best starters we could buy. Quartermaster makes them, and then we make a bunch of parts for them. We have 2 batteries in the car, one to take care of all the electronics, and the other takes care of starting the engine, although if there was some disaster we can override that, but we haven't had to do that. Right now we are using Braille Lithium batteries. They make some bitchin' batteries with huge cranking amps, and are super lightweight. I think the batteries we are using now have 1050 cranking amps, and we have something like two 1200 amp starter motors. A regular lead-acid battery would drop down to 8 or 9 volts, where this thing holds it at 12.7 or 12.8. It cranks the engine like you can't believe. When you are talking about 1/10ths of a second, you want it to start faster than the others."

As it was before, the engine bay is visually dominated by the cross flow airbox system with long rounded edge rectangular runners, and the engine operates at a higher RPM than the previous GT-1 car. In its final configuration, the GT-1 engine seldom saw 6000rpm, as with 500 ft lbs. of torque at 2500rpm it rarely needed to. The GT-2 design is of a similar school of thought, given the roughly equivalent inlet size vs. displacement ratio, but is significantly down on power compared to the previous car. Dan Binks noted at the debut of the 2009 GT2 Corvette that in his world of 6 litre V8s, there have been huge advances in efficiency across the last 30+ seasons in racing.

Binks – "In the days of the Can-Am with Morton, we were just basically pouring fuel in those things, something like 30 gallons for a 100 mile race. They chewed it up, made some power, and we didn't have any idea what the air-fuel was. Now, we can change the air-fuel ratio minutely with a switch right on the car. Let's say there is 10 laps to go, and we know we aren't going to make it any more than 6 laps."

"The driver can change to map 'whatever', as the engine guys and engineering staff have got it down. They know we are going to make it, and run out of gas... 'here'. With the 427s we ran 90 litres in 13 laps." At approximately 8.5 miles, they consumed 24 gallons to run 110 miles, which is 4.6 mpg.

Dan - "With the GT2 car it is probably closer to 6 mpg." Looking across 30 years of 5 litre V8 development, the fuel mileage has roughly doubled, while making about the same horsepower."

Another issue can be engine temperature fluctuation. If heat cannot be consistently managed, piston expansion causes galling of the cylinder walls on a tight tolerance engine.

Engine change at Le Mans

Superior alloys are of course, of help with this, but the tighter the range of temperature is controlled, the tighter the engine tolerances can be in response. In the Pratt & Miller Corvettes, constant temperature control for the engine is achieved by running the oil through the main water radiator, which serves to control the engine oil temperature as well. "You know, in Trans-Am, we used to run a heat exchanger on the transmission, the rear end, and on the engine. With our system, when a driver goes out for a warm up lap, we have already brought all of the temperatures up. As a result, the transmission is not at 50 degrees when we are wide open. We warm it up under the tent, and the transmission is at 180, the diff is at 180, and everything is warmed up before you go. It is easier on the parts. It is separate oil systems that all go through that central location, so sometimes it is the oil heating the water, and other times the water is cooling the oil. At places like Le Mans where

157

you are running when it is 50 degrees at night, and 100 degrees in the day, our water temperature is 180, our oil temperature is 180... it is a huge advantage. And now it is a non-decision. What's the oil temperature going to be? I know what it's going to be."

Was this all new for you at Pratt & Miller or was this used at Roush? "Yep, at Roush we did actually, and that's where we first started using heat exchangers, although in those days we never ran thermostats on the water system, but now we do, so it's way more linear. Everywhere we go it's going to be between 180 and 200 degrees, and you don't even have to think about it. In the old days there was just so much bullshit to worry about, now you just take all that stuff for granted."

Of course, in the rough and tumble world of endurance racing, it is best to have plenty of excess capacity in the case of the radiators or air inlets being compromised. So, the closer you push those parameters in saving weight or aerodynamic efficiency, the more likely you are to find yourself in trouble when the inevitable hot dog wrapper decides to enter the equation. Combining this with the small tolerances of the thermostatically controlled water temperature assembly, one can assume that the engine assembly is maximized accordingly.

Metallurgy also has a huge effect upon the clearances required. In the late 70s while running Arias alloy pistons in the iron block Datsun U20 engines, a 9 thousands piston to wall clearance was often insufficient to prevent cylinder scoring as the piston expanded under temperature and load. When switching to Cosworth pistons, the reaction was disbelief when the manufacturer recommended a 5.5 thou clearance. Yet the Cosworth metallurgy was superior to the point that it was indeed sufficient, and cylinder scoring was no longer an issue.

In complete contrast with endurance racing, the NHRA's top fuel dragsters and funny cars are truly unusual creations, their purpose built billet alloy blocks with steel liners containing what is essentially a slightly managed explosion. These cars having 8000 horsepower, fully 1000 horsepower is being fed from each cylinder, each having more horsepower than either a Formula One or Indy car and a life span of perhaps 4 seconds at full power between rebuilds. Electronic traction control is not allowed, but the designers have found a way around this problem. With a single gear and a spool differential, the only ways to control the amount of drive getting to the ground is either with wheelspin, the clutch, or the rpm. In a Wiley Coyote meets NASA solution, the teams have developed means for mechanically operated traction control through a multi-plate clutch.

The 5 disc clutch system has a mechanical timer controlled air gap that holds the clutch plates apart with compressed air. The timer controls the air-bleed from the air in each gap sequentially at a given rate in microseconds, providing the optimum launch control sequence. Each team has an extensive database on what would be the expected traction at any given drag strip, elevation above sea level, and temperature. This software program combined with the database, gives the data for the optimal settings for the timer, the on-board sequence being selected just prior to the run. Consider it to be electronic traction control with a mechanical implementation.

Given that these cars have turned the ¼ mile in approximately 4.5 seconds at speeds approaching 340mph, perhaps being strapped to the side of a spacecraft at launch would be the only equivalent. Before the start the driver holds on the handbrake in the staging area, and at the moment the lights turn green, the driver releases the handbrake and nails the throttle, starting the clutch pack launch sequence. If all goes well at the instant the car crosses the finish line, the rear wheels are driving (not spinning), the clutch pack is locked together, and engine is at maximum RPM. In the middle of the run, the driver is being subjected to over 5 Gs of acceleration.

Although spectacular, the specialized machines of NHRA top fuel racing have less relevance to what will trickle down to the production line in the future. To a lesser extent the same could be said for Formula One. Look for the DNA of the future high performance, high efficiency street car to filter down from lessons learned in professional endurance racing.

1960 Briggs Cunningham Team Le Mans Corvette engine

CHAPTER FOUR

POWERPLANT INNOVATION

The STP Lotus 56 Turbine Car from 1968

The history of conventional engine development has been a century-long saga of endless improvement in materials and layout. However, from time to time, truly unique solutions have appeared with varying degrees of success. For those who celebrate those designers who had the courage to explore roads less traveled, this is your chapter.

The Cummins Diesel Indy car

There have been a handful of diesel entries at the Indianapolis 500 across the decades, most with little fanfare to go with little in the way of results. In 1931, the Brickyard had adopted what became known as 'the junkyard formula', in an effort by the Speedway to encourage entries by something other than high dollar supercharged Millers, which had dominated the previous decade of racing there. Into this explosion of interest, Cummins entered a 360 C.I. four cylinder engine in a Duesenberg chassis, which finished 13th after running the race non-stop. For 1934, they returned with two entries, both supercharged, one of which was powered by a problematic 2 stroke diesel. Neither car finished.

Despite not having had much to show for their efforts, Cummins decided to return again in 1950, with a supercharged magnesium block 401 C.I. diesel in a somewhat conventional but effective chassis by the capable Frank Kurtis. The car started last, and was a mid-race DNF. At this point in time, there was nothing to indicate that a diesel engine car would or could be a serious threat at the Indianapolis 500. All of this was to change in 1952, as the Cummins diesel racer was to be the most innovative car seen at the brickyard in that decade.

There had been a huge loophole in the equivalency formula for Indianapolis, as the diesel powered cars were allowed the same capacity regardless if they ran atmospheric pressures or were supercharged or turbocharged. Although the 1950 car had

The upright and conventional Cummins Diesel Indycar of 1950

done nothing to send up a warning as to the potential, the 1952 car shattered convention as well as track records.

Cummins developed their aluminum block 401 C.I engine, into a turbocharged configuration that has since become accepted as standard fare for diesel engines. It was anything but that in 1952, and the car was to become the first turbocharged car to start the Indy 500. Interestingly enough, that was also the only time that World Champion Alberto Ascari had entered the 500, driving his 4.5 litre Ferrari. The Indianapolis 500 counted toward the World

Driver's Championship during the 1950s and it was to be the only World Championship race that Ascari did not win during the season. Ferrari's entry failed after 40 laps from a wheel failure, but as a result the 1952 '500' was to occupy a place of increased interest upon the world's stage.

The revolutionary 52 Indy 500 pole winning Cummins Diesel

Freddie Agabashian who was to drive the Cummins diesel, was excited from the beginning to be involved with such a convention breaking effort. Developed in a wind tunnel, the 6 cylinder engine was laid on its side, only 5 degrees off horizontal, allowing the driveshaft to pass alongside the driver, which allowed both an incredibly low center of gravity, as well as a tiny frontal area compared to the typical racer of the day. It also had the advantage of getting much of the mass down on the inside (left) side of the car. Magnesium was used where possible to get the massive engine down to as low of a weight as possible but it remained a massive lump.

Audi's Dr. Ulrich Baretzky is in charge of development for the Audi diesel program that has dominated the 24 Hours of Le

Mans, producing the winner in 7 of the past 8 seasons. – "I can't imagine… that was something completely apart at that time, more than anything else. When we started the Audi diesel program we covered a lot of information about what has happened before with the diesel in racing. There was also a BMW touring car diesel program for a 4 cylinder, but the program was cancelled for Le Mans."

The same year (1952), Frank Kurtis had debuted yet another design with a similar but less extreme 36 degree canted Offenhauser engine layout. This car nearly won the race and in 1953 became the pole sitter and winner driven by Bill Vukovich. This individual car had become known as the "roadster". Kurtis had begun a design trend that extended through much of the 1950s and early 60s with his semi-laydown chassis. This was again taken nearly to the extremes that had been exemplified by the 52 Cummins Diesel, with the George Salih / Quinn Epperly built Belond Special with its Offenhauser engine only 18 degrees off horizontal. That car won back to back '500's in 1957/58, by taking Kurtis' previous concepts to their engineering limit. The 52 Cummins Diesel had been a pioneering car, influencing a generation of Indy cars, made even more unique by its choice of powerplant.

The Turbine Cars

The Rover-BRM turbine car had its debut at Le Mans in 1963, with Graham Hill and Richie Ginther driving. It was considered an unclassified experimental design however it did finish the race (albeit unclassified as such) and put in a reasonable showing. The team returned to Le Mans in 1965, to compete as an official entrant in the 2 litre classification. BRM teammates Graham Hill and Jackie Stewart competed in this latest Rover BRM turbine car for the full 24 hours, achieving a 10th place finish. What upon first glance appears to be a stellar result was actually little more than an exercise in frustration. The entire field of prototype racers had failed or suffered major difficulty that year, and the race was won overall by the Ferrari 250LM (with the 3.3 litre '275' engine) of Rindt and Gregory... for all intents and purposes, a production car that hadn't reached the required 100 car production run that would enable it to be classified as a GT.

Sir Jackie Stewart - "I went to drive, of all things, a gas turbine car, a helicopter engine in a Rover-BRM. The car looked great but it was unbelievably slow. There was no engine braking at all, when you took your foot off the gas the turbine kept running, so we only had the brakes. In any kind of car we all drive you shift down and get engine braking, with this thing it had nothing at all, and brakes weren't all that good in those days. I said 'what do I do if we have a brake problem?' Because occasionally we'll have a brake balance bar break, or maybe only have front wheel brakes or rear wheel brakes. He said – 'Hmmm, I don't know.' I'm thinking 'Jesus, I'm going to drive the Le Mans 24 hours and you don't know what I can do if there is a failure?' He said 'well, you just get down as slow as you can go, and then you put your foot out the door.' The designer actually said that, God as my witness. It was at that time I sort of lost confidence in the team."

Jackie – "Graham Hill was the #1 driver for BRM, and I was the #2 driver. We tossed-up and whoever won the toss had to drive the first stint. The deal was that if that happened you would drive it into the sand bank at the end of the Mulsanne straight because we couldn't bear going around for 24 hours in this device. Of course, Graham didn't mean to do it, but he went in on the first lap, right into the sand bank at the end of Mulsanne. It swallowed a whole bundle of sand and it took the edge off all the turbine blades. So, instead of running 82,000 revs, which was what turbine could rev at, we now had to do 50,000, which meant that I got passed on the Mulsanne straight by a Triumph Herald."

Per Road & Track Magazine in February 1966, the Rover

25/150/R turbine engine was only rated at 126hp at 63,500rpm, with an Owens Corning ceramic heat exchanger. The car was only capable of a 0-60 time of 11.3 seconds in fully operational condition. However at Le Mans 1965, in its hobbled state it was likely producing well under 100hp. Stewart - "Jochen Rindt, one of my best friends, was co-driving with Masten Gregory, an American driver, in the winning 250LM Ferrari and they lapped me every 3 laps, if you can imagine. The thing lasted until the end of the race. We were the first British car home, which didn't say a lot for Britain at that time." The Rover-BRM Prototype had finished one lap ahead of Paddy Hopkirk in a 1.8 litre MGB, and 64 laps behind the winning Ferrari 250LM.

Needless to say, the racing world wasn't overly concerned about when the next turbine car would arrive on the scene. But as scant two years later at Indianapolis, an innovative turbine powered machine was to set the world on its collective ear, and that car was the STP Turbine Car, driven by Parnelli Jones. After that performance, there would no longer be any skepticism about the potential of turbine powered racers.

Parnelli Jones had been racing a very limited open-wheel schedule in 1966, with his own team. Parnelli – "What happened in '66 was that I built 2 cars, and after Indianapolis they were working on Dick Atkins' car, lit a torch and blew the side out of the tub. I felt an obligation to Dick and let him drive my car the rest of the year. I came back in '66 and ran the last race in Phoenix, led the race and blew an engine. I was thinking about not running the '67 race (Indy), not running at all. But I had mixed emotions. I had my own car to deal with and Andy was hounding me to drive the Turbine Car."

"First of all, you have to understand how I got involved with Andy in the first place. He asked me during tire testing to take a ride in the Novi. I went out the first time and ran faster than anybody had ever ran in it, and from that point on Andy was hounding me to drive for him. Well, I'd never drive the Novi

1967 STP Turbine Car as driven by Parnelli Jones in the Indy 500

because it didn't have a very good reliability factor. We started socializing a lot, he'd invite me to dinner and stuff like that, still trying to get me to drive one of those Novis, but we became close friends. When he built the Turbine car he said, 'I have something I want to show you.' I went to Santa Monica and saw the car for the first time, and the car was about ¾ of the way finished. He wanted me to drive it, so I told him that I was testing over in Phoenix and to bring it over once he got it finished and I'll take a ride in it and see what I think. That's where it all started."

"I took a ride in it and got all excited, it wasn't as quick as my car, but it was right there. It had a 3 second throttle delay time, so you had to kind of out-guess it. But the fact was that it handled good, and had 4 wheel drive. It seemed to handle decent, and at Indy I started second row outside and I stuck it up around the outside and passed all those guys." As the Turbine car flashed past Andretti on the first lap, Mario flipped Parnelli the bird, which pretty much sums up his impression of the situation.

Chris Amon – "That was the year Parnelli should have won it. It seemed to just go around the corners on rails; it was sort of glued to the track. It was almost in a different league, and it looked like almost a Sunday drive type thing when it came past." Parnelli – "If you watch the race, I could run about as fast as I qualified. The other guys, when they took on 75 gallons of fuel and took the 10 or 15% Nitro they'd were running out of it, then they didn't have enough to get back by me. In practice, they'd drive by me ½ ways down the straightaway."

Nitro was often added into the qualifying fuel mix, giving an inaccurate indication of race day performance. Was it ever used for a race fuel? Donald Davidson – "Not for the race, I don't think. In qualifying... yes. Very rarely would anybody try Nitro, basically it was a grenade."

As a result, the Turbine Car was to come to the start line with unreduced performance from qualifying trim. Parnelli – "They accused me of sandbagging, thinking that I was lifting but I wasn't. I knew their cars that they weren't going to have enough to get back by me. In qualifying I ran just as fast as I could possibly run. I qualified at 166mph, and was running 165mph in the race."

Parnelli Jones looks back fondly upon his '67 experience, although it left him just short of victory. What stands out from the Turbine car experience? Parnelli - "I got paid a lot of money for driving it, 100,000 dollars. I had a lot of fun during the month of May because they kept accusing me of sandbagging. I kept needling guys like Andretti and Foyt, asking them what they were planning to run on race day so I know where to set the screw. I was pissing them off left and right. I didn't know it was going to be as good as it was on race day. To this day they swear I was sandbagging but I tell those guys I had no reason to. If I could have run 200mph I'd have been glad to."

It gives one pause to consider that the throttle response of the Lotus 56 Turbine car was a big improvement over the previous year's car. Parnelli Jones – "They had a problem with the throttle delay time, but the Lotus wasn't as bad. Chapman was smart enough to use a fast idle, and that cut the delay time down. With the previous car, when you backed off at the end of the straightaway, they would still accelerate so you had to use the brakes to slow it down. That's the reason we had the 'flap' on my old one."

With the 1967 car, was there similarly a lag in power reduction when you dropped off the throttle? Parnelli - "It started to spool down right away, it wasn't as critical as getting it to come back on." The early jet engines had a tendency to throw blades, was that a concern with the Turbine Car? "I was a little concerned about that. But I had a little protection between the engine and the cockpit, that's where the fuel was, was in the middle. That's why it didn't hurt it so much when we took on 75 gallons on fuel. We were running the engine pretty conservative compared to what we went with in 1968. We didn't do it at Indy, but later in '68 we were melting the blades out of them from turning the power up so much."

The 1967 first generation STP Turbine car with the engine and driver side by side, had an air brake, essentially a large flap on the rear deck of the car, raised up to help slow the car upon the application of the brakes, similar to the solution Mercedes-Benz had used at Le Mans in 1955. At Le Mans, the disc brake equipped Jaguar team had a significant braking advantage over the Mercedes, but the 300SLR rear deck air brake helped to level the playing field. Parnelli had come up with the similar application at Indy.

Parnelli - "That was my idea, because of how the car didn't want to slow down when you backed off. I didn't have any problems with the brakes, but my idea after I first drove it at drove it at Phoenix was that you've got double master cylinders, one of the front and one for the back, and if you ever lost the front brakes you probably couldn't keep it out of the wall. With

The 1968 STP Lotus 56 Turbine Car

70% of the braking on the front wheels, and only 30% on the rear wheels, the spoiler (air brake) was hooked to the 2nd master cylinder for the rear wheels to hold the back end down. If I did lose the front brakes, the flapper on the back would help hold the back end down and make the rear brakes work better, get better traction. You don't use the brakes that much, but when this thing spooled up, the only way you could tell it to slow down was using the brakes. The flapper provided some download to help you slow the thing down... it didn't want to slow down when you backed off."

The Lotus Turbine Car of 1968 was a massive refinement over the previous years' design which had the engine alongside the driver. With Colin Chapman's Lotus 56, it was shaped like a doorstop, very similar in appearance to the Lotus 72 Formula One car which it had inspired. The Lotus 56 featured 4 wheel drive, as had Parnelli Jones' 1967 STP Turbine racer. Both the Lotus 56 and 72 had the inboard disc brakes, were wedge shaped, and a technical leap forward in comparison to the rest of the paddock, although the inboard brake shafts (or the presumably stronger driveshafts in the four wheel drive Lotus 56) carried an inherent risk of breakage which could render the car uncontrollable under braking. The Type 72's debut was fully 2 years later at Zandvoort, and it was to win the 1970 and '72 Formula One World Driver's

Championship, although 1970 Champion Jochen Rindt lost his life in the Type 72 during practice at Monza, the car turning sharp left into the barriers under braking for the Parabolica.

It was a tragic loss, and Rob Walker withdrew his Lotus 72 driven by Graham Hill, due to concerns over the safety of the car. As Rob Walker pointed out in his December 1970 Monza race coverage for Road & Track, he and Graham went to inspect the shattered Lotus 72 as they had feared a front brake shaft failure similar to as had occurred with John Miles' car in Austria. They found the right hand brake shaft had broken, which would result in a hard left turn upon brake application, although in fairness it is impossible to be sure that breakage was not from crash damage. Graham Hill subsequently called Maurice Phillippe, the Lotus designer, and had him provide newly designed brake shafts prior to the next race in Canada, although the factory Lotus team did not compete there. Jochen's fear of not surviving his two seasons at Lotus had sadly been well-founded, telling Rob Walker earlier in the season that he would win the championship this year and then retire.

Joe Leonard was not originally scheduled to drive the Lotus Turbine, instead scheduled to drive the 1967 first generation Turbine car previously driven by Parnelli, but a series of sad misfortunes to some of the greatest drivers of the day gave Joe the ride. Leonard – "First it was Clark, but then he got killed. Then they were going to put Jackie Stewart in it, but then he had a shunt and broke his wrist. So then they put this guy Spence in there. He was flying around, and I said "Parnelli, I need one of those cars." The Lotus would press down (aerodynamically it was a wedge), and it was practically a ground effects car. When you'd get behind a guy in dirty air you really had to watch it."

On May 7th, a month to the day after Jim Clark's death at Hockenheim, Mike Spence crashed his Turbine car into the turn one wall and was killed when the front wheel slammed into the cockpit. 5 days later Joe Leonard wrecked his 1967 Turbine car,

The STP Lotus 56 was the last Turbine car to lead the Indy 500

also crashing into the turn one wall. That 1st version Turbine car never raced in anger again, and Joe Leonard was given the ex-Spence Lotus 56 for qualifying. Leonard put the car on the pole position for the race with a lap over 171 mph, breaking all previous one and four lap records, to start alongside Lotus teammate Graham Hill. It was the first time that teammates had started 1-2 at Indy since 1949.

Adjusting fuel/air mixtures in a Turbine car was a truly unique situation, and rather than adjust the fuel system mixture for changes in weather, one could also change the fuel used. Joe Leonard, pole position at the 1968 Indianapolis 500 recalls – "It was a wet year at Indy, and most of practice I did maybe 4 or 5, maybe 8 laps and then have to pull in when it would sprinkle. Actually, when I qualified I'd only had about 43 laps in the thing. They used 'White Fuel' when it was cold weather, because it supposedly gave more power, and you'd use whatever is best for your circumstances. It wasn't multiple fuels; it was only a couple or 3. It was just a big stove, is what it was, and if it burned hotter it would make more power... to a point. When you go past that point, it would make less. When they dropped the green, I took off and led a few laps, but we hadn't used the usual jet fuel. The car was kind of lazy, like you'd turned the spark back."

There was more to it than just using whatever fuel appeared to be best. Parnelli – "When they'd drop the green, the car wouldn't take off. Andy Granatelli had made a deal with Standard Oil to run gasoline instead of jet fuel, as their American Oil company was sponsoring us. You could use anything (for fuel) you wanted, but it didn't have enough lubricant and it froze up the fuel pump drive on the yellow flag. If Andy hadn't agreed to that deal, we'd have been alright."

Parnelli – "There was no rule on what kind of fuel you could run. Andy made that decision, but it was a bad decision because we'd probably have won the race in 1968. I ran gasoline when I ran the Lotus in 1964 at Milwaukee and Trenton, but that's the last time I'd run on gasoline. I went straight back to Methanol. Formula One ran on gasoline, so when Lotus came to Indy they liked that gasoline got better mileage. When I won Indy in 1963, the Lotus made one stop and I made 3."

Hadn't gasoline been outlawed as a permitted fuel in the aftermath of the 1964 MacDonald/Sachs deaths at Indianapolis? Donald Davidson – "I wondered that too. I had thought that it was, but in 1965 it was not (outlawed). It was highly discouraged, and there was some discussion about gas being banned, but it was not. So, what they decided to do was to discourage people from using it. They put in the 2 mandatory pit stops for 1965, and you had to hook up the refueling mechanism. The thinking was that the advantage to gasoline was to get better mileage. But, if you had to stop twice anyway, you may as well use methanol."

Parnelli Jones – "From what I understand in 1968, Chapman had tried it (gasoline in the car) and found the same problem but he didn't let Andy know. I don't have any details on that, but that's what I'd heard." With the decision to switch fuel, Granatelli's gamble had sealed the fate of his Turbine cars.

Bobby Unser won the 1968 Indy 500 in the Eagle/Turbo

Offenhauser, but it wasn't a sure thing until near the end when Leonard's broken Turbine car coasted to a stop. Bobby – "The Turbines were definitely faster than we were, and we were the fastest of the piston engine cars. Andy Granatelli had the Turbines, and they were exceptionally good cars, and Joe Leonard was an exceptionally good driver. Art Pollard wasn't nearly as good, and Graham Hill wasn't as good on an oval track, he wasn't as quick around Indianapolis. We were the underdogs, but Granatelli thought that he had us beat so bad that he decided to run gasoline in the Turbines instead of jet fuel, which made it run hotter and cut back the power. He got 100,000 dollars from the gas company, and that's where he made his mistake. He thought that he had more of an edge than he did."

It was a poor gamble to take, and it cost Granatelli the Indy victory that he coveted. Leonard continues – "I led for about 10 or 12 laps, and all of a sudden here comes Bobby (Unser) right down the long straightaway, and here comes Ruby... they just blew right by me. I thought "Holy Toledo, I'm in for a long day". All was not lost, as the Lotus 56 had advantages elsewhere that helped to offset the reduction in power. Joe Leonard recalls the advantages of the 4 wheel drive – "When the track started to get oily, it started to slow down and the race started coming back to me. I started going better with the four wheel drive, going through the corners on the outer edge. The Turbine had an abundance of acceleration on the short chute, that where I could do a lot of passing."

Parnelli was similarly impressed with the handling of the 4WD Turbine cars, which allowed outside passes in the corners. "Wasn't anybody giving them any credit about how good they handled, even the old car (1967 version) you could pass people around the outside in the dirt. It made me appreciate four wheel drive, but the problems with it are too much un-sprung weight, along with more moving parts." Four wheel drive was later experimented with by almost every Formula One team, all having seen the advantages from Indianapolis, but the 4wd cars proved inferior to the standard 2wd designs.

Braking in a Turbine car was one of the shortcomings. Joe Leonard – "There was no engine braking, absolutely none. When you backed off the throttle, there was no compression. Another thing, you notice when you are landing at an airport and the only compression effect you get is if they reverse the engines." There was no system to reverse engine thrust to provide any kind of brake assist. Leonard – "I wish they did. We went one step further, the way that car was, Colin Chapman had designed it with the inboard brakes. We got to thinking about this, and thought we'd go one step further... "Why not run an 8 disc system on there, run them like a regular race car with discs out on the wheels?" We tried to redo it, my feet didn't fit up there very well under that differential and the four wheel drive anyway. Parnelli set it up with two levers that were separate. What I had to do was to lean my one foot to the left and use that one brake for a couple of laps. There was hardly any room in there, especially with my size 12 shoes. We could last about 15 or maybe 20 laps hard, and then the brakes would fade out again, because of the lack of compression."

One can only imagine driving such a car in race conditions. Joe – Well, with the Turbine what happened was that you had to anticipate. You'd get in down there behind a guy... with no brakes. You'd ease into the corner and stand on the throttle while easing on the brakes because you had to watch how fast you'd be coming up on a guy. With the four wheel drive I could get through the corners fantastic, probably 5 miles per hour quicker. I'd have to get on the gas and hope like the devil... I almost ran into the back of a couple of guys whose cars weren't handling real good. The truth is that you had to make these decisions really quick. If they didn't move, I'd have to get out of the throttle and then after I hit the throttle again it would be 1...2....3... before it would start going again from the throttle lag."

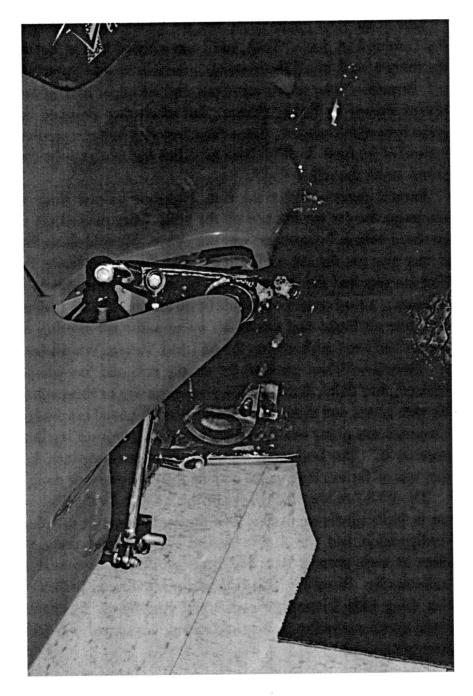

The front brake assembly on the Lotus 56 – 4 disc version

Late in the 1968 Indianapolis 500, Joe Leonard was leading in the Turbine Car. Joe – "Yeah, and I was within 9 laps of having the thing won, it was disheartening... there is no other word for it." Parnelli – "The yellow came out, and we might have gotten beaten anyway by Bobby (Unser), but when they dropped the green it wouldn't take off. Remember how they had run gasoline instead of jet fuel? It didn't have lubricant and froze up the fuel pump under the yellow flag."

Parnelli Jones – "After the race, Firestone wanted Andy to campaign the car for the rest of the year. They needed me to go along with it, because Joe was our driver. We told them that if they give me the car, we'll run it." For the season finale, the Turbine cars had the daunting task of racing around Riverside raceway... a road course, with little or no brakes. The 67 Turbine car's rear air brake that would lift up to assist the slowing of the car had been outlawed, so the 68 Lotus Turbine was without it. Parnelli – "They wouldn't let us, the rule said 'no winged devices', they didn't like that. They were starting to cheat a little bit with wings, and that's why this car (the 68 Lotus) is a wedge. Chapman was pretty smart, and it's why the thing has a big long nose on it." The bodywork served to provide downforce, but that was of far less help under braking than the previous design.

The 1968 Rex Mays 300 was to be the last race for the Turbine car in Indianapolis car racing, and the Turbine car in this final configuration had the 8 disc system (inboard and outboard discs at each corner) that had been previously discussed at Indianapolis. Parnelli – "We had inboard/outboard brakes on that thing with 2 complete pedals and everything. 2 separate brake systems completely, for road racing. Front and rear too." It wasn't enough.

Complicating the issue was the USAC championship had come down to this final race, between Mario Andretti and Bobby Unser. In this era of tire wars, all the Firestone cars were to be at Mario's disposal, and all the Goodyear shod cars were at Bobby's.

As it turned out, when Mario's car failed, they brought in Leonard to hand over the Turbine Car. Parnelli Jones – "Mario was trying to win the championship. Clint Brawner, his mechanic, came over asking 'if we need your car ½ way through the race and Joe got out and Mario got in, he'd get ½ the points. Can we have your car if Andretti needs it?' So, in the race Brawner comes to me and says 'Pull Joe in, Mario needs the car.' I said, 'look, the car doesn't have any brakes, I'm telling you'. Brawner said 'you're just back-pedaling, you don't want to give us the car', and I told him… 'look, you can have the car, but I'm telling you, it has no freaking brakes. I tried to emphasize that to him, you know…"

Joe Leonard – "It was stupid, if a guy had trouble with his car, he could jump into another car and still get points. Somebody could have really gotten hurt. I'm considerably larger than Mario, and so we put in a big piece of foam. We had previously done this, in case he wrecked the transmission or for some reason that his car wouldn't go. I had been running along in fourth or fifth with the brakes hardly working and I told him "No brakes Mario, watch it."

Mario Andretti – "Actually I drove the car earlier in 1968 when they let me get into it, but I just did a couple of laps at Indy. I said 'Man, this thing's a piece of cake.' I think in 2 laps I had gone as fast as I had with my own car… Oh my God what an advantage they had. I was totally impressed." Joe Leonard – "Everybody bitched about it, but they all wanted to try it to get the feel of it. It was a unique car to drive… it wasn't like driving a race car, there was a lot of differential there."

Taking over a Lotus Turbine mid-race on a road race circuit was a somewhat different proposition. Mario – "When I got into it at Riverside, it was during the race and the thing had NO brakes. The turbine engine had no engine braking; the car never went to idle, as it would idle at like 60 percent (rpm). When you got out of the throttle it almost felt like the engine was still pulling… zero engine braking. There was no way that it could have been competitive."

Lotus 56 turbine car steering wheel and gauges

Joe Leonard – He couldn't hear me very good, and he sailed down into turn 9 and crashed into Pollard. It was ironic that he went into the side of Pollard (in the only other Turbine car), who still had a little bit of brakes left." Mario didn't get the message about the brakes from Leonard or from Parnelli's voiced concerns to Clint Brawner, and was simply unprepared for a race car without either brakes or engine braking. Even a conservative approach was insufficient. Mario – "I could feel it over near turn 6 and figured I'd give myself plenty of room. I think I braked right at the kink, stood on the brakes and the thing wasn't even TRYING to slow down." The Turbine Car era in Indycar racing was over, although a few half-hearted attempts were made to build a car for 1969 that conformed to the newly reduced intake restrictor, again restricted well down much as it had been after Jones' stunning 1967 debut.

Meanwhile, the Turbine engine was also to be a factor in prototype Endurance racing. Ray Heppenstall created the Howmet TX Turbine Cars for the 1968 Endurance racing season.

The turbine engines were installed in McKee chassis, while far from being state of the art, were surprisingly effective. The heat from the exhaust was directed straight out the back of the bodywork, which had some less than stellar effects upon the competition. Mike Rahal (Bobby's father) – "The Howmet turbine car... I was on the grid behind him and the heat coming off the turbine was melting the Plexiglas covering over the headlights of my Porsche 906. It had the most unbelievable Banshee sound."

Not something you see on every race car

Shocking most, the car managed to qualify 3rd for the 12 Hours of Sebring, and finished 3rd at Watkins Glen... the only podium finish ever achieved by a Turbine car in a World Championship of Makes event. 1968 had marked the high point as well as the end for the concept in International racing, and other than an unsuccessful F1 variant of the Lotus Turbine car, it was the end of the genre.

4 Wheel Drive had also been used by various race cars across the eras, most memorably perhaps by the Alfa Bimotre (the last version with engines fore-aft). In the early 60s, Ferguson had

built their P99 Formula One car with 4 wheel drive, but its racing career ended after a non-championship win at a wet Oulton Park in the hands of Stirling Moss. By mid-1969, the F1 paddock having recently had its high wings clipped, were collectively concerned about a lack of traction from the ever more highly developed 3 litre engines. This concern brought about new 4wd cars from Lotus, McLaren, and Matra. The Lotus 63 scared off just about everyone who drove it, which given that those concerned were Lotus F1 drivers that was saying something. The additional weight and complication could have been a worthwhile tradeoff for traction increases in the pre-wing era, but with the downforce generated from low rear wings and front dive planes, these aerodynamic developments were sufficient to increase traction to a degree that the overweight 4WD cars were of inferior performance except in the worst weather conditions. 4WD in Formula One became a fruitless exercise by the end of the 60s, and with the exception of the Lotus 56B turbine car that ran a bit more successfully in 1971, they had all disappeared from the grid by the start of the 1970 season.

The Chaparral 2J fan car

Perhaps one of the most unusual aspects of the 1970 Chaparral 2J was that it was powered by both 2 stroke and 4 stroke rear mounted engines. The aluminum block 427 Chevrolet engine provided power to the rear wheels, and the 2 stroke snowmobile engine powered the active ground effects system, in this case sucking the air out from under the car and blowing it out the rear through 2 large fans which were operated by the 2 stroke powerplant. Lexan skirts sealed the perimeter of the car to the circuit. This design came from the GM equivalent of the Lockheed Skunk Works after the banning of high-wing Can-Am cars as used in 1969, which had provided their aero downforce directly to the rear uprights. A suction solution provided sprung downforce, as with the winged bodywork configuration that the competition used in 1970, except with the Chaparral the downforce was pulling (vs. pushing) down onto the sprung chassis regardless of the car speed.

Advantages included a huge speed advantage through slow and medium speed corners, where the Chaparral generated more downforce than the winged competition. Disadvantages for the competition included being blasted by clag and anything that the car drove over, vacuumed directly into the faces of those behind. When the Monterey Historics had their salute to Chaparral, Vic Elford drove the 2J off-line through the corkscrew section and the clouds of debris coming out the back bordered upon the unbelievable. Mike Rahal – "I drove against Jackie Stewart when he was running that crazy car that Jim Hall had… the sucker car. I was behind him on the grid at Watkins Glen, all this #%$# came flying out the back."

The biggest disadvantage for the Chaparral driver was the unreliability of the active downforce system. As the Chaparral mechanics were fiddling with the temperamental fan system I asked Vic if this reminded him too much of 1970… Elford's stone-faced response was "Yes… yes it does."

A fan failure must have been lovely for the driver's state of mind while entering a high speed corner. It would have been the aero equivalent of having the wings fall off the car. Did Vic ever have a fan failure at high speed? Elford – "Yes I did, in turn 9 at Riverside… right in the middle of it, of all places. Because of the way it would sit down on the road, when at static ride height way up in the air, only about 2 inches of each rear tire would be on the road. Those big wide tires at the back would go into positive camber. Well, in the middle of turn 9 the fan failed, the rear of the car came up in the air, the rear tires went to positive camber and it was total oversteer… going from one side to the other, but I managed to make it around without hitting anything."

Chris Amon had a ringside seat. "I can remember following

The Chaparral 2J sucker or fan car of 1970

When the 2J runs off line, it blows enormous amounts of clag out the rear of the car in the face of the competition.

the sucker car with the 707 March at Riverside. Riverside was always a bit dusty anyway, but I was getting sandblasted as it was picking up everything off the track. I remember being right behind him once coming out of turn 9 when the 2 stroke engine stopped and he had a huge sideways moment. How Vic held on to it, I'll never know. I gather they were generating enough downforce that the carburetors on the two stroke couldn't cope with the G-loading, from what was being said at the time."

Another downside was the technical complexity of the rear half of the car, in a real world racing environment. Elford – "At Laguna Seca we never did the race. I was on pole position of course, but in the warm-up on Sunday morning, the big engine broke. The whole rear end of the car had to come apart to get at the engine, the whole lot. Where with most cars you could change an engine in a couple of hours, with this it was a full day's job for 2 or 3 mechanics at the workshop."

Vic Elford – "It was a great car to drive, as it could do things that no other car could do. With the fan system it worked at any speed, it didn't rely on speed to have the air going over the body pushing down. Where it really worked the best was under braking and in slow corners, because it wasn't speed dependant. The balance was so calculated, it actually was totally neutral." When the car was operating properly it was otherworldly in its cornering speed, and devastatingly demoralizing to the competition.

Elford – "Yeah at Riverside, I passed Denny Hulme around the outside of turn 9. It took care of him. He went in, sat on the pit wall and sulked (laughing)."

Interestingly, most of the innovative cars in this chapter had a sonic signature that was truly unique. The Chaparral 2J, when heard on approach, sounded like the leaf blower from hell as the only thing that could be heard was the un-muffled 2 stroke engine howling away while exhausting out the top of the rear bodywork. As the car went past, the rearward facing exhaust pipes from the alloy 427 Chevrolet drowned out the leaf blower sound as it blasted away. It was entirely bizarre, making noises like nothing before or since.

The complexity of the dual powerplants and fan system caused enormous problems during the 1970 Can-Am season

Cars with fan driven suction downforce were banned for the 1971 Can-Am season, but for 1978, Brabham's Gordon Murray revived the concept for a Formula One application. The car cleverly used the single rear mounted fan to also cool the car through the horizontal radiators, and with this integrated package Murray could make the argument that the fan and shrouding was just part of the cooling system. This had the desired effect of keeping the scrutineers from telling Brabham to remove the fan, as the car could not run for long without it. The car won in it's only Grand Prix appearance, with Niki Lauda winning the Swedish GP of 1978 before such fan driven suction downforce designs were banned again. History had repeated itself, as with the high wings of the 1966 Chaparral 2E having shown up in F1 two years later (before being banned in just under a year) the suction based design of Chaparral had now shown up in F1 eight years on. Imitation is the sincerest form of flattery, and perhaps no company has pioneered radical design solutions to the degree it has been by Chaparral Cars.

Vic Elford was reunited with his Chaparral 2J. There were fan problems, again, much as plagued the effort in 1970.

So, is it normally aspirated or not?

Originally in the early 1950s, the equivalency formula for Grand Prix racing was 4.5 litre normally aspirated, vs. 1.5 litre supercharged. In one of the more memorable weekends at the Long Beach Grand Prix, Ferrari showed up in 1981 with 2 of their standard V6 dual turbo Type 126 Grand Prix cars, and also the new 1.5 litre Comprex supercharged version. Ferrari made the poorly received argument that due to the nature of the design and the text in the rulebook, it should be allowed the full 3 litre displacement as would be used by a normally aspirated engine, vs. the 1.5 litre allowed for more traditional supercharged or turbocharged designs. Otherwise known as a pressure wave turbocharger, it used the pressure waves from the exhaust to pressurize the intake charge. The Comprex car was easily recognizable due to a large bulge in the rear bodywork to enclose this taller version of the V6 powerplant with all the Comprex system plumbing atop it. The car only ran in practice, quickly proving to be inferior to the twin turbocharged version. It was never raced.

The Audi R10/R15/R18 TDI and Peugeot 908 Diesels

The Audi R10 diesel program grew out of the incredibly successful Audi R8 Le Mans program of the early 2000s, which won 5 times at the 24 hours of Le Mans from 2000-2005. Such was their dominance that the R8 swept the podium at Le Mans in both 2000 and 2002, when the car made well over 600hp from its 3.6 litre direct injection V8. Perhaps the most remarkable feature of the Dallara-built chassis was how the entire rear transaxle and suspension assembly could consistently be replaced in less than 5 minutes, sometimes even faster. The one year that the car lost this prestigious race was in 2003 when the Bentleys finished 1-2, using a 4 litre version of the Audi R8 powerplant (at Le Mans there were entirely different rule packages for closed vs. open prototypes). For the last 3 years it was campaigned, the R8 with mandated and smaller airflow restrictors was down as much as 100 hp. This 2004 spec Audi R8 again swept the podium at Le Mans. The last win for the car at Le Mans came in 2005, campaigned by the American team 'Champion Racing'.

Dr. Ulrich Baretzky has been the director of the Audi engine program, through its R8 successes on thru to the latest R18. Ulrich – "It was a really good experience working with the Champion team. They brought a lot of their own ideas, from a different culture. That was worth a lot, it's not only the factory team that has all the knowledge, and we did lots of learning together."

What prompted the decision to go with a diesel engine? Dr. Baretzky - "It's a funny story. The diesel... the story starts in a bar, in Ingolstadt during 2002, really... honestly. After 2 or 3 beers, somehow, someway, we came to the point where we discussed running diesels at Le Mans. This was the first moment of the idea. Most people don't believe the story that we weren't talking about sex, women, and cars, and that we talk about motorsport." As if there was ever any doubt, this should confirm that the best ideas are often found in bars.

At what point did the development of the R10 begin? Ulrich - "It started in 2003, and in the beginning I was very much against it, we had never made a diesel engine before. But almost like being struck by lightning, as I realized that if you didn't do it and somebody else did it, you would regret it the rest of your life because you missed this opportunity." Without the commitment on the production side to commit Audi to diesel technology, it would have been pointless to pursue development of an Audi diesel racecar. "Yeah, why go with a diesel? So, we started to discuss it with our production development people, it was not easy. When we started we had asked for partners, maybe Bosch or Mahle for the pistons. We said, 'ok, we'd like to go to Le Mans, run and win in LMP1 with a diesel.' They couldn't say that it was impossible, but that it was very close to being impossible. But, they said that they would help us, so we went on."

Was the appeal the denser energy charge of diesel fuel, with more stored energy in a given volume of fuel, hence the higher thermal efficiency? Ulrich - "At that time, we had no idea whatsoever where we would come out with the power. In the early design of this engine, we decided to go with a 12 cylinder to get the lowest loads per piston possible. Then we decided to make a mule engine from a 4 litre production Audi V8, everything production... while designing the crankshaft and conrods according to the bore and stroke ratio of the V-12. That was when we started to learn about the difficulties, over the next 6 or 7 months. We destroyed blocks, pistons and cylinders, I can still see the face of the engineers as it didn't make any noise, it just went. There was no knocking or anything like we were used to from the gasoline engines. Spark ignited engines have a tendency to knock and destroy themselves, diesels don't do that. The diesel engine didn't do anything; it just went 'bang'. The piston was melted, which was the smallest possible type of engine failure you can have, as the crankshaft pressure goes up and then you know it's done, before everything is falling to pieces." Those lessons learned from the mule V-8 were then applied to the first V-12.

Allan McNish using all the road and then some – 2007 Audi R10

Dr. Baretzky continues - "Then came the very first prototype V-12, a huge engine, 700mm (27.5") long. We had gone with an alloy cylinder block, which was also a revolution for a diesel. A lot of people had come to me and said that an aluminum block for a diesel will not last, but I said that you will never see me go racing with a cast iron cylinder block. Never, ever. I had to fight for that, and we never had a problem with it. We had no liners, the block was Nikasil coated."

What was redline for the V-12? "4800, five thousand, and it's stayed about the same up until now. A diesel is limited by combustion speed. If somebody tells you they've got a diesel that is revving up to 7000, just smile because he doesn't know what he's talking about. You can rev a diesel up to that, but you will not get any power." One imagines the torque numbers were off the scale with the 5.5 litre V-12. "I'll say, you get a LOT of torque, so they have huge loads on the pistons and huge loads on the bearings and everything. This is the experience that you have to go through first, to forget everything you knew about gasoline engines, you had to re-learn everything new for a diesel. With the R10 we had to limit the torque voluntarily for the gearbox, or it couldn't stand it. Even with the upgraded gearbox we had to limit it because we were in excess of 1100 NM (greater than 811 ft-lbs). And when I say more, I mean it was a LOT more."

With the announcement of the R10 diesel racer, it seemed every race fan and motorsport journalist in the country made themselves a note to go see this car. As with the Indy Turbine car or 6 wheeled Tyrrell, the chance to see the debut of such innovation may only occur once in a generation. Baretzky – "I believe that. I was getting more and more aware that what we are doing was a little bit like your trip to the moon. We had seen it, we think that we may get there... maybe not... but you can see it and it touches you every night when you look at it. And you know it's a slight possibility to get there, but you have to try it. The more we worked on it, the more we became aware of the importance of what we were doing."

Allan McNish is one of the pre-eminent endurance drivers of the past 2 decades, being the last to win overall at Le Mans for Porsche (1998), he raced the Audi R8 at Joest in 2000, followed by a stint with the Toyota and Renault F1 programs. He returned to Audi in 2004-5 to drive their highly developed R8 endurance racers. For 2006, the Audi Diesel R10 appeared upon the scene, with a 5.5 litre V-12 diesel engine. The car was nearly silent as it circulated the track, eliciting comparisons to the "Whoosh-mobile" Turbine cars of the late 1960s.

2008 version of the V-12 Audi R10 powerplant assembly

What was the initial experience of the early Audi R10 for the driver? Allan – "At the first test at Sebring, going into turn 13, I wasn't sure if I'd shifted down to 3rd, if I was in 5th… didn't know where I was, I couldn't hear it. Normally you hear 'wrinnng wrinnng" when you go down gears… there was nothing. There was no feel, we needed a gear display just so we could get used to it. There was actually a discussion about putting audio of the engine into the drivers' earplugs, so we could hear when we downshifted. It was more different than I expected, but after a few tests I got used to it. If you are sitting with something screaming its head off right behind you, whether it's a kid or a big engine, there is the fatigue aspect to it. It is important to keep that threshold as low as possible, but I'm pretty sure that (noise reduction) wasn't in their philosophy, it was a by-product."

McNish and Baretzky at Le Mans '12, photo courtesy Audi Sport

Dr. Baretzky – "I will never forget the first test of the car at Sebring. There were no spectators, just the guys that worked at the track. They came running and said 'that's a silver ghost'. It is so supernatural just to see it go by but you don't hear the noise. It was absolutely mysterious. Allan was driving that first time, and he jumped out of the car, went straight away to me, shook my hand and said 'Thank you, thank you for the car.' I had never heard this from a driver; I think it will never happen again… and from a Scotsman (laughs), I'll never forget that. And I'll never forget the first race we had at Sebring."

The debut for the car had gone anything but smoothly. Ulrich Baretzky – "I had broken my leg skiing 2 weeks earlier, had to get screws in my broken knee… I had told the doctors they had 2 days to fix it because I had to go to America. They told me I was mad, but I had to; it was the most important race of my life, I would have gone if they had to carry me. At Sebring we had an awful problem before the race because of the oil tank that was provided by others. It had oil level sensors in it, and instead of fixing them to the tank, they had taped it in. In the hot oil all the time, the tape fell off and went into the entry for the oil feed to the oil pump. So the oil pressure would go down and we'd have to change the engine. This happened 3 times, so it was our very last engine which we raced."

There were still more problems - "We had qualified on pole, and in the warm-up I saw the engine oil temperature going up. The race was starting 2 hours later, and we couldn't change the engine as we didn't have another one. We thought it had to be something in the heat exchanger, so we decided to change it as there must be something wrong. We had 2 crews of mechanics, who dismounted the engine from the running car and got the heat exchanger out of the other one. When we dismounted the heat exchanger we could see that at the entry for the water to cool it down, it still had the plug in it. Somebody had forgotten to pull the plug out, so it had no cooling at all. We put in another one, but had missed the grid and had to start for the pitlane. So, I was standing there on crutches with a cast, in my fireproof suit." The Audi R10 TDI came from behind to win its first race. Baretzky - "It was extremely hard and extremely satisfying on the other hand."

Allan McNish - "I started at the end of the year (2005) with Emmanuelle Pirro and we agreed that it would probably take a season to really understand how to drive the R10... to use the torque to your advantage. Sure, you could nail the throttle and go straight ahead, but you had to have tire management in mind as we didn't have traction control then. You had to really work with the car given the advantages and also the disadvantages. There were weight distribution issues and things like that in the beginning. It was the first time that anyone had actually done it (race a diesel in endurance racing). Definitely it was one of those journeys that started off where we didn't really know where it was going to go. There was a lot that was new from a team point of view, not just from the drivers."

Was there a significant drop in redline when you went from the R8 gasoline engine racer to the diesel R10? Allan – "There was a drop. With the gasoline car you need to use revs to get the power. With the diesel, first of all you don't have that rev potential. Secondly, with the diesel you don't use the horsepower to go, you use the torque. Michelin had to redevelop a tire to withstand the torque we were putting through it, as the original tire couldn't take the load or the heat when we dropped the gas pedal."

There was no traction control allowed on the R10 diesel, which likely made for a huge challenge. Dr. Baretzky – "In the beginning it was just the driver, it was a nightmare. The only thing we could do at the time was to limit the torque and the boost. So we had a cutoff for the boost for the 1st, 2nd, and 3rd gears to avoid that. We gave up power." So you had a pop-off valve that limited the manifold pressure at certain rpm in certain gears? "Yes, only 4th and 5th gear was free... in the dry. In the wet we had special mapping and the driver could reduce everything to an acceptable level. The driver has to change the mapping; it is not allowed to do it from the pits. There were multiple maps, between full power, saving fuel, rain, yellow, or whatever. But in the rain with a lot of mass in the rear, the problem was more with the front to keep it from aquaplaning."

Allan McNish - "Because of the weight of the engine... because of the placement of the engine... the particle filters, the gearbox and everything, you basically ended up braking in a straight line, turning it as quickly as you could and then getting on the pedal in a straight line." So, the Audi R10 was a point and squirt car? "Exactly, the apex speed was quite low." Ulrich Baretzky – "Allan (McNish) was complaining an awful lot about a lack of balance and everything in the rear. Today he's complaining that there's nothing in the rear because it's such a small engine (V6-R18)... drivers... you know, you can do whatever, and they are always complaining about something. I don't listen to them anymore (smiles). Ok, the R10 was not an easy car to drive, but on the straight it was very fun because it would pull away from everybody. I remember at Miller, Pirro came from position 12 and overtook 8 or 9 cars after the green flag in only one straight."

The 2008 Audi R10 at the Sebring 12 Hours

Allan - "We're sitting here in 2011 and this was in 2006. Five years ago would you have ever thought that a diesel car would dominate some of the biggest races in the world? No. And five years ago would you have ever thought there would be so many diesel cars being sold in the US by premium brand manufacturers?"

Starting with 2007 there were 2 major manufacturers racing diesels in LMP1, with the arrival of the 5.5 litre 100 degree V-12 Peugeot. They finished 2nd at Le Mans, as strong showing for their first effort. Soon after I had congratulated Sebastian Bourdais, and mentioned that it had to be a dream for him, being a kid who grew up in Le Mans watching his father race at the 24 hours. His response at the time was "Yes, all but one position." Sebastian looks back - "We were happy back in 2007, just to finish was great. The V-12 was much easier to deal with than now (2011), because the powerband was much wider. The difference with the diesel is that you actually get a kick when you upshift into the peak of the torque. You follow the shift lights so you are always on top of the curve."

Were there further developments of the R10? Dr. Baretzky – "The basic architecture never changed, even the arrangement of pumps and things stayed more or less the same. We went from aluminum to steel pistons which allowed us to lower the crankcase as the piston crowns became much lower. What we didn't expect was that straight away we got 1% more power. We never raced it in the V-12, but had started development to where we knew how it would work so that we could take it 100% to the V-10, which would never have allowed us to use aluminum pistons. The reason it worked is that aluminum has a factor of heat expansion 2 times that of steel. So as the clearance is increasing, you get less friction and get a power advantage. When the engine is cold, you nearly cannot move (turn) it."

In 2007 at the season's final race at Laguna Seca it came down to a straight fight between the lighter, pole sitting LMP-2 Penske Porsche RS Spyder, and Dindo Capello in the Audi R10. As one would expect, the R10 was incredible coming off a yellow flag restart and the Audi came into the double apex turn 2 on the outside of the Porsche, shockingly managing to hold the outside position and pass for the lead on corner exit. So much for low apex speeds. Anyone watching in turn 2 that day was left stunned. McNish - "Yeah, I know... so were we. I thought it was talent (smiles), but no, we'd never seen anything like it. When it first happened it was like... 'what happened there, say again?' Well, they (the Porsche) had struggled with tire warm-up. We had made a quite clever tire choice and also the weight actually helped at Laguna because it's such a slippery circuit. The weight of our car and the loading it put onto the tire, warmed the tire up quite quickly which would be negative at most races, but was positive there. We could generate quicker tire temperature than what the others did." The nimble Porsche, upon getting its required tire temperature, was now all over the R10 for the remaining laps, but could not get by.

For 2008, McNish was to get his first Le Mans win for Audi with the R10, in a classic race-long battle with the Peugeot team despite being anywhere from 3 to 5 seconds a lap slower in qualifying. That narrow victory against all odds became the storyline behind the racing film "Truth in 24". It was clear to all, that a new car would be needed, and soon.

The 2nd generation of the Audi Diesel prototype was the R15. Dr. Baretzky – "The R10 car had been basically designed for a V8 petrol engine. We changed our minds and then went for the diesel, so it was an imbalanced car. They didn't want to stretch the car to build a new one, so we fit it in there. The R15 should have overcome the problems that Allan was calling out about this weight distribution thing. We moved the entire engine forward by about 200mm (8 inches) and we made the engine smaller by one cylinder (in length), so the mass centralization was much more in the center of the car, to solve the problems of the R10. We no longer had to reduce power in the first 3 gears, as we had traction control with the R15. With a diesel, the traction control is much easier, it reduces or increases the amount of fuel injected using direct injection. This is something we developed with the R8, when we developed mapping for yellows, to get the best out of the fuel economy."

Allan – "Going from the R10 to the R15, the engine was (physically) smaller going from a 5.5 litre V-12 to a 5.5 litre V-10, which was partly to help the balance of the car, and the management of the chassis packaging. There was a turbo boost reduction, and we had a fuel cell reduction as well, with 65 litres of fuel instead of 80. It was still a bit 'point and squirt', but I have to tell you that I think the R15 was a very underrated car. It was underrated because it lost a Le Mans (2009), and in that race we didn't perform that well as a team, as a group. We were a bit underpowered, but we were fighting against a factory that was very ON. They (Peugeot) were really up to it, and they deserved the victory."

The V-10 diesel powered Audi R15

Simon Pagenaud was to drive the Peugeot 908 at Le Mans from 2009-11, and he gives his impression of racing a diesel prototype. "With a gasoline engine car, when you reach maximum rpm you can feel it because it is screaming in your ears. With the diesel, when the power goes, it goes very quickly through the gears. It is a lot of shifting. If you go above 4200 rpm, you lose power so you have to shift quite early. And you don't really sense the right engine noise when you shift up, so you actually have to look at your gear lights on the steering wheel." The Peugeot featured a 6 speed transmission, and given the rpm at which the power falls off, there is no need for a rev limiter in the car. Simon – "No we don't have one, we don't really need to."

One could say the same about the Le Mans that Audi won the following year (2010), where the updated Audi R15 was still very much the performance underdog but by running the perfect race, they had swept the podium of another Le Mans. Allan –"Yes, 100%. Since then, the competition level has gone up so much now, to where if you are any percent off, you lose. The R15 was up against some pretty tough competition, and after that the regulations changed mid-season which hurt us a lot. There was all this stuff around about the front of the cars... to be honest it was all the stuff you don't want in sport. It compromised us and made us have a change of philosophy in 2010. If we had known these regs at the time of design, we'd have had a closed car. The R15 had huge potential that wasn't realized."

Dr. Baretzky – "I have to say that the V-10 was one of the least varying engines we have ever made. We had kept the 90 degree architecture from the V-12. It ran from the very beginning, never made us any problems. It was very reliable and very powerful as the 2010 V-10 made more power than the earlier less restricted V-12. It is an interesting thing, to see how the power reductions under the rules relate to powerplant development. What we discovered with the R15 program was that a diesel engine is very sensitive to the length of the intake system. With a boost pressure of 2.6 bar, the engine was extremely reactive to this torque-wise. It was 2009 already, time was running short and we couldn't make a complete development program to cover the loads. So, that was something we experienced in 2010 with the R15, and this was for sure one of the highlights. We knew on the other hand, that the R15 was kind of a dinosaur, a huge thing more or less outdated. It is not the style of the time, and we don't need such huge engines anymore. That's why we discussed about the reduction to the size of engine that we have now."

It was somewhat of a surprise to see Audi go from the V-10 to a V-6 with the R18. Baretzky – "Yes, and it was a surprise also to Peugeot (the Peugeot diesel is a V8). The reason is simple...

it would have been boring to make a V-8. We have more V-6s in production than V-8s, and I thought given the choice we had some advantages. First, the V-6 is very compact, very short, which would allow us for the future to integrate any kind of energy recovery system that you would like, behind the engine. Another thing was the weight, and the third thing was that we wanted to develop technology for downsized diesel engines. To develop the power means that you have that much more load per cylinder and this requires technological solutions to keep this engine going."

The end of the road for the R15 at the 2011 12 Hours of Sebring. McNish felt it the best balance of chassis & engine to date.

Ulrich Baretzky continues the saga to the final race for the R15 – "In 2011 at Sebring, the R15 had the weakest engine of all. We had to adopt it (the V-10) to the rules, had to reduce the power dramatically to be in conformance with those rules. We had a smaller restrictor, so we had to re-map the engine and there was a reduction in boost. And then, I think for the first time, the car matched the power of the engine. Before that, I think the car was over-run by the power. The car and the engine were now on the same level. Allan came to me and said it was fantastic to drive. I told him… 'For the first time, you don't complain about this car. From day one, you complained about it. Now you come with the power all reduced, to say it's fantastic.' We could have won the race if he hadn't had the accident. It was a great car, the best R15 ever, that's for sure." McNish – "In its last race, Sebring 2011, that was probably its best race. I know we won there with it in 2009, but in 2011 that car was singing." Still, the car finished 1, 2, 3 for a podium sweep at its final Le Mans in 2010.

Looking up under the front of an R15 toward the cockpit area could best be described as a wide-bodied formula one car. Allan – "Yes, and when you strip it apart, it looks stunning, and I have to say that with the R18 it looks even better. We've gone from a V-12 (R10) down to a V-6 (R18), and the whole development and efficiencies that we've now got out of it; it's been quite mesmerizing over the last few years. It's now a better packaged car, a better balanced car, and a better feeling car." Ulrich Baretzky – "It was a real challenge and this engine was the opposite of the V-10 in the R15. This engine really made us problems… we were really struggling with it."

Was there ever a chance of pulling the plug on the V-6 and going back to the V-10 that had worked so beautifully at Sebring? "No chance, there was no chance it was this one or nothing. We couldn't have run at Le Mans but only as a grandfathered car with no chance of victory at all. It was the R18 or nothing. And we had been developing it since September 2009, 2 years ago. You have to remember that the V-12 took us 30 months, and the V-10 which had a little bit bigger of a cylinder bore took us 20 months. The V-6 engine took us less than 16, and it was also steel pistons from the beginning."

Was the problem the big bore engine? Dr. Baretzky – "The problems weren't the pistons, the problems were the bearings. There were also a lot of strange things going on with the injection, as of course the bore was far bigger than with the V-10 so it had far more loading on each piston as the pressure went up as well.

The American debut of the R18 was at the 2011 Petit Le Mans

In the R10 it was about 45 hp per piston, with the V-6 we have about 90, so the load per cylinder has doubled. The boost is a little bit higher than it was at the end of the R10 project. It shows that we have reached almost the same power level that we had almost 10 years ago with the (gasoline powered) R8 and this is a diesel engine of nearly the same size, which shows the progress that engine technology has taken in the last 10 years. That's incredible. I was surprised myself, and the fuel mileage is a LOT better. In 2001 our qualifying time was something like 3 minutes and 31 seconds, this year we made 3 minutes, 21 seconds." Getting more for less? "Exactly, and that's exactly why we are doing this. Doing things that nobody else is doing... it's like we've discovered a new planet. It will be interesting to see where all this ends up, but I'm quite optimistic and we've applied some of these ideas about diesel technology for the future, what we will do."

The new closed cockpit Audi R18 hadn't run at Sebring in

2011 because the time was too short, there were still continuing development problems until the team got to Le Mans. If you have to pick a place, Le Mans is a good place to have things come together. Although 2 of the cars were destroyed in massive accidents, the surviving R18 was in the lead. Coming off the final pit stops after 23 ½ hours, the R18 equipped with new tires was 6 seconds ahead of the lead Peugeot 908. Turning the fastest lap of the race on the final lap, the new R18 had won the 24 Hours of Le Mans on its first attempt by just 14 seconds.

McNish – "With the V-6 turbo, you actually drive it more like you would with a petrol car; it is about momentum, as you have to roll that speed into the corner. We can carry more apex speed than we could before, and then control the power coming out." As the new R18 is a momentum car, vs. the point & squirt torque monsters of previous years, one assumes it has increased the challenge of getting through traffic. Are there issues with keeping the turbo spooled up for quick throttle response? Allan – "That's not a problem." Dr. Baretzky – "There are mainly 2 reasons for this. Number one is that we are using only one turbocharger now and it is a VNT turbo, which is a variable turbine nozzle system, which avoids any turbo lag. That's why it doesn't feel so different between a normally aspirated gasoline engine and the turbo-diesel now. You hit the accelerator and the car goes. Our problem is that because of the efficiency, the temperatures in our engine are much higher than production engines, so we needed to develop a system that works between 800 and 1050 degrees centigrade and that is quite a lot. It is not ceramics, as that is not allowed… it is steel. We developed it with an American company, Garrett. They are very good, but they suffered a lot, and we suffered as well, but we made it together. It was the hardest journey, we had started with the V-10, we used it in the last version of the V-10 but we didn't promote it. With the V-6 we wanted to promote it, you cannot feel that (any lag) as it's always keeping the revs up. Even the ACO came to us and said 'when you are shifting, you have no drop in pressure!' Yeah, because it is closing down and keeping the speed up, and then is opening again when the shifting is finished. Thousandths… actually a couple of Milliseconds…. It is incredible, and we never have problems with it. The single turbo, we couldn't have done it without this technology… we would have made it like the Peugeot, with 2 turbos. Our turbo is right in the middle of the engine, it is a breakthrough."

Dr. Baretzky continues – "With the R10 we had the turbo lag of course, because in the beginning we had the old technology with waste gates, so you'd have to wait until the pressure was coming up. The turbo was smaller and the engine was big displacement, but nevertheless you had a delay in response." Small wonder Allan McNish loved the last version of the R15, with big torque, hugely improved balance, and very little turbo lag. As for the R18, Mc Nish comments – "The problem is just keeping the car's momentum up. I'm sure it's the same down the road (at Peugeot)."

No doubt it is also a momentum game at Peugeot, but their drivers can only wish that keeping the turbo spooled up in traffic on the 2011 car was resolved as over at Audi.

Peugeot driver Simon Pagenaud – "The turbo kicks in at about 2500 rpm, and it's a very narrow powerband which makes it a bit tricky in how you have to drive it. It is very important to have the turbo early-on, in the corner. The redline is pretty much the same as the older one, it is at 4200 rpm. The V-10 had more torque initially; this new one is a little bit more… metallic… in the sense that it's more abrupt. You don't have much torque, there is more to gain higher up between 3800 and 4200, where before there was more to gain lower. In a corner like Radillon at Spa (with the V-10 car), you would actually shift up at the bottom of the hill, it would pull better. It was incredible; we would short-shift it basically. This is the big difference, this year is the opposite, and it is much more like a gasoline engine higher up in the revs." What is the driving technique to keep the turbo spooled up? Simon – "Sometimes when you go into a corner on the brakes, you hold the brake and start tapping the throttle slowly, to spin up the turbo. Once it's up, it really goes. Otherwise if you go really hard for the throttle, there's a hole in the power."

The 2011 V8 Peugeot 908 was to win the Championship over Audi, narrowly losing Le Mans by a handful of seconds

So the trick is to get everything spooled up and pressurized while in the corner, so when you need the power on exit, maximum boost is available? Simon - "Exactly, but it doesn't take much time to build up." The Peugeot 908 endurance racer has pedals that are arranged go-kart style for a variety of reasons, not the least of which is to make such sensitive application of both pedals simultaneously. Simon Pagenaud – "The cars stop so fast these days you don't have time to go from one pedal to another. Back in 2006 I used to right foot brake but realized when I got to Champ Car I thought, "Man, if I'm going to right foot brake it will be very difficult because those cars stop so fast, I'm not going to have the time for it." Sebastian Bourdais – "Yeah, but the problem is that when you do that, you overheat the brakes so there is a limitation. You also burn a lot more fuel. This year with the V-8 the powerband is much narrower and until you get the boost, since the engine is much smaller, you get nothing." So, you need the 6 speed more than you needed it before? "We could use an 8 speed (laughs). If you get in a big hole, you have to downshift quite a few gears just to get out of it. When the boost is not on, there is not much going on."

Dr. Baretzky – That's the problem, and we don't have it now. I just make the engine as bulletproof as possible." McNish - In terms of the powerband (the R18), it is a bit narrower. The redline has been going lower and lower, every time you change the restrictor… you put less in, you get less out. In engine performance, when they are restricting you back so much, if you can stand still you are doing well. If you've got a wrong balanced engine, then it doesn't matter how good the chassis is. That's the big difference in going from the V-12 to the V-10 to the V-6, is that you have a more nimble chassis in a lighter car that you can package a bit better and get the performance that way. Ultimately if you look at pure car performance, lap time performance, then you have to say they've moved forward very well. The big question over here… 10 years ago, performance was horsepower, and now the performance isn't just horsepower."

Anthony Davidson was the third driver of the #7 Peugeot. "You need momentum on the exit, that's what it's all about. You have to make sure you can get into the braking zones ahead of the traffic, get the move done as soon as you can. You drive like you've just done a bank robbery and you've got the cops behind you. That's got to be your mentality… 'I ain't stopping'. If you don't, Audi will be. Last year we could arrive at the corner, downshift a bit and power past the traffic on the exit. Now we can't. I can agree with slowing the LMPs down, but they didn't really slow GT down as well. If they had done it with both, then it's no problem. Now we are basically driving Formula 3 cars, we survive on momentum. We used to hear the LMP2 guys complain about that last year, trying to overtake the GT cars. Now we feel their pain. The car is improved aerodynamically over last year and we are actually quicker in the corner, but our ultimate lap time is slower because we don't have the acceleration." There is sad irony in the fact that Ant subsequently had an enormous accident at Le Mans 2012 in the P1 Toyota hybrid, due to a wandering GT car making a move in the braking zone that could best be described as clueless.

What about engine braking which the enormous compression ratios required for a diesel engine to operate? Simon Pagenaud – "Both of the diesel engines (V-8 and V-10 Peugeot) don't really have much engine brake, you lift off and it doesn't really decelerate. It's a funny thing, it was even more the case in the old car, you lift off and it wouldn't stop so you have to use the brake a lot. Getting ready for Le Mans, it's a big focus. The carbon brakes are different than steel. You have to use the carbon brakes properly, by using them really hard. If you try to save your carbon brakes by braking more easily, you are actually going to use more material. Like with any other carbon brakes, they operate at very high temperatures, around 900 degrees centigrade."

Have the tires changed to softer compounds due to the reduction in torque from the R10 to the R18? Allan – "No, not really because the loads onto them are just as high, now it is downforce related. It has changed the tire construction but I wouldn't say it's gone a lot softer. It changes every time we develop a new tire, during the season sometimes." Peugeot may have had the dominant car in 2011, winning most of the events and the championship, but victory at Le Mans, the Holy Grail of endurance racing, eluded them.

Sebastian Bourdais looks back upon the profound disappointment of again losing Le Mans, his home race. "Now, having finished 2nd three times, this year was heartbreaking. You push, you push, you have the perfect race without one problem… and you come in 2nd by 14 seconds. You start saying, 'what could we have possibly done?' I first went to the race when I was pretty young; we were living about 60 meters away from one of the corners. My Dad was racing himself and I grew up at the race tracks. It still is my home town, I moved to Switzerland when I was in F1, but we came back… we came home. That's why there is really nothing that can make up for not winning it. If someday I am lucky enough to win it, it will probably be one of the very best days of my life."

Dan Binks – "I know what it meant to me, and I can't imagine growing up there and have it slip away that many times. To be up there in front of all those people is unbelievable, and when they play your National Anthem, it just doesn't get any cooler than that." And now the Peugeot is gone. Binks – "That's really a bummer, by the way. That caliber of race team just doesn't getput together that often. For it to shut down…"

Making what was well beyond a last-minute decision in early 2012, Peugeot pulled the plug on their endurance racing program and Sebastian Bourdais' dream of that elusive home win in a French car went along with it. It was similarly a disappointment for Frenchman Simon Pagenaud. Simon – "I had already decided to go full-time Indycar, but obviously it was heartbreaking to see something like that happen. It was a fantastic car to drive."

There is little doubt that the French manufacturer learned valuable lessons that will result in improved efficiency across their entire range of diesel vehicles. Audi continued to fly the diesel banner with lightweight variations on the 2011 R18, called the R18 Ultra, and the e-tron Quattro Hybrid car is covered in a subsequent chapter of this book.

Ulrich Baretzky – "Of course, we have developed the engine, as you do every year. If you stay with the same engine you lose. It is a development of last year's engine, you cannot do a new engine every year. We got a draft of the new rules on Monday and now we have to think about how we attack that. It will take some while…"

Sadly, some horrendously poor adoptions of gasoline engines to diesel fuel in the 1970s and 80s poisoned the American market for diesel technology as the products were noisy, smoky, and unreliable. The VW diesel Rabbit did nothing to dispel this as their pickup truck could best be described as a noise factory with an echo chamber. This perception has been hard to shake, and as recently as 2010 a particularly oblivious auto journalist at the LA Auto Show voiced the opinion that Americans don't like diesel cars as they are noisy and smoke a lot. Dr. Baretzky – "And then you listen to our race car… incredible. It is so difficult to change the mindset of people, once they have an image in their head, it is very difficult to get it out… without cutting their head off (smiles)." McNish – "That perception is changing very quickly, I think. You look at the number of Audis that are sold with diesels it is gaining ground very quickly."

Audi, along with Peugeot, have achieved what previously would have been considered impossible. They have shown that the terms Diesel and High Performance are no longer mutually exclusive.

Diesel dominance was the surprise story of Endurance Racing

CHAPTER FIVE

TIRES AND BRAKES

Mario Andretti driving the 1921 French GP winning Duesenberg

Racing has seen massive changes in tire technology from the 1960s up through the present. Looking back upon his experiences at the 1958 Race of Two Worlds at Monza, Stirling Moss explains the tire technology of the day. "Well, the Americans came over and it rained for practice, so I told my mechanic to start it up as I wanted to go out on the circuit was like when it was wet. The Americans came over and asked me 'what are you doing?' and told me that they don't race in the wet. I said... 'That's all right, Luigi Musso, Phil Hill and myself... we'll just split the money between the 3 of us if you aren't going to race.' So, were quite happy when the rain came, I went out to see what the car was like. They came along and had me black flagged! We didn't have slicks, you see. In America you had slicks, and they were undriveable... while in my entire career I never used a slick. I'd done about 5 laps, and they got all excited and came rushing up to me afterwards asking what it was like. 'A little bit slippery here and there...' If it was wet or dry, it didn't make any difference to us, we just went a little bit slower. In principle, you had the same tire, wet or dry."

There were differences between dry and rain tire patterns, but no differences in the compounds of the tires. That all changed at the 1961 German Grand Prix. The shark nose 156 Ferrari was the superior car of the day, Phil Hill taking 5 pole positions and the World Championship. However on the twisty circuits such as Monaco, Stirling Moss in the Lotus was able to contend. Phil – "In practice, I broke the lap record at the Nurburgring, the first under 9 minutes in that car. It was an accident, really, because the car happened to fly so beautifully and land so beautifully. Every lap you went faster, every lap was that way... until the race, where the track was damp. We wanted to use the wet weather tires but the circuit was only damp and Dunlop didn't trust our car on them."

Stirling Moss – "Yes, they were called the 'green spot'; they had a little green spot on the side... a different compound for wet weather. It was dry and I put them on, the Dunlop mechanics went bloody berserk saying 'you can't go out on those tires, it's dangerous'. The tires were faster in the dry, until they wore out. I told them without them I didn't have a chance to win this bloody race against the Ferraris, they are much quicker. They insisted that it was very dangerous, but I told them 'sorry, but I've got to use them.' It was a big to-do." Phil Hill – "Moss, with his lighter Lotus ran them anyway. Moss came in on rags, incidentally. It paid off for him, he won, but the tires were shredded. That was our introduction to the rain tire. It wasn't just the tread pattern, it was the actual rubber that was different. It changed the world for tires, you can't imagine how many lives it has saved the world over. It was a giant leap for that year." Looking back upon his bold gamble that had paid off, Stirling Moss comments – "Bravery and stupidity are very closely related. Whether I'd been brave or stupid, I don't know… but obviously I wanted to try to win and beat the Ferraris. The only chance I'd got was on the wet tire. It's dodgy, but one takes that risk, you know."

From that point forward, it became an ever escalating race between manufacturers to find the best possible compound and tread pattern. In the case of McLaren, it paid the bills. Chris Amon - "In 1965 with McLaren I was doing a huge amount of tire testing with the original M1A, because for the McLaren team that was about 90% of their income. We were getting paid about 10 dollars a mile, or something. It was when Firestone first came into European racing, and the M1A became the tire test car, some weeks doing 1000 miles a week. It had an Oldsmobile (aluminum) in it, 4 liters and probably with about 300 horsepower, and they were relatively reliable to where were getting probably 1000 miles out of an engine. The right person could rebuild one quickly as they were pretty simple. The Firestone people would show up with 6 or 7 different constructions or compounds of tires, and it was a very interesting year. It did me a lot of good, and it was amazing to see the progress that Firestone made. Initially, the differences in the tires were actually quite big, with one maybe a second a lap quicker. As the year went by, it was coming down to tenths of a second as the tires got better. I have to say that right up until the time I stopped, I always enjoyed the testing. In the last 2 or 3 years that I raced, I did very little testing, primarily because the teams I was with had no budget to test... and I really missed that.

Amongst Formula One drivers, Chris Amon became noted for having otherworldly recall as to characteristics of the different tires he had tested. Firestone engineers were known to provide false information to test the consistency of driver feedback, by putting on a new set of tires which had been previously tested while telling Chris the tires were something new. Chris – "I thought the mechanics had made a mistake and put the wrong set of tires back on." The 'switcheroo' didn't work, further validating the accuracy of Amon's feedback.

The tire wars between manufacturers had reached a crescendo during the mid-late 1960s, yet it was still an era where a tire manufacturer would defer to reality and allow their signed drivers to switch to a competitor's tire, if the circumstances warranted it. Le Mans 1966 was a classic example. Chris Amon – "The fact is that we were the only car contracted to Firestone, because we were both contracted to Firestone. The first part of the race was intermittent drizzle and we were running intermediate tires that had never been tested at those sorts of speeds before. I had at least 2 sets of tires in the first hour that were throwing the tread off, and everytime we had a pit stop we were getting further behind. At a certain point he (Bruce) put me in the car and went and argued the point with Firestone that either we put the car on Goodyears, or we withdraw. Firestone said, 'put it on the Goodyears.' By then we'd lost a lot of time, so Bruce just said 'lets just drive the door handles off the thing.'

This was the same decision made by Jochen Rindt and Masten Gregory the previous year, when they thought their Ferrari

250LM had no chance, they tried to drive it into the ground so they could walk away. Instead the car held together to win Le Mans overall in 1965. History was to repeat itself. Chris – "With 3 or 4 hours to go, before the decision was made to hold station, we were comfortably ahead. When the 'hold station' thing came out, Ken (Miles) actually ignored it. In one ½ hour stint, he made up a huge amount of time on Bruce, who was holding station and lap time. I still get a bit about it to this day, because I see Greta Hulme every now and again." Ken Miles' co-driver was Greta's husband... and yet another Kiwi, Denis Hulme.

Le Mans 1966 was to be both one of New Zealand's and America's greatest sporting moments, as the black and silver car had won the race driven by Kiwis McLaren and Amon. Chris Amon – "It was very special, and as it turned out was probably the pinnacle of my career. I guess you never got quite the same degree of satisfaction out of a sports car long distance race as you did out of a Grand Prix, because it wasn't an individual (driving) effort. Unfortunately it was clouded by the finish, as Ken Miles felt he was the resident Shelby driver and should have won the race."

By 1968 the Dunlop shod Matra had a massive advantage with their wide central groove rain tire. Jackie Stewart used that tire to great effect in miserable conditions at the German Grand Prix. Race reports of the time referred to Stewart having such a huge lead after the first lap that people began to wonder if the rest of the field had crashed, due to the long delay before another car appeared. They also had advantages in the dry given their new compound, the Dunlop 970.

Paul Butler was the Dunlop tire engineer for F2 car racing in Europe during the 68-69 season before eventually becoming Race Director for motorcycle Grand Prix racing. 1968 was a watershed year for Dunlop's F1/F2 program. Paul – "That year in F1 they had the central groove rain tire, which was like having 2 motorcycle tires which had huge water dispersal. The 970 compound was Formula 2, where it started. When you asked 'what were my most memorable moments in racing?', I said Zandvoort in 1968, which was where that 970 compound was tried for the first time in the dry. It had started as a wet weather compound used in 1967 and it was the first time that the engineers had worked up the courage to try it and see if it would last in the dry, and it was 2 seconds a lap quicker than anything else."

Jackie Stewart with the Dunlop shod Matra MS-80 in 1969

Butler continues - "We tried that 970 compound on the bikes in the year that John Cooper beat Agostini (1971 Race of the Year at Mallory Park). Cooper had the 3 cylinder BSA, Ago was on the MV, and Read was on the Yamaha. I told each of them that the technicians want to try this compound and told them that we'd like them to try the tires. Read didn't want them, Cooper used them and of course won the race as they worked really well. The construction of the casing was conventional, and I would venture that it was the most successful compound that Dunlop ever had."

By the mid-1970s, tread had disappeared and the dry tires became slicks, ensuring the maximum rubber footprint in any given width. And those given widths were increasing quickly to ever wider rims and tires. Along the way there were innovations that changed the design approach for future generations. Perhaps the biggest leap forward since the advent of the racing slick was the development of the Gatorback rain tire of the 70s. The hand cut motorcycle racing tire is where the idea for the innovative Goodyear F1 rain tire came from.

Kenny Roberts, 500cc World Champion 1978-80 – "That whole Gatorback thing was motorcycle derived that then went to F1. I had to cut my own intermediate tires, because we didn't have intermediates. When I was cutting a pattern, Tim Miller who invented the Gatorback, asked "Why make those big ones and little ones, why don't you make them all the same?" I told him that if it's cold, I want the little ones because they get hot from the friction and then the little ones heat up the big ones, so when the heat gets high, the little one wears on and the heat transfers to the big ones. He was a Goodyear race technician, and they brought him to see the Formula One racing. He started looking at the rain tires, and they were worn out on the edges but not in the center. He asked "Why don't you put little knobs in the center? Let me do a tire." When Miller first cut one, they put it on a rim and everyone was just pissing themselves laughing, it just looked so weird. All the drivers laughed at it, one guy said he'd try it... guess what... 2 seconds faster per lap at Hockenheim. The little knobs cut through the water a lot better than the big knobs, and they got warm so you could use the whole tire. That's where it all started."

The 1980s brought radial tire construction and it wasn't long before the earlier bias ply designs were obsolete for road racing. Eventually it reached a point where there were 3 choices... slicks, intermediates (often a grooved slick), and monsoon wets for heavy rain. Attempts in mandating grooved slicks were a somewhat unsuccessful attempt to slow the cars in the ever escalating duel between new regulatory restrictions and engineering innovation.

Of course, tires are as critical to safety as they are to performance. The greatest driver of his generation was Scotland's Jim Clark. His 1968 death in a F2 Lotus was most likely due to tire failure. Having tire failure on the tree-lined Hockenheim circuit had sealed Clark's fate. Later, in the case of Nissan's GTP effort, they achieved 4 consecutive championships for Geoff Brabham from 1988-1991. It wasn't always so successful, as Bridgestone tire failures dogged their earlier efforts. At Riverside, Eliott Forbes-Robinson had a massive accident in turn one, thanks to a favor from his teammate Brabham. Geoff - "I was still doing Indycars so I just did the odd race. When I logged in, I normally qualified and started the race. At Riverside I actually felt sorry for EFR and told him 'look, why don't you start the race for a change.' So 10 laps into the race the tire failed, he goes backwards into the fence and breaks his collarbone. As it turned out, it was one of the good decisions I'd made." Hell of a favor? "Exactly... what buddies are for." Don Devendorf – "Actually a turbine blade from a Porsche had punctured the tire."

The glory days for the Nissan effort began with a switch to Goodyear tires. Don Devendorf – "Fortunately for us, Bridgestone wouldn't sign up after I laid on them a 400-500,000 sponsorship. I told them 'this tire is causing us so much damage. I want to get compensated for the damage caused by your tire failures, and I want sponsorship money.' They didn't go for it, which actually was great because Goodyear was sitting there waiting. The Goodyear guys knew from some Trans-Am thing or something like that, where they had Bridgestone and Goodyear... they knew there was such a marked difference between them side by side. The Goodyear guys knew that there were 3 or 4 seconds a lap in our car. In testing at Riverside using an interval of the track, using the Goodyears and the lower horsepower restrictors, we were 2-1/2 seconds faster than we'd ever been there before."

Devendorf – "At Charlotte, we had just bolted on the Goodyear tires, and the car was instantly faster. Within 2 laps I was almost 5 seconds a lap faster. That's where the bell housing broke and the car just steered up into the guardrail, sliding on the tub as the suspension had all collapsed. So, here you are on this thin carbon fibre honeycomb toboggan."

The Trevor Harris designed Nissan GTP ZX-T racer was their best

Devendorf continues - "Turned out the whole side of the bellhousing had pulled out. So we designed a girdle for it… an exo-skeleton for the thing. When we finally did the new car (the 88) we measured it and I think it was 8 or 10 times stronger torsionally than the Lola car."

The Trevor Harris design (the 88) was a superior machine in all aspects and the combination of Nissan and Goodyear dominated the class for years. However, as the speeds increased, and despite the change to Goodyear, tire failure returned to become a recurring nightmare for the Nissan GTP effort in their later years. 1991 at Elkhart Lake was one of the worst. Geoff - "The rear tire blew just before I got to the braking area on the front straight. It went backwards and took off, that's why I got hurt. I did 4 ribs in, and I actually didn't wake up until I was in the helicopter 50 minutes later. We wrote that off as being a freak thing. The race after that was 6 weeks later and was a street course, Del Mar. Then the next year at Daytona we used a different car, and then we had 2 street courses... Miami and West Palm Beach. Then we went to Road Atlanta, which was the first fast, high load circuit that we had been to with that car since Elkhart Lake. In the first 10 or 15 laps, Chip's tire blew and he had a really big accident."

It was a massive accident with the car strewn up the hill after the 'gravity cavity' at the end of the long straight. Geoff - "The problem for me was that I could tell what had happened. After the yellow came out, you could see pieces of tire first, and then you saw the wreckage. I remember radioing in and saying 'Look, Chip's had a rear tire failure. What are we going to do?' Stupid wisdom, we decided to keep going with doing more pit stops and changing the tires more often, just to get through to the end of the race. I think there was only about 10 laps to go, at full noise at whatever speed we were doing, in the dip the rear tire goes again. The only time I've ever been frightened in a race car was then. I understood what had happened to me at Elkhart before, when it went backwards. All I remember is just praying to myself... 'please don't take off, please don't take off'... over and over because if it had taken off, I would have gone into the crowd. I went into the bank backwards and ended upside down."

Trevor Harris was the engineer on the cars. Trevor – "It was a sheer overloading of the tires. There were a number of other cars there that almost had it happen. Toyota almost had the same thing happening, and they caught it. It was just a combination of speed and load, all those cars in that era made a lot of downforce. Half way down to the hill to the dip, the tire just couldn't take it anymore. Luckily we had two drivers that walked away from their cars, in essentially identical accidents."

IMSA had narrowly dodged a bullet, a potential disaster including a large number of spectators. The nightmare wasn't over for Geoff Brabham – "The problem was that the roll cage collapsed and it pinned my head between my shoulder and the road. The Marshalls didn't know what to do, I was stuck there forever. Actually it was my crew that came around from the pits, jumped the fence and they were the ones that lifted the car up so I could get out. I had been stuck there for quite a long time, and luckily it didn't catch fire. It quite damaged my neck a little bit, and I didn't realize how much it had been damaged until I did a test for the next race, and I could only do 4 laps, as I couldn't hold my neck up. For the next race we only had one car left anyway, and Chip had a problem with his shoulder from his accident, so we shared the car. Neither of us could do a whole race, and after that we just went back to running one car."

Don Devendorf - "Ultimately, Goodyear designed new tires for us, and went from a 27" to 28", later in 1992. They had to get a bigger tire because it was overloading the tires. At least Goodyear, when they did something it worked... the Bridgestone tires were another story." The Nissan IMSA program was essentially destroyed at Road Atlanta due to tire failure, and the team was disbanded early in 1993.

While in Trans-Am racing during the mid-1990s, Dan Binks of Roush racing was finding advantages in a series with limited tire options. A big part of their success was tire management, but not so much what the driver Kendall did. Binks - "Trans-Am cars are rough, tough, and made to run into people, but with the little tiny 13" steel brakes, you've got to take care of them, and the Goodyear bias-ply tires were junk... 100 miles was Russian Roulette, how much do you use? The game in Trans-Am was always, "who has tires left in the end?" Dan – "In the beginning we would go to the track and buy tires there. The tires would be

2 weeks old, they had just made them. They were bubble gum, and never had time to cure on the shelf. So, in 95 we started buying tires and putting them on the shelf in the beginning of the year. When we needed them, they would be hard enough."

Binks played the tire game in Trans-Am better than all others

There were teams that would put a heat cycle onto the tires, scrubbing them in, to increase the durability vs. running "stickers". Dan Binks – "Usually we didn't use hardly any heat cycles, we would just have them in the shop and mark the dates on them. Ours were probably the oldest tires on the grid. Not that many people were doing that... it would say 400-240 on the tires, but it wasn't brand new. There was no way to control what we ran if I buy them at the track. We would play it by ear; I'd know that at a certain track we should run these fronts, with these rears... I came up with a couple of combinations, and we had plenty of wheels that had the other combinations mounted already."

In comparison to warehousing aged tires to achieve options, motorcycles have been the beneficiaries of some of the most advanced tire technology, with different compounds at each side and the center, for optimum performance at any given circuit layout. A track with primarily left turns will overheat the left side of the tire due to the continual load, if the ideal softer compound for the right side is used for the left side. Also, the contact patch is miniscule in comparison to the cars, where lean is not a factor. As a result, tire choice and development is ever more critical with the bikes than the other disciplines of racing. Al Ludington – "In Miguel's (Duhamel) heyday, he would give really good feedback to Dunlop, so… we did the majority of the tire testing for Dunlop. Well, pretty soon we had a tire that suits our bike pretty damn well. Same with Mladin, as the Yoshimura guys came up with an instrumentation package that was very advantageous for Dunlop to chart tire temperatures, wheelspin, and things like that. Couple that with really good feedback from the rider, and pretty soon you have a tire that suits that GSXR pretty well. That's what Mark Donohue called the 'unfair advantage'. You become their tire tester and guess what? Pretty soon the Sunoco Camaro has tires that suit it pretty well."

Ludington continues - "Doug Polen had testing ability to the point where he would say 'You know, this feels like that 2193 that I tried 3 years ago, only with a different profile and a little bit different edge grip.' The guys would all go 'Holy S##t, the guy remembers that?'

The proven technology of tire warmers has become part of most racing series, but there are still limitations upon the effectiveness. Tom Houseworth, Crew Chief for World Superbike Champion Ben Spies – "You've got to load the tire. The tire warmer heats it from the outside on the surface and sometimes gets hot all the way to the wheel… which is great to help you get going,. But it takes load at the rear or the front, to generate heat in the carcass because with the tire warmer there is no movement, it's like using a hair dryer. And once you get to operating temperature from loading the tire and proper deflection, now your pressure comes in. Tire pressure is important, 0.05 (psi) up or down."

Nobody gets more out of a contact patch than the racers of Moto GP. Dani Pedrosa on the dragon teeth under full power - 2012

What about the tire spring rates, for which charts had been made available in AMA Superbike? Tom - "You know that's funny, I used those for years, but not in MotoGP. I guess these guys are too smart for that, and it's totally critical." Is it considered privileged information? "That is correct. The only time I ever got that was with Dunlop in the AMA. This is a spec tire, and everybody is on a need to know basis."

In the GT1 wars between Corvette and Aston Martin of 2005-6, Corvette found that regardless of what was done to the drivetrain and chassis, it all still comes down to the contact patch of the tire. In recent years, Michelin has been the tire of choice for the GT category to the point where in the ALMS allowed larger engine air restrictors for cars that struggled to maintain the pace. The unspoken truth was that the lack of pace was due to running different tires. However, no such performance breaks occur at the 24 Hours of Le Mans, so having the right tire becomes even more critical to Le Mans success, than with the American series. Pratt & Miller learned this when switching from Goodyear to Michelin.

Dan Binks – "It was unbelievable. As racers you get 1/10ths of a second, ½ of a second change maybe from a guy getting used to a race track. When we put those tires on for the first time at Road Atlanta, it was 'you've got to be kidding me.' We had just got done racing there on Goodyears, and we had in the neighborhood of 700 laps there, we were pretty comfortable with what we had. Literally on lap 4, we were nearly 3 seconds faster. It was so much faster that the gearing wasn't even close. It was like 'you can't make this stuff up.' I would not have ever believed that it could change that much. At that time they were doing Formula One stuff, and everything in Europe. Goodyear had quit doing F1, and I'm sure their engineering budgets were cut back… and it showed."

BRAKES

Braking areas are now amazingly short, as carbon disc/ carbon pad braking systems now permit ever shorter braking zones. Such was not always the case. Looking back upon the pre-WW1 era, the 4 cylinder Peugeot Grand Prix cars of 1912-14 were the most innovative racers in the sport. The Peugeots with their twin overhead camshafts, 4 valves per cylinder, dry sump lubrication and plain bearings (later changed to ball bearings) on the crankshaft, set the engine design pattern for generations to come. In 1913 Jules Goux won the Indy 500 with his GP Peugeot, while Georges Boillot had won the French Grand Prix in 1912, the most important races on either side of the Atlantic. Despite these innovations, the Peugeots had a largely convetional braking system, cable actuated rear drum brakes along with a brake on the transmission. However, the 1914 GP Peugeot had brought braking innovation to match those they had achieved with their engines. 4 wheel brakes were a feature of the new car, revolutionary in an era where all other cars had 2 wheel (rear) brakes.

The clash of titans between Mercedes and Peugeot in the 1914 French Grand Prix was the stuff of legends, and sadly served as the preface for the long and bloody First World War that erupted in less than a month. In the immediate post-war era, the next major innovation in braking systems was with the 1921 Duesenberg. The car as raced in America was typically equipped with rear drum brakes, but going up against the 4 wheel brake French Ballot racers would require the Duesenberg team to make modifications. Harry Miller had installed a 4 wheel hydraulic braking system on a race car 2 years earlier, but it was otherwise unheard of. The American Duesenberg team arrived with a hydraulic operation system for its 4 wheel drum brake system vs. the cable operation used elsewhere through the field. American Jimmy Murphy won the 1921 French Grand Prix at Le Mans with this Duesenberg, ahead of the Ballots of DePalma and Goux. Murphy had achieved what has only occurred once in all the years since (Dan Gurney, Eagle – 1967 Belgian GP). An American driver had won a Grand Prix in an American car.

Soon after, Duesenberg became the first car manufacturer to produce cars with hydraulic 4 wheel brakes. From this point until the early 1950s, braking systems were largely a refinement of the 4 wheel hydraulic drum brake. Historians often point to June 1953 as a defining moment, when Jaguar arrived at Le Mans with their proven C Type factory racers, newly equipped with Dunlop disc brakes. However, such theories overlook the fact that many cars previously running at Indianapolis Motor Speedway had already been equipped with discs. Donald Davidson – "They claim that Le Mans in '53 was the first major race with disc brakes, but this was after Vukovich had already won the 500 with disc brakes... not that he used them a whole lot." In fact, the revolutionary pre-war rear engine Miller Indy car had 4 wheel disc brakes, as did many Indianapolis cars before 1953, such as the pole winning Cummins diesel Kurtis of 1952. Some production cars had also adopted 4 wheel disc brakes, such as the 1949 Crosley Hot Shot.

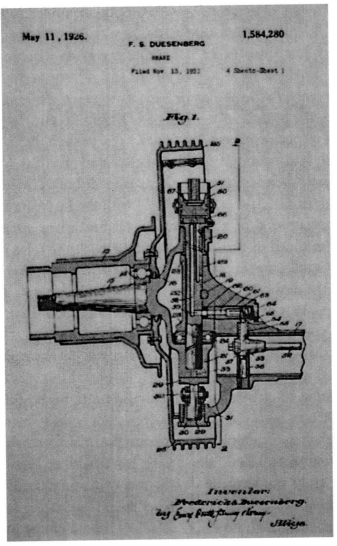

The patent for Duesenberg's internal line hydraulic front brake

Drum braked equipped cars, their drivers accustomed to having to conserve the brakes, were immediately outclassed. The quote – "I make my cars to go, not to stop", has been both attributed to Ettore Bugatti for resisting the superior hydraulic brake operation in favor of cables, and to Enzo Ferrari, for staying with drum brakes in the 1950s. Both paid a price in competitiveness as a result, while others responded in innovative ways. The most interesting response was from Mercedes-Benz.

The American driver, John Fitch, was to experience those innovations first hand, when he was brought onto the Mercedes factory team for Le Mans due to his stunning 5th place overall finish in the Mille Miglia driving a GT class 300SL. In a similarly legendary performance, Moss with the proven 1955 Mercedes 300SLR had won the Mille Miglia, and for Le Mans they introduced their latest innovation... the air brake. Mercedes had dabbled with such concepts in 1952 with the Le Mans 300SL, but this latest version of the Mercedes air brake was approximately 24" x the width of the body behind the cockpit. John Fitch – "It was hydraulic, operated by a lever about 6" long that extended out of the dash. When you wanted the brake up, you moved the lever up. You could move it up however far you want. In other words, you wouldn't have to have it all the way up... you could drop it down with the same lever. After you get through the turn, drop it down to the middle."

Sadly, in Fitch's debut race with the team, his co-driver in the 300SLR was involved in a massive crash across from the pits, as debris was scattered throughout the main grandstand. 83 spectators were killed, along with his co-driver Pierre Levegh. It was truly the darkest day in racing history, leading to the withdrawal of the Mercedes factory team from racing for the next 30 years. Although their air brake had been a clever response to the superiority of the disc brake, it was only a few years before the solid disc brake had become standard fare for all forms of racing. Mercedes was clearly on the path to discovering something else, the aerodynamic benefit from the increased downforce when the airbrake was partially deployed in the corners. However, it would be another decade before the benefits of moveable wings or spoilers became fully implemented by the wizards at Chaparral.

In this era, the benefits of the disc brake revolution weren't yet felt within endurance racing GT categories, as the cars could only run the type of brakes available on the production models. The trials and tribulations faced by the drum brake shod Corvette team headed by Fitch in the late 1950s, was enough to fill a book in itself. The brakes were so poor that drivers had to apply the brakes far before they could see the upcoming corners, in Dick Thompson's case, by developing a system of counting at the beginning of each straight, so he would know when to brake.

One of the 1960 Cunningham team of Corvettes for Le Mans

Dick Guldstrand is known as "Mr. Corvette" for his lifetime of involvement with the car. Dick – "The earlier drum brakes were absolutely awful. When you hit the brakes, you didn't know where it was going… it would go left one time, and change lanes.

You couldn't warm them up. There was just nothing you could do, and they never fixed them. In fact, that was so bad that Duntov walked away from the Corvette and Fitch took it over in 1956. He finally got them to work a little bit, and they started winning races. Of course, Duntov came back into the program and then improved things considerably."

The 1960 Le Mans Corvettes were entered by Cunningham, and had Alfin alloy drum brakes. With those cars, Corvette was to win the GT class in the 24 Hours of Le Mans. Dick – "It was an improvement, they could drive them and they were a very competitive car. Then the original Grand Sport had solid discs."

It was somewhat better for Bondurant and Guldstrand in the 1967 24 Hours of Le Mans, driving the Dana Chevrolet 427 Stingray. However, even with the 4 wheel discs of their time, they would have to lift and wait until after 2 or 3 seconds of deceleration from engine braking before applying the brakes. It was the only way they had a prayer for the brakes to last through a stint.

1967 Dana Chevrolet 427 Stingray - Bondurant & Guldstrand

Dick Guldstrand - "It was the first time that the brakes had ventilation on them, ventilated discs. We had some special pads from Andy Porterfield, a very good metallic material. They were the best working brakes that we ever had on a Corvette. They kept that braking system on the car from 1965 or 66, straight through to 1982. It had exactly the same brakes for all those years. It was conserving them... that was what we learned, that's what Duntov kept telling me. We made those brakes last over 12 hours in that race."

Meanwhile in America's USAC Champ Cars, variations onto standard disc brake systems were being adapted to the Indy Roadsters in their final years as well. Joe Leonard recalls the braking effectiveness during the Indy Roadster era – "At the last race of the 1964 season at Phoenix, Foyt was on the pole and I was in the 5th row. Foyt told me... I want you to go hard about 2 or 3 laps, then I want you to cruise." I asked him "What do you mean?" Foyt said, "Lookit, listen to me... go hard for a couple or 3 laps, then go easy for a lap or two." Most of the field was rear engine cars, and there were only about 5 of us roadsters out there. On about the 4th lap the brakes were nice and cool, and I thought... "Hey, this isn't bad." Next lap coming down into turn one, I was up in the marbles and flinched because I thought for sure I was in the wall. Then I knew what Foyt was talking about."

AJ Foyt – "They just didn't last very long. We'd put double brakes on all our stuff, but you still had to be real careful. We'd have one disc at each wheel, but we'd have 2 sets of calipers on each." The discs weren't so much the problem as the pad construction/area and fluid? AJ – "Yeah, it was the pads."

At what point in the USAC Champ car era did the effectiveness of the brakes become a non-issue? AJ – "I'd say 1965 or 66." So, was the problem of brakes more a result of the increased mass of the car during the Indy Roadster era? AJ – "It was that, and we had problems with the brakes back then. The calipers weren't that good, and the pads weren't either. On the Coyotes, we always did the single calipers." Soon, solid discs gave way to vented discs, and for most applications the era of Indycar brake management were over.

One of the most prominent exceptions was with the Turbine cars of 1967-68. The inboard brakes of the Lotus 56 were insufficient given the lack of engine braking, and the end result was inferior to even what the racers had during the roadster era.

Typical double caliper, single disc setup on an early 60's Indycar

With the development of the ventilated iron disc brake and multi-piston calipers, the solution was set for the next 11 years, until Gordon Murray's ever-innovative Brabham designs began to implement technology brought in from the Concorde supersonic jet, which first flew in 1971. Undoubtedly the technology found its way to military test aircraft well in advance of that civilian application, however Concorde's carbon brakes and pads led to a F1 revolution and they remain the highest state of the braking art available today. However, Murray with his Carbon/Carbon braked BT-48 Brabham of 1979 wasn't the first to attempt a racing application. Paul Butler, former F2 and motorcycle GP competition manager for Dunlop, later to become the Race Director for MotoGP – "Harry Hunt was the Dunlop motorcycle tire importer for the west coast, and he was working on carbon-carbon brakes in 1973/74 with Hercules, the people that McLaren subsequently worked with for their carbon tubs. I've talked with various people who thought they were there for the pioneering days of carbon brakes. I asked Gordon Murray if he'd known that Hunt was working on carbon-carbon brakes for motorcycles so many years earlier, and his reaction was 'No, good Lord…' Harry had spent a fortune on it, but backed out in the end because it was getting too expensive."

Cockpit adjustable brake bias is currently allowed in Endurance racing. Binks – "I would say that the drivers might adjust it a ½ turn or one turn in their stint. The guy who has to adjust it the most is when it gets into the night time, as when the sun goes down you have to adjust it a fair amount. The biggest adjustment we make now is obviously for the rain, but the kind of adjustment we might have in the dry stuff is one or two turns. The driver tells us if he's moving the brake bias, so when the next guy gets in we can tell him that it's moved 2 turns to the back or whatever. In endurance racing, since the cars have no cockpit adjustable sway bars or wings, so the options are to adjust the car during a pit stop, or find a way to adjust the balance of the car during a race. As for adjustments during pit stops, Binks adds – "The rear sway bar extreme adjustment range is 2-1/2 turns, something like that." However re: cockpit adjustments, the answers vary depending upon if you are talking with the GT category drivers or those in the high downforce prototypes.

For the GT class, one option for handling adjustment is to use brake bias to help the rear of the car rotate. It seems like it would literally be a moving target depending upon the speed of the upcoming corner. To get the brake bias right, one has to understand that as the car slows it loses downforce from the rear diffuser, and hence cannot take as much rear brake bias as the speed decreases. Jan Magnussen – "We play around with that a lot; we use it to change how the car drives. If you have a lot of understeer turning in, you can wind the brake bias to the rear, to get the rear to turn in on the brakes. You go to the front if you are oversteering, so you can play with it to get it to change how the car drives."

'09 Corvette GT2 front brake for the debut race at Mid-Ohio

It is an entirely different world with different techniques in the prototypes. Allan McNish – "The only things we've got is brake balance and traction control. We play with brake balance but never to lock the tail. We've got far too much downforce to be locking up the rear, we can't do that. If we do that, we're off the circuit. But we do tune the brake balance to work with the car as you go through the stint, and the same with traction control. It depends upon the tire and the track as well." Bourdais concurs – "Not with the prototypes, these cars don't like it. As soon as you introduce some slip, you lose the aero. Yes, we adjust the brake bias to compensate for tire wear to what the car is requesting, but not in terms of chassis balance. The only tool you have to save your life when the rear goes away is traction control... and that's all."

What about if you begin to pick up a bit of push, or if things get loose? Simon Pagenaud – "If you look at the Peugeot when it sits in the pits, it's a big wing, like a plane. Or if you look at the front you'd say it's got a massive front wing like you'd see on an Indycar. The influence of it (the underbody wing) is so important, as mechanically the car is not as good as you think it is. An Indycar would have more mechanical grip, but the Peugeot gets a lot more grip from the aero. You try and try different ways to get your splitter as low as possible in the corners, and then you control your ride height with your braking. So for example, if the car is oversteering or very loose on corner entry, you lift off the throttle slowly and you go onto the brakes slowly and then harder, to avoid the rear being light on entry. Those cars are very sensitive to what you are doing with the brake and throttle... very sensitive."

Conversely, to adapt to understeer on corner entry, the driver initially goes onto the brakes harder, which gets the front of the car lower to create more downforce on the nose, and also the tail gets light. Simon – "It's all about finding where you need the most

235

brake pressure in the corner. You can break up the segments of the corner based upon where you need the aero grip. Sometimes it can be a bit more difficult and it's not easy if the car is loose on entry and then gets push in the middle, like it was today."

Looking up the air exit, the extent of the underbody wing is clear

Johnny Mowlem explains their baseline setup at Dyson Racing and how they use brake adjustment techniques to change the dynamics of the car setup – "For a low grip circuit we run maximum downforce on the wings and various panels on the car. You can do the same thing, if you have an understeering car you might look at changing more weight to the front, or maybe trail braking a little just to keep the weight transfer to the front tire. We would use brake bias adjustment during a stint with the fuel load lightening, and you do actually favor the brake bias quite a bit as the fuel load lightens. The way the weight distribution of this car is, it's pretty neutral. I think the Audis have been incredibly clever at making their car reasonably neutral, especially as they developed the V-10 on thru to the R18 now. There is some pitch sensitivity with any car, and maybe you can get out of it with stiffer springs, or get a lot less pitch with anti-dive, the things you can do with the suspension. The Lola is roll sensitive, and it is different with some changes in the rear suspension geometry."

There is obviously interplay between braking and downforce, as the harder the tires are pressed into the pavement, the greater the force needed to lock them up. At the rear of the GT1 Pratt & Miller Corvette is a massive multi-straked diffuser, and its effect upon the car under braking is hard to over-estimate. The faster the car went, the greater the grip under braking. Dan Binks - "I think you could lock them up, but that big diffuser helped hold the back of the car down. Let's say you stand on the brakes at 150mph, the driver can push as hard as he wanted on the pedal. At big speed with that big wing and big diffuser, the driver could just mash on the brakes. But when he got down into the 70-100mph range, then he had to be careful to modulate the pedal. There are no power brakes on the car, just power steering. It would be awesome if you could take off rear brake bias as the speed reduced legally, but I believe the rules say the brake bias has to be driver controlled. Before you know it, we'll have anti-lock brakes, and that is where it's going."

There were many drivers in the Pratt & Miller GT1 cars, including NASCAR drivers Dale Earnhardt and Dale Jr. Dan Binks – "Dale Jr., he didn't know enough about the car. He would look at the data and see where he was off, and try to go a little bit better here or there. The biggest thing for those guys running NASCAR cars, when they come to drive our cars, is the brakes. Our cars stop SO MUCH better. Big diffuser, big carbon brakes... when Boris Said came over he just couldn't believe how it stops. They will stop faster than you can imagine, even compared to the Trans-Am cars that Boris was driving at the time."

There was a time when the team incorporated electric fans into the brake cooling system, to keep the temps from soaring during pit stops, but no longer. Dan - "When you came into the pit lane, they'd all turn on and blow air on the calipers. The hardest part for a caliper is when you stop, when you are running on the track there is air moving by them and they stay cool. Now, with the brakes that we currently run, with the brake fluid that we currently run, it's just unbelievable. We've got the brakes where they are organized enough so they don't overheat, so we don't need the fans anymore. It's taken a long time, but it's working out. In the old days, we'd have to bleed the brakes 10 times a weekend. Now, we only bleed them for race prep. The fluid is amazing, I think the advertised stuff is in the 650 degree range, but that is being conservative. I would have lost a years' pay because this guy came up to us a couple of years ago saying 'try my brake fluid'. Over and over... I kept telling him that we were good. So, finally he gave me 6 bottles, I put it in, and it was one of those 'ah-hah' moments. The brake pedal was stiffer, and it's not like it had bigger master cylinders or something. It was stiff like that, no matter what the brake temperature was like. Endless RS650, this is the deal, and it doesn't matter what kind of car it is, it works. In the old days high-performance fluid was crazy hard on the seals, and it's not like that now." Technology marches on, and those bottles of 550 we all have on the garage shelf are now the setup of the past.

What is the protocol for brake changes at Le Mans with a 2012 GT2 car? Binks - "At Le Mans we usually have to change the front brakes only. We can change both front rotors and front calipers in between 50 and 70 seconds. All new stuff, basically." The cars have 4 rotors and 8 pads. "The rules are that you can only have 2 pads per corner. There for a while we had like 8 pads per corner, and there were pads getting loose... this is way safer and they eliminated all that. The GT2 brakes are getting closer to the carbon and compared to 2009 we are a lot better on the brakes. The pad compounds that we are using now (2012) are awesome. They brake good and are not susceptible to lock up. You can get pads that will stop the tire, but the drivers can't modulate it. Now we have great modulation and great performance. But when we went from carbon/carbon to the GT2 brakes it was a big deal for the drivers. It's not as good as the carbon as those bite so hard when it's hot that it's unbelievable. With iron stuff, it's almost backwards, the bite is as good as it gets and then goes away as you go through the zone where it gets hotter and hotter. It loses efficiency, where the carbon is just awesome. You just need to mash it, and be done. On and off, that's how those things love to be used. If you drag 'em or trail brake, then the brake wear goes out of sight. But if you drive every lap and use them like it's qualifying, the brake wear is way less."

Michael Messina, sportscar program manager for Brembo, explains the issues with how an easier drive application causes increased carbon brake system wear. "What causes that increased wear is the amount of time the brakes are used, not so much how they are used." Trail braking obviously increases the amount of time the brakes are in use, so hence using that technique with carbon brakes results in increased wear.

Meanwhile, over at Flying Lizard Porsche, Team Manager Eric Ingraham comments on braking strategies and the differing specifications of braking systems used at the variety of tracks that make up professional endurance racing – "For the sprint races we run the standard configuration... Brembo calipers front and rear, but for the longer races you start changing what you do depending if you have pad changes or not, thicker pads or not, rotors..." As always the optimal configuration for the car depends upon the task at hand, one size does not fit all.

One might assume that Le Mans with its hard braking at the end of multiple straights would be the ultimate test of brake systems. It isn't. Michael Messina – "The 24 hours of Daytona is harder on the brakes. At Le Mans there are long straights for the brakes to cool down, after each hard application. At Daytona, the brakes are still hot when being used hard to slow the car and that is hardest on them."

Typically the cars require a pad change at each corner to complete a 24 hour race. The teams are often reluctant, saying they would prefer to use a pad compound that would last the distance. Michael Messina – "We could do that, but over 24 hours, the reduced braking efficiency would result in about 7 or 8 additional minutes lost. How long does it take to do a pad change? A minute? So by using pads that can run the entire race, you then lose 6 or more minutes of track distance covered in that 24 hours." The only advantage would be that there would be one less task to be fumbled in the middle of a night or early morning pit stop. Messina also sees less of a revolutionary improvement in the GT class braking systems since 09 than Binks, attributing much of the improvement to tires and aerodynamics. Whichever aspect of the package gained the most percentage-wise, the end result is a considerable improvement in braking power.

One of the long-time traditions of qualifying at Indianapolis was to pull the pads/pistons back in the calipers to insure absolutely no brake friction for qualifying. Mauro Piccoli (Racing Market Director) of Brembo explains recent developments. "This is something that we do not want ever, not just with Indycar. We know that we must not have any drag in the system, and every time that the driver goes for the brake, it will always be the same pressure curve." Rubens Barrichello – "Obviously you don't want is to have any touch of the brake pedal at all when you are running, but you need to have the pedal there." It is one of the key challenges for any brake manufacturer, to achieve a zero drag system while being unused, yet also to have that same system 100% ready and firm upon the initial pressure application.

Brembo made reference to the Indycar brake calipers being the same spec front and rear, which they would not do with other cars. What are the front/rear ratio numbers on a 2012 Indycar vs. a sportscar? Mauro - "The brake balance on an Indycar is around 54-55% in front. The only difference between the front and rear is going to be the hats. The pads and calipers are all the same. Formula One, today you have a brake balance that goes more like 58% to the front. Now you have a very wide front wing and a very small rear wing on a Formula One. And in Formula One, everything is stretched to the maximum, so the front caliper is different from the rear, the installation of the 2 is different and the life of the part is less. In Indycar we were trying more to minimize the consumption of the parts."

What is the 'sweet spot' in temperature for the current carbon brake systems. Mauro Piccoli - "I would say (for Indycar) around 400 degrees C, with a 50 degree variation. And Formula One is more or less the same. A Le Mans car runs at a lower temperature, it has to last 24 hours quite unlike Formula One does. The problem is the middle of the race, as you can always have problems with the ducting, or some debris going into the brake ducts. You don't have everything under control. Carbon works very well from 300 degrees up to say 500." So, for the 24 Hours, would you suggest starting out with something like 350 degrees C as a baseline setup, leaving room for unforeseen issues? "Yeah, we always suggest it, preferably at the bottom of the range so you still have room to avoid any overheating problems."

Mauro continues - "Now you have telemetry on the braking. What is the maximum travel, what is the maximum temperature, maximum pressure... you have total feedback while the car is driving. You download the data and that tells you what the car is doing." The old school method is still useful, and it isn't always just digital pyrometers and sensors in use today. "We still use thermal paint, and it gives you a quick indication of the temperature that it is running. If you lose the data, at least you have an idea of what temperature range the disc was in."

High speed ovals like Indianapolis can present a real problem as there is likely to be no temperature in the brakes when it is time for a pit stop. Rubens Barrichello – "What Tony (Kannan) has done in the past, is just before you go into Turn 3, you are actually laying on the brake pedal a little bit. The temperature goes up quite rapidly; you just need that minimum temperature. You also have the consideration that the car is pulling to one side (an oval setup), and when you come into the pits you have to be careful with that because the car wants to go off to the side."

The driver can change around the master cylinder sizes so that they can have different sizes to get a different pedal feel. Mauro - "They run from 16mm all the way up to 22mm. In the beginning of the season, everybody tested every size to see how the pedal feels. It seems that most of the field is between 19 and 22, the most common combination is 19 front and 20 rear. Kanaan is 22 front, 22 rear, as he likes a pedal that is rock hard." Rubens – "I could see some of the guys at Sebring (pre-season testing) complaining about locking, and the behavior of the brakes. But, the carbon brakes are so good, that they work. It's up to you to modulate the pedal, and work on master cylinders. I kept telling them how good my brake pedal was the whole month that I tested. They were telling me that it was the same kind of system as Formula One, but in F1 they try to make it so light. At Indy you are carrying 200 kilos more, and it is safety all the way. Just for example, I run a softer master cylinder than Tony, just because he likes a stiffer pedal. He likes the feeling of being an animal, and you can see his size (laughs)… he's an animal anyway. He goes deep into that pedal, and I like a little bit more to modulate."

Out of the entire field at Indianapolis, if you were to paint someone Green for an Avengers movie, it would be Tony Kanaan. Does Tony's superior physical conditioning play a role in his use of the largest master cylinders available? Tony – "I'm a stronger guy (laughs). No, I'm not trying to prove a point. I compare it to, if you are going to run and go to buy a shoe, you might like a stiff sole, and I might like a softer sole." Is there any performance advantage to be had? "It is just a matter of preference, it's not a performance item, it's just the way I like it. It's probably a reflection of my personality. I jump on the brake pedal really hard and I like to have it without a lot of movement." Are there any compromises in your ability to modulate the pedal? Kanaan – "No, not at all. I don't think it makes me better or worse, it's just the characteristic that I like."

2013 Indianapolis 500 winner Tony Kannan has a unique brake setup

Of course, any system can be compromised by a poor installation within the chassis, as was the case with multiple issues on the Lola Nissan at Le Mans. Don Devendorf – "One year we were running the Nissan engine Lola at Le Mans and were a lap ahead of the Jaguars with a whole extra stop worth of fuel. At around near 13 or 14 hours, we developed a fuel leak. The carbon fibre chassis had carbon fibre spurs that wore through and cut the cell bladder. Unrepairable… you'd have to take the car apart to change it."

Don continues - "That was the car where when you stepped on the brake and as the linkage travelled, the leverage ratio got worse instead of getting better or staying the same. We discovered that problem in testing before Le Mans, so at our shop in England we cut the whole front floor of the tub out, put in a flat panel replacing this aerodynamic whoopee thing, and put in a whole new brake linkage system. So although our car had cast iron brakes, and the factory Nissans had carbon brakes, our brakes worked… everything was working. So, in the race we were just killing them, leading the race." As always, racing is all about the package, being sure that maximizing any one component or assembly is not at the expense of something else.

CHAPTER SIX

SUSPENSION

The 1976 Tyrrell Project 34 six wheeled Formula One

In suspension development, the spring rates had skyrocketed during the late 70s and early 1980s in Formula One. Alan Jones, one of the tougher characters in the game, had commented during his years in the FW07 from 1979-81 that he was concerned over the potential for spinal injury from the cars being sprung so hard, the cars hardened and slammed toward the track surface to keep the aero downforce at an optimum relationship with the track. In that era of F1, the cars essentially had most of their spring rate coming from the tires and suspension flex than from the springs, as the lowered cars pounded their way around, as aerodynamics trumped all other concerns.

Dan Binks recalls the spring rates in the early ground effect tunnel car era. "We had 3 or 4 sets of springs, with the ground effects cars. The Frisbee Can-Am car, it would lay over big time so the front was fairly stiff, I would say 1100# or 1200# (lbs. needed to compress one inch), but the car didn't weigh very much. The rear springs were maybe half of that so it wouldn't lean over so far, maybe 700#. The front of the IMSA Lola T-600 was in the 1000# range... we thought 1000# springs were ridiculous on a car like that. SCCA Sports Racers (CSR, DSR) had 125# or 150#, they didn't run any spring rate compared to what they do now." With the advent of high spring rates, the popular rocker arm suspension had become essentially an un-damped leaf spring. As a result, it wasn't long before solutions had appeared to address this problem, the use of pull rod and push rod suspensions.

As was so often the case in that era, Gordon Murray had again led the charge with his pull rod Brabham front suspension of the mid-1970s. With sports car or "hammerhead" noses, the F1 designers of that era were less concerned about the aerodynamics of a cluttered front suspension, and Murray's designs featured exposed semi-outboard shocks, all the way through to his BT46 of 1978. With the advent of narrow noses with either large dive planes or continuous front wings hung below, some teams lagged behind in improving the package. Although it was a Grand Prix winner in the hands of Mario Andretti, the pre-ground effects Lotus 77 viewed from the front, was an aesthetic horror show.

Mario Andretti won the 1976 Japanese GP in the agricultural appearing Lotus 77

With their Lotus 78 ground effects car of 1977, the front aerodynamics had been extensively improved over the Lotus 77, although the Lotus maintained rocker arm front suspension, despite the obvious inherent compromise given the high spring rates. The 1979 Brabham-Alfa BT48 being a ground effects design, the airflow entrance to the tunnels were an obvious concern and the suspension units were moved out of the airflow with lengthened pull rods. Their similar BT49 Cosworth powered version was to win the World Championship in 1981.

Somewhat surprisingly, Williams had persevered with rocker arm front suspension with their FW07B, the 1980 Championship winning design. Perhaps it was the belief that less tunnel airflow obstruction was worth dealing with the rocker flex, perhaps not...

but for whatever reason Williams changed to pull rod front suspension for 1982 with their new FW08, having narrowly lost the '81 drivers championship to Piquet in the Brabham.

Almost unbelievably refined in comparison to the Lotus 77, the Lotus 79 was the dominant car of the 1978 Grand Prix season

Mario Andretti raced the FW08 at Long Beach Grand Prix in 1982. Mario – "I tested at Willow Springs, which is high speed, to get familiar with the car. It was awesome and the car was really good, but for some reason or another when we got to Long Beach, they kept that setup on there. I told them that we can't run a setup that stiff around Long Beach."

Mario continues – "Keke Rosberg was my teammate, and he had a really soft setup on the car, and I told them 'That's the way to go'. I had a hell of a time. I had Frank Dernie as my engineer, and I just couldn't understand... he kept saying this was how they'd been running it. I was like on a pogo stick with the car." Willow, being one of the highest speed road racing circuits in the USA, demanded spring rates commensurate with the available downforce. A bumpy street circuit of reduced speed requires an entirely different, more compliant approach.

Keke Rosberg's pullrod FW08 won the driver's title in '82

Regardless to having blown the setup on Mario's car, the pull rod suspension concept was sound, with the slender rod in tension while under suspension compression, although more prone to flex on rebound when in compression. One downside of early pull-rod suspension was the aerodynamic effect that placed the spring/shock units in the tub on either side of the footbox, making for a wider overall monocoque. A secondary concern is that it was more difficult to work on and spring changes and/or shock adjustments can take up additional valuable time in a session, vs. the pushrod system that can place the linkage and shocks at the top of the tub, instead of alongside the footbox. That said, the pull rod suspension was an improvement in comparison to previous rocker designs, and the Williams FW08 was the chassis that Keke Rosberg drove to the 1982 World Championship.

Murray responded with his slender 1983 BT-52 Brabham-BMW that Piquet took to the next years' World Championship. The car now employed pushrod suspension front and rear actuating inboard vertical spring/shock units. In time, the concept of placing these spring/shock units on top of a narrow chassis with pushrod actuation proved to be the superior approach when air management under the chassis became the most critical aspect of aero development, and it remains the most common design in use today. As always, there are prominent and highly successful exceptions such as the rear pull rod suspension used on the Red Bull RB5/6/7 chassis of Adrian Newey. Craig Hampson, long time Newman-Haas engineer – "Yeah, but it is because everything is aero there." No question that the primary reason for the recently revived use of pullrod suspension was that aerodynamics trump mechanical advantages (and everything else) in the modern F1 car.

Sebastian Bourdais - "Previously when I was racing at Indy, our car was a G-Force and the car seemed a lot more straightforward. It seemed to react much more like a Champ Car. The Dallara wasn't a car I could identify with, so strange... the recipe to try and make that thing go fast was to forget what you've seen and learned in Champ Car because anything you've seen there is complete nonsense on this car. With the Champ Car I would go with a very stiff front end to get some stability. If you do that with this Indycar, forget it. The thing will not be responding at all... washes out in the corners, you can't brake. The springs I had to run were like nothing I had ever seen before. If my engineer Craig (Hampson) knew what kind of springs we ran front to rear on the Indycar, he'd be like 'WHAT???' Every time we'd go on the shaker at Newman-Haas, they say 'you've got to soften up the front, its better on the rig'. We'd try it on the track and I could never drive it. Now, I come to Indycar and we go from 2500# front to 1400# front. It was ridiculous; I would have never believed you could drive a car that soft."

Bourdais's front pullrod Dallara Indycar – 2011 Baltimore GP

"With the 2500# springs it seemed over-powered by the stiffness, it was just bending everything and the car would act really funny, we were losing grip at the front and it was making the rear of the car loose on turn-in… it was the weirdest thing. I think the whole thing would kind of bend and then take a set. I don't know if it was the chassis, or the whole assembly with the pull rods, A-arms, and rockers. With the Champ Car you could go stiff at the front and not have to worry about what the back was doing. That is what we had to learn from the car. The car never went on the shaker, so we didn't have info… we didn't really know where we were, or where we had to go. You have so many combinations, but if you don't go on the rig to get some kind of idea…"

Of course, one cannot directly compare spring rates between different chassis, as the rocker ratios can vary substantially across manufacturers. That said, the issue that Bourdais struggled with was likely due to the pullrod front suspension used on the previous Dallara (thru 2011) chassis. Craig Hampson – "It's true that you would run softer front springs because the front installation on the old Dallara is a pullrod, which is softer. With pullrods, you can't get it as stiff because you are putting forces through the upper wishbone that you wouldn't normally have on a pushrod car, and that was common across the entire field. I wouldn't call it a problem; it was just different and required different characteristics."

The JPS Lotus Renault was a successful pullrod car

Hampson continues – "Every car has its own personality and it's going to have some quirks… some that are good and some things that aren't so good. Certainly taking last years' setup and bolting it onto this new (2012 front pushrod) car, isn't going to work. It's a whole different package. Inherently a pushrod is a stiffer installation, and you can run stiffer springs."

Gordon Kimball – "That's the problem with pullrods, and not only that, but the more suspension travel you have, the more it works against you. The geometry gets worse and worse. But the brilliant thing is that the link is in tension, so you can make it small all around. Which is great until you find yourself in rebound, although most of the time the pullrod never goes into compression unless you are running hellacious rebound in your dampers. Except for when the wheel is in the air, it always has load on it and it always is pulling on the pullrod against the spring. There are pluses and minuses for both solutions; it just depends upon which you value more. With Newey's cars (Red Bull rear pull rod suspension since 2007), I don't know if it is aerodynamic, or just lowering the center of gravity, which is what most are doing it for… to get mass down low. With a pullrod, you can put them (dampers/springs) right at the bottom."

Meanwhile at the front suspension, everything has universally gone push rod, as the current thinking is to get everything as high as possible in order to pack the maximum amount of air into the underbody of the car. Gordon Kimball – "And that's where the money is, or at least it seems to be. And that is why everybody is running pushrods, except for that silly thing that Ferrari has done."

Front pullrod suspension made a comeback in Formula One with the 2012 Ferrari. With the high and shallow tub configuration of the current breed of F1 chassis, the small angle (from horizontal) for front pullrod operation could well prove a difficult challenge for Ferrari to overcome. Craig Hampson also shares his concern over the effectiveness of a nearly horizontal front pullrod installation from a geometry perspective by saying "I don't know much about the Ferrari, but it sounds like that wouldn't be very good."

It certainly seems that the geometry is working against them. Gordon Kimball – "The loads are huge and then you've got a lot of parasitic deflection. They did it to lower the center of gravity, and they went for radical. The flipside is that everything has got to be incredibly stiff because the loads are so high. I don't think it's all that clever. The more deflection you get, the more the pull rod and the top wishbone come together, and your mechanical advantage goes away, whereas the pushrod, it works better and better. But, it is all trade-offs, packaging, center of gravity, and geometry."

Despite showing mediocre speed in testing, Ferrari was to win the 2nd GP of the 2012 season at Sepang, primarily due to a brilliant driving performance by Fernando Alonso. It would not be surprising if the changing semi-damp conditions helped, as their front pullrod suspension design may be less effective in dry conditions while running stiffer springs. Of course, just to confuse all attempts at analysis, when the series got to Spain, the Ferrari of Alonso was now on the pace in the dry. The lesson is that although there are mechanical advantages of pushrod over pullrod front suspension in an era of high nose F1 cars, other factors may tip the scale in favor of one solution over another. By the midpoint of the 2013 season, the front pullrod Ferrari had remained a factor at most races, possibly because most Grand Prix tracks are billiard table smooth. That was not always the case.

At the final Long Beach Grand Prix for F1 cars (1983) they had revised the course layout to eliminate the Ocean Boulevard section, and the Linden Leap. Where the bottom of Linden met the new course, there was a series of bumps at the intersection, and the F1 cars approached this area at approx. 140mph under full power, and there was never a more vivid example of how the various suspension solutions were succeeding. If Mario had felt the stiffly sprung FW08 was a handful around Long Beach in the previous course configuration, he would have found the issues had multiplied for 1983.

In the Friday morning practice session, you could see the cars jumping and banging around from the end of the back straight, and upon closer inspection showed in graphic terms the variety of suspension solutions and their effectiveness. The Toleman chassis fared worst, as unable to cope they immediately retired to the pits with deranged suspension. The robust Tyrrell was in its element, and Ken was telling all who would listen that it's a street course, so you build a car that can cope and get on with it. Meanwhile the hydro-pneumatic Ligier chassis simply floated over the bumps, clearly the most successful design in reacting to the bumpy street circuit. However, nothing could prepare one for the arrival of Rene Arnoux's Ferrari. Slamming into the bump at full cry, the front would bounce up, and then the rear wheels would impact the bump with all the weight having transferred back just prior to the impact. The resultant impact kicked the rear tires at least 18" off the ground amidst the sound of the front wings slammed into and dragging along the pavement. Arnoux never lifted, so the revs would soar until the rear wheels dropped back down, and the shock load to the driveshafts must have been enormous. Track conditions on a bumpy street course can shift the design priority to survival.

1983 also coincided with Dan Binks arriving at Conte racing. Those early days at Phil Conte's shop taught Dan the benefits of keeping accurate records, despite being an era of less than precise setup repeatability. Dan – "When I first went there to Phil's (Conte's), they didn't have scales, nothing." Phil Binks – "When Danny went with Conte, there were 2 things that I gave him. A Dunlop camber/caster gauge, and a weight checker with the dial indicator to check the corner weights. They didn't have scales at Conte racing, and told him what I knew about using it (the corner weight scale). The corner weights were way, way off. Bailey asked him where he got that? Dan said 'my Dad gave it to me.' Not everybody had those things then."

Dan – "We had 2 blocks; we'd put the front tires on those and the rears on the scales, and then switch it around. It was really a shot in the dark, but we started to get some repeatability. We started to pay attention to that stuff, writing everything down; even if it didn't work we wrote it down and tried to pay attention to it."

Corner weights were always part of the setup at Penske

Racing, even back in the 1970's. Rick Mears – "We didn't do a lot with corner weights on the road courses, where we'd just square it up, but on ovals… yeah, we were always playing cross weights and corner weights on ovals. And all that's been different over the years depending upon car design and tire design. Some cars like left front corner weight, other cars liked right front corner weight, there were different engineered settings that could make either one of those work."

Dan Binks - "We'd talk to Fred (Fred Puhn, the author of the excellent book, 'Make Your Car Handle') about it, in those days you used a steel bar with fishing line for checking the toe, wiggling it back & forth so that it was the same on both sides… plus or minus 30 thou, probably. Now you do 10 or 12 thousandths as an adjustment. The stuff you used in those days for a road racing team was pretty primitive, it was so random. That's why they wouldn't go that fast. The shock absorbers were horrible, we just bought them from Koni and I think they had 3 or 4 adjustments, you had to take the shock off and push it all the way in, and that was the adjustment. That didn't happen very often, we couldn't tell what it was or should be anyway. It was 'put it in the middle and hold on.'

Where were the roll centers on the suspension of these early ground effect prototypes? Dan – "You know what… I didn't even pay attention to that stuff. They had designers at Lola who said where they found it to be. We didn't mess around with roll centers, we just moved the ride heights up or down at the end that was having trouble."

The Can-Am Frisbee demanded a slightly different approach. "Morton had his own Frisbee, and had also been running Phil's Frisbee before I got there, so they had a pretty good ballpark setup. Morton was a pretty consistent development driver, but we didn't know enough. He was one of those guys who was interested in what we were doing. But, we weren't doing things like putting baseline tires back on, 'A – B – A' stuff. It was more

"I think that's better, leave it that way", and we'd go to the next thing. I think a lot of times we got farther away from where we needed to be, but everybody was in the same boat. We were all working with about a 75% setup, rarely did anybody hit upon a really good one."

After leaving Conte Racing mid 1985, Dan moved to the Malibu Grand Prix team with their GTU Mazda RX-7 and IMSA lights Alba-Mazda. Dan – "The RX-7 was horrible; it had a 3 link suspension that had 2 roller rear links, and one upper link. When I first got there, it had roll oversteer. It would toe out, and roll. You have a McPherson strut car, so it already won't turn. It's got a ton of caster, no power steering, so you are trying to make the thing turn and then as soon as you load up the rear suspension, it turns for you. It was just a nightmare trying to make the thing work. Jack Baldwin would drive around it, he would grab the steering wheel as hard as he could and just manhandle the thing and made it work for him, so it was hard to work with him on development stuff. Jeff Kline was more technical asking "Why is it doing this, and why do I have to drive around it?" Ira (Young) just didn't go fast enough for it to make a difference, but he was the Money Man. I just didn't know enough about it, how to attack it. What do I have to do to make the car not toe out in bump? So, we started moving stuff around, lowering the front as much as we could on the control arms. It had big problems, you couldn't lower it anymore because it would be in the seat rails, and it was a flexy flier, a unibody RX-7. Those cars just weren't all that good but in those days I don't think the drivers knew that the car could get that much better."

Dan had the support of the team to try some changes. Binks –"Clayton (Cunningham) was pretty open to things, saying don't cut the old suspension mounts out, so we could go back to the previous setup, but if I could make one of these go around a race track that would be great. At that time, maybe 50% of the things we tried were better." This was an era 25 years ago where data acquisition was essentially non-existent. Dan – "The MSD box for the engine was our electronics."

'86 GTU Mazda RX-7 of Tommy Kendall at Cleveland
– Photo courtesy of Mark Windecker

It is best to keep in mind that this was a time when suspension development wasn't particularly refined. Dan – "We would put a tie wrap around a shock absorber to see how much travel it gets, it was before the science projects." Binks was later to help work on Bruce Short's Mazda RX-3 in Bruce's attempt to win the 85 GT-3 Championship at the Runoffs. That search for help was likely a result of Bruce's modifications to the rear suspension of his car the previous year. As a competitor racing against Short in 1984, I wandered over to look at his "new" rear suspension and noted along with David Vegher's mechanic James McNiff, that the revised design had raised his roll center to a point above the rear differential. My comment was "That isn't going to work." The response… "Yeah, I know. Don't tell him (smiles)."

Dan – "The Mazda RX-7 had a panhard rod, and with some

adjustments, it got the roll center to down within about eight inches above the ground, with the front about 2 inches above the ground. In those days that was common." The panhard rod had provided a simple way to get the rear roll center down into the ballpark, despite the obvious asymmetric loading upon the chassis by tying one side of the chassis to the opposite side of the suspension.

Within a few years the state of the sports car art was shifting. Dan on The Cars & Concepts Beretta – "The car handled plenty good enough. The first car I had with a really low roll center was the Chevrolet Beretta in 1988. On either side of the transaxle/independent quick change it had CV joints and had double a-arm wishbone suspension all the way around. It had a Watts link that connected to a plate on the bottom of the diff. We had bushings in there so we could adjust the roll center 1/2"down, centered, or 1/2 "up." Wherever the Watts link connects to the diff is the roll center, and doesn't suffer from the asymmetric actuation of a panhard rod design. What were the results from these slight adjustments? Dan – "We actually ran it higher at some of the street tracks. I actually thought that was going to be backwards. But it helped you turn, and when you lowered the bar, it wanted to go straight. Several times we tried it, and I was sure it would be better lower. It took a while before Tommy (Kendall) could tell us why it wasn't better. Once he explained that it wanted to go straight, it sort of made sense. When you lower it down, it lifts the back up, plants both tires and wants to go straight. It became kind of a game, and when we moved it up a little bit, it would turn a little better."

Tires and wheels were also an issue. "Terry had designed the car for the wheels (10s & 12s) to have so much offset, that scrub radius determined where the sway bar holes could go, which placed them in the middle of the control arm, ½ as effective as they could have been. We were getting some deflection from the control arm which was causing trouble, and we just couldn't get the bar big enough." One typically wants the pick up points for the sway bar to be as far out the control arm as possible, for maximum leverage and precise control.

When you have so many variables, how do you know which variable to focus on first, or in what order? Spring rates, sway bars, roll centers, how do you know which direction to go? Dan – "Early on, I figured out... or at least with our little Trans-Am car, the front sway bar was not an adjustment. Any time you softened the front sway bar, it would turn better... for a little while, but then the rear tires would be gone. We decided that the front bar was mainly off limits. The rear sway bar was a little tiny one on those Trans-Am cars, and the biggest problem was that the rear tires wouldn't go 100 miles. If the front sway bar was less than 1000# per degree, then you could start playing with bringing the rear sway bar on. The Beretta, it had a 1000# front bar, and then we made a 1200# bar, and I think we finished with a 1300# bar. A 1-3/8" .125 wall bar running across the front of the engine bay, we thought we would never have to run it full stiff. Sooner or later, it ended up full stiff all the time. That car was pretty bad, Riley had designed it for General Motors, and his standard bar was about 1500#, which would be more like it for a V8 car. We did a lot of trial and error."

One cannot help but wonder why such massive and heavy sway bars were being used in the late 80s. Niki Lauda's 1976 Ferrari had a sway bar slightly larger than a pencil which provided the same torsional resistance as a long heavy steel tube at a fraction of the weight. Even my (Norm DeWitt's) D Production Datsun 2000 in 1980 had a custom built Speedway Engineering rear sway bar approximately 16" long of 1/2" diameter for weight savings and mass concentration over a thicker bar running the full width of the chassis. As is often the case, convention ruled over concept at the time, and an attentive mechanic/engineer could find design advantages.

Ride heights and suspension pickup points were another

variable. Dan - "We needed to raise or lower the front if we needed more front grip. Or we could mess around with the height of the mounting points for the rear 4 link. We could give it more straight line grip but it would make the car push in the middle of the corner when you started squeezing the gas on. So, you could raise up where the 4 link mounted, as you could move it up or down an inch at a time at the frame."

Toe settings are another method of adjustment. Perhaps no story on using toe to adjust around a chassis problem is more extreme than the struggles of the Gurney Eagle team in 1981, trying to find a road course setup for the CART race at Riverside Raceway.

Geoff Brabham drove the Pepsi Challenger at Riverside in 1981, and comments upon his experiences with the BLAT Eagle. Geoff – "Mike Mosley won an oval race with it, the car was good, a normally aspirated car. The team was running on a pretty small budget, we didn't even have a diff setup; we had a spool which they used on the ovals."

Trevor Harris - "It was running a spool because that was typical of what you were running on ovals. The differential on the car was built by Pete Weismann, and he had built an unlocked system for his rear end but we at All American Racers didn't own one. We put in an order for one, months and months before the race, because at Riverside we needed a differentiating differential, a limited slip or something. But he didn't have one on the shelf. In those days, Weismann had major delivery problems on anything you ordered from him. It got up to a week before the race and we were calling him frantically asking where our proper differential was, and of course he hadn't finished it yet. It got up to race time, and there we were."

Trevor – "All we had was the spool, and we were stuck with running what we had. We were the only ones running a Weismann, and there wasn't anything weird about it except it had a locked differential on a road course, and nobody ran that (in

Indy car) on a road course as far as I know. The last thing you want to do is run around the tight turns 6 and 8 at Riverside with a 100% locked differential in the car. Trevor continues - "We took the car to Riverside and sure enough, the car understeered like a pig. At the track we machined down the front swaybar to be as small a unit as possible. We were running the largest swaybar on the back that we could get, and it still understeered. So, I started toeing out the front end. As I toed it out, it understeered less and less, but it was still doing it a lot. Then I started toeing out the rear. That's a tool that you can use and I've used it a lot on tight road courses. As I toed it out, it decreased the understeer very

The innovative Pepsi Challenger, a BLAT Gurney Eagle

notably… so I just kept going. There's no rule book on this stuff, and everytime I toed it out more, the lap times got better. The numbers were freaking everybody out, as nobody including me had ever run so much toe-out on ANY car, much less an Indy car. When you say toe-out to anybody with an Indy car, they look strangely at you."

Geoff Brabham - "We ended up running just unbelievable amounts of toe out on the rear to make the thing turn. It was like a half inch or more, just ridiculous to try and counteract the effect of the spool, which can make the car difficult to turn. The only way we could fix it was to keep adding more and more toe out. It didn't seem to have any effect on anything but the turn-in so we just kept going. It was to the point that I told Trevor that 'I don't want to know anymore (laughs). It feels good, but if I knew how much toe out it was, I might think it was bad.' But, it worked, the car was great to drive, and we stayed with it (qualifying setup) for the race."

Trevor - "One thing really great about Geoff, is that he definitely could tell me what the car was doing. Finally it got to the point where the limit to run toe-out at the rear of the car was his ability to feel safe going 190mph at the end of the straight. It finally got to the point where it was just too hairy for him. My recollection is that we were running 5/8" toe-out on each rear wheel; it had so much toe-out that when you looked at the car sitting there, you just knew something was broken on it. It just didn't look right, neither at the front, nor the back. But we kept going quicker and quicker with the car to where he qualified on the pole, and broke the old track record set by a 917 Porsche (Mark Donahue's Sunoco Porsche 917-30)."

Geoff continues - "Trevor was my engineer at Nissan, and we ran toe out on that all the time as well, to get the balance of the car and make it turn like I wanted. That car was really sensitive to toe out changes on the rear, so we used to run a 'reasonable' amount. It never affected how it put the power down." Trevor

Harris - "The starting setup was always with a slight amount of toe-out in those GTP cars. It was a useful handling tool in helping the car to get around tight corners. Part of it was that they did put the power down so well. If you've got a car with no downforce, some of the reasoning is a little bit different."

So, maybe you have a mechanical setup to avoid understeer at lower speeds, which then is overwhelmed by the aerodynamic downforce at higher speeds, to achieve a car that is somewhat neutral everywhere? Trevor - "Yep, you can end up with that as an end result. The word 'toe-out' should not be a bad word."

Geoff - "Actually with all that, the Eagle was quite good to drive and we'd got it quite well balanced at the end. I think I was on pole by nearly 2 seconds. When we started the race, I'd pulled out such a lead on the first 2 laps… I used to rev it to something like 8000, and by the third lap of the race I would shift at 6000, and was still pulling away. It was a walk in the park, but when I came in for my first pit stop they cross-threaded the nut on the rear wheel, lost 5 or 6 laps and that was it. We had the race."

Cars & Concepts was to build a Beretta Trans-Am car for the 1989 season, leaving the GTU wars behind. Binks – "In the Trans-Am, basically we copied a Riley chassis. With the rear suspension, we had tried to keep it as simple as possible. In those days they were all 4 link cars, but ours could also be an upside down 3 link (with the triangular linkage to the top of the differential carrier, one upper link, with 2 lower links). A couple of other guys tried a single upper link, which didn't work that good. It never really handled right, compared to having the Watts link on the bottom (with the previous 1988 GTU Beretta design)." The upside down 3 link had raised the rear roll center to similarly ill effect as with the Bruce Short RX-3 rear suspension at the 84 Runoffs.

1990 brought a new chassis for the Trans-Am, hoping to build upon their 3rd place finish in the 89 Championship. Dan – "We built it, but Riley designed that car from start to finish, and won the Championship. At the end of the year, Trans-Am was coming to an end, or at least it was for us. Tommy got hired on to drive the Intrepid and that's when I went to Pratt & Miller."

The Intrepid was a cutting edge GTP car, with enormous downforce unlike anything else on the grid. Dan – "It was a double A-Arm car with front rockers, which was kind of cool, having a rocker ratio of about 2 to 1. We were running about 2000# springs in that car, which was unheard of. It was the first car that I had ever worked on that had really big downforce. We had done the first winter test with that car at Firebird, I used to like going out and watch the car run... nowadays that's unheard of, leaving the pits. I would walk around, watch practice, and then call back on the radio saying "it looks like this..." I was watching the car on the track, and the front tires were actually smashed down to almost zero. You could see that it had no sidewall in the fast esses. I called on the radio and said "STOP, take a look at the front tires." "Yeah, there are stripes all the way around them, what is that from?" They thought it was from hitting curbs or whatever. It was actually the outer rim trying to cut the tire in half. It had so much downforce it was squeezing the tire down to nothing."

Dan – "At that time we had been running low tire pressures, kind of like what we'd been doing in Trans-Am, where you'd start with 15 or 16 and maybe get up to 25 pounds before you were done. The Intrepid had Goodyear radial tires, we didn't know... at that point we ended up adding 5psi all the way around, that's how far off we were. It was new uncharted territory for us. Same with the springs, in the beginning it was less than 2000#, but we wore the bottom off the car a couple of times against the track. Riley wasn't big on packers, little shims on the shock shaft that wouldn't let them go down anymore. They'd do packers on Indy cars and other stuff, but he wasn't big on that for road racing."

Riley's attitude is understandable, as when the spring unit is bound up with packers, it just automatically transfers the load to

265

the loaded corner of the car, akin to grounding the chassis onto that corner. Today, there is the more common 3rd rear spring design, which keeps squat to a limit with a changeable variety of spacers and rubber packers. Rick Mayer of Level 5 motorsports in P2 – "We usually call it the 3rd.... the rear 3rd or the front 3rd. It's not so much a spring; they call it packers because it's used to pack the gap... it is to control the ride height, to keep the rear end off the ground." So you can maintain a softer spring setup at the corners with the 3rd spring (packer) design? Rick – "Yep or you can have a different rear ride height. Otherwise you have to run so much rear spring or a high ride height to keep the car off the ground. This way it sits on the packer going down the straight so you don't have to drag the bottom of the car. It's still as low as it can be aerodynamically; it's just sitting on that packer instead of dragging on the ground. It's used a lot in NASCAR, but they only go left and it's a whole different game."

Ray Evernham was the crew chief for Jeff Gordon during his glory years of the mid-1990s (Cup titles in 95, 97, and 98). – "There are different durometers of rubber and plastic, different combinations of what they can do. It's just a matter of what the tire really wants. Technology doesn't stop; people are going to continue going faster, further, higher. I'm sure that there has been a ton of development on that."

Rick Mayer – "If you have it too high, it makes it loose on entry. If you have it too low, it understeers going off. Trying to find just the right ride height that you want dynamically, this is what we use to control that. And you don't want to get onto the packers in the corners because it upsets the car, but you also don't want to squat down the straight and drag the skin off. You need to prop it up on the straight enough, but you want to be off of that going into the corner because it would upset the rear." Prior to joining Level 5, Rick Mayer was the Engineer for Risi Ferrari in the GT class. Were the packers used as much on the GT cars as on the prototypes? At Risi, we would use it just to keep the chassis off the ground. I never used much rear packer, front rubbers we would use sometimes, but not rear. It upsets the car too much, but you don't want to bottom the car either, you'd rather have the rubber there (on the shock shafts)."

There are javrock planks under ALMS prototypes that are only allowed to have 5mm of wear on the 25mm planks before the car is disqualified for being too low. This is the same issue that cost Michael Schumacher the 1994 Belgian Grand Prix, when his Benetton failed post-race scrutineering due to excess plank wear, no doubt helped by a mid-race spin over the curbs. Having been there that day, there was a lot of javrock dust coming out from under the car early in the race when carrying a full fuel load. Best not to roll the dice too aggressively when it comes to lowering the ride height without using a 3rd spring/packer design.

Steering systems could also have a great effect upon suspension settings. Binks looks back upon one of the revelations from his Intrepid years. "The Intrepid was the very first car I had ever worked on with power steering. Running power steering allowed us to run much more caster than we had run in the past.

Binks wrenching away on the Intrepid in 1992

As a result, there were several different things that we weren't able to do before. What happens is that you can then run less static camber. A lot of the guys at that time were running 2.5 or 3 degrees of static (negative) camber. Without the power steering you could maybe run 2, 3, or 4 degrees of caster, but you could never run more than that, the driver couldn't turn the car. With the Intrepid we were running 6 or 7 degrees of caster, allowing you to take 1 or even 1.5 degrees of the static camber out. That flattened the footprint of the tire out, and allowed it to stop way better." The power steering also was a learning curve for Tommy Kendall, as his style of hanging on to the wheel led to unexpected issues at speed.

Tommy – "I finally got my Intrepid for Lime Rock. In that car, I used left foot braking for the first time, and so for the first time I didn't have my left foot to brace myself. I also didn't realize how much I was using my arm on the steering wheel to hold myself in place. The car had power steering due to that level of downforce and so coming down the hill, the car was darting all over the place, as I was making constant steering corrections to hold myself in place. It was an eye-opener, and it was really tough physically on your neck. We ended up having to do major seat work, to re-engineer the entire seat with side support. For my lower legs I made a big bowl for side support... but I was using way less energy and was not having to hold myself in place. The body was isolated for the first time. I learned a ton about seating then, and had a version of my seat for the rest of my career. People would say, 'that's stupid looking'. I ran it even in the NASCAR cars. But, eventually all those guys went with that kind of seat."

There are also safety advantages to having power steering in race cars, as Rubens Barrichello explains regarding the 2012 Dallara Indycar. "What I would like to see is to create a power steering. Right now the steering wheel has so much kickback, that when you touch a curb... I haven't seen anything like that before. That is the thing that strikes me the most. If that front wheel touches a wall just slightly and has a kickback… that's where people break their wrists and that is what I am afraid of. You have a lot of drivers here with wrist operations, and I'm pretty sure it has to do with that steering wheel. The steering is a lot quicker in Formula One because you have the power steering, this one you are not able to correct the steering so much because it is so heavy. It is a safety issue and I would like to see something done."

As for the suspension, the Intrepid's layout was completely subservient to the aero package. Dan – "They compromised the suspension for the aero, those cars had really short uprights with the control arms way up on the transmission to make sure they weren't in the airstream. Of course this was a Bob Riley designed car and I'm just a kid from San Diego who read Carroll Smith's book… I didn't even ask."

With the beginning of the Roush era in 1993, Dan was involved with the GTS Mustang, which was to win the Championship. Dan – "That car had a carbon fiber tub, with a transaxle, an entirely unique car with wishbones all around. It was the real deal for then. It was sold to Sarel Van Der Merwe, who then won the Championship in South Africa with it, running in some FIA class."

For 1994, Binks moved over to the Trans-Am effort for Roush. Jack had worked with Riley on the cars in the early 90s; the Roush car was an evolution. We moved the suspension pick up points a little bit. So, at the beginning of the Mustang era, we ran a 4 link, but in the middle of 1995 we ran an upside down triangle bar wishbone at the bottom (like an a-arm with the top of the A connecting to the underside of the diff, 2 mounts forward on the chassis) and took the watts link out. By taking out the 2 lower links, it got rid of the bind, we only left the 2 upper links so it wasn't a 4 link anymore."

Kendall – "We ran a 4 link in '94 and part of '95. I wanted

to know a lot about the shocks in terms of understanding conceptually what we were trying to do. The bind made sense because we had real problems with tire wear and it wasn't linear. I don't know what the benefits are, but I knew that (triangle lower link) was their big idea, and that was what they wanted to do. The car deviated dramatically from the Riley cars. I oftentimes didn't know exactly what they were doing at all. I was giving feedback and doing 'better-worse, like it, or don't'."

Although diagrams for a 3 link suspension are diagrammed in Fred Puhn's book, it wasn't commonly used. Where did Dan get the idea for the 3 link? Dan - "At the Runoffs, I think Walter Preston had been the first guy I'd seen with this, on a Datsun 200SX. I wasn't sure if it would work with the power that we had, so we got this crude A arm made, put it together and it was like 3/10ths of a second faster around our skidpad."

There was far more going on under the back of the Roush Mustang than most competitors had ever expected

Binks continues – "We were used to doing changes that would get us 3/100ths, 5/100ths, until we ran out of tires and were done. Kendall said 'This is unbelievable; I'll be able to kill 'em.' But, now we were putting so much load into the differential housing that it was breaking the tubes and all that stuff. It was a learning curve getting it stiff enough."

Putting that link on the top of the differential, similar to the 1989 C&C Trans-Am Beretta, would have moved the roll center way up. With the single triangle bar at the bottom, it kept the roll center down under the differential, as it was with the previous watts link. A standard problem with the 4 link suspensions of the time was a binding issue that occurred as the suspension moved up through its travel. Dan – "The 4 link works really good, but as soon as you start to roll, it binds up and acts as its own sway bar because it's all bound up. This was a 3 link, but everybody else had been doing it upside down (mounted on top of the differential). We had to put a rear sway bar back in, people would look under our car and see a 1-1/4" or 1-1/2" rear swaybar on it, and they would freak out wondering how we were doing it. We never had the car left with the tires off it, we never let anyone see, and would have blankets over the back. If somebody saw it, they could just copy it and be as fast as we were." The blankets were eventually replaced by a snap-on cover, and there was to be a beneficial aerodynamic side effect from that as well.

There were other reasons behind their ability to use a large rear sway bar, and that was low spring rates at the corners. Marge Binks –"The SCCA knew they were doing something but couldn't prove it… couldn't find it. Inside the car, over the back axle, there was an Igloo cooler with hoses leading to the driver… for the cool suit. Well, there was a hole in the bottom of the cooler, and there was a shock absorber mounted there. There were shocks and springs at each corner of the car, but the rule book says, 'shocks and springs'… it didn't say 'FOUR shocks and springs'. The SCCA tried everything they could to figure out what they had done, but couldn't find it. On a 2 wheel bump, this shock would help, but on a 1 wheel bump it didn't do much, so you could run the outer shocks softer than you could without using the 3rd shock."

As a result the car was supple over the bumps, common on the street courses of the day, and this proved to be a huge traction advantage. This helps to explain how they ran the larger rear sway bar than others, given that the roll stiffness wasn't coming from stiffer spring rates, nor from any binding of a conventional 4 link rear suspension. Dan Binks – "People just weren't smart enough to follow that at the time, they just assumed we were cheating. Dorsey is still convinced to this day that we had traction control." Marge Binks – "The rule book didn't say how many shocks; Dan said he could have ten shocks if he wanted. You read the words, not the intent, and find the loophole in the rules."

Kendall wasn't much of a believer in the 5th spring system. "The 5th spring was in 1996, but it never was the secret of our success. That was the greatest mind-f**k, where we hid it in a Thermos. To this day, I think most people think that was the secret for our success. I wanted to understand, but the reality was that there were only 2 places where I felt we got a benefit from that. Testing at Homestead going into turn 1, where you got a little bit of horizontal load and a hard brake zone, I thought it was a little bit better... doing 'with it, without it'. It was negligible, far from conclusive. It was all anyone focused upon after that, but it was a total non-factor. At first people thought... 'oh a drink bottle'. Then they thought, 'what it a drink bottle doing back there?' So then they started focusing on it. We did run it the rest of the time, and it would be a cool story if that was where the advantage was, but in my mind it wasn't a factor. It's quite possible that unbeknownst to me, they sorted it. They were starting to do simulation for the first time with that car. Doug Louth was an Intern from college in '93, and when he graduated in '94 he went to work with us as our engineer. Now he oversees all the engineers at Pratt & Miller. It's funny, as even though I was at Roush, I think of that as being the Dan Binks/Doug Louth car. It was Binks and all the guys."

Kendall continues - "That car was torn down over and over, more than any other car x 10. The SCCA called and said they wanted to see the car again, and that they were in the lobby. Sneak attack..." Dan Binks also felt the pressure from others who were searching out other advantages - "I think in the end, Will Moody (Ron Fellows- Sunoco Camaro) was doing some of that too. Will was a pretty sharp guy and paid pretty close attention to what was going on." The Roush Mustang exploited every angle imaginable.

Years down the road, similar designs are still being used at Pratt & Miller. The 2010 GT2 car also employed the 5th spring technology that they developed in the mid-90s. Dan – "We employ the center spring so you can take side spring rate out. It is similar... very similar to the previous design. Some things never change, you can get the ride rate down and it will still hold itself up under aero loading." But, eventually the 5th spring rear suspension design went away on the Pratt & Miller Corvettes.

Dan Binks – "That happened a while ago, in 2010. Just more traditional stuff, we run this stuff pretty stiff. The engineer guys have never taken it to the extreme, back in the old days we'd be all over the place. Now it's in a normal range. 50# increments under 2000#, over is in 100# increments, and the normal spring change is about 100#. It was always 4 shocks because that's all that was allowed, with a ride spring like other people have. Technically we have rub blocks on the rockers, with 4 blocks under the frame, which keep us from destroying the bottom of the floor. With these cars, we are able to change the floors pretty easily so we put the ugly ones on for Laguna Seca and Long Beach and save the good ones for Road America, Le Mans, and places like that."

The baseline must be substantial by this point. "Exactly, even with the comparison from GT-1 to GT-2, even that information helps us. In an 11 or 12 year program, you've got a lot of info to check out."

The Roush Mustang of Kendall/Binks/Louth had other unique rear suspension developments from Dan Binks and Doug Louth, which were a contributing factor to their success. Was it something like the clever system in Forghieri's 1979 Ferrari 312T4 GP car, which controlled chassis pitch with tension cables? "No, but that's the kind of stuff that everybody fights, it doesn't matter what kind of car you've got. If the weight transfer can be smoother or less abrupt, it's going to be faster every time. We used the ride spring in the center so that we could soften up the outside springs, but we also started using that spring for pitch control, to try and keep the car from jumping onto the front. You had a shaft with a spring on the top and a spring on the bottom, that typically you would pre-load each about 1". There was a heim joint on the axle housing with a ¾" diameter rod with threads on it so you could pre-load it. Whatever spring rate you chose, you could take that off the outside springs. When it unloads one spring, it loads the other so it tries to hold the car in the middle. We did all of the pitch control at the rear suspension. We tried it on the front as well, but it's been not as successful as with the rear."

Essentially they had installed a push me, pull you device that kept the rear car at the desired range of pitch reduction that would eliminate pinning the front of the car. "Right, the Pogo Stick pitch control... you pre-load it so that you can get through tech and all that. The biggest problem with most of these cars is that if the nose gets too close to the ground, the car gets loose. So, the key is to keep it from jumping onto the front of the car so hard. With the car flatter, the driver can get in deeper and more under control than he used to." So, the key is to avoid weight transfer from the rear, rather than running packers in the front? Dan – "Exactly, lets say you had a total pitch of 1 inch... if you could by running this, reduce the pitch by ½"... that's a huge deal. At that point we didn't need things like traction control as our car was so much better than the cars anybody else was running."

Another area of focus was wheel bearings and exotic coatings or construction. Binks - "Early on, the bearings almost wouldn't move, it took a while for them to get run-in. So, some of the wheel bearing stuff we did was to get them sent out to be graphite sprayed at this place in Florida. It was a spray, and it was really thin almost like water, that they would bake onto the bearing at some temperature. When you got these back… you'd swear it was a sewing machine bearing, it had perfect spin."

Binks was the wizard of Trans-Am in the mid-90's

"We'd put a little grease on them, even though they actually would recommend using no grease. I was always so scared to run anything with no grease, or virtually no grease, that I always chickened out. In the end we were using spindle oil from those hot CNC machines, almost like water. You could get away with maybe one ounce per front wheel bearing. This was before we started using ceramic bearings. We use ceramic bearings now without any spray on them. We actually found out at Roush when we had a bunch of people doing NASCAR stuff together with Ford, and we found this bearing coating. We actually used oil instead of grease with some of the cars on the front wheel bearings. In the rear of the Trans-Am car, the rear bearings were in the rear end oil."

Working on the Ackermann settings was another area of large improvement during those years of Roush domination of the Trans-Am. Binks – "In Trans-Am, we learned about Ackermann adjustments, most of the time we had too much Ackermann. Those cars had a problem where they would cup the inside tire real bad. Turn one at Mid-Ohio, the left front tire on the inside would just rip the rubber off it and wear the inside edge off. I was trying to figure out what in the heck was causing this. Well, we started looking at pictures... where is the steering wheel? As it turned out, the inside tire was turning way way too much. So, we started to take that out, almost making them turn one to one. You'd put it on a turntable and turn it 10 degrees with the right front tire... and it would now turn 10 degrees with the left front tire. In the past, the setup had been turn the right front tire 10 degrees, and the left front inside and unloaded tire would turn 12 or 13 degrees."

While these 3 link vs. 4 link multi-shock suspensions were being developed at Roush racing, in Formula One they had moved to the Space Age in comparison. Early efforts at active suspension cars such as by Lotus in the late 1980s had achieved largely mediocre results, but by 1992/93 the cars were of staggering efficiency. Hydraulic rams at each corner of the car were controlled by computer, adjusting every few hundredths of a second. This permitted the chassis with its fixed aerodynamics to be at the point of optimum ride height regardless of track surface. Watching these cars with their wheels moving up and down over a choppy surface while maintaining a static ride height, was the stuff of dreams for the aerospace designers of the day. Taking it even a point further, there was a button on the Williams that once depressed, changed the attitude of the car on the straights. The car itself, through its adjustable suspension, became a movable aerodynamic device... trimming the wing by reducing the angle of attack for the overall vehicle, or stalling the diffuser.

Active suspension had also found its way into IMSA prototypes. Don Devendorf – "Remember when Chevy bought the fully active suspension from the Lotus Formula One cars? They had the full active system in the Corvette GTP car that Lola had built. I remember at Columbus Ohio, where you could look at TV pictures of the cars going around, and the Chevy and our car were the 2 ones that looked the best and most stable, and yet we didn't have the active suspension. In practice, they came roaring into the pits for a fuel and tire change. They plugged in the air hose, the car jacked up and the active suspension thought 'hey, I'm getting too high' and pulled all the wheels up into the wheel wells. This actually happened."

This engineer's dream came crashing into reality at Spa-Francorchamps in the worst possible place. Alex Zanardi, driving the Lotus in practice, arrived at speed into Eau Rouge. This corner is a 6th gear flat out challenge for even the bravest drivers of the day as the bottom left-right flick coincides with a drastic transition from downhill to steep uphill. Upon corner entry, the light indicating hydraulic system failure flashed onto the dashboard and the car essentially reverted into a carbon toboggan instantaneously as the car dropped onto its tub, careening into the barriers. Zanardi had one of the most violent accidents in F1 history, and was indeed fortunate to survive. As a result, all of this clever implementation of computer controlled hydraulic suspension sans springs came to an end at the conclusion of the 1993 season.

On the Grand Prix motorcycle side of the equation, before

being outlawed, one wondered if our future the computer controlled hydro-pneumatic suspensions with infinitely adjustable ride heights, could revisit the technology from the Formula One cars of 1993? Stuart Shenton (Suzuki MotoGP Technical Director) - "It wouldn't work; the system would be too complicated and too heavy to go on a motorcycle, keep it simple. Motorcycles don't need to be complicated, why do people think they have to be complicated? The simplest ideas are the best." Sensing the potential for ruinous cost impacts upon the series, MotoGP banned active suspension.

Al Ludington – "One of the things that we had a big leg up on was that we were one of the first guys to get into the Computrack and really started sorting through our geometry in 94. Once you could get it quantified through Computrack, then you could say 'Where are we? What is the impact?' Find out that 'Jeez he likes the 102mm better than the 89mm of trail.' So we had a head start on that, and we had a huge advantage for 3 or 4 years. We were testing for months at a few different race tracks, getting our heads around swingarm downslope, rake & trail, getting a lock on the geometry. We found that once we got the bike setup where the rider wanted it… and with the Hondas in particular, once you found 101-103 degrees of trail and 13.5 degree downslope on the swingarm, it was basically where you wanted it and stayed the same at every race track. We found the window that the bike wanted to operate in." That was the basic setup geometry for many years of American Honda in AMA racing.

One would think that from a geometry standpoint, a long swingarm, perfectly level at static load, would be optimum for chain adjustment and provide the most constant wheelbase as it moved through it's travel between unloaded conditions (over a hump) or heavily loaded (through a dip), but that has not proven to be the case. Jeremy Burgess – "That is because we are trying to create an anti-squat ratio. Companies have tried to remove this by placing the sprocket on the swingarm, or by putting the swingarm in direct line with the sprocket. But, it doesn't seem to work like that, as the bike needs a certain amount of anti-squat ratio. It is an important part of the setup on the motorcycle."

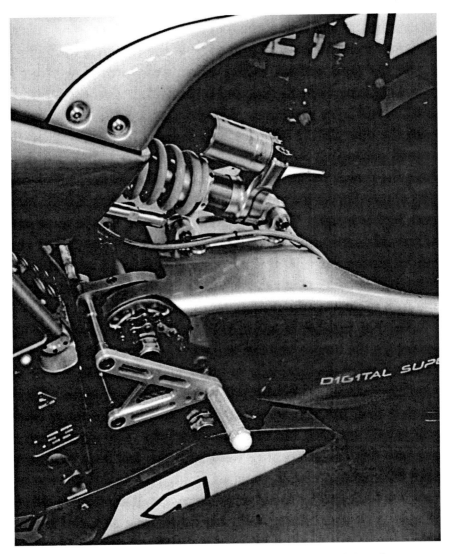

Swingarm downslope, and final drive on the 2011 MotoCzysz

Al Ludington – "When you've got the right downslope in the thing, what happens when you get on the gas is you get your instantaneous moment where the bike rocks back, and then what you want to see is the separation between the seat and tire. Basically you are trying to put the tire on the ground. When the seat goes up, that's the anti-squat and that's what gives you the grip. If the thing goes flat (swingarm) and goes negative where the tire and seat come together, the tire just spins. It's no different from the control arm angle at the rear of a car."

In the zero carbon racing scene, swingarm downslope is following accepted practice, and is similar between the 2010 and 2011 MotoCzysz machines. Michael Czysz – "If it is different with the new (2011) bike, it's only down a hair because of the overall packaging, as the wheelbase is shorter. And you don't have the power pulses (as with a combustion motor) which may play somewhat on that anti-squat. But, you do have, for the most part, higher torque. We are always coming out, for the most part, at second gear speeds. It's a freaky thing for everybody and until you've ridden the bike it doesn't really sink in. I get frustrated now driving every single day when I pick up the gas and wait for the rpm to pick up the power. With this, you go."

Another variable is swingarm length. As a function of the geometry, the longer one can make the swingarm, the longer the point to point distance axle to pivot, and a lesser degree of arc would occur as it moved through its travel. Al Ludington – "Yeah, there is that, but you start weighting the front tire more which will reduce wheelies, but gives up drive grip. The manufacturers got into this era where they went with the real long swingarms with the engine up front, short up front... a lot of times you had to come back and band-aid what they were doing on this side of things. A shorter bike typically has more drive grip, and another thing you've got to keep in mind is the closer the wheel couple, the tighter the radius it can scribe comfortably. So as the wheels move farther apart, the radius that the bike can scribe efficiently gets bigger. Everything on a motorcycle is a compromise. Look at a set of forks... that's got to be the stupidest idea for a suspension because when the thing is leaned over the things want to bind. It's a turd, but it's a well developed and highly polished turd."

Burgess elaborates upon the challenges of engineering the overall package – "You are overlooking the fundamental thing that makes a motorcycle move, and that's the engine. You have to transmit the power from the engine and clearly you won't do that by going longer and longer, you won't have the weight on the swingarm to give you any traction at all. If you move the rear axle back, you have less weight on the rear, and conversely if you move the rear axle forward, you have more weight on the rear if the bike's weight remains the same. If you move the front end forward, away from the rear, you again add more weight to the rear. Bring the front end back, and you put more weight on the front, but you need to have a wheelbase that allows the motorcycle not to be too nervous. What we do know is that much of what you do on a motorcycle is related to where on the engine that the countershaft sprocket is built. And the countershaft sprocket has to be placed very close to the swingarm pivot. But there is a lot of engine, other than that sprocket. You can cast the engine so that there is weight below the sprocket, or you can cast the engine so that there is weight above it. This is one of the things that make the engineering part of a motorcycle so tricky... and all of this weight turns. So many variables with linkages, swingarms, and everything else... there are so many pieces to the puzzle. If any one of those pieces of the puzzle is wrong, and it isn't always visible to see, such as the crankshaft and the rotating parts inside the engine... and once you get the power there, you have all sorts of stresses that you have to compensate for, to achieve what should be the ideal dynamics of the bike." A motorcycle is a far more complex dynamic package to model than any racing car.

Mid-year 2011, Valentino Rossi was to get a development update 800 Ducati with a similar rear suspension to the 2012 model currently undergoing development. Jerry Burgess – "What we have gone to is a completely different design for the rear part of the motorcycle. We have a new swingarm... if you think of the where the wheel is touching the ground, there is a line of force between that point of contact for the tire, the center of the swingarm, and the pivot, and that line of force is more direct. With the swingarm essentially upside down, the line of force is straight and we can control it more. Yamaha did it first, and the only reason I can see that we have copied it is that line of force, that you can make a better, more linear swingarm."

The clever Yamaha rear swingarm as described by Jerry Burgess

Indeed, when looking at the conventional 2011 Ducati swingarm used by Hayden, those force vectors that the swingarm has to resist more closely resemble a 90 degree hinge. Burgess – "Yes, to get strength in something that is shaped like that... whereas when you go the other way where it's all in-line with where the forces are coming from, your high school physics with vectors tells you that you want a direct line with where the strength needs to be. And we believe the linkage is more in-line with the linkage that works on that type of system without putting long straps down the side. It's more in-line than what the other companies are doing... not a copy, just more the right way to go." The end result is a lighter yet more rigid and improved structure.

While on the subject of linkage, the MotoCzysz electric bike that won the 2011 TTXGP on the Isle of Man, has carbon pushrod suspension that actuates horizontal fore-aft mounted spring/shock units mounted above the battery, something akin to a typical formula car layout only with the pushrods running fore/aft vs. side to side. Above the frame rails where one normally would find a gas tank, there is instead a shock cover. It should be mentioned that Shuhei Nakamoto of HRC was looking over the suspension on the MotoCzysz, and he smiled when I asked how long it would be before carbon pushrod suspension showed up on the Repsol Hondas.

As with most "innovations" there were others who had headed down that same road in the past. There were design sketches done by rider/designer Philippe DeLespinay for Morbidelli 20 years ago, with a forward pointing a-arm suspension operating a push rod to the shock linkage. It was not entirely unlike the BMW GS suspension of the mid 1990s, except it used pushrods vs. installing the spring/shock unit in a conventional location (as with a standard automotive lower a-arm mounting).

Of course, pushrod suspension that allows placement of the shock/spring units atop the tub on a F1 car is to narrow up the tub and increase underbody aerodynamics. With the MotoCzysz, the resultant lowered CG and the tighter aero packaging could provide significant advantages, but the real purpose was to achieve a later-day Seeley concept. With this solution it wasn't so much using Seeley's line of force from swingarm pivot to the steering head idea so much as using pushrods to get the spring/damper units up into the desired connection points near the steering head. The initial developments of the MX monoshock rear suspension of the early 1970s (eventually adopted by Yamaha's GP team in 1973) were for similar reasons, which was to get that connection point up by the steering head to reduce frame flex. The resultant long travel rear suspension that resulted was almost an afterthought.

Innovative pushrod suspension in the 2011 MotoCzysz

Michael Czysz – "We decided to take all of the loads into the neck area of the frame. It was easier to drive that force up to where we want it, than to have it down where we don't want it. And we had problems with a slightly restricted amount of front travel by trying to bury the shock between the radius of the tire and everything else. We thought about raising the triple clamp, but we are trying to get lower and lower for aerodynamics. I just felt it was all fighting against each other. Once we made the hard decision to take that element (front shock) out, which was really the hard engineering… then we thought we'd put the other one (rear shock) up there too. Actually it worked out in enabling us to extract the batteries relatively easily as well. And it's a joy to work on, I love it. I think the Moto GP teams appreciated it, and guys like you appreciate it, but it was lost on everybody else, including the majority of the TTXGP teams as they didn't know what was going on or why. I think this bike has been a little bit underappreciated from that standpoint. It has a full carbon fiber front end (the oval tube fork design). Aerodynamic and flexible lowers…"

The trials and tribulations of the carbon framed Ducati, with their repeated attempts to engineer in the sufficient amount of compliance in yaw, have found a different solution at Motoczysz. The flexible lower sliders of the fork system have an engineered-in amount of deflection, which allows for a rigid carbon frame without compromising the front-end feel. Michael – "That's why we don't care about that with the carbon fiber frame. Rossi… the poor guy got 7 frames in one year. There is no doubt in my mind that carbon fiber is the right choice for the frame. Zero doubt, regardless of the problems that Ducati is having, it is the perfect frame material of the future. The geometry and the shape have to be right, but you have more options. We can't pick the grain structure of the aluminum it will have its normal grain structure. With the carbon fiber it's all in the way you lay that stuff up that matters. We did something different; we had that since day one and carried that through. If you had to get flex, you want controlled flex. Would you want to do it over a long distance, cross frame, or over a short distance to flex in one direction and not in the other direction? To be completely honest, we've backed off a little bit on that lateral stiffness, and we have less stiction than a conventional fork. And the new carbon frame (in the 2011) is more sophisticated than the previous frame."

Jeremy Burgess – "As for the pushrod suspension, we've had leading link suspensions, center hub steering, and all of that. Of those I think the center hub steering is the most interesting, but I don't think it will come until you get a specific tire company to develop the right tire." Center hub steering eliminates the front forks from the equation, with swingarms front and rear; it has a pivot to allow the steering of the front wheel. The most commonly seen recent application, if the word common can ever be used to describe a Bimota, is with the Bimota Tesi. Burgess – "The Elf Company did it and it had the 87 Honda engine... in the same year as Wayne Gardner won his championship. There was a business association between Honda and Elf at that time, Elf developing things like single sided swingarms which were never used on the 500s, but were used on 250s and four stroke bikes, and they continue to be used to this time. Ron (Haslam) had one of those and the standard bike, and by the 4th practice session, he went back to the standard bike to qualify and get his place in the race, which gave him, fourth in the championship. It wasn't that bad, but he always raced the regular bike... that year he had that option."

There is also something to be said for taking the best ideas in the pitlane from as many sources as possible. Tom Houseworth – "I wanted guys who had other ideas that had come from other companies. The best ideas are the ideas that you get from other people. Trust me, you poach stuff and that's just the way it is. You come up with your own ideas, but you can't come up with 100 ideas, you can come up with a couple. You've got to get the other 98 from somewhere. There are too many smart people in the world; you can't think that you're the smartest. So, I wanted guys from other manufacturers."

Also, there might be data that could be shared between divisions of a manufacturer competing in numerous racing series. For example, was American Honda privy to the developments of the Honda World Superbike team? Al Ludington – "We were privy to their data, but different race tracks and different riders, stuff like that makes it different. Their setting bank didn't really work well for our circuits or our riders, but you could see trends. Once you get a rider who is really comfortable on his bike... once you get a baseline, it tends to work everywhere. Maybe a click here or a preload, or at Mid-Ohio where you might make the front a little bit more nose heavy to handle that kind of stuff. I was working with Jamie James, and we had a good baseline on the OW-01. We changed it a little bit for Mid-Ohio putting a little weight on the nose which helped with all those downhills. So, we go to Topeka and I ask him if he wanted to leave the Mid-Ohio settings or do you want the baseline? So, we left the Mid-Ohio settings to see what we've got. Jamie is struggling, and when he comes in I asked him what he thinks. 'Well, you know you've got your old easy chair there with a certain kind of pattern. Then you get yourself a new one, sit in it, and it just ain't your easy chair.' So, I ask if he wants to go back to his old settings & he says yes. He goes out for the next session, comes in P1 and says 'Got my easy chair back!'

Comfort and confidence is everything, and a confident racer is a fast racer. Al – "Sure you can go out there and do that one lap, but you might have to pucker up and close your eyes to do it... but we need to figure out how you can do that every lap with a high confidence level, because whoever can do that is going to win the race."

Moving across to the NASCAR truck series for 1998, Dan Binks became the car chief for rising star Greg Biffle. Greg recalls some of those innovative early efforts to build a better suspended mousetrap – "We fabricated a lot of stuff, and the feel Danny had for fabrication... axle housings... we'd be trying something every time we showed up. NASCAR is real strict about the type of suspension, you have to use 'truck arms'... but I feel like we pioneered the soft spring era. We went to Texas and ran softer springs than anybody had ever heard of; put it down on the rubber bump stops, qualified on the pole and won the race. Randy Goss (Crew Chief) got pissed at me for running too fast, I could hold it flat all the way around the track and we were 6/10ths faster. He was 'what are you going that fast for?'" There is something to be said for not showing your cards.

Thinking back to how Bob Riley resisted the "packers" that would effectively do the same to the suspension of the Intrepid, did this have the expected effect of immediate weight transfer to the outside wheel? Biffle – "That's something that we fight... but really, it seemed to load the tires pretty evenly. That's what we are doing today, so the technology that we kind of did in 99, we're doing now. If the downforce will overcome the grip by sealing the car, that will overcome the grip that the tire has through the contact patch and will make it turn. I remember when we went to Kentucky, and went softer... softer... softer, we're taking 300# rear springs, cutting them and putting them into the left front, trying to get the softest springs we could... it was crazy. Keep in mind back then on a mile and a half or bigger, you'd never run under a 1500# spring. Now we are figuring out how to run 500# or 600# springs... pretty amazing. Keep it real soft to get it down to the race track, & we keep 'em down there, that's where we make the best aero. Seal 'em off, keep the air out from under the car."

Biffle, Goss, and Binks may have been innovating with such developments in the truck series, but the best Cup teams had already been working with coil bind and light spring technology for a few years. Ray Evernham – "We actually had stuff like that back in the mid-90s, but we used straight stuff. Back when I was a crew chief we didn't use packers. We got into coil binding and stuff like that, but it was really expensive because we had to design springs. It was more about size and air dam height than it was about mechanical grip. It's not technology that I really liked, as I've always been kind of a mechanical grip guy, but it does make a difference aero-wise. But it is a very very expensive technology, and you can't turn back the clock and un-learn... things will continue to develop. I know that right now, the guys can make as big of a difference by changing a 1/16th of an inch of packer than we used to be able to make by changing an entire spring."

NASCAR truck racer Timothy Peters recalls more recent developments – "I came into it back in 2005, and there was no bump stops allowed by then. Everybody did the coil bind trick with light springs, to try to get the front end close to the ground. When you coil bind these trucks on a mile and a half track, aero overrides mechanical. You do whatever you can to get the body down on the racetrack."

The necessity and advantage of sealing the car to generate downforce, live on in NASCAR today. The proper car setup for NASCAR oval track racing is an art form, unique to itself. Goss, Binks, and the team had found a new Everest to conquer, and along with Greg Biffle, they had become the team to beat in their 2nd and 3rd seasons. For good reasons, NASCAR collects the damper units for testing during the race weekend, to check that they only provide damping, and have no provisions for locking onto the shaft, which would enable the shock units to hold the car down at the precise optimum height for aero.

There are of course additional ways to play the game. David Murray, ALMS Ford GT driver – "I'm sure that over the years, they have figured a way to make those bump rubbers a progressive rate. That way there is somewhat of a spring rate once it goes down, before it bottoms out solid. They could be working on the balance of those bump rubbers front and rear, so that it doesn't unload one end or another instantly. The bottom line is that stopwatch." David Murray was correct, as further refinement of these bump rubbers/packers has become one of the key developments in NASCAR today.

To a certain extent this is a bit similar to the twin chassis Lotus 88 that Colin Chapman pioneered in the 1981 Formula One season. The rules required a 2.5 cm chassis and bodywork clearance from the track when the car was measured in the pitlane. So, Chapman used the normal bodywork with a downforce generating underbody, only he put it onto light springs so once the car was up to speed, this sprung body settled down onto the separately sprung monocoque chassis, effectively sealing the ground effect tunnels to the road. All the downforce developed was then transferred directly to the chassis through the fully compressed light springs. The car circumvented the 2.5cm ride height clearance rule, made to limit the available downforce by removing the seal from car to road surface. The car only ran once in anger, in a practice session at the Long Beach Grand Prix, before being outlawed by the FIA... while the same sanctioning body approved Gordon Murray's solution for the Brabham with self controlling hydraulics that lifted the car to the legal height when slowing for the pit entry, and then lowered the car back down onto the road shortly after leaving pit lane once the car began to reach operational speeds. Go figure...

By comparison, suspension designs are severely limited under the GT rules in ALMS. Dan Binks – "In GT1 and GT2, the suspension needs to be within the realm of where the production car is. The rules state that control arm pickup points need to be within a 1" sphere of the stock locations. With the current GT2 rear suspension it has independent upper and lower A-arms just like the production car has, and the toe link on the rear side that connects to the upright, is just to set the toe. As for packers, nowadays we don't... but normally the packers that we use are mostly for places where you hit the curbs really hard like Mid-Ohio or Road Atlanta, so you don't wear the bottom of the car off. In GT1 is was more of a big deal to get that science figured out, but in GT2 the front ride height is so high with that 50mm block that you have to clear, now it's a long ways from the ground. In the old days we used to have rubbing blocks made of aluminum or titanium. Now these cars (GT2) have less and less of those pieces. It's a tradeoff to get it soft enough to get it down where you want it..." Lessons learned in NASCAR trucks have found new road racing applications.

Binks continues regarding the suspension adjustments of the GT2 car – "We have offset plates where the hole is in a different spot, and where the upper a-arm mounts to the chassis we have the serrated pills that you can move up and down 150 thousandths per notch pretty quick. On the lower arm it has spacers." At the upright, where it mounts to the A-arm, the holes are just in different spots. We know if we change those plates 1/16", then the toe changes 'this' much, and the camber changes 'this' much. It just makes it easier to change instead of having a heim joint up there. Some of the GT-1 cars had JRZs or whatever, but I would say from 2002 until now we've been on Penskes (3 way adjustable gas shock/spring units). They help us out a lot and our guys are comfortable with them. They are close by, and those guys help us out as much as they can. We have our own in-house guy who takes care of all of our shock builds and everything, and he's been the same guy forever... Kenny Caparella.

What is the current thinking with Roll centers? "I think that most of them are pretty close to the ground plane, plus or minus 3/4" on either end. In the old days, if I didn't do it, it didn't get done, and now we have our entire engineering staff working on stuff like that. They look at it and ask us to move this washer or that washer and move the roll centers up and down in pretty small numbers."

In speaking with various prototype drivers, they concur that typically their roll centers are underground, but not by much. Johnny Mowlem of Dyson Racing – "Where are the roll centers on the modern day prototype? I think both are below the ground now. I don't know the exact numbers, but I do know that the rear was quite a long way below the ground, and we've actually moved it up." So, the current thinking on roll centers, at least with Lola prototypes, is various amounts of subterranean.

Although not currently allowed under Le Mans rules, cockpit adjustable sway bars were pretty standard fare in most forms of racing by the 70s. Of course, it is helpful if the driver can remember which way to turn the knob. Andretti's Lotus team in the late 1970s came up with a memorable solution. Mario - "The linkage was such that it could be installed reversed, and I told them we had to make sure it was only installed one way, installed properly. It was a knob on the dash, so when you wanted to soften the bar, you pulled it out. For stiff, you pressed it in. The mechanic said… 'Just so you don't get confused… Hard – Push it In, Soft – Pull it Out." Always best to end a chapter with something we can all remember.

An example of the pounding suspension can take around a street course, in this case at Foch corner during the 2011 Pau Grand Prix

CHAPTER SEVEN

WEIGHT, POLAR MOMENT AND CG

Typical Watson style offset chassis with the engine and drivetrain vertical but 6" or more left of chassis centerline

In the 1940s, the Indianapolis 500 had been dominated by either designs from European Grand Prix (such as Wilbur Shaw's Maserati) or American dirt track Champ Cars. The dirt cars were surprisingly effective given that they looked positively prehistoric when placed alongside cars such as the Kurtis Novi or Shaw's winning pre-war Maserati. Frank Kurtis had developed a purpose built car for the 1948 Indianapolis race, powered by an Offenhauser. That car later was to win the 1950 Indianapolis 500 with Johnnie Parsons driving. One of Kurtis' dirt track Champ Cars was to win with Lee Wallard in 1951, but it was the end of an era.

For 1952, Kurtis had designed the pole winning and radically innovative Cummins Diesel (see Chap 4) along with a somewhat more conventional "roadster" driven by Bill Vukovich. Kurtis had taken the laydown engine concept from his Cummins Diesel and applied the lessons learned to his next generation KK500 Offenhauser powered racer. That car had the engine location only moderately (36 degrees) laid over to the right, but the entire drivetrain package was shifted to the extreme left side of the car, getting the engine bottom end, transmission, and driveshaft over to the inside. The actual advantages in lowered frontal area in the engine compartment were limited with the "roadster" vs. the extreme laydown of the Cummins Diesel racer, as the twin overhead cam engine design of the 'Offy' was such that the left bank cambox was now standing nearly vertical within the chassis. However the bulk of the engine weight now was far to the left side of the chassis, and as a result the driver could sit next to the driveshaft in a lowered seating position. It proved to be a winning combination.

Vukovich led the Indianapolis 500 in 1952 until the steering broke with a handful of laps to go, and then returned to win the race in 1953-54 with that car. Vukovich died while leading the 1955 race with a different roadster, and it was also marked the end of domination by the Kurtis machines. The stage was set for new cars by A.J. Watson, the most successful of the last generation of front engine Indy racers, all of which featured an upright Offenhauser engine. The term "roadster" appears in quote marks for this era, as the term historically referred specifically to Vukovich's 1953 winning car. 'Indy Roadster' much later became more of a generic description for those varied designs of the mid 50s- mid 60s.

The Watson was a significantly lighter chassis than the previously dominant Kurtis roadster of 52-55, and one result of the lighter weight was a less rigid chassis. The Watson took their designs in a different direction from the semi-laydown Offenhauser powered Kurtis, although it shared the concept of moving the engine centerline to the extreme left side of the chassis, typically 6" or more off-centerline. Watson was to offset the sprung chassis towards the left wheels, again moving the CG towards the inside of the car. The next generation of laydown roadster design at Indy... the Epperly/Salih car, was to provide the main opposition to the Watson. That experiment in lowered CG with the aero advantage of reduced frontal area was to follow the more extreme laydown path blazed by the Cummins Diesel of 1952, to become one of the most significant cars in Indianapolis Speedway history.

Donald Davidson, historian for Indianapolis Motor Speedway - "George Salih's concept to lay the engine on its side... personally that would be my favorite car. If they said you can take a car home, I'd take the '57 winner. Salih and Howard Gilbert built this thing in the garage next to Salih's house. The engine was laid 18 degrees from the horizontal. Quin Epperly did the body, or 'skin' as they called it... it wasn't a factory entry at all." In this era of homebuilt specials, this car set the bar highest (lowest?) of all.

If there is any driver who conjures up images from the glory days of the Indy Roadsters, it would be A. J. Foyt. He arrived upon the scene out of Texas, at a time when Watson, Kurtis, and Kuzma were from Southern California, the center of gravity for the

Indycar design scene. A.J. Foyt - "99% of them (the builders) were from California, and 99% of the drivers were from California. They always told me that if I wanted to be an Indy driver, that I needed to come to California. I think it was because there was so much more hot-rodding going on there, which means more racing was going on in California. The owners could see the drivers more out here so they'd pick a California driver. How I got picked was Clint Brawner. At Salem, Indiana, which was where Bob Sweikert, a super race driver, got killed... well I had won an IMCA sprint car race which was pretty hairy and I guess that's where I stood out. Clint told Dean Van Lines' Al Dean that this A.J.... it looks like he's going to make it pretty good. And I always ran very strong and very fast on the high banks, probably because I was half crazy and brave. That's where most of your top Indycar drivers in them days come from... from the high banks. You had to be pretty brave to run fast on those."

A. J. Foyt's first Indy ride was in 1958 driving the offset engine Dean Van Lines Kuzma roadster wrenched by Clint Brawner. It was Jimmy Bryan's Championship winning team from the previous season, and that Kuzma roadster had been the winner of the Monza Race of Two Worlds. One could hardly have asked for more going into their rookie season. A.J. – "It was the same car, same mechanic, same crew... the only thing different was that my Daddy would change the right rear tire. It was a pretty good car for a rookie. I was kind of nervous because they'd won the National Championship 3 times. That was a big load of shoes to try to half-way fill. Bryan now drove for George Salih in the laydown."

For 1958, Jimmy Bryan had moved on to drive the 57 winning Salih/Epperly Belond Special. This was the same Salih laydown car that Sam Hanks took to victory in the previous years' Indy 500. Foyt's Dean Van Lines Kuzma car had offset suspension to get as much of the chassis weight as possible to the inside or left side of the car. A.J. – "They were all offset a little bit anyway, and

and the ones that weren't… they would do it with the wheels, different offsets." At the end of the day, the Salih car was to have taken its second Brickyard victory in a row.

The most successful of the laydowns — the George Salih car

Phil Reilly - "George Salih was the shop foreman at Meyer Drake. He was a very well regarded chief mechanic and he was the one that made the (laydown) engine. The Belanger Special that won in 1951, he was the chief mechanic on that, so he was a top flight guy. He had this idea, that Louis Meyer and Dale Drake (Philip?) supported… they gave him parts to do this (the laydown engine). He built the first one, which is in the Belond car, and it is still in the car in the museum today. The next year, several people wanted them, so Meyer Drake built a version, and it then became something you could buy from Meyer Drake. Part of the advantage for the Belond car was George. He was arguably the best mechanic in the place for that era along with Ray Nichols and a couple of others. Both Hanks and Bryan were as good at Indianapolis as anybody, and better than most, so they really had a good team."

The laydown was looking to be the setup to have, and for 1959 A.J. was to drive a new laydown chassis designed by Kuzma, again wrenched by Clint Brawner. Things didn't quite work out as planned. A.J. – "It wasn't worth a damn. It was a real good short track car, but it didn't work real good on the speedway. I was still kind of a rookie back then, but I just never liked that car at Indy. I mean, we ran decent in it, but that was when Watson's cars were really hot… they made 'em lighter and they were good cars. I ran good with Clint, but mechanical problems kept putting me out, and Bignotti always had motors run fast. I'd drove Midgets for him and Jack London out here in the Bay Area, we were hitting it off pretty good, me and George."

Ex- AJ Foyt and George Bignotti Kuris/Epperly 500J laydown

For 1960, A.J. was to drive the Kurtis/Epperly 500J laydown at Indy, wrenched by George Bignotti. A.J. – Kurtis really had better Midgets than anything. I wasn't really happy with it, myself. Like the year before… short track it was good. I just didn't know how to tell Bignotti how to do it." Foyt had multiple finishes in the top 4 at the Trenton and Milwaukee races that season, yet could only muster 16th on the grid at Indy. It was the twilight of the Kurtis era, and for A. J. Foyt it was back to the offset upright chassis for the following 4 seasons and a stunning run of success.

Parnelli Jones also had experience with these successful designs at Indianapolis during their glory days, both with the final version Epperly laydown of 1961 as well as the Watson. Parnelli —"Frankly, the Watson roadster was quick, but it didn't have that solid feel like the laydown did. The laydown car seemed smoother, it didn't have any vibration or anything like that, and it felt like it was one piece. We tried to get the weight on the left side of the car, on the inside... that was the whole idea. The Watson would shake a little bit through the corners. The laydown that Epperly built, Tony Bettenhausen was supposed to drive that car, but he got killed. Tony almost set a new track record with that car in tire tests. Lloyd Ruby drove it in 1961, and man... that's the one that I really wanted to drive, I really fell in love with that car. I still feel that was the nicest roadster... the Autolite Special, it was fabulous. The other ones Epperly had done before had the engine laid over to the right (as with the 57/58 winner) instead of to the left. With all that weight over on the inside, it was like a super-modified. But, I guess things worked out best for me and I ended up driving a Watson roadster."

Phil Reilly - "Even Quin Epperly, who built several of them (laydowns) and was the biggest advocate of them... he was a good friend of mine for years, and said that there was never a clear advantage. But, the last itineration of the concept was a really good car. Parnelli will tell you today that it's the best race car he ever drove. He said, 'if I'd gotten that car, which I was supposed to get, I would have won this joint 4 times in a row.' Bettenhausen had the same reaction, and that's why he got Lindsay to buy the car, and the rest is history. That car was clearly better."

The Mid-Continent Securities Special was another sponsor of the Autolite car, different paint jobs at different times, same chassis

Tony Bettenhausen was the fastest car at the Speedway in practice with Epperly's Autolite car, but Tony didn't live to qualify the car as he died while testing Paul Russo's car. Ruby had been the 2nd fastest qualifier, being handicapped by that time being set during the 2nd weekend of qualifying. The Autolite car was the ultimate version of the laydown concept, as the crankshaft and transmission were now rotated around that crankshaft axis 180 degrees with the cylinder head now sticking out the extreme left side of the chassis for the highest amount of inside weight offset possible while maintaining the aero advantages of the laydown design. Lloyd Ruby drove that final generation Epperly car to finish 8th in the 500.

Phil Reilly - It (a typical laydown) has about 60 lbs of weight bias to the left, not much. The Autolite car was considerably more. Quin's cars were the best... by a wide margin they really were the best cars. But Watson had a huge advantage in that he was his own chief mechanic, and he went to every race, developing the car. He knew what was needed. Quin would build a car, hand it over to the team, and then he'd never see it again. Some of those teams were good, other were not so good, and he didn't have any control over that. He used to get so mad at some of the guys, asking 'why do you have that setup on the car, it's ridiculous.' They would say –'well, that's what we did last year.'… that sort of thing." I think it was less to do with the car, than with the team."

Note the engine is rotated to the left around the offset drivetrain

Bill Akin currently owns a number of Indy Roadsters, including the Autolite car. Bill – "Let me tell ya, I had the car (the Autolite car) over by the pool at the hotel one day. Parnelli was talking to a bunch of people about how great it was… well Foyt comes up behind him and says 'pushin piece of s**t'. Parnelli turned around and say, 'Hey that was a great car.' Foyt – 'Pushin piece of s**t'. Foyt drove that car for 2 races after he and Bignotti split up, he went and drove Milwaukee and Trenton for Hopkins in late 62. So, he drove the Autolite car, although by then it was the Mid-Continent Securities car. He ran Ward ragged in the 2nd

Milwaukee race that year, but Mr. Foyt did not like laydown cars. Lloyd Ruby drove the Autolite car at Indy after Bettenhausen got killed. He had the 2nd fastest qualifying after only 5 laps of practice in the Autolite and I asked him what happened on race day. He said, 'well, basically the motor all f**ked up, running so rich that raw fuel was spraying in my face. Lloyd loved that car. When they were going to name part of the interstate up by Wichita Falls for Lloyd, he and his buddies came to get the Autolite car and take it up to Wichita Falls and run it around out there. I said, 'Lloyd, Parnelli's going to be there. That chain with a padlock that you used to lock your golf cart over at the Speedway Motel? Well, you'd better lock the steering wheel of that sumbitch or Parnelli will be in it and gone."

Parnelli reflects upon the reasons why the upright Watson design became the final refinement of the front engine Indy Roadster. PJ and mechanic Johnny Pouelsen were to raise the art of the Watson to new levels. "I don't know... I guess a lot of it had to do with reliability. He (Pouelsen) was a race driver himself, from California. He always had an attitude about trying to make the car better and we did. I drove the Watson in 61, 62, 63 and 64, and every year we improved the car. We were the first ones to have the air intake on the outside in 63, which Foyt came along and copied in 64."

Foyt's version was best described as a major refinement of the concept. A. J. Foyt – "When I won again in '64 it was with a Watson. We did a lot of work on the front of it, for ram-air on the nose. The nose was really different, but we weren't getting the pressure that we thought we should have. I told them to put a slot down in front of it, and that made the air go straight in. It was working good, but a guy named Whitey Haubold from Douglas Aircraft said it would work a lot better if we altered that (the area just in front of the intake). The car was all painted and everything, so Bignotti cut it and bent that part down."

AJ Foyt's 1964 Indianapolis winning Watson-Offenhauser

Parnelli was similarly moving forward with what was to be the final refinement of the Indy Roadster. "We rebuilt it every year; we built a whole new body shape on it, with a new cowl. We built a new lower streamlined oil tank which got us in trouble a little bit (a crack in the oil tank nearly resulted in the car being black flagged which would have cost PJ the '63 Indy win). In 64 we built an aluminum rear fuel tank and that one bit us because the aluminum wasn't strong enough to hold 75 gallons of fuel and it warped the tank and the fuel got away from the pickup. That's why I had to make an early stop, and then it caught on fire in the pits. When they were all the same, you just try to make yours just a little bit better than the next. There weren't wind tunnels and all that stuff available for us." Did the team do "tuft testing" as was prevalent in Formula One, where small strips of yarn were attached to the body to photograph the airflow? PJ - "No, not really."

And all the while, the question of laydown vs. upright had

continued to where everything was about to change in favor or neither as the rear engine cars had returned to the Brickyard. Davidson – "The big decision was, 'which way to we go? Do we want an upright or a laydown?' It was interesting to see how that played out, because typically the upright "Roadster" would win."

Meanwhile in Formula One, Porsche was using the same logic with their low CG 'boxer' opposed cylinder engines. From privateer efforts with 4 cylinder models, to the 1962 factory 8 cylinder cars, there were obvious design advantages. Ferrari was to pick up the theme with their flat 12 GP cars of 1965, and by 1970 their 3 litre F1 cars were also to follow suit. Two World Championships for Niki Lauda in the flat 12 Ferraris of 1975, and 1977 were to follow. Such were their success, that when Alfa Romeo entered F1 as the engine provider for Brabham, they followed that same 12 cylinder boxer layout. Legendary French V-12 manufacturer Matra, designed and tested flat 12's in recognition of those CG advantages. However in the midst of all this success, the advances in underbody aerodynamics pioneered by Lotus during 1977 meant an engine that was narrow at the bottom, could allow larger ground effect tunnels, and increased downforce. This obviously favored narrow V engines, or ideally, in-line engines. The era of the flat 12 was widely thought to be over and for 1979 Alfa Romeo produced a V-12, abandoning their boxer layout of the previous 3 seasons. Bucking the design trend, Ferrari's Mauro Forghieri persevered with a flat 12 in the 312 T4. Despite their aerodynamic handicaps, the Ferrari was used to great effect by Jody Scheckter and Gilles Villeneuve, who finished one-two in the World Championship. It was the final championship for the boxer engine in Grand Prix.

With the ban on tunnel cars for 1983, the ideal layout for powerplants in GP cars was again in play, with the semi-laydown 4 cylinder BMW that carried Piquet to the World Championship. Gordon Murray was to try a more radical version of the same concept with 1986's Brabham BT55 'flying skate'. This car had a full-laydown 4 cylinder BMW powerplant, built that way for all the same reasons as Salih's Indy winner. With the end of the tunnel car era, the concepts of reduced frontal area, and lowered CG were rational enough to warrant the return of the laydown or boxer engines. For whatever reasons, the laydown 4 cylinder BMW turbocharged powerplant was less powerful than its upright counterpart, a design which had previously won the World Championship. As a result, the 'flying skate' was not a successful design, sadly costing driver Elio de Angelis his life in testing. This Brabham had marked the end of the road for laydown engine design in Formula One.

Soon after those 2 wins by the Salih-Epperly car at Indy (57-58), the rear engine revolution arrived. Donald Davidson – "The rear engine cars came in again... like they did before, from 1937-51." Harry Miller's brilliant yet unsuccessful rear engine 4 wheel drive racer that entered for the 1938 Indianapolis 500 had centrally located pannier tanks on either side of the driver. That car also used a 6 cylinder engine laid over similarly to what was to appear on the post-war Kurtis "Roadster" of Vukovich 14 years later. Miller's layout advantage is obvious both from a traction standpoint with the rear engine, as well as having a centralized fuel load to keep the handling more consistent, with less variation in CG and reduced a polar moment for the car regardless of the fuel load. These were lessons previously learned in Europe by Auto Union with their rear wheel drive, rear engine V-16 racers of 1934-37, and were further refined with the 1938 V-12 car.

The European 750kg GP formula of 1934-37 had been meant to contain the ever-escalating speeds by imposing a maximum weight, but it had the completely opposite effect. It had led to a technological explosion of ever lighter and more powerful cars, as with only a maximum weight limit, the sky was the limit. The German government financially supported these efforts as a showcase for German superiority... keeping in mind their master race propaganda of the day.

The mid-engine Auto-Union V-16 Record car

Although Germany's racing color had long been white, the paint had to be removed from the Mercedes Grand Prix cars before their debut at the 1934 French Grand Prix, as that was necessary for them to reach the 750kg weight limit. The legend of the Silver Arrows had begun and continues to this day, its origin primarily being due to the weight of paint. Auto Union's Hans Stuck had a stellar first year with Dr. Porsche's rear engine V-16 racer and would have been European Champion of 1934, but that title did not officially begin until 1935. Their greatest driver, Bernd Rosemeyer, was to become European Champion of 1936.

This story of European innovation and success was to have an entirely different result at Indianapolis, as the rear engine/four wheel drive Miller, though brilliant in concept, was a complete failure on the track. Donald Davidson - "The '38 car arrived very late. Ralph Hepburn was the driver and didn't make the qualifying time, rolling out as they shut the track down. In 1939 they had 3 cars and George Bailey qualified for the outside of the second row, the first rear engine car to qualify for the 500. The last start (for the rear engine car) was in 1947, with one of the '38-'39 cars. They had very little success, in fact when Bailey went 47 laps in 1939, that's the farthest a rear engine car went until Brabham (in 1961)."

The rear engine cars were to spark other innovations. The Harvey Aluminum car of Mickey Thompson was the first to run the small wheels with lower profile tires. Parnelli Jones – "They were 12" tires, and that was part of the creation of the 15" tire. The tires would change from year to year. One thing was that we developed a good tire for the '63 race, which we didn't have in '62. 1963 was the first year that we went to 15" tires instead of the 18s. The 18s were skinny, where the 15s were a little wider. To get the ground clearance we jacked it back up, it had a solid front axle and you could change it a little bit."

Parnelli continues – "I had done the track testing for the 18" tires before and I was trying to get them to build a 16" tire and make it wider. They said 'Oh, you can't do that'... the engineer was giving me this bullshit. I told him 'you run the wider tires like that on the stock cars, don't tell me you can't run a wider tire like that on an Indy car.' I was really mad but I finally got them to make them. They had made their first 15s for the Lotus, because it couldn't run the big 18s. I told them if they gave me those tires 'I guarantee I'll break the track record right now.' They said 'oh bullshit', so I had Halibrand make a set of wheels for me, and fly them in. When I first put the 15s on, I went out and broke the track record first time out. They should have listened to me, but they think they know more than anybody else."

A.J. Foyt – "Mickey Thompson wasn't no dummy. Like the Indycar that Dave MacDonald got killed in, I think it had 12" wheels when we were running big 'ol 18" wheels." Why didn't the smaller wheels catch on immediately with the roadsters?

A.J. – "Back then it was monkey see, monkey do... and you didn't have the kind of money that you have today and didn't have that many big purses. I think that probably kept everybody where they were. An Offy motor back then was 12 or 13,000 dollars and the car was something like 10,000. If you had a 100 or 200,000 dollar budget, man you was BIG TIME."

Despite the aforementioned financial limitations, were the drivers of the Indy Roadsters pulling out all the stops to compete with the new rear engine racers? Parnelli – "We were. We didn't have much of a problem in 63, but '64 was the first real good cars. I also had a Troutman and Barnes rear engine car in 64, but it didn't handle well. I later took it to Trenton, but it bit me over there and I went back to the Watson roadster."

The fuel loads during this 2nd rear engine revolution at Indianapolis, brought yet more design challenges. Joe Leonard – "Now they scrape the cars with a full load of fuel, and they only carry about 40 gallons. When I drove the Yamaha Eagle in '66 we used to carry about 75. With about 75 gallons of fuel, the car handled like crap until you got about 20 laps or so. Then it would get pretty good but when it got light it would float around on you. It wasn't no trip to Paris, that's for sure." With such a massive fuel load, the drivers would set the car up on a medium fuel load to just have a chance of hanging on to it the whole time.

Ironically, in recent years for Formula One, the rules no longer allow fuel stops, requiring the cars to carry enough fuel to complete an entire Grand Prix distance. Thankfully that is no longer the case in Indycar. Rubens Barrichello compares his experiences with the two. "Here (Indycar) the fuel tank is pretty small and I was surprised that from low tanks to full tanks, that the balance doesn't change very much, it's actually a pretty good car for that. In Formula One, every gallon is a 1/10th of a second. You have 10 kilos for qualifying, and 150 kilos for the start of the race. Even when we had 60 kilos in the car and refueling, we went from 60 to zero... and it was a lot. Here the balance is really good, full tans or low tanks, it doesn't make a difference." Does the balance of the car change from tire degradation across the usual stint? "Well... it does if you abuse the car on full tanks."

In the Trans-Am series, the Roush/Binks/Louth Mustang had a massive CG advantage over what the others were racing. Dan Binks – "In those days there were 2 or 3 cars that were good enough, although there were a lot who were close, like the Simos and Tom Gloy. Those guys were racing cars that they bought... Riley's cars... and just for instance, they were hundreds of pounds heavier than our car. They got down to the minimum but they didn't have any weight. We had tungsten all over our car. We sent an engine to Riley and Scott, so they built us a brand new Mustang. We took it home and it had about 25# of ballast. Our car's CG was lowered by 1.1 inches with 208# of ballast, so they weren't even close."

Exactly how was the super-light Roush Mustang keeping its advantage with a paddock full of inquiring minds? Dan – "We played it pretty close to the chest. We screwed the ballast into the floor, but not where they could see it. Under the seat, on the front of the passenger compartment on the floor, we would put it in places where we could cover it up. We would have 3/4" thick bars of tungsten that you could just lay on the floor, which was about 50% heavier than lead, so you need a lot less of it. It was expensive, about 1000 bucks for 100 pounds.

In the days of the Kendall/Binks domination of the Trans-Am series, they would add weight to the car that won. With the sort of winning streak that the Roush team was on, the challenge was keeping an ever-heavier car competitive. Of course, the weight was added low within in the wheelbase, so the net effect was an ever lowering CG and an ever-smaller Polar Moment.

Dan - "We made some pretty big changes on making the bodywork light, and used magnesium sheet metal in some of those cars. The rules said that you had to use aluminum. If you look up magnesium sheet metal, it has 2.7% aluminum. Well, in my book, is that really aluminum or is it magnesium? Well, it has 2.7% aluminum, then I'm going to say the rule book doesn't say it has to be 100% aluminum… it just says it has to be aluminum. If you look at regular 6601 aluminum, it's not 100% aluminum either as it has other things in it, so…"

Well ahead of the curve, a big part of the success of the Roush Mustang in Trans-Am was the low CG and small polar moment

What was the effect upon the settings of the car from the lowered CG and smaller Polar Moment? Dan – "It just seemed that it changed direction better, and when we messed with that, it seemed like the car wanted to stay flatter." All of that would make sense as a car typically will respond more quickly with a low polar moment. Also, the lower the polar moment and CG, one could also expect a lessened tendency for fore-aft pitch as there would be less mass bouncing around at the ends of the car. Dan – "We made some pretty big jumps there at the end, that last car we raced for Jack was pretty special. By the end, we were way up on the spring rates. Our car had 300 pounds of ballast, and theirs had virtually none. That was how we were able to move the CG down so far. That and we basically took everything off the top, and put it on the bottom. From the windows being thinner, to the roof being carbon... every time we ran that car, if it needed a piece of bodywork, it was brand new. We never painted it more than one time. There were enough customers that when we were done with a hood, we sold it. That's the kind of stuff you need when you are winning championships, you need the best car and Jack allowed us to spend that kind of money so that we had the best stuff. The Ford motor company was behind us, and although we didn't waste money, we had the best stuff."

Lowered CG doesn't translate into improved performance in the world of motorcycle racing. A classic example was the Honda 500cc GP bike of the mid-1980s, especially with the "upside down" 4 cylinder machine of 1984.

The mechanic's nightmare, the 1984 upside down 4 cylinder machine had the exhaust pipes running over the engine, with the fuel tank under the engine. Had team mechanic Jeremy Burgess thanked his lucky stars that his rider Haslam had avoided the upside down 4 bike? Burgess - "Except that I was (working on it) as the thing wasn't working any good. I've still got burns on my hands from getting the plugs off that thing. Every night you had to pull the exhaust pipes. The exhaust pipes went vertical, so carbon would fall back onto the piston face through the exhaust port. I mean it was a nightmare. I remember working on it on a number of occasions; in particular with Freddie, George (Vukmanovich), and Erv (Kanemoto) at Laguna Seca. It was an engineering disaster, really, but Randy (Mamola) won the British Grand Prix on that bike. It had lots of power, but all that was lost with the amount of work to get that thing to the start grid. You just couldn't do it; everything was so difficult in the way it was done. Every week the fuel tank was cracking, and you couldn't go a weekend without cracks in the swingarm or the frame. You don't want to be building race bikes at the race track. It is a tool for winning the race, for the riders to use. Don't build it here."

Stuart Shenton was also a team mechanic at HRC and dealt with the constant struggle of the fuel tank being slung under the chassis, to further lower the CG – "The damn bloody fuel tank was always cracking. My job was to get somebody to weld up the fuel tank all the time, the way it was hanging off the chassis… the weight and the way it was mounted, it would crack. And the sloshing of the fuel load around in that tank drastically changed the handling as the fuel load was reduced."

The next generation machine was more conventional and won the 500cc World Championship in 1985 (Freddie Spencer) and in 1987 (Wayne Gardner). Gardner recalls his first season with the factory team – "The Honda in 1986 had a lot of understeer. It was very hard. I was constantly thinking it was me all the time, and Jerry (Burgess) couldn't understand it as well." Of course, given the unique riding style of Freddie Spencer, this arrangement was likely ideal, as his turn-in points were different from the other riders, and that style meshed with the machine's idiosyncrasies. Team riders like Randy Mamola could never feel comfortable with the understeer of the early 4 cylinder Hondas, but this issue was never more the prevalent than with Wayne Gardner.

Gardner – "Honda at that time had no idea. They had no understanding of how the bike would be working or how it should be working. Their philosophy was to push the weight down low. Remember the upside down bike, with the fuel tank underneath and the exhaust pipes above? The philosophy at HRC was to get the center of gravity down as low as possible. What they were doing, that they didn't realize at the time, was that with the low CG the bike wouldn't steer. The higher the engine is, the more the bike wanted to go around the corners. Engine position was extremely important, and for some reason Freddie (Spencer) and Erv (Kanemoto) worked around what Honda's philosophy was. Every year they pushed the engine farther down, it just became more difficult to get the thing around the corners. We were changing the rotation of crankshafts in the bike, everything to try and get rid of the understeer. Typical Honda, it was never short of horsepower. In 1986, I finished 2nd in the World Championship, but I think it was more about brute horsepower than anything. In 1987, they were still going with that philosophy, but had improved the bike quite a lot, and I won the Championship."

Jeremy Burgess - "What Wayne had in 1986 was a crankshaft that rotated in the wrong direction. And this phenomenon would cause the front wheel to lift. You would almost have to set the bike up to trip over itself into the slower corners, to get it through the fast corners when the crank was really spinning and it would take the weight off the front. The Japanese could see how hard Wayne was riding the bike in 1986, and this (crankshaft direction of rotation) was fixed in 1987. They realized that to compete with Eddie Lawson you needed a better bike. The whole bike was an improved bike and with it we won the Championship. Also, you only had to look at the 0C vs. the 0D (87 NSR500) bike to see that it was a big step. It was a completely different engine, as the carburetors were between the Vee instead of in front of the engine and out the back. For 1986 all the pipes were under the bike in a sort of spaghetti-like maze." With the crankshaft now turning opposite to the direction of wheel rotation, a wider Vee design allowing the revised carburetor location along with 2 up 2 down exhaust routing and a host of other improvements, Honda had won their third 500cc Championship.

Gardner – "In the beginning of 88, when I was still with Jerry (Burgess), they pushed the engine down. It wasn't until mid-year 1988 that we started to realize where we'd gone wrong." Burgess reflects upon the modifications that occurred mid-1988 – "I had moved the swingarm pivot down by a significant amount, so when we got the swingarm angle where we wanted it, the steering angle was too steep because it didn't have adjustability. So, we had to cut the frame and kick the front out... and Eddie was getting away." Gardner finished 2nd in the 1988 Championship.

Jerry Burgess and Valentino Rossi – a combination for the ages, sadly ended for 2014. Burgess has been at the tip of the technological spear for 35 seasons, engineering World Championships in 500cc Grand Prix or Moto GP for Gardner, Doohan, and Rossi.

Wayne Gardner – "We were really struggling early in 1989; we just could not get this thing to go around corners. At Le Mans, Suzuki with Kevin Schwantz was next to us... well, my motorhome had tinted windows, and I could see Schwantz's bike. So, I brought over some of the bosses from Honda, and they sat there all day taking photos of the Suzuki. They took the photos back to Honda Japan, and blew the things up to scale, measured everything and realized that the Suzuki engine was mounted extremely high and theirs was extremely low. After that, in 1989, they started this different engine placement philosophy, deciding to try it, cutting and hacking the chassis around while pushing the engine up. It really took off from there, and by 1990 the thing was fantastic.... and it all came about because of the photographs they got of the Suzuki chassis. They realized their philosophy had been incorrect, and they got that sorted out just in time for Eddie (Lawson) to win the Championship."

Jerry Burgess sees far more to the equation – "I'm not sure you could influence Honda in that way. The biggest thing that changed in 1989 was Eddie Lawson and Erv Kanemoto put 13 different chassis through the 1989 bike. They worked furiously. It clearly came from Eddie Lawson's experience on the Yamaha, and the fact that we went to a full deltabox chassis. I believe the 1990 bike at 115 kilograms was the best bike they ever made, and a few of the chassis engineers felt the same way. It was a big step into carbon fiber, and the rear subframe had gone. It was super light, and then of course when the rule went back to 128kg and we made the engine cases out of aluminum and some other things. From that point on, the chassis didn't really change until Valentino rode it in 2001, when we lifted the engine up and back 10mm to get more rear grip."

The upcoming era of Honda's 500cc dominance was born from the lessons learned and hard work of that 1989 season. Lawson did not stay to bear the fruit of his labor, moving on the Roberts Yamaha and a season of injury, and it was Mick Doohan who was the ultimate beneficiary of the incredible efforts expended during that 1989 season.

Al Ludington sees issues with the obsession over CG locations and fore/aft weight distribution on motorcycles – "One thing that a lot of people get hung up on, is the front-rear weight split and CG. I'm like... ok, that's all fine and dandy, now take your 350 pound motorcycle and put a 180 pound rider on it. Move

315

him all the way to the back of the seat, then to the front of the seat. Now stick your leg out and lean way over to the side. The CG can move in a radius of 2 or 3 feet. Static CG, unless it's really way out there, means nothing. This isn't like a car, where a guy is bolted down into his seat. They are to the point now where they can barely turn their heads with the HANS devices and stuff like that. With a motorcycle, the rider is 1/3 of the weight of the overall machine and has this huge area that he can move around in."

The rider can use this moveable weight to great advantage. Ludington – "If the tire is spinning, he can slide his butt back on the seat to try and get some grip. This brings up the argument… 'are you better with a bigger rider or a little tiny rider?' Well, with a little tiny rider you get a good power-weight ratio, but you lose a lot of the ability to compensate for the motorcycle. Maybe we gained in acceleration, but we lost in every other dynamic aspect. An ideal rider would have a 150 pound head, with really long arms and legs, so he could put that head wherever he wanted… down next to the front axle or back over the swingarm." Has Al known any riders that he suspected had a 150# head? "No, but it seems the more they win, the bigger and heavier their heads get."

Tall and lanky, Ben Spies was able to move that weight around to his best advantage. At the 2008 United States Moto Grand Prix.

CHAPTER EIGHT

AERODYNAMICS

Jim Hall driving the innovative Chaparral 2E, a car that stunned the competition at its debut during the 1966 Can-Am series

Reduction of drag was the predominant design goal of the day for aerodynamics up through the 1950s. Perhaps the most beautiful examples of low drag aerodynamic design in GP racing were the 1954-55 Mercedes W196 Streamliners, with their full width center seat bodywork. The cars suffered from instability and understeer, as at the time, combating aerodynamic lift did not appear to be a priority. Still, their success on the fast tracks was undeniable, and their influence was immediately felt in America.

1937 Auto Union Grand Prix Streamliners by Ferdinand Porsche

A. J. Foyt – "I don't think a lot of people knew a whole lot about air then, other than make it kind of clean. The one who made a car that did everything right was Sumar… Kurtis had made a nice aerodynamic car where the wheels were covered. Chapman Root owned all those Sumar cars, and that was a beautiful car." On the heels of the Mercedes Streamliner success in Grand Prix racing, Root had brought his Sumar Streamliner to Indianapolis in 1955, which even included an enclosed bubble canopy over the cockpit. With the enclosed fenders it more closely resembled a Bonneville LSR car, than an Indycar.

1955 Mercedes W196 Grand Prix Streamliner

At Italy's Race of Two Worlds in 1957, Tony Bettenhausen had pushed the Novi around the high banks of Monza at a searing 177 mph, backing it up in the race with a lap of 176.8 mph... a world record for closed course speed. A. J. Foyt – "They took the Sumar to Daytona and set a track record, but Marshall Teague got killed in it." Before his death in February 1959, Teague had turned a lap of 171.8 mph around the Daytona course, and no doubt he had his sights upon Bettenhausen's record lap when he was killed. Quinn Epperly had previously produced a Kurtis based streamliner, the Belond Miracle Power Special for the 1955 Indianapolis 500, but that car was unsuccessful.

Similarly, for 1956 the British F1 team Vanwall created an updated racer, a joint effort of Colin Chapman's spaceframe chassis and Frank Costin's aerodynamics (Costin formerly having been with the De Havilland Aircraft Company). The distinctive design was one of the earliest to introduce innovations such as the low drag NACA intake duct to racing. The car, although relatively tall, was highly effective and its striking design was to

319

set a trend. The 1957 Maserati 250F lightweight, which was to win the World Championship for Juan Fangio, resembled the Vanwall in many ways, although built without the high tail or the elegant and efficient NACA intake. Although Stirling Moss narrowly lost the World Driver's Championship to Mike Hawthorn and Ferrari in 1958, the Vanwalls of Moss, Brooks, and Lewis-Evans (sadly killed at that final race) were to win the World Manufacturer's Championship, the first year for that prize category.

Epperly Streamlineer built for Bill Vukovich to race at Indy in '55

While these low-drag exercises in F1 development were taking center stage, a young Aeronautical Engineering graduate in 1959 from Milan Polytechnics found his first employment opportunity came with Ferrari, who seeing the writing on the wall, was seeking an aerodynamicist. Gian Paolo Dallara – "I was ready to go work for the Aermacchi factory (Italy's premier aircraft manufacturer), but Ferrari was looking for an engineer and asked one of the professors if he had someone to suggest, as they were doing aerodynamic tests. At the time they were not looking for downforce, all that came much later."

There were clues, as the Lister factory team had riveted in place additional infill bodywork behind their tall front fenders, in an attempt to keep the airflow better attached to the fender line, vs. the turbulent negative pressure areas behind the front fenders on the dramatically curved original design. The result was the Knobbly Lister, a flowing and reduced lift design... a car which provided great success for Lister in 1957-8. Race car crew chiefs and engineers began to note that negative pressure from turbulence resulted in aerodynamic lift, and solutions to counter the turbulence began to appear in their designs.

By the early 1960s, high speed stability problems became noticeably improved with the lip spoiler at the rear of the sports prototypes and GT racers of the day, such as the 1962 Ferrari 250 GTO. This spoiler became more prominent upon the Lola GT the following year, which then inspired the similarly equipped Ford GT40. The Kamm tail design of these cars was deemed to have similar performance to a long tapered version, which was always more cumbersome and vulnerable in a racing situation, although Porsche found success with long tail versions of their endurance racers throughout the late 60s and early 70s.

Ford had tried the same with their Ford GT program at Le Mans in 1965. Chris Amon shared the long nose/tail 7 litre car with Phil Hill. Chris – "That '65 car had a much longer nose and tail on it than the '66 car. I seem to remember it was something like 10 or 15 mph quicker on the straight than the '66 car. It was very quick and I remember it going something like 230mph. The downside was that there was really no such thing as downforce in those days, it was just minimizing the lift, and it certainly wasn't as stable at high speeds as the '66 car."

There were aero issues with the car that caused serious handling issues in the region of 180mph that then smoothed out again over 200. Amon – "Towards the end of the straight, you had that very high speed right hand corner (the Mulsanne Kink). It was ok flat because you'd gone through that stage where it was

321

squirrely." So, the last thing you'd want to do was to lift for the Kink, as it would then place you into the squirrely zone? Chris – "Exactly."

All this aero development was to pale in comparison to the radical pace of development in the United States by Chaparral Cars. Their Chaparral 2 with the nose mounted aero trim tabs generated front downforce, along with the rear spoiler which eventually became an adjustable wing at the end of the rear engine cover with the 2C.

The Chaparral 2 influenced a generation of racing car designers

Mario Andretti had been paying attention to the design features on these innovative cars from Texas, as well as the Kamm tails of the Le Mans prototypes of the era. Mario – "In 65 and 66 we had the Brawner Hawk, and the big problem we had with that car was the gearbox overheating because of the shrouding of the bodywork in the back was too close and there was no airflow whatsoever, so they decided to make a much bigger body for 1967. We thought we'd give it a ducktail, to give it some shape like on the sports cars we'd been driving. So, I'm shaking the car down in Phoenix just before it gets shipped to Trenton and it's flying the front end. We realized that we were getting downforce in back and were panicking over what in the hell we were going to do."

As with their rear bodywork, the team took another lesson from the innovative sports car designs of the day. Mario – "I remembered watching the Chaparrals with their chin spoilers, so along with Jim McGee we just made some kind of cardboard spoilers for the nose. They were going to make them in fiberglass for Trenton, but they were running out of time, so they made 'em out of wood. When they showed up at Trenton the nose weighed about 30 pounds... I was so upset. But, the shape of it was there, and I went out and set a track record. For the next race they made them lightweight, out of fiberglass. We were the first ones to actually use that with a single seat car."

Ride height was another key consideration with aero setup, especially on high speed ovals. Joe Leonard reflects upon the early Gurney Indy Eagle of 1966, which he drove at Indianapolis. "It was a bad car, Len Terry did the engineering and he decided to raise it up. At Indy, if you can lower your car 1/16th of an inch, you gain 2 miles per hour."

Jim Hall's legendary success with the 1964-65 Chaparrals proved that his aerodynamic concepts worked, and the next step was the radical 1966 Chaparral 2E Can-Am car, with its high wing. The system was operated by a pedal which when depressed would trim to a near-zero downforce configuration. Moving from the wing pedal to the brake pedal dropped the wing into maximum downforce, the struts connected directly to the rear uprights, so as not to compromise suspension movement. A technical tour-de-force, it was years ahead of its time, fully 2 years ahead of when Formula One adopted high wings mid-way through the 1968 season.

When you stood on the wing pedal on the 2E, it also closed the nose inlets for more top speed. Chaparral team driver in 1966-7 and 1961 Formula One World Champion, Phil Hill, confirms the innovations of the car. "It did, it was an invisible aerodynamic thing. It was great, and the 2F was even more so. It had combination mechanical and spring loaded gadgets in the front rather than just mechanical to close the openings in the mouth of the car. A spring loaded door. Actually, it wasn't the radiator outlet (or inlets) any more. The radiators had been moved to the rear of the car in front of the rear wheels. The closed inlets were there to deflect air over and under the car, and these were closed off in unison with the big wing on top."

What was the paddock reaction to first sight of the high wing Chaparral 2E at the first Can-Am of 1966? Chris Amon – "It was something else, mind blowing at the time. It showed where Jim Hall and his guys were at really, great thinkers. It probably didn't give them the advantage that you would have expected it to have done. Maybe they never had enough front downforce to counterbalance the rear? I can remember Bruce (McLaren) saying 'My God, what are we going to do now?' Jim did some amazing things."

Chris Amon looks back upon the Chaparral 2F endurance racer from 1967 with similar wonder. "My most vivid memory of that car was at Brands Hatch, which was a bumpy track. That thing at Brands was just unstoppable. To develop that into an endurance car with the degree of reliability that they managed to achieve was huge. Jim Hall certainly had a great operation."

This innovative machine also had some spectacular failures. In 1966's season finale at Stardust Raceway in Las Vegas, the wing control broke on the 2E, the broken wing flipping back & forth with the angle of attack going from full downforce to full lift. What was that like to hang on to? Phil Hill – "That was terrible. I came into the pits and they took the wing off. That was like sending somebody out with a loaded revolver." One can only imagine the handling of the car sans wing, when the chassis was setup for maximum rear aero downforce in the corners, and to achieve a balanced setup the chassis would have had massive oversteer without the wing. The Chaparral 2E/2F/2G series of cars had blazed this aerodynamic path from 1966-68, and Formula One was to follow in their footsteps during the 1968 season. The downside of the Chaparral experience was nothing in comparison to the catastrophic high wing failures that plagued Team Lotus in 1968-69, comprehensively destroying the Lotus 49 of Jackie Oliver in practice for the 1968 French GP.

Jim Hall with his 1966 Chaparral 2E Can-Am car

Jackie Oliver – "It (the high wing) was the right thing to do, but we were like test pilots in those days. They just stuck it on the car and asked if it was better or if it was worse. It was better. Colin stuck one on my car at the French Grand Prix, and I suspect it was too high and too fragile, and I had a big accident opposite the pits. I think the rear wing fell over backwards and as it went over it picked the rear wheels off the ground. It was such a big accident, you just wouldn't know. They were the first experiments in aerodynamics with an aerofoil shape. Everybody understands airflow now, but then they didn't really understand it. This had been around with airplanes for years, but they didn't realize it would work well on race cars when going upside down… flying into the ground. They shortened them, and then they ended up banning them."

At Monza in 1968, always having something new with which to dazzle the Tifosi at home, Ferrari had the debut for a new hydraulically controlled rear wing (above the engine) that was connected to the brake pedal as well as the shift lever… and was also equipped with a manual override. Chris – "It was hydraulic. If you were in first, second, or third gear, the wing was automatically down, or when you hit the brake pedal it came down. When you got off the brake pedal in the higher gears, the wing would come back up again. It's amazing how quickly you get used to these things, and I'd pretty much operate it with the (override) button all the time. It was good to have the automatic mode, as I think it was a backup in case you forgot, but it quickly became second nature." Probably easier to remember what the button does, when you don't have thirty four buttons like on the modern F1 car steering wheel. Chris – "(laughing) we had one."

The front row at Monza had every variety of aero package imaginable. On pole was John Surtees in the Honda, with its high rear wing mounted to the uprights (unsprung downforce), and small trim tabs on either side of the nose. Chris Amon was on the outside of the front row with a hydraulically operable small rear wing mounted above the engine onto the chassis (sprung downforce) and small trim tabs off the side of the nose. In the middle of the front row was Bruce McLaren, running no wings at all. Each car would have its great aero strength. The Honda was best of all in the corners, the Ferrari strong everywhere but not stellar anywhere, and the McLaren a rocket on the straight when it wasn't falling over itself trying to keep pace with the winged cars in the curves.

Chris – "Yes, it was a bit like that, but that Honda had a lot of straight line speed anyway, so John could run a bit of drag because the thing really had a lot of horsepower." Everything sounds all well and good for the Ferrari approach, as long as the system worked. As had happened with Phil Hill at Stardust raceway in the '66 Can-Am, Chris had his turn to experience total failure of the wing control system during the '68 Italian Grand Prix. Chris – "I had activated the wing going into the first Lesmo because in those days the Curve Grande was sort of flat so you were doing 200-odd mph by the time you got to Lesmo. I put the wing down and I had the oil line fail to the wing. It just swapped ends, hit the guardrail running backwards and the posts blew up. I did a quadruple summersault through the trees. What caused the accident was that one of the guys hadn't done up one of these oil lines where it came off the oil pump on the side of the engine. He had done it up finger tight and got distracted and never got to tightened it with the spanner. It was the only time that something like that happened in my entire time at Ferrari."

Mario Andretti had also practiced with the Lotus 49 sans wings at Monza in 1968, when some teams ditched the wings in favor of less drag on the high speed Italian circuit. He then drove the high wing Lotus 49 at Watkins Glen, putting the car on pole for his first Grand Prix start. Similar to Jackie Oliver's car in France, the high wing 49 had the struts from the wing mounted directly to the uprights, transferring the downforce directly to the un-sprung wheel/tire assembly, not compressing the suspension of the chassis. Mario – "Exactly, that's the way to do it. You had the downforce directly on the un-sprung weight, and the car was still soft enough to negotiate the slow corners where the downforce is at a minimum. So, you had the best of both worlds."

What was it like to step into a high wing car for the first time? How long did it take for a driver to begin to explore where these new limits were given the vast improvements in cornering speed made possible. Mario – "Well, you just go by the seat of the pants. We all try to have the best possible feel for the car's limit of adhesion; it's just a higher limit. That's what downforce does for you... you get to that level and then you say 'I can go faster next lap', until the next lap and you are too fast (laughs)."

The front wings of the 49 were essentially dive planes mounted on either side of the standard car's nose, and on the sprung portion of the car. Any downforce created would have been acting to compress the front suspension vs. the un-sprung application of downforce at the rear of the car. Also given the comparative size of the wings involved, the center of aerodynamic pressure would be well back in the car. Was chronic understeer at speed a characteristic of the late 1968 version of the Lotus 49? Mario – "No, not necessarily… we found a balance, and that was enough. The car actually was very nice to drive; there was nothing unusual about it from that standpoint." Jackie Oliver – "You could adjust it, that's the thing with the wings. You stuck the aerodynamics on the back and the front and then could adjust it."

Brabham took the same concept to the next degree with the Biplane, which had its debut at Monza in 1968. Having a similar rear wing mounting at the uprights, their high front wing instead mounted where the suspension connected to the tub. As with the late 1968 Lotus 49, it had unsprung downforce at the rear, with sprung downforce at the front. Why wouldn't one attach the high wing to the front upright for optimized unsprung downforce at each end of the car? Mario – "That's a good question. In those days… at that point, it was in the infancy of the aerodynamic package for the single seat car. If you think about it, since there was no rule to prohibit that, why wouldn't you have that connect to the uprights? Well, it probably would have made the car so positive to drive, so twitchy down the straightaway, that it was undriveable." Perhaps the steering would also have been too heavy? Mario – "Probably that too, but it would have made it too positive, very quick on turn-in and all of the undesirable parts which would have negated the secure feel that you'd get from the rear wing. I'm fairly sure that would have been the case, and I'm sure that Colin (Chapman) thought about that when they tested, but I was not part of that development."

Jackie Oliver – "It wasn't the best solution, the best solution would be to have the downforce on the unsprung part of the car, but you couldn't do it on the front very easily. The trouble was that with the front wheels steering, where can you put the load? At the back it was easy, but at the front it was much more difficult as the fixed part of the suspension was inside the front wheels." This configuration of high rear wing along with front bodywork mounted dive planes, allowed Team Lotus to win the 68 Championship for Graham Hill, and that was also was used to great effect by Jochen Rindt in the Tasman series of early 1969.

Interestingly, when the Lotus 49 adopted a high front wing for the 1969 F1 season at the season opener at Kyalami, it was mounted far outboard on the front suspension alongside the uprights vs. the inboard attachment of the Brabham. Another difference was that the Lotus also had dive planes of varying length mounted onto either side of the nose (one suspects the variety of dive plane lengths used by Rindt, Hill, and the customer car of John Love, were a driver preference item). Colin Chapman, always at the forefront of adopting innovative technology, with all of the resultant risk and benefit, had taken the design to what he likely saw as its ultimate configuration. This next generation high wing Lotus 49 might be best described as a Triplane, adding both additional sprung and unsprung downforce to the front. It was not a great success, as not only was Jack Brabham's Biplane on pole position, but Jackie Stewart's extensively redesigned Matra MS10 with a similar wing configuration to Tauranac's Biplane, dominated the race. It appeared that sprung downforce at the front was the superior solution.

Ron Tauranac, the designer of the Biplane Brabham, explains his concept of sprung downforce at the front and un-sprung with the rear. "The Biplane was a long time ago & was short lived because of regulatory changes. Putting the wing on the uprights puts the load direct on to the ground via the tires. This is good for the rear as it does not reduce the ground clearance.

There are many reasons for not doing it at the front. One: putting the wing load on the chassis reduces the ground clearance at the front providing chassis rake which improves down force from the chassis under side. Two: by un-weighting the inside front wheel in cornering the weight is transferred diagonally to the outside rear, this reduces the tendency to over steer when applying power on corner exit. Three: with the front uprights swiveling to steer, it would be difficult to provide a safe connection from the wing to the upright." It is interesting to note Ron's comments about chassis rake given the early season controversy over the similar rake used with the 2011 Red Bull RB7 F1 car, showing that some ideas aren't always as revolutionary as they may seem.

Ferrari meanwhile was struggling to find a better mousetrap in the wake of Amon's horrendous crash from wing system failure at Monza. Chris – "Interestingly, during the Tasman Series in 1969, we had a fixed wing on the Dino. The principal competition was Rindt and Hill in those Lotus 49s with their huge suspension mounted wings. We were really struggling with the Ferrari because of the drag from the wing in a straight line. One of my New Zealand mechanics developed a system using 2 actuating solenoids off a truck. They developed it between the 3rd and 4th race in the back of a utility truck. He had it so that if you held the button, it kept the wing up, going down the straights. When you let go of the button, it was exactly like the Chaparral (2F), and the wing would go into the down position. It was actually a much better system that what we had on the Formula One car. I think we would have put that onto the Formula One car later in the season, but after Lotus had their problems in Barcelona, the wings were banned."

As Amon had referred to, the high wing era of Formula One was about to come to an end when the GP circus arrived at the bumpy and twisty Montjuich Park in Barcelona for the Spanish Grand Prix. Lotus reverted to the nose with the largest dive planes, extended almost to the front wheel centerlines, likely having determined along with the other manufacturers that the front sprung downforce configuration was the best option. The car was again similar to the late 1968 configuration only with an even larger high rear wing connected to the uprights. One is reminded of a particular exchange after the British GP in 1968. Chris Amon – "After Brands in 1968, somebody said to Colin Chapman, 'weren't you afraid that the Ferrari would get past you'? He (Chapman) said 'Oh, Amon can't pass people.' My response to that was 'Nobody in their right mind would follow a Lotus that closely, in case something fell off."

Interestingly, Sir Jackie Stewart had brought the new Matra MS-80, which was designed for high wings front and rear in the same configuration as the final version MS-10, yet the MS-80 raced with only the high rear wing mounted at Barcelona. Jackie – "That was the biplane thing. Yes, we felt it was too dangerous. I had them off. But, we knew that the rear end (needed it), because of wheelspin. Keep in mind that there was no aerodynamic technology around at that time… these wings just did it." With just the high rear wing in place, Stewart won at Monjuich Park in the Grand Prix debut for the Matra MS-80.

Jackie Stewart – "That was the race where Jochen and Graham crashed when the wings broke, big accidents on the very fast part of the circuit. The wings were just ridiculous; it was a short lived so-called improvement." Graham Hill's rear wing had failed at speed, followed a few laps later by an identical wing failure on teammate Rindt's car at the same point of the circuit, and his Lotus 49 then cannoned into the barriers. Even the typically more conservative and stout Brabham design was similarly affected at Montjuich Park, and Jacky Ickx also suffered a rear wing failure.

This series of mishaps eventually led the FIA to ban the high wings from Formula One after the first practice session of the Monaco Grand Prix weekend, less than one year after they had first appeared on the scene. Jackie Stewart – "Of course, it was quite a big change for a car suddenly to be wingless, after having been set up for wings."

Tony Adamowicz was the American Formula A Champion in 1969 with his Gurney Eagle, also equipped with a high rear wing on upright mounted struts, and dive planes on the nose. Tony – "Where things got really bad back in that period was when a lot of the manufacturers started going lightweight on the struts. It was not the area to try and save weight. We never had a failure with the Eagle."

Tony Adamowicz's Formula A Championship winning Eagle

Were there efforts to go the Biplane approach in F5000? Tony – "It was allowed, but the problem was where you mount these wings, structurally. First of all you have to look at the application. Running the struts down to the rear uprights was relatively easy. It was experimentation back in the day because nobody really knew, nobody had definitive accurate information, and it was always a guess.

In 2011, Adamowicz was to find that running the original un-modified 1969 high wing configuration had been an accident waiting to happen. Tony – "Thank God for pictures as we could see at Watkins Glen, they (the vertical struts) were bending. We put a ¾" tubing down inside the 1" equivalent streamlined tubing and welded it. A picture tells a thousand words. It didn't have drag links; we (recently) added those from the roll hoop back to the vertical struts to keep the wing from having any chance of wanting to tip. It had to work with the suspension so that it moved in the same plane, not changing the wing angle."

1969 was also a year of high rear wings throughout the Can-Am field, mounted thru the bodywork to the rear uprights, with one prominent exception. Why did the Ferraris persist in continuing with the chassis mounted rear wings, when the entire rest of the paddock had gone to the unsprung downforce upright mounted configuration? Chris Amon – "Ferrari wouldn't. Pretty much from the first time we ran wings at Spa in '68, Ferrari said that we will not have wings mounted onto the suspension. With the Formula One cars on a bumpy circuit like Brands Hatch, the Lotus with the big suspension mounted wing was just phenomenal. We could run with them, but it was a real struggle. It wasn't just having to run higher spring rates, in those days the suspensions had quite a bit of camber change, particularly with the little Dino. We were getting a lot of negative camber going down the straights, because the wing was pushing the chassis down, which in turn was giving us a lot of camber change. It was a real problem." The downside of large chassis mounted rear wings continued…

Chris Amon – "Early-on in the Can-Am series during 1969 I told them that unless we had a suspension mounted rear wing we are absolutely dead ducks. It was going to be difficult enough to beat the McLarens anyway, or to even run with them. Ferrari said 'you get one made in America and I don't want to know about it.' And we did, so the 613 had the suspension mounted wing. It made a huge difference. But, you know, Ferrari was an amazing guy. He knew those things were dangerous and ultimately of course he was proved absolutely right."

Although Ferrari was no fan of the upright mounted high

wings, did Ferrari ever run a high front wing connected to the tub like the biplane pioneered by Brabham? Chris – "I don't think we did. Piers Courage ran in the Tasman with one for Frank Williams, but I'm not convinced that it did much more than the nose spoilers. Unless you were in traffic, the nose mounted spoilers were running in clean air. But I never really thought those high front wings gave you any advantage. It was different at the rear, as of course a low rear wing wasn't running in clear air. However a high rear wing was in clean air, which was advantageous.

At the end of the 1969 season, the high wings were banned from the Can-Am series and F5000. It was the end of an era, but it wasn't long before the next aero leap forward started to creep into the sport.

For 1970, March introduced their first F1 car, the 701. This car had inverted wing bodywork extending out from each side of the monocoque, between the wheels. It was essentially a ground effects car, without the outer sidepod fences that would have somewhat sealed the "tunnel" and forced the air across the bottom of the wing section, instead of spilling off the side. Mario Andretti drove the STP March 701 in 1970 – "We were testing in South Africa with the March 701. I was not thinking of the aerodynamic downforce, I was more thinking of the drag factor. We were down on power because of altitude, so I said 'We should just free the car up from a drag standpoint... why don't we take off the sidepods?' The sidepods weren't doing anything; there was nothing in them, no fuel or anything... it was aesthetics. Those sidepods had the shape of a wing, and as soon as we took them off, the car really flew the front end, and we had to use a lot more front wing, and that was a drag penalty. This means the sidepods were producing downforce and had moved the center of pressure forward. Removing them lost that and moved the center of pressure back, so we put them back on... those pods were functional."

Chris Amon was now Mario's teammate at March, since he had just left Ferrari. "I'd actually signed a contract for 1970, but I was getting so disillusioned, with the flat 12 breaking and I thought that I couldn't stand another year of frustration. I went to Ferrari and told him that I thought it would be better for both of us, if I moved on. One of the parts of the agreement to let me break the contract was that I would still do some sports car races for them, so I did Brands and Monza. Ferrari said to me as we parted company... 'I'll win a race before you do.' He was part right, because he won a Grand Prix before I did, but I won a Formula One race before they did (winning Silverstone's non-championship race in a March 701). As the years went by, a lot of my decisions were brought out of frustration... I never should have left Ferrari."

The March 701 contained the secret that only Andretti noticed. He was to use that knowledge to great effect with the Lotus 78

Chris Amon, known for his testing skills, also had the opportunity to note the advantages of the March sidepod, but it passed un-noticed. "I don't remember ever running without them actually. I can remember Mario running without them, and

I think we would have taken some interest in that at the time, but I don't remember it ever being talked about. Of course, I've blocked out much of that very frustrating year as I spent most of it arguing with Max Mosley, and in that I certainly wasn't alone. Leaving March was an easy decision."

The March 701 was also raced by Jackie Stewart, but he and Ken Tyrrell never saw the car as anything but a solution born of desperation. Jackie – "Well, there was nobody else who would sell us a car. Lotus wouldn't sell us a car, and neither would Brabham. I think to be frank with you that we realized very early on that the March wasn't going to be something we could live with for long. It was quite quick, I put it on the pole for it's first-ever race, which was the GP of South Africa in 1970. I also won the Spanish Grand Prix, which was the only Grand Prix that it won. By the middle of the season, Ken Tyrrell decided that he couldn't race it anymore, so we kind of accepted that it was going to be a bad year. It was a frustrating experience to drive it. I'd had a bad year before, with the H-16 BRM, but the Matra had shown itself for 2 years, both in 68 and 69, as 2 great cars (MS-10, MS-80). But '70 was a disaster, and it was not a good car to drive. I don't think we ever took off the sidepods, I don't recall that at all." The aero potential in those inverted airfoil sidepods had only been noted by Andretti.

Multi-element wings had yet to make an impact, although anyone who looked at an airplane wing at landing or takeoff could see the slot and 2nd element positioning when a high lift configuration was called for. Jochen Rindt was to win the 1970 Monaco Grand Prix with a 3 element rear wing for the Team Lotus 49 mounted over the engine cover/rear wheels, a design feature of the upcoming Lotus 72. The Lotus wing resembled an inverted venetian blind as much as anything else, vs. what eventually became more standard, a main element with a smaller rear element. Such a dual-element rear wing had its debut on the flat 12 Ferrari later in 1970.

For 1971, Andretti had signed to drive the Ferrari flat 12 F1 car, taking his first F1 victory in South Africa. Mario - "They had a boxer, and the good thing about the boxer engine is the center of gravity is nice and low. But the rest of it... we were still in the infancy of wing development, and quite honestly the rear wing was too far forward, forward of the rear axle and was not all that effective." Ever consider taking the sidepod design from that previous year's 701 March and sticking them on the Ferrari? Mario – "Never crossed my mind... no."

1972 had been a year of massive speed increases at Indianapolis, and Jerry Grant was to turn the first 200 mph lap in a Gurney Eagle with a wide and rearward mounted 2 element rear wing. Robert (Bob) Liebeck was one of the many aerodynamicists who came directly from the aviation industry.

Liebeck's wing on Jerry Grant's Eagle was the first to break 200mph average speed on an oval, at Ontario Motor Speedway

Bob - "I was working for McDonnell Douglas, and I did it (work for Gurney) as a consultant after hours. They were just starting with multi-element wings, and what they were doing at the time was copying airplane wings. It's like on a transport airplane so that this flap could be retracted and then you get a smooth conventional airfoil rather than one with all this camber. When you see the flaps go up, they all fair in."

Looking at Jerry Grant's 1972 Eagle that turned the first 200mph average lap, Bob remarks – "If you were doing it right, this hump (at the exit of the main element) would not be in there. But, this worked ok... he went 200mph with it." Dan Gurney – "To push that car to that speed with very little practice means that you had to have enormous confidence backed up with the ability to do it. You were into territory that all the best in the business had never been into before."

Bob Liebeck – "Another thing is the leading edge of this wing I did modify and gave it more what I'll call 'nose camber', so that the flow would stay attached... and it worked. The only thing modified on this over an airplane wing was the leading edge, as it drooped up. It comes up more than a stock wing." Bob confirms that the multiple vertical strakes that occur every foot of wing width weren't used for aero effect. "They were just for support." The world of straked wings and diffusers was to be far into the future.

Pointing at the rear vertical piece at the trailing edge of the smaller rear element, Bob relates how for once racing cars influenced aviation. That is rare. Bob - "Yes it is. This was the phenomenal thing, called a 'Gurney Flap'. Dan was the creator of this in 1971. I just went back to the wind tunnel at McDonnell Douglas and confirmed. I tested this on just a single airfoil and you get more lift and lower drag. Now, all cars do this. Later we put it on the MD-11, but we built it in so that it is a trailing edge wedge (vs. vertical lip). At Boeing now, the 747-8 has this."

Bob – "The way Dan encountered this, was he had a Ferrari

coupe, and he was all over the road on the Mulsanne straight. He decided to put a piece on the tail that went straight up. All of a sudden, 2 things happened. The car went straight, and it reduced the drag so that it went faster. So, then he said (looking at the Eagle rear wing), 'why not do this?'

Another advantage of the Gurney Flap is that you can quickly change to different heights. Bob - "What it does is think of a wing the right side up. When you go to high lift, the flow doesn't want to stay attached to the upper surface. The aft facing step of this has very low pressure. You'd think this would be 'draggy', but it's more 'draggy if the flow is separated. Having that low pressure area behind, reduces drag and adds downforce. I published a technical paper on this in 1973, and I looked the other day at the number of Masters and Phd's that had been written on Gurney Flaps... I mean he's a legend in aerodynamics for this. I manage an airplane program at Boeing and teach aerospace engineering at UCI (Irvine) and MIT... this thing is magic, aerodynamically."

Bobby Unser reflects on his early days at Leader Card Racing and the difference when he arrived at AAR. "We were a small company, and I went to a giant company. One who had the ability and had some real live engineers, the ones that can make things go faster. They had fabricators who could make the stuff that believed in you. We could make the thing go fast because we were in the high-tech part of the industry. And it wasn't just the Gurney flap; it was what the Gurney flap went on. No human being on earth tested as many wings as I did. Dan had good people, he had the world by the ass, and he was so smart himself. But I wasn't nearly as smart with the '72 Eagle, as I was when the PC-7 came along."

A few years later, the sidepod of the March 701 again crossed Mario's mind at a Team Lotus brainstorming session and the resultant design was the most aerodynamically significant car of the 1970s, the Lotus 78. When Mario arrived at Lotus in early/ mid 1976, the Lotus 77 was anything but a clean effective design, with the front rocker arm suspension and exposed shock/spring unit mounted directly in the airflow, outboard of the tub. Mario – "Colin knew it; we knew we were stuck with that car. We said 'Let's make the best of it, finish off the season.' We got better and better with it, got some podiums and did finish off the season with a win, but we just improved the car mechanically." Turning to the Lotus 78, Mario explains the genesis of that landmark car – "Let me explain something, and this is something that for some reason, some people have amnesia about. At the end of 1976, at the end of that season with Lotus, we all sat in a room back at the factory in Hethel... the Engineers and I were there, and there was a general conversation about a wish list for what we'd drive for the next year. At that point we were really searching for the aerodynamics, and I made some comments about how nice it would be to have downforce without a drag penalty. Then I brought up something to Colin..." Mario told about his experiences six years previous at Kyalami in testing, when the March 701 sidepods had produced downforce. Andretti – "I told Colin that it would be more effective if we put fences on them, and that's how the Lotus 78 was built. Colin had expanded upon it with much bigger sidepods, as the March's were relatively small, and Colin put a fence down the whole side. We were testing in Hockenheim and in the Bosch curve, the right turn at the end of the straight, I noticed that when the car would roll, that I was really gaining some downforce on the left side of the car. So, Colin quickly sent the boys into town to buy several sheets of plastic and he closed the gap (between the sidepod outer fence and the ground)."

The rapid development of the sidepod skirt had begun. Mario – "I went out there and the car felt fabulous for about 2 laps. They (the skirts) would wear, and the grip would disappear. Colin didn't know what to do, so he put brushes on there. It diminished the effect, but it remained more constant. For a couple of races, the brushes, that's what we had. We tried rubber, but instead of being straight it was at an angle so it would flex and not really wear out right away…we had all kinds, but ultimately wear out toward the later part of the race when you really needed the downforce. In those days, like today, you had to run a full fuel load that would run the distance, which means the car was quite heavy and lower at the start. You were really wearing the skirts off in the first 10 or 15 laps of the race. As the car got lighter, the gap got bigger and bigger… until he came up with the moveable skirt, the sliding skirt which was the ultimate."

The moveable skirt would ride up and down within a track on the inside of the fence, keeping an aerodynamic seal on the sidepod. At speed, the car could drive on the ceiling, so great was the downforce created. The sliding skirt ground effects cars of the late 1970s generated so much aero grip, it was said that there literally might be no limit as to the potential cornering speed on high speed sweepers, with sufficient downforce from the underbody aerodynamics. In the Ost Curve in the pre-chicane Hockenheim, the cars would turn into the corner at maximum velocity, a concept previously unthinkable. Mario Andretti – "Obviously with the speed the downforce increases just because of the air velocity. But, there is a limit somewhere, regardless."

The Lotus 78 was a game changer, although it had a primary weakness. The center of pressure of the sidepods was too far forward, and required running a large rear wing to balance the car. Mario –"That was the big drag penalty, the Lotus 78 was just a brick down the straightaway… it was terrible. The car was just barely finished in time for the start of the season." However, Mario's 77 season was almost over before it started, when the fire extinguisher exploded alongside the footbox during practice in Argentina. "They had put the fire extinguisher right behind the oil cooler in the front, never realizing the temperature factor… there was no effort to measure it. Argentina was in the heart of the summer, and it was blazing hot during that practice day. The thing blew up like a bomb, and busted the pedals so I had no brakes at the end of the pit straight. Luckily it was a pretty fast right/left and it blew up early enough that I was able to downshift like crazy and make it through. I broke a bone in my right foot, but I still raced with a fiberglass sole in my shoe." Many saw the new car as big trouble for the competition. Chris Amon – "The Lotus 78… that was unstoppable."

Mario Andretti won 4 Grand Prix in the 1977 season, including what remains the only win for an American driver in the long history of the Formula One United States Grand Prix (USGP West – Long Beach). Teammate Gunnar Nilsson also won the Belgian Grand Prix at Zolder, and with 5 wins, Lotus finished 2nd to Ferrari in the Constructor's championship. Mario had finished 3rd in the Driver's Championship, Nilsson in 8th. Better things were on the horizon for Team Lotus.

The next generation was the iconic John Player Special that brought Andretti his World Championship, the Lotus 79. The sidepod tunnels were extended into the rear section of the car, to move the center of pressure back on the car. Mario – "Yeah, we were learning more and more about it. We were trying to get the center of pressure much closer to the middle of the car, so we won't have to use so much rear wing to balance the car." The car was immediately a pace setter, and across the season, the Lotus 79 was dominant.

In Sweden, Gordon Murray's Brabham fan car made its F1 debut; essentially a similar concept to the sucker car built and campaigned by Chaparral in the 1970 Can-Am series, with a large powered exhaust fan mounted at the rear of the car. The vacuum created literally sucked the car down to the track, vs. using aerodynamic means to achieve the needed downforce. As with Jim Hall's Chaparral 2J, the car was greeted with derision, as the car tended to vacuum the track while depositing all the clag and debris into the face of the following driver. While Lauda in the Brabham sucker car had defeated Andretti in that year's Grand Prix of Sweden, it was to be the only time the car was permitted to compete.

The dominant car of 1978 – Colin Chapman's Lotus 79

One cannot mention Andretti's championship year with the Lotus 79 without giving a nod to his teammate, the great Swedish driver Ronnie Peterson, who had returned to drive for Lotus in what was to be Colin Chapman's and Lotus' final World Championship. Mario - "We were really good friends, I definitely liked the man in every way. We were totally honest with one another, which is not always the case. Ronnie was one of those drivers who would compensate with his driving instead of trying to help himself with the chassis. He was not very technically minded, and he was basically running my setup… but my setup was changing through the weekend." It was one of the great tragic ironies from that era of Grand Prix racing, as Mario's clinching the title at Monza coincided with the death of his teammate the following morning from complications suffered during a first lap crash in the Italian Grand Prix.

Sadly, it was a similar experience to that of Ferrari's Phil Hill, the only other American World Champion, who had lost his teammate Wolfgang Von Trips to a savage crash in the 1961 Italian GP at Monza, the race where Hill clinched his World

Championship. History had repeated itself in the worst of ways. In a double blow to the Formula One fans of Sweden, Gunnar Nilsson died a month later, a victim of testicular cancer. The Grand Prix of Sweden was never held again, the event simply unable to recover from the loss of both of their national heroes in rapid succession.

The following season in America, Rick Mears was driving the previous seasons' non-ground effects Penske PC-6 in the 1979 Indianapolis 500, during those early days for ground effect car developments at the superspeedway. Was the combination of the two design philosophies a dangerous mix? Rick – "There was probably not as much as you'd think, because we were on the early edge of the ground effects. After year or two of development of the ground effects car, it would probably have been... but back then we were just getting our feet wet with ground effects. The PC-7 that Bobby (Unser) was working on, that we called our 'semi-ground effects car'... our first attempt. Being really early in the development, we didn't understand the center of pressure, or what moved the center of pressure. It was trial and error, and we were just getting into it. We were all over the map with it, and what was the right center of pressure one day, was the wrong one on others depending upon springs, setup, length of tunnel, where the leading edge was removed, the shape of the leading edge, the shape of the top of the radiator... it all came into play. With those blocks you could stack them in different ways, but it took a while to figure out the best way to stack those blocks. There just wasn't a huge gain at that point."

Rick reflects upon his decision to run the old car. "The main reason I wasn't in that car the first year, was that Roger gave me a choice. I was new... I was still really green and had been running the PC-6 for a year. From their standpoint, they didn't know if the 7 would go all day or a half-day or whatever. Because I was familiar with the 6 and knowing what I had, I stayed with it. Bobby had done all the testing (on the PC-7), he didn't want me testing or getting any more experience than I absolutely had to get. Teammates… he had done all the development on it. Bobby would say, 'I wasn't put here on this earth to make Rick Mears go fast.' I understood, as your teammate is always your biggest competitor."

Bobby Unser – "I put in thousands of hours testing that car, it wasn't good when we started out… there's no race car in history that was. That's what I did for a living… but I ended up with the best one, how come he wanted one of mine? That car was 100% ground effects, we had sliding skirts on it, that thing was at the top of the development all the time. All the ground effects stuff was done in Albuquerque, I had a small wind tunnel, 1/6th scale, and I built the models. It never quit going on, it was going all the way through to the PC-10. I did all the wings, and I did all the tunnels… Superflow made it, and I converted it. The idea was that your downforce underneath was somewhat free (vs. with the wings), in other words… not much drag. This (the PC-7) was really a big test bed. You've got to remember that in the beginning with these things, we weren't any smarter than the hitchhiker on Hwy. 66. We had to learn it… trial and error."

Derrick Walker – "What Bobby Unser had was a device that would facilitate flowing air through cylinder heads, and he had made a makeshift wind tunnel out of it. He'd make a very small ground effect tunnel that he would put in this thing, and when the air would flow underneath it, he would measure the pressure, the vacuum effect of the air passing underneath this shape which vaguely resembled what the underbody did. He would flow these things night and day, and he would send things back to us and we'd make them in metal, as in those days we were making them so fast, and we weren't into carbon at that point. We'd try them on the car, and sometimes they'd kind of work, and sometimes they didn't. It was as basic as that."

Bobby Unser with the Penske PC-7 ground effects car

Bobby Unser had nothing like the usual relationship between development driver and team, as he had a significant role in the continuing re-configuration of the car. Unser - "I had a drawing board in Albuquerque that we could draw on. That's where my learning came from, at Penske they would let me do whatever I wanted. Colin Chapman came up with this stuff; all I did was to take his ideas and invented ways to go fast. I'd test the models, see which ones were good and send a design to Pennsylvania (Penske). 2 weeks later we would be testing it on a race track. For Jim Hall or Patrick, or anybody, it would take them a full year to do that. We'd do it in 2 weeks."

One notes that the PC-7 sidepod has a horizontal split where the lower ground effects section extends well forward of the air intake above, for the radiator. Bobby - "That was a trade-off.

The front tire is an air pump, not so much lift as drag from the air disturbance. I was trying (sidepods) that were skinny or wide. To go to the rules limit, or not? Ronnie and I, I'd guess we designed 50 of those."

Was there an advantage going to the maximum sidepod width despite the turbulence off the front tires? "Yes, for sure. Then we made a moving ground plane, to simulate being on the ground. John Barnard thought a moving ground plane was an effective thing and changed the numbers, so I made one. Talk is bullshit, just do it. I was looking at Formula One for the concept, not to see if it should be an inch longer or an inch wider. We had sliding skirts on this car (the PC-7), we had hundreds of tests." What was the wearing surface that the PC-7 ended up using? "I knew you were going to ask that, I've got them in my garage in Albuquerque. They were running the sliding skirts in 1979, and then the rules makers said 'no'. Now I had to design other types of skirts, and I went through more than you'd ever believe. I had to get them as close to the sliding skirt as I could, and we didn't have exact numbers like they have today. But I had good numbers... repeatable numbers. I was like Jessie James... I shot from the hip. I didn't finish high school, and wasn't as good an engineer as John Barnard, but I made the cars go fast."

Derrick – "The first ground effects car we did really wasn't full ground effects; it was a tunnel that we put on the bottom of the race car. I had photographs of Formula One cars and other such like the Chaparral (the 1979-81 John Barnard designed Yellow Submarine) later. The PC-6 went to a PC-7 from just basically raising the fuel cell up and we drew up an underbody, a tunnel underneath it The fuel cell instead of being down on the ground, on the flat bottom like the '6' was, it was raised up a couple of inches. We didn't have a wind tunnel program going in Europe; it was very much like 'seat of the pants'. We were starting to copy that Chaparral design, John Barnard's car. All that time we were just designing them as we thought they should look. We'd make them, put them on the car, measured them, tested them, measured them, and if it worked we stuck with it."

Walker - "A lot of things that Bobby tried, we tried. Some things sort of worked. But, there was probably more of it came from the drawings or just making it. We'd change profiles on Friday, and go find out actually what the shape did. We'd there is no way that everything that was designed for a Penske at that time, came out of Bobby's tunnel. There was a lot of stuff thrown at it by the designer of the car, me, and a couple of guys in the shop. Another thing that was going on, was as we were finding these big chunks of downforce, we were also finding the penalties that go with it. At that time most of the Penskes at that early stage were 'normal' race cars. There were rivets, aluminum, and steel bulkheads, and they flexed like crazy. So when we started to get bigger numbers of downforce, we found these things were flexy-fliers."

Would Bobby Unser give you a lot of stuff and some of his ideas made it onto the car? Roger Penske – "Bobby thought he did more than maybe he really did, but he was helpful. Some of it stuck on the wall…" It was one of the rare examples when a driver made a significant contribution to the design of a revolutionary car, whereas most are limited to providing feedback to the engineers and designers.

Roger Penske - "Bobby was a special guy; he always had stuff going on that he never told anybody about. He was a hell of a driver and the PC-7 was a great car. He helped us develop the front entrance with the small wing planes that we had at the entrance into our radiator, which was very key in the development of that car. We were very close and he did a great job for us."

Unser had found his perfect home at Team Penske. Bobby – "Ronnie Dawes and myself, we would make up sometimes one or two (underbodies) a day, working until about 1 in the morning on our wind tunnel. When we came up with something we thought was good, I'd send 1/6th scale drawings overnight to Penske

Racing in Reading, Pennsylvania, and then be finding a race track to try it at, could be Phoenix, or Ontario... my choice, I could do whatever I wanted at Penske. He would allow me that. Penske just let me do whatever I wanted to do. It was the first time I'd ever got that. I used to somewhat have that with Dan (Gurney), but not like with Roger." It sounds like Roger was getting a good return on this driver. Unser – "Well, he figured that out after about a year or so (laughs). Nah... he always was good, the easiest man I ever drove for in my life."

Roger Penske – A passion for searching out any advantage

Penske's legendary pairing with Mark Donohue was very much a similar situation. Roger - "Mark was very key... being an Engineer by trade from Brown University, and he really gave us a lot of input. We've had a lot of smart drivers… Gil de Ferran was also great at testing and helping us. Overall, we've got a lot of people doing their jobs, and I think Bobby was one of the greatest."

Given the challenges from all others on the grid, one would think that teammates increased their odds of success by working together. Mears – "Well, if they're smart they do. Working together with your teammate is how you lift your team above the other teams. That's why I fit in so well at Penske early on, and didn't really know why at the time. It was because my brother and I had always worked on the team concept way before I ever got to Indycar. We'd sit down and talk about what we were doing into turn 2, what we were doing into turn 3… what did the car do when you did this? We would help each other at night, because if we knew we could help each other to get an advantage over the rest of the field, all we'd have to do is to race each other and that would be a lot of fun. Emerson and I talked a lot about that sort of stuff, he and I thought along the same lines. He was really good as a teammate, I could count on him. We had similar feel, he'd go out and qualify after adding a turn of front wing, and I could go up to him and ask 'what did it do?' He'd say 'it did this here, this there'… and I knew that was what it did… we spoke the same language. So, I was comfortable putting that turn of wing in, and then going out and making my run. He understood the value of teammates working together, there was never any BS." Using the old Penske PC-6 to great effect, Rick Mears got his first of four Indy 500 victories in 1979.

By 1980, Mears was now in the ground effects Penske, while learning to adapt to the new world of setup. Mears – "When we started getting into ground effects, the aero was making the mechanical things work differently than they had worked in the past. With ground effects, you had to start stiffening things up to get grip, the opposite of what the rule of thumb is… soft is more grip, stiff is less grip. We didn't have that problem until we started sucking the things down and started bottoming out. Nothing was routine, the engineer would say to do 'this', and it might be the opposite of what I'd thought… I had to be open. But the first time, you had to think about it and put the trust in them that it would be ok, even if it was contrary to what you thought. I'd better be open to it, because they went to school for it, I didn't. So, it was a matter of me saying 'Yeah, do it, I'll try it, put it on.' You'd try something, and log what it does… and you might not use it for 3 or 4 races down the road when you might say 'the last time I felt this, we did that, and it affected this.'

Mears continues – "We were always trying something. One time at Michigan we were out to lunch, I had qualified lousy. The night before the race we decided that we had to do something, as we were just terrible. Normally, it would absolutely be only one making change at a time, but we were junk. So we built a new car overnight, reshaped the tunnels to move the center of pressure. Back in England they were just getting into the modeling, and we weren't sure we were fixing it; these were still the early days. We didn't have the telemetry to read what was going on where, as it was all trial and error… a best guess on shape from what we had learned so far. We changed spring, we changed wing angle… we changed everything on that car just before the race, started the race green with no practice. The first turn was interesting… believe me, I tiptoed."

Tales of the cars from this sliding skirt era border upon the realm of legend. One hears examples of where the limit might be 150mph for a combination of mechanical and aero grip for a given corner, as the car could not generate sufficient aero downforce at that speed to complete the corner any faster. However, the same corner could be taken at 170mph purely due to the increased aero downforce possible at that higher speed, if the driver could bring himself to pursue that leap in corner entry speed. Was it really that much of a leap of faith in the aero package to drive an early ground effects GP car at the limit? For

Mario Andretti, the answer was no. Mario – "Nah, that's something that never entered my mind. I think as a driver you have a feel for the limit of the grip and that's where you take it. If you improve the car on the mechanical side or the aero side, you just go faster."

Rick Mears concurs that it all just comes down to grip – "They used to say in the ground effects era, 'Oh my God, if you just get this car sideways you are gone.' They used that as a reason to do away with ground effects. Well, if I get the car so far sideways that the bottom isn't working anymore, I'm already gone. With a flat bottom car, I'd be gone too. A lot of that stuff was BS, grip is grip. The only times I can tell you the difference is if it affects my speed trap times. If you put on more wing and it didn't affect my drag and trap speed, you could have told me it was a softer tire or you could have told me it was a spring rate change… grip is grip. The only reason to differentiate between aero, mechanical or whatever, is that you are trying to make it more efficient… any combination of the above.

Does the car hit that magical endless aero loop where the faster it went, the more downforce it made, and the faster it went… and the more downforce it made? Rick – "It does compound itself to a point, but it always comes down to a combination of settings and getting a little bit more of an edge. It was that combination of cambers, toes, spring weights, tilt, whatever….coming up with a better combination."

There was a point where Mears almost joined Andretti during F1's sliding skirt era, as in 1980 he was auditioning for a future ride with the Brabham F1 team, testing the car that was to win the World Championship during the following season. Rick Mears – "I ran the car at Paul Ricard first. It was the right year, the right time, the right car, Nelson ended up winning the championship with that car and I'd have been his teammate the year he won. Ecclestone called me and said 'let's do a test.' I went to Roger and said that I've got an opportunity here to drive the Brabham and Roger being Roger said 'that's a decision you've got to make, I'm not going to keep you from doing it. Go do it.' Part of this was this wasn't long after CART and USAC had split. It was so early in the planning that I wasn't sure if CART was going to take off or not. I saw this as an opportunity to get my foot in the door someplace else, if CART didn't go. I went to Ricard and did the test, ran ¼ to ½ second off Nelson. The first time I got the thing warmed up and went into one, ran it in, downshifted and got on the brakes… it stopped so much quicker that I had to drop another gear, pick up the throttle and drive to the corner. You talk about grip, this had grip, and being lighter… their weight limit was 3 or 400 pounds lighter than ours with more grip… it stopped in a shorter distance."

Mears continues – "Bigger tires, bigger brakes, bigger tunnels, it had more everything… but it was still a race car, which was the best thing that I learned from it. If before I was going to brake at (shutoff marker) 4, now I'm going to brake at 2. If you can only brake at 4 and get through the corner on the limit, then that's what you do. It's all relative, and still about finding the limit."

The next test was on home turf for Mears. "Then we went to Riverside, I had been on their home track but now I was on a track that I knew. They had added chicanes, and it was basically a Weisemann gearbox test. I was 2 or 3 seconds ahead of Nelson around there. Once I drove the car, it was just a race car. Yeah, there's a lot of grip, but the only thing different is your numbers. If I had never driven a Formula One car that would have always been in the back of my head. The main thing for me was that I got it out of my system. Bernie and I had come to terms on everything with the contract, the money was good, and it was up to me to make the decision. I didn't need to prove anything to the world. I liked the Penske organization, and by then I could see CART was taking off."

Mario's final year at Lotus was to be 1980, with the Essex Lotus 81. "That car had the same problem as the 80 (see the

Chassis - Chapter 2). The 81 was a continuation, they sort of slimmed down the 79 and with very aggressive pods and diffusers. In fact it was so aggressive to obtain the ultimate downforce that we didn't have to run front wings." It was nearing the point that the wings were no longer used for downforce given the drag penalty, instead just being used to trim the car for balance.

There were some changes required in Mario's driving style during the sliding skirt era – "I always liked to use the curbs… I was one of the first guys to REALLY use the curbs, but you had to watch it, because if you stick a skirt up there… that's it." The sliding skirt seemed to provide the best of all solutions, until 1980 in a test at Hockenheim when a skirt on Patrick Depailler's Alfa-Romeo stuck in the up position. Entering the Ost Curve at maximum speed, the expected downforce was missing, and Patrick crashed to his death. As happens so often in racing, the loss of a competitor triggers the needed safety changes. Regulations were changed for the 1981 season, and sliding skirts were no longer allowed.

For 1981, Mario Andretti signed with Alfa Romeo, given their strong performance at the USGP (Watkins Glen) of 1980, with Bruno Giacomelli leading most of the race. "It was basically the same car. Mario - "It was electrical that put him out at the Glen, he just almost lead from flag to flag. I was thinking this was going to be Alfa Romeo's time to win some races, and that's why I joined. The big problem we had with the Alfa was that somebody decided to do a rule that minimized the ground effects by raising the cars. They would have a box that you had to clear on your way out of the pits, and a box to clear on the way into the pits."

The 2.5cm ground clearance rule led to some inventive cars such as Chapman's Lotus 88 twin chassis car, with the bodywork and tunnels independently sprung from the chassis. However, the one that was somehow deemed acceptable by the FIA was from Brabham's resident wizard, Gordon Murray. Mario – "Brabham, which was owned by Ecclestone, devised a hydraulic system for the first race in Argentina, whereby you would go out of the pits and then lower the car. When you came back to the pits, the hydraulic system would raise the car, and they allowed this system to be legal. For me, this was a big bone of contention, because Alfa Romeo knew that it was illegal (or should be). There was no way I could convince Carlo Chiti (team manager) to install something like that. He would not... Chiti just stubbornly dug his heels in, and I had some big arguments with him. So, we would run softer springs to suck the thing down to some degree, and it was just an awful waste of time and the car never would work."

A side effect of the hydraulic solution was that the cars would drop down onto their rock hard springs that would allow the ground effects sidepod bodywork to function for optimal effect while in near or full contact with the ground. Most of the suspension travel available was said to be the sidewall flex of the tires. Everything had deferred to aerodynamic advantage, except it appears, at Alfa Romeo.

Mario – "We were testing during that summer at Paul Ricard, and I said... 'Look, we're just testing... lets just run the car at the proper ride height that we should be running.' We were top 3 in times; all of a sudden we were quick and competitive. I said that was where we need to be, and still he would not install the hydraulic system. A couple of times I almost walked away and said 'I'm quitting.' At Belgium, in the morning practice, I was clamoring for a setup and Chiti would not give it to me. After practice, he then said 'Well, now you could do it, because we're in such trouble.' I told him 'You know what, I'm packing up... I'm leaving.' He chased me through the pits to get me to change my mind."

After the frustrations with Alfa the previous year, Mario was completely fed up with Formula One. "I was, to be honest with you... yeah." Mario Andretti had no full time ride in the 1982 Grand Prix season, although he got to race 2 of the most impressive cars of that era. First was the pull-rod suspension Williams FW08 at Long Beach, which was less than memorable when they ran a Willow Springs derived setup on the car. In 1980, Jan Lammers had shocked the paddock by putting an ATS on the 2nd row of the Long Beach grid, following a Willow test session. Showing the herd mentality that sometimes is F1, many teams scheduled pre-race testing at Willow Springs during the following years. In the case of the FW08, it simply didn't translate to the streets of Long Beach.

Fortunately there was to be a last hurrah at the track where Mario had first debuted in a F1 car (in practice with the Lotus 49 – 1968). It was also the track where as a child, Mario and his twin brother Aldo Andretti watched Ferrari's World Champion Alberto Ascari race in the 1954 Italian GP... Monza. Aldo – "As kids we were overwhelmed at the time, being there was a dream for us. We wanted to be involved so badly, but there was no way." Mario – "The first Formula One race that I ever saw was there, Ascari fighting with a Ferrari, an underpowered car at the time, fighting against the Mercedes of Fangio." The Andrettis had seen Ascari's last Italian Grand Prix. Mario's final Italian Grand Prix was also to be at Monza in a Ferrari, and it was to be memorable.

The Ferrari effort was more comprehensive than the Williams ride at Long Beach. "It was fast, I had tested at Fiorano with that car the week before. I arrived Saturday morning with the idea of shaking the car down a little bit, and then run a full day Sunday. I started feeling better and better with the car, and I ran 87 laps that day (Saturday). I got it exactly the way I wanted it, and at the end of the day we put a qualifying setup on it, I set an absolute track record that lasted four years. We didn't need to run on Sunday, I gave everybody the day off. The setup was a little bit different for Monza, but it was a known setup... the aerodynamics were a little bit different." Mario was ready for his final Grand Prix, the Italian GP.

When Mario says the aerodynamics were 'a little bit different' it was not an exaggeration. "In 1982 with the Ferrari at Monza, we ran the front wings reverse to create lift, not downforce... we had so much downforce in the front. A lot of people don't know that, and we weren't the only ones, either. Can you imagine if you lose a front wing? It would be like really pinning the front end. It was the complete opposite... if you lose the front wing now, you fly." Although this was fully 6 seasons into the era of ground effects design, the proper location for the center of aerodynamic pressure was still not well understood and in the case of the F1 Ferrari, it was centered well forward of the optimal location. Gradually it became clear that the optimal center of pressure was further back on the car, a lesson that could have been learned from the success of the high rear wings on the Chaparral 2E/2F or Lotus 49 from 15 years before.

The Malibu Grand Prix GTU team was another who took lessons from the Chaparral 2E/2F, in this case regarding the radiator closures. Phil Binks – "With the RX-7 at Daytona, they put a flapper valve in the radiator to limit the amount of air going to the radiator on the oval. A third sway bar link operated it, and it was good for 3 mph on the oval. On the banking you had the prototypes up high, then the 'Lights' cars, then GTO and down on the inside GTU. Well, this GTU car was going as fast at most of the Lights cars. It was so fast they couldn't stop it, Clayton had to go with water cooled calipers." Dan Binks – "It wasn't legal, but we did it. It worked off a sway bar adjuster in the car." Kind of like the wing pedal in the Chaparral? Dan – "Exactly... 3mph with an RX-7 was gigantic, it was a big deal."

Kendall remembers the radiator closure as serving a different purpose. Tommy - "What got us in trouble at Daytona was the mixture, we still had manual jetting and when it got cold it leaned out and hurt the engine. So, for '87 they came up with an adjustable mixture knob and a lever that closed off the radiator based upon the engine gas temperature. There was a lever to close off the radiator, used mainly for night running and pace cars to keep the engine from getting too cool. There were so many levers and gauges in the car, you couldn't tell if it was brake bias or sway bars or what… at last count we had 17 gauges, one was on the floor of the passenger seat which was measuring airbox pressure. Basically, we had data acquisition before there was data acquisition."

Meanwhile back in CART, Rick Mears had use of what was the greatest design advance since John Barnard's Yellow Submarine Chaparral of 79-81, the Penske PC-10. Rick – "The 10 was a quantum leap, the best car for its time, it had everybody covered due to the downforce and the tunnel shape. They changed the skirt rules from what we had already figured on, and we had to really re-work that car. It wasn't so good mechanically, that was being masked by the downforce. It was quick, very good."

John Barnard's Yellow Submarine was dominant in 1980

Derrick Walker – "I can remember at Phoenix (1981) when Johnny Rutherford flipped over and ended up on the roof. We were all diving for cameras, to take pictures of the underbody while it was upside down... and we weren't the only ones taking pictures. So, now we had a couple of pictures of the Chaparral and got a good look at it. We didn't make exactly that underbody, but it was interesting to see what their shape was. That was a complete car that was designed for ground effect. We had cars that were still a technology behind... that we were trying to band-aid into being ground effect."

Bobby Unser - "When Johnny Rutherford turned over Hall's car at Phoenix one time, within 2 days I had already made up a model and run it on my wind tunnel. I didn't take the picture, somebody did it. I went to a Goodyear engineer and said 'I want to know the width of the tunnel and the length of it. Jim Hall didn't know what he had, and Barnard didn't have figures on it either because it hadn't been to a wind tunnel. But Bobby Unser did." Needless to say, the flow bench in Unser's garage was again humming late into the night.

Derrick Walker - "At a later date, there were some people who tried to put a ½ of a race car in a wind tunnel and flow air across it, which I actually saw in Indianapolis. There were all sorts of attempts to try and create a proper ground effects car. The only time that it all started to make sense was about 1982, when we looked at Formula One and how they were sealing the underbodies to the race track. So, then we were into sliding skirts for a while and then it really worked. At that point it was almost where the shape of the underbody was immaterial as it had so much suction that it worked very well. It really turned the lights on for the cars."

What were the skirt developments like in Indycar in the early 1980s? Derrick – "We also had a blade or honeycomb board they had a 3/8 of an inch wide ceramic edge on it. Of course, they banned that because it was cutting up the race track. The old pavement was no match for that 5' long ceramic blade on each side of the car. Then they banned the sliding skirts, so we got into having flexible rubber skirts so that the car would suck down when the car was at speed. That was the 1982 PC-10, and that was the one where it really worked well. We tested it with the airflow pulling down and it sealed. When it came into the pits, it had all the clearance you needed to get through tech."

As a result of these developments, the Penske PC-10 was a landmark design, the cream of the 1982 crop. Derrick – "It was, it was the most dominant car we'd had for a long time. Just about everything on the car worked, and the shocks were a big part of it. The underbody, the ground effects worked really well. We actually ran the car during practice at Indianapolis in 1982 without any wings on it. We took the front wings off, and we had a very flat rear. It had so much ground effects that it didn't need the wings. But, when you got into traffic, it wasn't quite good enough. In the end we had really small wings, and we had

The 1982 Penske PC-10
– Photo courtesy of Ken Anderson

all kinds of things that year in what was a really dominant year for us."

The business end of the Penske PC-10, perhaps their greatest car

One would have to precisely nail the proper center of pressure to run on a superspeedway without wings. Derrick – "The center of pressure... we hit it right. We knew exactly where it needed to be, and after adjusting it a little bit, it came alive."

Their nemesis proved to be Patrick Racing. Pat Patrick had secured the services of Gordon Kimball for 1981-83, and the team achieved victory in one of the closest fought Indy 500s in history. Kimball - "We took the John Thompson car and re-did it for 1982, and we won all the 500s that year. At Indy in 82, Rick was just coming at us (in the PC-10)... when I saw Rick coming I thought 'Man, we're just toast'. Rick is quick, and when they went into turn one I thought, this is over. He tried to make the pass, but mistimed it and Gordy slammed the door. When Gordy came out ahead I was surprised and it took Rick too long to get the momentum back. There wasn't enough time left."

The most shocking part of the result was that the PC-10 had been such a tremendous car that the perception was that every other team had brought a knife to a gunfight. Kimball – "Yeah, honestly we won those races, but we didn't have the best car."

Sports car racing was far behind the technological parade that was the open wheeled racing in this era. The Lola T600 was the first venturi, or tunnel car designed for IMSA. Dan Binks – "In 1983, the Lola T-600 had a big wing... a banana wing is what I called it, with huge drag. That's what everybody had in those days; they weren't really sensitive to angle of attack. They were so curved that it was more of a spoiler. Thinking about it later, I'm not even sure that it worked, it might have stalled... we didn't know. At that time people were going to the wind tunnel, but not enough to make it work. We were doing things like moving the wing around... better or worse... better or worse, relying upon the driver and the stopwatch. We'd think it would be better and that was it."

The GTP program was considerably more advanced at Nissan. Tony Adamowicz - "Electramotive also had their own wind tunnel with a moving ground plane... it was state of the art. That became really important in the development of the car, as it had its aerodynamic issues. Eventually that car was made into an IMSA Championship winning car." With 4 consecutive drivers' championships (88-91) for Geoff Brabham, Nissan left its mark on the series. However, not everyone shares Tony's enthusiasm for the cars that emerged from the Nissan wind tunnel.

Trevor Harris – "I was working for Electramotive in 1985 we'd done a short course program and won the stadium truck series with Roger Mears. The T-810 project was initiated in 85 with Lola with Yoshi Suzuka doing the aerodynamics on it. Don Devendorf recalls the struggles with the T-810 Lola – We qualified really well, and would be leading races when something would go wrong with the car, like hmmmm, the suspension would pull out. It was like each part... the CNC parts, or it was the carbon and aluminum honeycomb bulkhead coming apart, so we would have new stuff made in L.A. It was 'discovery, fix, discovery, fix' all the time. At Laguna Seca something was wobbling in the steering, and when I came into the pits, the axle was broken and the disc and caliper were what was holding the wheel on. Both axles were broken, as it turned out. So, we changed axles and carried on. We had contracts where if we didn't start the race, there were huge penalties. It would have cost us 50,000 dollars.

It had weird downforce, a kind of unstable downforce where it made so much downforce at the front it was like it was all on the nose. In turn 9 at Riverside, when it got loaded on the banking, you literally couldn't steer it at all. Going into corners, it was so unstable that when you got on the brakes it would change lanes."

Were you running toe out on the front of the car to help it turn in the fast stuff? "Those are subtle things, this was radical. That car was so bad aerodynamically. We were there when they did the wind tunnel test, but Eric (Broadley) had this bright idea where without any testing, he completely changed the tunnel design on the car he gave us. Yoshi measured stuff, and said, 'this wasn't the same'... I mean it was off by inches. That was when Trevor came on-board."

Trevor Harris – "I remember the first meeting we had in your office. You said that you had to go and do some test somewhere, and I said that we aren't going anywhere until we fixed that problem. By 1987 the car had evolved really good aerodynamics, but the chassis was pretty deficient, so I got hired by Kas Kastner to design a new chassis for that car. The 88 car, the chassis was mine. The rear suspension was essentially what the earlier car had, but I did a completely new front suspension, using the Lola uprights. The upright itself was a good piece, but the rest of the suspension was not. The 88 car was easy to drive and it was not aerodynamically sensitive to ride height changes. The 88 car, from the driver's point of view, was always very forgiving, and it was easy for me to set up."

Geoff Brabham – "The NPTI car that they brought out after that, it was nowhere nearly as good a car. It was an aerodynamic brick, and we had to run a lot of rear wing on it to affect a balance. It wasn't generating downforce from the tunnels, so therefore you just had to have huge wings on it. I remember when the NPTI car came out they told me that we would have to run a totally different top gear because this car was going to be so good down the straight. It was actually the opposite." Stories abound of the Nissan GTP cars making anywhere from 5000 to 9000 pounds of downforce. Geoff Brabham – "I wouldn't believe all those numbers if I were you. To be honest, and this is my own view, the wind tunnel that we had at Nissan at that time was totally ineffective and it didn't work. The 1988 car was a really good car, by far my favorite."

Geoff Brabham's favorite Nissan – the 1988 GTP ZX-T

Don Devendorf – "The problem was that it (the 90 NPTI car) wasn't as stable. It had good numbers at the right ride height, but when it actually got down to it, it didn't. That was what was good about the 88 car, in that you could have a lot of suspension travel without affecting the downforce. It was stable and consistent, which allowed the P car to run softer springs because it was so compliant. The suspension was actually working."

Brabham - "But the engine was just really good; the NPTI had a huge gain with the engine. In my opinion if we had put the engine from the NPTI into the 88 car, it would have been a rocket, but obviously that would have been politically incorrect. At Watkins Glen I remember that I had a problem with my race car and I had to jump into the 88 car, which we had as a spare, to qualify. When I jumped in it, I could not believe how weak the engine was.

Single turbo engine installation in the favored Nissan 88 chassis

"I realized that the engines we were now running were so superior to what we'd had in the 88 car, and it crossed my mind at that point... putting the engine into the 88 car would be just as good if not better."

Did anyone seriously consider taking the later NPTI engine and dropping it into the 88 car? Trevor – "That probably would have been extremely effective, but not at all politically correct given all the money they had spent on the development, etc... but there was more to it than that. The earlier car used a single turbo engine, and the later car used twin turbos. The intercooler system on the later car was totally different, so you couldn't have taken the later engine and installed it into the earlier car, as it wouldn't have fit the intercooler system on either side. That twin turbo configuration demanded a whole different chassis." Devendorf - "Ultimately we were developing over 800 foot pounds of torque out of a 3 litre engine, they were astounding numbers. We discovered that because of the restrictors, the only way to make horsepower was with very high boost pressures at kind of low engine speeds. Until 1991, I mean those guys couldn't touch us. I mean, it was the Nissan show; they weren't in the same ballpark, trying to figure out what to do."

Despite enormous horsepower and torque, Geoff was stuck with the difficult NPTI chassis – "When the Toyotas got their act together... I remember the last year (92) at Elkhart Lake, we were 3 seconds a lap slower than the Toyotas, and I was 2 seconds quicker than the next person. The reason was that the Toyotas generated downforce from their tunnels, and ran quite sensible amounts of rear wing. Whereas we did the opposite and we had so much drag. It was further proof to me that the wind tunnel we had then wasn't able to produce a decent aerodynamic package. The chassis was good. One thing that Trevor always did and I think it was his greatest asset, was that every car he did put the power down like nothing else. It was unbelievable how the car always put the power down, but it wasn't aerodynamically effective."

Trevor Harris – "The 90 car was very difficult to set up, mostly because it had aerodynamic issues that were never really fixed. The car was capable of being very quick, but what we didn't know was just how sensitive it was to ride height changes. I think some of the attitudes that we wanted to run the car in, that were demonstrated by wind tunnel work... you couldn't practically run the car that way. Geoff probably told you about him giving me a ride at Elkhart, to prove to me just how bad it was. I got in the car and there was no seatbelt for me, hanging on for dear life. When I was in it, Geoff was driving it at maximum speed. He wasn't backing off; he was trying to demonstrate to me the serious aerodynamic problem that the car had.

Aerodynamic nightmare – the NPTI of 1990-92

Trevor got the ride of his life. "It wasn't lacking in downforce, it had an extreme sensitivity to certain ride height combinations. What Geoff demonstrated to me at Elkhart was he told me the car was getting into some sort of vertical oscillation going down the back straight. Going down that hill it got to the point that the vertical shaking was so bad that I could not see. Forget controlling the car, it was moving vertically very rapidly and it shook my glasses off. It was unbelievable. I believe the car made very good downforce, but the trouble was that under some conditions it made so much that it would suck itself down to the ground. Once it got down to the ground, the airflow and downforce would leave, so it would pop up vertically and then re-institute that same sequence."

Solutions? "Well, we ran massive spring rates on the car at Elkhart, but the solution was to just change the ride heights. We were running astronomical spring rates, my recollection was that we were running 7000#, but it didn't make any difference. At that kind of spring rate, the rate of the tire dominates and is what drove the spring rate at the wheel more than the rate of the spring in the suspension. You could have doubled the spring rate on the suspension and the wheel rate wouldn't have changes very much, being primarily a function of the tire spring rate."

Trevor - "There were certain ride heights that I couldn't get away with, a combination of front and rear. So, I don't think the car ran with the optimum maximum downforce, but you simply couldn't run it that way and get it out of the vertical oscillation. If you are looking at wind tunnel maximum numbers, the earlier car didn't make as much downforce, but that 88 car could run at any ride height front and back that you wanted and not be aerodynamically sensitive to it. One day after my ride, Geoff was going up the back straight at top speed and a tire exploded. The tires were actually being aerodynamically overloaded, it turns out. It took the wing off the car, and Geoff ended up flying very high in the air, and was lucky to live through the crash." Don Devendorf – "I went to see him in the hospital and he looked like one of those guys that rode a rocket sled... just bruised all over."

Geoff Brabham - "I ran the Peugeot at Le Mans in 94, and that car was incredible. We were only running 25% downforce for Le Mans, but still in the fast corners it had more downforce than any car I'd ever experienced. It was running small wings; the car was generating all the downforce from the underwing. That thing would just rip your head right off your shoulders with the downforce, and I never experienced that with the Nissans. It just reinforced for me that aerodynamically the Nissan wasn't very good. The astronomical downforce numbers that Nissan would quote, you should take with a pinch of salt, you know. They probably saw those numbers in the wind tunnel, but the tunnel was giving them false numbers, in my personal opinion."

Nissan was ready with a new car for 1993, the P35 chassis, but the new V-12 engine was a disaster. Don Devendorf – "It had something like 30% to 40% less power, but in the wind tunnel with all the attitude stuff... it was really stable like the '88 car. That car had the same characteristic where it was really stable to where you could run softer suspension. The aerodynamics of that (P35) car was not as sensitive to height." The hopeless nature of the new V-12 meant that the excellent P35 chassis never raced.

Despite all the challenges with the later car, the Nissan was the dominant car from 88-90, and the stage was set for the next generation radically high downforce GTP car which debuted in 1991. There is little doubt that the most aerodynamically unique car from Dan Binks' 30 years of racing would be the Pratt & Miller Intrepid. Dan Binks – "The thing was just so fast and made so much downforce... it was just awesome to work on it. I was working with Riley on a day to day basis... him basically having designed everything and told us what to do and we did it. It was really the first time we had an engineer... we had several engineers at that time, Kurt Rohrick, and Riley. It was the first time I could ask if we should go up or down on the springs... up until that point in Trans-Am I had been "engineering" or "winging it" in those days. This was my first time to not be used in that capacity, where I was just making sure the thing was bolted together right."

Dan - "Where it made all it's time was by NOT slowing down. There were rumors of the car generating 7000 pounds of downforce, but I don't know that for a fact. We took it to the wind tunnel at General Motors and it pegged the scale so it made a LOT of downforce." The car had exceeded the tunnel's capacity to measure.

Wayne Taylor in the 1991 Intrepid
– Photo courtesy of Jerry Howard

Phil – "When they took it to the wind tunnel, they ran it up… shut it down… ran it up… shut it down. The guy kept saying 'something's broke on the thing, at 113mph it's showing 6000# of downforce. It really has that much? Holy s**t, we can't tell you much after that.' They couldn't even measure it. That was an incredible car."

Wayne Taylor – "I had the first car for the initial testing. It developed so much downforce and the faster that you went, the harder it would suck itself to the ground. The Intrepid was nothing like anything else that the group had worked on. I had moved to America to drive for MTI Racing, which was Jim Miller. We were running a Spice-Chevrolet with a sort-of redesign by Bob Riley. We only had the experience of running the Spice around when the Intrepid came out." The Spice was an aluminum tub car, and the step up to the Intrepid must have seemed like a step into the space age. Wayne – "For that era, it was… for racing in the United States. Although, when we did that initial test at Firebird we had the Spice there as well and it ran comparable lap times. We were puzzled as to why the Intrepid wasn't faster straight out of the box. So, for the first race at Miami, they put Tommy in the Spice and I was in the Intrepid. From then on, as we went to race tracks and kept developing it, we just kept going faster and faster."

At Lime Rock they realized they were pushing the limits of human capabilities. Wayne – "Tommy and I, we couldn't keep our legs up. Danny made these brackets inside of the cockpit to hold our legs up. The car went around the corners so fast that we could not hold our legs up, and we had to have our legs strapped so that we could stay on the throttle. An amazing car…" It had reached the point where Taylor literally could not keep his feet on the pedals as they were being pulled off to the side with such enormous force.

Tommy Kendall - "I finally got my Intrepid for Lime Rock. In that car, I used left foot braking for the first time, and so for the first time I didn't have my left foot to brace myself. We ended up having to do major seat work, to re-engineer the entire seat with side support. For my lower legs I made a big bowl for side support… but I was using way less energy and was not having to hold myself in place. The body was isolated for the first time. I learned a ton about seating then, and had a version of my seat for the rest of my career. People would say, 'that's stupid looking'. I ran it even in the NASCAR cars. But, eventually all those guys went with that kind of seat."

Once Kendall could be held in place at the controls, he smashed the track record. Tommy – "In qualifying I lowered the track record by 2.2 seconds, at a track where you normally lower it by 10ths. We were in our own world. The race started and I took off, and was started lapping the field pretty quickly. I was leading and had just lapped Wayne, who I think was running 3rd, and I was behind the Jag which was running 2nd.

Wayne – "We were really competitive as expected, but in

qualifying when I got out of the pits my clutch exploded, so I was at the back of the grid. In the race they radioed that Tommy was coming so I pulled to the left and lifted off, so Tommy came by. I tucked in a half car length behind him in Big Bend. Well, in this corner where we were normally flat, Tommy hit the brakes and I had nowhere to go, so I drove right into the back of him. That was the beginning of a bloody nightmare, to be honest. How could anybody in that organization believe that I took Tommy out deliberately? It was incredibly disappointing."

Kendall – "There was a combination of Camel Lights cars, and there was a little bit of a stack up, it was the accordion effect. Wayne got into the back of me, and turned me around. The car wouldn't start as the battery was too small to restart the motor when it was hot. We learned that the hard way, so I sat there for 4 or 5 laps."

The Cardinal Sin for any driver is to take out his teammate while being lapped. Tommy – "It was the first time we had been in the same car (Intrepid), and that morning was the first time that Jim Miller had said 'I know I don't really have to say this, but I can't help myself and I've got to say this. Under no circumstances are you two to ever touch each other.' It was a disaster all the way around, Wayne had a bad day. He ended up getting into a couple of other people, taking out Parker Johnstone, the lights leader, putting him on his head. He was not popular with a bunch of folks that day. I was young and racers are ego-centric, and you only see it from your perspective. I was thinking that you had just sat us down this morning and said it was unacceptable, he took me out when he was lapped, and it was a win… I wanted him to get fired. In my mind I was thinking, 'why wouldn't you fire this guy?' But the reality is that guys rarely get fired… it made for some tension." Binks was equally disappointed. "We were going to win Lime Rock by a lap, but then Wayne ran into Tommy."

Kendall - "At Mid-Ohio I was on the pole again there without having any practice due to a sticking throttle, and qualifying was the first time the car ran. Wayne and the Jag got around me at the start. At New Orleans Wayne won a really weird race in the rain." It was the only win for the Intrepid. "No... can it be? Wow, that's just staggering. We should have won about 7 or 8 races that year. It stuck in my craw, because he got the first win in the Intrepid, and I thought I should have gotten the first one. I got hurt in the next race at Watkins Glen. The ratings must have been really high because everyone I talk to was watching that race on TV."

Dan Binks – "The weekend Tommy was hurt, we were caught through the trap at 168mph at Watkins Glen. The Porsche 962 that was on the pole went 211mph, with almost identical lap times. It was ridiculous... what we had to do was get off the pit sequence compared to them. You didn't have to slow down much for the corners, and that's why when Tommy crashed that car, it was such a big wreck. He was carrying so much speed through the corners compared to the Porsches, which had about the same horsepower." Of course the opposed cylinder boxer motor was always going to be a massive compromise for underbody aerodynamics in the tunnel car era. Dan Binks – "Right, they paid a price for that, but in a straight line that car was obviously slippery."

Phil Binks – "At Road America they had the pole, but it was 18mph slower than the 2nd qualifying car. In the Carousel it had registered 4.8 Gs of side force. Think about that." Wayne Taylor – "In qualifying I think I was almost flat through there, it was just ridiculous. You weren't flat through there in anything else, not even close. I remember at Road America qualifying on the front row next to one of the Joest Porsches. On these high speed tracks we'd lose an enormous amount on the straightaways, as with the amount of downforce it produced, it was very draggy. But even with all that drag, we were always up front." The Intrepid was purely a dedicated downforce machine and it showed in the trap speeds.

Wayne Taylor – "I remember at the last race of the year at Del Mar, we were doing single car qualifying. I had taken pole there in '89 with a Spice-Pontiac, and I'd gotten a few poles and track records during the year ('91). Coming into the pits at the end of my pole run at Del Mar, Dan Gurney came running out into the pit lane with his thumbs up. I had qualified the car over a second faster than anybody. The factory Nissans were there, the Jaguars, the Toyotas… the car was incredible. Unfortunately at the first pit stop when I was about to lap the entire field, the clutch exploded so we didn't finish the race. If you look at the results of the car, it's maybe not that impressive, although I won in New Orleans when it was raining."

One would think this would be the ultimate GTP car in the rain, with all that downforce. Wayne – "Yeah, it was good. It was just an amazing car. It's just a pity that they did not continue to develop that car. When I think back upon all the GTP cars and all the other cars I've driven over the last 21 years that is still the car that gets most people's attention. That whole Intrepid thing was so great, the car was so unbelievable."

Aerodynamic development isn't just the province of high-end premier class machinery. Dan Binks was involved with a Formula Vee campaign in SCCA Nationals. "I did a couple of those cars in the early 90s; I helped my father-in-law build a car called the Adams. We won the Runoffs with my brother-in-law driving it in 1995.

The car was a unique aerodynamic exercise, a vertical emphasis and really narrow and pointy at the ends, named the Adams Aero. Dan – It wasn't super aerodynamic, but that was the one, you sat upright. It was something they dreamed up, I did the chassis stuff. We basically built the car for Mid-Ohio. It was a transition time for us, we had gone to Road Atlanta for the Runoffs a couple of times, and when they announced it was moving to Mid-Ohio, we decided that now we would build a car, knowing it would be there for a few years. In 94 we ran a lot of races and finished 10th,

I think… and then we built a new car and changed some things around for 95. We led every lap and nobody passed us, it was pretty impressive." The bottom line is that in even the most cost restrictive classes, or with the most unlikely machinery, there can be room for substantial aerodynamic improvement.

There were also minor items that proved to have significant aero benefits, discovered during that same era. At Roush racing with the Trans-Am Mustang, they had installed snaps around the perimeter of the rear window so when the car came off the track, there was a cover snapped into place to keep prying eyes from seeing the rear suspension. That was only part of the story. Phil Binks – "They found that the snaps tripped the air, and made the rear wing more effective. The wind would come over the back and separate, the placement of the snaps would help to control the airflow over the rear deck of the car. With the cover off, the snaps served a different purpose." Dan - "The snaps were vortex generators. They actually helped, believe it or not. In the wind tunnel, we tried vortex generators, but I said they were never going to let us run that, but they let us run snaps because they thought they were to hold on the cover. It was so wacky, it worked. It was all about, 'what can you get away with'. Those cars were so much better."

In Sports Car and Formula car racing manufacturing, none can claim anything close to the long term success enjoyed by Dallara Automobili. Frustrated with his position as aerodynamicist for Ferrari since 1959, Gian Paolo Dallara was ready to move on. Mr. Dallara – "After about a year at Ferrari, I was needing the racing, I was crazy for racing… and so I went to Maserati. My first activity in racing was testing at Monza with the Cooper-Maserati 2 litre with Roger Penske driving. At the same time we were racing the birdcage, but it was fragile, and then Maserati stopped racing. In 1963, I went to work for Lamborghini." While at Lamborghini, Gian Paolo designed the Miura chassis and the Espada, before moving on to work with DeTomaso on a F2 car, and then his first

F1 design, the DeTomaso F1 car for Frank Williams and driver Piers Courage in 1970, the effort ending in tragedy when Courage perished in a fiery crash at Zandvoort.

Gian Paolo founded Dallara Automobili in 1972. Currently, Mr. Dallara's firm is the exclusive manufacturer for Indy Car, Indy Lights, the World Series by Renault, and GP2. They also hold approximately 90% of the F3 market, and have constructed such legendary sports cars as 1993's Ferrari 333SP, and the dominant Le Mans winning Audi R8. After a stint with Scuderia Italia in Formula One from 1988-1992, Dallara returned to Formula One in 2010 with drivers Bruno Senna and Karun Chandhok at HRT Hispania racing (formerly Campos). Needless to say, Dallara has expertise in every major discipline of racing car design.

Andrea Vecchi, wind tunnel manager at Dallara, discusses the challenge - "It takes months of time and effort, both in design and production."

Wind tunnel model for the 1989 Dallara F1 car

"The designer sends the images... the Cad files, to Roberto, who then translates the data into what the prototyping machines can read. This is the first material that we used, from back when we started up with rapid prototyping stereotography in 2001, starting off with epoxy resin. Then we moved on and bought a second machine, to use the ceramic based blue material, called blue soap." Think of Roberto's job as being similar to programming a CNC (Computed Numerically Controlled) milling machine, only this final product is bits for aero development models.

Further developments in rapid prototyping material proved to be of better use. Andrea - "We changed from the blue to the white material, which is also ceramic based. The white ceramic material is called Nano 2, and the yellow-gray one is called Nano 4. The Nano 4 epoxy based material is a big improvement over the old material and we use it for main bodywork parts on the wind tunnel model. The ceramic based white Nano 2 material is very similar to the blue ceramic, but is superior in certain applications for a few reasons that I won't bore you with. A laser solidifies the layers of liquid resin, a 1/10th of a millimeter at a time. There is also a metal coated material that is painted black and it is a lot stiffer when you start testing at 50m/sec, and the forces on the model parts become very big. What happens is the scale model is 50% and so something that is already thin, full scale, becomes even thinner here... but the speeds are still very high, and just the ceramic material is not strong enough." Again, necessity becomes the mother of invention.

Using that electroplating process, Dallara can achieve the desired stability of the parts to get accurate data from the 50% or 60% wind tunnels used at Dallara (2 rolling floor wind tunnels are used at their factory in Parma, Italy). One of the surprising features of the F1 Dallara wind tunnel model is the weight of the wheels, roughly equivalent to the F1 car wheel/tire combination, and one is completely unprepared for the weight when handed a wheel/tire assembly. The relation of wheel/tire to rolling ground plane reacts differently if the actual un-sprung loading of the assembly isn't accurate, and it is also safe to assume that the spring rate of the tire must also be representative of that used by the tires on the actual car. Just the variety of "tooth" to the rolling ground plane "belts" can also make a difference in the readings, although they have developed mathematical factors to adjust the data for this, depending upon the of the moving ground plane belt used.

Interestingly enough, looking over the current generation F1 wind tunnel model, the various assemblies are made from numerous small pieces, a wing end plate perhaps having as many as 6 different panels. One would think that all the additional fasteners vs. the smooth finish of the final car assemblies would have some detrimental result upon the wind tunnel data, but that does not appear to be the case. Does rapid prototyping save untold time over fabricating carbon pieces in an autoclave for the aero model? Andrea Vecchi – "It depends upon the type of carbon fiber you are using, it can be very quick when using pre-impregnated carbon fiber, which is used for parts that don't require a lot of stiffness. If you are doing the top of a car, then you have a lot of different types of carbon fiber... they have the honeycomb inside, you put the carbon fiber with one layer going in one directionality, then another layer with another directionality... thicknesses depending upon if you think there would be more of less pressure, more or less temperature... which is why you have such a big variety of carbon fiber, and a variety of sandwich systems that you can make. The loads can vary a lot from one area to another, the nose box, for example." It should be pointed out that there is still a lathe in the corner of the F1 model shop and they verified that it gets used; old world mechanical fabrication skills remain of value.

In 2009, Nick Wirth mentioned at a technology conference in conjunction with the Long Beach Grand Prix, that aerodynamic simulation by computer now allows for approximately a 99% accuracy, to where when a part is produced the chances are overwhelmingly likely for a positive result in the wind tunnel and test track, thereby reducing the wastage of mass fabrication of potential solutions, most of which end up being unusable...

a waste of time and material. It seems that such conclusions would fly in the face of justifying such laborious work for wind tunnel models. Wirth's conclusions are not universally accepted.

Mr. Dallara – "CFD - I do not agree completely, but I believe it has changed the attitude of those in Formula 1. I believe in the wind tunnel with the models you can see things you cannot see in the CFD. With the model you have the results but sometimes you do not know why. There are a lot of people with doubt, they realize it is not 100% right, maybe 80% is right."

Simon Marshall, former Lola and Delta Wing design engineer, is of the opinion that this number is in direct relation to the quality of the CFD operator and program. "It depends on who you use and what program. The program is a lot of it, but so is the person who is applying it. The guys at Total Sim (England) know how to use it and know what they should see, so they drive it towards being sensible."

That said, racing history is full of stories where something also worked in the tunnel, yet did not have the predicted result at the track, adding yet more variability. Dallara – "Yes, it is true, perhaps they did not exactly predict the deflection of the tires. The results are good, but with the model there are ways where you might not reproduce properly what is going on, because maybe you are not producing the vibrations, something in the way you are testing." Dallara uses two, with both 60% and 50% rolling floor wind tunnels. The Toyota F1 program used a full scale tunnel, without much apparent advantage. "The Toyota team had the most expensive of resources, everything you can have… and they did not succeed… very strange. You have to play with the same order of magnitude, or be smart with your research. If you are smart with 50%, you can possibly get a better value, but if you are at 1/10th, you will never compete. A low budget company can maybe perform well in one race, but not in the long term. But it is true that not always does the company with more money win."

As an example of doing more with less, in 1988 Dallara had returned to Formula One with Scuderia Italia cars initially designed by Sergio Rinland and driven by Alex Caffi, later adding second team driver Andrea DeCesaris for 1989. Budgets were tight in relation to other teams of the day. Dallara – "The team was run by Scuderia Italia, and they attracted the sponsors… something like it was supposed to be with the Spanish team (Campos, then HRT). But it was a different situation at the time, because the budget was maybe 1/10th of what it is today. It was 3 million euro for the full season, not much time in the wind tunnel, very few mechanics… you could buy an engine and the performance would be very similar to that of the Ferrari." Caffi's 4th at Monaco and DeCesaris' 3rd at Canada helped secure Dallara's 8th place finish in the manufacturer's championship for 1989, a result they matched in 1991. 3 million Euros went a very long way within the highest echelons of racing in 1989.

The high dollar Toyota saga in Formula One is proof positive that clever use of adequate resources and information can trump unlimited budgets, to a degree. Examples include Force India-Mercedes, or Brawn-Mercedes running ahead of McLaren-Mercedes in 2009. Mr. Dallara - "They survive with a well-mixed cocktail of components and people working just enough… it is possible until everything collapses. Such a company has to rely more on individual persons, and they are more fragile. Look at Red Bull, they had just enough so that one person (Adrian Newey) made it grow." Another example might be to consider where Brabham cars might have been without Gordon Murray, the designer for their cars in the mid 70s-80s. "Sometimes there are some… Supermen… who make it happen." Of course, the stability of such a company can be seriously in doubt if their superstar designer decides to move on to another firm.

Obsolescence of the package is another item driving the ever increasing budgets, mostly driven by aero development. Each year the designers strive for a smaller and more aerodynamically efficient package which is then shrink-wrapped around the new generation smaller engine. Options are gone to retreat to the previous engine, short of using the previous chassis as well, which would doom the effort to mediocrity at best. There is no looking back in Formula One.

Of course there have been stunning advances in recent years, with the high pointed tub and under-slung front wing pioneered by Benetton in the early 1990s, which set the design concept for the next generation of GP cars. Gordon Kimball was at Benetton during this era. "Flavio sold me a deal, as he was fed up with John's character. John (Barnard) had already done a high nose car, it was there when I came to Benetton in June or July of '91." The high pointed nose with under slung front wing eventually became the design solution of choice, the idea being to pack as much air as possible into the area underneath the tub where it could then be used to create downforce.

There were many designs to route the exhaust into the diffuser area, what is known now as the "blown diffuser". The F1 teams eventually abandoned the concept given the differences in downforce between throttle-on and throttle-off conditions, and the effect upon handling. With a mid-season update in 1998, Ferrari's latest solution now routed this airflow out the top of the bodywork ahead of the rear suspension. At the time, these upward "periscope" exhausts equated to a gain of 2 or 3/10ths of a second in lap time. Formula One was moving away from the blown diffuser.

Further focus on the underbody led to such innovations as the double diffuser, which became a big part of the Brawn F1 success story of 2009. Taking over the still-born Honda F1 design, while gaining access to a Mercedes engine package, had resulted in a potent combination.

However their budget was small and they barely had enough parts available to get 2 cars to the grid for the first GP of the season in Australia. Incredibly, Jenson Button was to win 6 of the

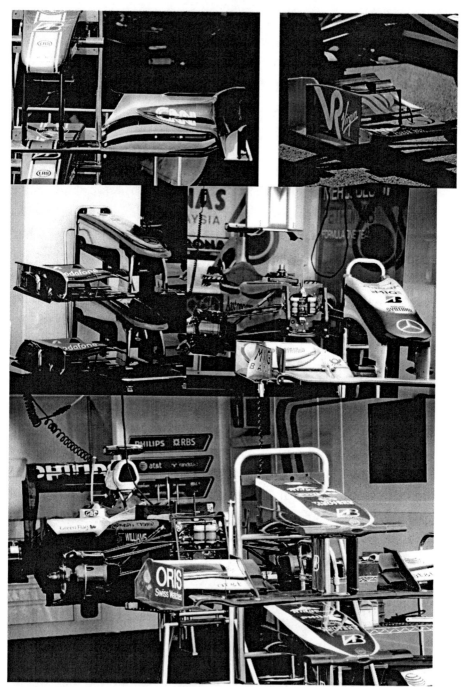

Scenes on the pitlane at Monaco 2010. Note the variety of design solutions for the ideal high downforce front wing configuration

first 7 events. There were serious doubts in the paddock if the double or stacked diffuser designs were legal, as there were vertical openings that led to a second level of diffuser above, adding significantly to the downforce. Toyota and Williams had similar systems, but none were as effective as the Brawn. The protests were soon dismissed and the Brawn GP team won both the World Driver's Championship as well as the Manufacturer's Championship.

The 'blown diffuser' also was making a comeback. This design was taken to extremes by Renault in their 2011 car, with the exhaust moved well forward in the car to create the maximum effect across as much of the underbody as possible.

At the same dime, designers resolved the variable downforce problems of earlier generations of blown diffusers, with the engine mapping now being modified such that airflow from the engine was now maintained even in an off-throttle application. The result was to finally achieve that optimal use of engine exhaust to compliment aerodynamic flow. Of course, after 25 years of development and the eventual discovery of an optimum combination, the use of off-throttle airflow to the diffuser was banned.

In the American Le Mans series, most lean toward being true believers in CFD programs, vs. endless development in wind tunnels. Slight rear bodywork tweaks developed with CFD had resulted in large gains at Jaguar, as confirmed by their designer Ian Callum in discussions prior to the 2010 season. The Pratt & Miller team similarly uses CFD programs to develop the cars. Binks – "There are a lot of things you can do for that, but the engineering staff has been working hard at it, using a lot of CFD stuff working on the body panels, and we have a new tail." For confirmation, the team does actual aero testing to back up what they appear to have discovered in the CFD programs. Dan Binks - "We go to Oskoda 2 or 3 times a year. It's a big skid pad, 12,500 feet long, pretty cool. It just goes up and back in a straight line basically, as we just use the runway. Its great information and the key is getting there on the right day when it's not too windy."

The GT1 car made use of straked diffusers, which are not allowed in the GT2, now GT class. Binks - "Doug Louth and his group studied that over and over again, and it looked like everytime you went to more strakes, you had more downforce, and it was more consistent downforce. I don't know if it was a drag reduction device as well, as those cars had a lot of drag and a lot of power. But the biggest problem with those strakes was that they kept getting knocked off."

Straked rear diffuser on the 2008 GT1 Corvette at Sebring

"It was one of the best rules that the ALMS has made, when they decided there would be no strakes at all. The diffusers just last forever now, vs. before where every practice session we were putting one on because the old one was missing 3 or 4 strakes."

Did you ever play around with strakes under the front of the car? "We have, but we didn't see much there. The problems get back to where they get knocked off. Let's say you do gain from putting strakes under the front, but then they get knocked off and now you are dealing with an aero disadvantage as the pieces are not there anymore. And the other problem is that if you run over it, you get a flat tire. So, we tried them, but decided to stay away from them. That's why we put them at the rear, so if they fall off, they flatten somebody else's tires (laughing)."

Jan Magnussen – "I did one season with the C5 and locking up the rear wheels was a big issue there under hard braking, but the diffuser helped that problem. And it was a really big problem for us when it was bumpy. The GT1 car was sensitive to the under wing, under the nose. So, we played around with the attitude of that, it would have quite a bit of an effect. It was not a critical thing with the GT1 car, but it's still there in the GT2 and is still used, but there is way less downforce."

The GT1 car aero grip would go from stuck to gone, much like in the prototype classes. Dan – "The GT1 car was so aero sensitive, it wanted to be tracking all the time. These (the GT2 cars) are better at that, you can slide them around. We are better with downforce than we were with the early GT2 cars, but you can still slide them big-time, drive through the aerodynamic downforce, and still save it. I would say it is accurate to say that it is somewhere in the middle now."

By mid-2010 the GT2 car was far more refined than at its debut mid-09, lessons learned from running that partial season. Binks on the 2010 Le Mans effort – "We spent more this year on our Le Mans aero package, than we'd ever spent in one year… all this before we went to France, doing wings and underbody stuff. I don't know how many wings they did, but there were literally tons." The wing that Pratt & Miller developed has a flat section across the middle of the wing, in the area of higher turbulence coming off the sloped rear windscreen area. The result is a twisted wing profile that presents the greater angle of attack over the aerodynamically cleaner rear fender area at each side of the bodywork. Apparently there was a big payoff, as the GT2 Pratt & Miller Corvette was clocked at 182 mph in a straight line, faster by one mph than the fastest of the GT1 cars at Le Sarthe. Were the Corvettes running a low downforce setup to get those trap speeds? Dan –"Ours wasn't that low. It had more downforce than we expected to go there with. The drag number went down because the new wing was so good."

2009 debut of the GT2 Corvette with twisted rear wing profile

"We were in good shape, we had good downforce. When we take out the aero to go fast on the straight, it doesn't handle as good, or stop as good. So, our normal deal is a little more downforce than the competitors, so you've got something to fight with. You can have a fast race car, but if you can't fight inside and outside, you are going to get beat every time. You know, as soon as you take downforce away, it doesn't stop. It transfers all the weight to the front so you've got to keep rear wing in it." The aerodynamic silver bullet is sufficient downforce with less drag, and it appears that Corvette has found that elusive win-win scenario.

As one might expect, similar solutions are found in the ALMS GT pitlane, in this constantly improving manufacturer battleground. David Murray, driver for the Robertson racing Ford GT program — "The big development for this class over the last year are twofold... tires and aerodynamics. In this class, a couple or 3 tenths move you up a half dozen grid spots. We go back to the wind tunnel every chance we get, and find whatever tidbits we can for less drag and more downforce. Porsche isn't sitting around waiting for Ferrari, BMW, or anybody else to gain an advantage. Last year we went to race in Japan and by the time we got the car back and unloaded the container, we'd lost 2 months development time and it showed at Sebring." As a result, the team was forced to play catch-up for most of the 2010 season.

There is no substitute for testing and development as the team found with their new 2nd car at the final race of 2010, the Petit Le Mans. David — "We think something came loose in the front aero, and we had so much front downforce that it started chattering and hitting bottom in front. We raised it after the warmup, but then that changed the balance of the car, so that now we had understeer during the race." The car was unable to achieve its full potential due to this minor aero problem and the resultant missed setup, dealing a severe blow to the small team that had sat on pole for the 2009 Petit Le Mans.

Andrew Smith is the team manager and resident technical guru at the Ford GT team. Best known as "H" (along the lines of Bond's "Q") this former alumni of Tom Walkinshaw Racing (TWR) and Eddie Jordan Racing (Jordan F1), has developed a similar rear wing, his version hung from an overhead cantilevered pair of support plates that loop up from behind the wing, reminiscent of the wing support solution on the Audi R15 and Peugeot 908 prototypes, which have their overhead wing supports mounted in front of the wing. H- "We put the wing at the most rearward point of the car, it had previously been about 50mm forward, and now (vs. an underside pylon type wing support) the whole of the underside of the wing works, 100% of the working surface of the wing… for about a 5% increase in downforce. It is twisted so that in the greenhouse section, it presents a lower profile. We are trying to make it 100% effective all the way across the car." Again, the wing angle is increased in the area of cleaner airflow, and then reduced in the center where the air is more turbulent.

Other than the obvious benefit of the twisted wing profile on a closed car, the lessons one can take from recent developments is that it is more important to keep the bottom of the wing clear of obstructions with support provided at the ends or from above, and that the wing should always be mounted as high as possible and placed as far back as the rules allow.

The challenge was increased with the 2011 ALMS season, as the rules require a single wing configuration to be used for the entire season. Corvette racing's new design raises the leading edge at the center of the wing to a negative downforce configuration at the leading edge of the wing, somewhat matching the slope of the rear deck lid. One assumes that with the newly mandated compromise, and Binks' stated preference for giving the driver some downforce to work with, that the wing retains a substantial amount of downforce. Dan – "The way that the wind goes over the car, the back window pulls down, so you actually need to get some wind going under the wing in the middle." Under the new rules, the angle of attack for the rear wing can be adjusted as needed. Binks – "That's the key. It is roughly parallel to the window with the sprint package."

Things changed again for 2012 and 2013. Binks – "It's got a new rear wing, now they've let us move the wing up so it's less swoopy, as it's not as close to the rear deck (and window). We moved it 75mm and it was a pretty big change, our aero guys are sensitive to all that stuff. The BMW and Porsches are way up there, a long ways from the body, and it becomes less important to have the swoop in the center for the rear deck lid... you wouldn't think that 75mm is that much, but it's a big deal."

"The lap times are close to the old GT1 car, how about that? We have way less power and the tires have come a long ways in 5 or 6 years. The wings are still way smaller than on the GT1 car, when you walk up to one of those old wings now, you just think 'oh my God.' The guys who work on our whole aero system, they are so smart."

"Between the wheels it (the underbody) has to be within 5mm of flat. Then the diffuser behind can be anything you want behind the rear wheel centerline. No strakes... the strakes would always fall off; they were a big pain in the ass. It was so much work taking care of the diffuser when it had those things on it. Anything happens and they are wrecked. With the wider body we went to the bigger front tire, and that worked all of last year. There were all sorts of rules and they just said 'screw it', so the rules changed from 2000mm to 2050mm wide. The only car that was being built was the Ferrari and they had built it to the wide spec for 2011, when everyone else was running the narrow spec. So, we did the wide body for 2012, we were just playing catch-up."

Is the 50mm wider car an advantage? Dan - "A wider car at a place like this (at Laguna) is for sure. At Le Mans, maybe you could argue that you don't want a wide car, but we've been able to run a wide car just fine. We want people to walk up and say 'hey that looks like a Corvette' vs. bringing a BMW that doesn't look like a street car. They've got one down there now (Z4) and it isn't even close. We want them here, don't get me wrong, but that car doesn't look anything like the street car. The M3 was cool... it had a couple of flippers here and there, but anybody that walked up said 'ok, that an M3.'" Binks has a point, and it probably isn't good when the production class starts heading the way of slope nose 935s. Dan - "We all ran those cars in the 1980s, and I thought we were past that."

As the GT cars inch back towards being IMSA 935s, Indycar has inched towards open wheel cars that often resemble prototypes. The new 2012 Dallara Indycar, has similar characteristics on the limit to the GT1 Corvette or ALMS prototypes, as to the narrow relationship between 'stuck and gone'. The Dallara rear diffuser has a pair of side fences, or strakes, under the rear of the car. By channeling the air and keeping it from spilling over the sides, the generally accepted figure is approx. 200 lbs of additional downforce is added for each side fence left on the underbody. As always, on the Superspeedways, it's a delicate balance between being able to navigate the corners quickly, vs. straight line speed. In qualifying at Indy, many of the teams/drivers ran a negative 10 degree setting on the rear wing, in an effort to trim out the car as much as possible. Negative 10 degrees or 10 degrees of wing lift, was the maximum allowed at Indy 2012.

This was uncharted territory for Jean Alesi. "With our Formula One cars, it is not like at Indy. There they designed the wings for different kinds of tracks, so we would have a package that was designed for… Monza." So, you would have an entirely different aero package for each different track? Jean – "Exactly, we don't deal with a wing we used in Barcelona, and then we have to go to Monza with it. The flaps would be modified…"

Sebastian Bourdais – "When you try to make a road course underwing package work on an oval, it is very difficult. So, everybody is using the rear wing to take downforce away from the car. But the extreme levels you are seeing is getting out of hand, running the rear wing nose up and all sorts of crazy things. I haven't seen figures but when the rear wing is at minus 10, it is probably lifting the back of the car. These trimming levels are strange, trying to get as much downforce off the car as you can."

Scott Dixon – "With the old car, you really couldn't do it, but with this new car we've run it at Indianapolis at minus 10. Earlier on, when we did the test at Texas we were limited to minus 7 degrees. The difference is nothing drastic; I think you lose another 100 – 150 lbs of downforce." At Indy, the decision was made to increase the boost available to the teams for qualifying, and it was back to uncharted territory.

Scott continues – "The effect depended upon the team. For us, it was trying to trim out the car as much as possible to make up a little bit of the difference on the Chevys in qualifying trim. We were still minus 10, but the efficiencies are different in relating to the floor. At Indy you could run the side walls (fences or strakes) on the floor, whereas somewhere like Texas you can't run those. The floor is much more powerful than the wing. At Indy, at one point in qualifying, we ran with both side fences off and a loss of 400 pounds of downforce, while still running minus 10 on the wing.

Dixon had taken everything out, trimmed the car to the maximum. "We were trying to, but you get to a point at Indy where the straight line speed picks up, but you start scrubbing so much speed in the corner. You are still flat, but you still lose so much." What was the magic combination for 2012 qualifying? "We qualified with one side wall on, still minus 10 on the wing." Is there a difference with which side fence is left off the car? "I think they are pretty even. If it had been a cooler day, like in the morning, we'd have run with both sidewalls off. For the race everybody ran the sidewalls, and ran wings between zero and minus 4… cranked a lot more in to where you'd have had about 400 or 500 pounds more downforce."

American motorcycle flat track racers of the 70s and 80s had turned their deft skill at handling a barely hooked up machine, into years of American domination in Grand Prix racing. Rarely in recent years has the bullring been the road to success for open wheel car racing, with the obvious exception of Tony Stewart. For every rule, there is an exception and in 2012, Midwest sprint car specialist Bryan Clauson had his Indycar debut at Indianapolis, taking the path that once brought generations of American drivers to the Indy 500. Bryan – "Yeah, I think it's exciting for everybody involved with that type of racing to have me here. Everybody was pumped up about it, and it's good to see that enthusiasm for the 500 back. We all loved it even when nobody was coming out of that form of racing. When you have somebody there and you can say, 'that's one of our guys,' it just makes it that much better." Feel the weight of the Midwest upon you? "Yeah, a little bit. Some of it is self-induced, but it's so passionate, and I want to do well for them. I love that form of racing so much. I put the weight of that world on my shoulders."

Is there any correlation to the modern Indycar, coming from a background sliding around the bullrings? Bryan – "They don't move around a whole lot, it's pretty glued to the track. We're at these really negative angles because this car produces so much downforce. We're at negative 10 and still not as light on downforce as the other cars were last year, and that's the limit. You just can't get 'em to where they were last year, and that's why everybody is maxed out. But you won't see -10 on race day, I promise you that. Trust me, none of us will tell you that we want to go out there and run negative 10 for any extended period of time. But to get the speed for qualifying, that's what you had to do."

Clauson had the car snap around on him on his 4th lap of the qualifying session. Bryan – "To this day, if you'd stopped me at the flag stand at the end of the 3rd lap, I would have said, 'we're good, don't change a thing.' And then it stepped out. We took the data from the first 3 laps and when you lay them over, everything lays right over the top of everything else. We've watched it a hundred times, and looked over the data for hours. You just have to chalk it up to Indy being Indy."

Simon Pagenaud – "When it snaps, as you saw in qualifying, you're gone, you're in the wall. You are flat, and I wish the cars had 1000hp and a little bit less wing. I think it would make it more exciting for the drivers. It would be better for us to drive in, and have to lift if we had so much speed going in. If you can reduce that lift... that makes you a better driver. Right now, I don't see what makes you a better driver than the others. In qualifying I was flat, and Briscoe was flat. It's not in your hands as a driver on the racetrack here."

Simon Pagenaud brings his setup sensitivity to Indycar

A combination of less downforce and more horsepower would make for a better show, and perhaps the talents and techniques of drivers like Pagenaud or Clauson might have a greater opportunity to shine. However, the sorry trend is still toward high downforce cars with low horsepower engines.

Parnelli Jones concurs – "The problem with Indycars right now is that the engineers are running the show. They keep coming up with the ground effects and everything else, while the horsepower stays the same... so, the cars are just so anybody can drive them."

Oriol Servia - "We are supposed to be rocketships on wheels. I remember in my rookie year of 2000, I had 870hp. They were amazing to drive and they were amazing to watch. You wanted to see the good guy, like Montoya when he arrived. He was the guy with the most car control that I ever saw. I was a driver, and I wanted to see HIM drive. When you have 500 hp instead of 900, there are maybe ten guys who can do that, instead of one." Oriol has a point, and it should only be a select few who can deal with such machines at their absolute limits. Those with true talent will shine through.

There is little doubt that high downforce cars with restricted horsepower can turn quick lap times. But if the downforce can be taken away from the cars, and the horsepower increased, the lap times average speeds may be similar in the end. Rick Mears has a theory that is elegant in its simplicity… The Goose Theory. "I've always been one that wanted less downforce instead of more. Over the years we gotten more and more downforce, more and more grip, which raises the corner speeds and you hit the wall harder. So, to me my preference would be to go the other way with less downforce, put the driver back in it more… less corner speed, and more horsepower to go down the straightaway and keep the lap times up. If you just go up with 1000hp and leave the downforce alone, then you are going to want more downforce because you will be reaching the corner faster, and it's a catch 22 that keeps going. Over the years we've raised the corner speed and the straightaways have stayed the same… the gap between our fastest and slowest have gotten narrower and narrower. Some years ago a 10mph split between the highest speed and lowest speed was good. Now if you are over about a 4mph split, you're bad… it's constant all the way around."

Rick continues – "Even when I was driving I'd do tests to reduce the downforce, go out and drive it, and come back and say 'ok, this will work'. I've got to drive it, but it puts me back in the car and things happen slower. You aren't leaning on that string as hard waiting for it to break; it's more progressive when things do happen. So, they'd take it off my car and go put it on somebody else's like Michael's. They'd go out and run 3 laps, they'd slip and slide and they'd say 'oh my God, you are going to hurt somebody.'

Oops, can't do that, and out the window it would go."

"The more grip you use in aero, the more you lose when you get behind somebody. Here they always wonder why we can't pass... why we can't get up to somebody. It dawned on me, so I went up to some of the guys and said 'Are Geese considered to be a highly intelligent bird? Well, they know better than to fly right behind each other. If I fly behind my (goose) buddy, I lose lift. We're just geese upside down and here you are trying to make us fly behind each other and it doesn't work. They want to know why we can't run right behind each other in the turns, why we always have this gap between the cars. You'd have to run up high or down low. Geese know they can't fly behind each other. How come they don't let airplanes fly right up behind each other? It is because of the turbulence, the dirty air."

Mears - "In the earlier years it wasn't as critical on the short tracks, but when we get to the higher speed ovals like Indy or Michigan, as we didn't rely on the aero quite that much, the aerodynamics wasn't that refined. As we've made the cars more efficient, and aerodynamic, and taken the horsepower down, you can't get to the guy. Even on road courses... at Edmonton, the first time we ran there Will (Power) was leading the race and he around to lap somebody. They were all lined up and there was this same gap between 1st, 2nd, 3rd, 4th, 5th, 6th. Will was catching Marco at 2 seconds a lap, Marco was having a bad day. Now this is a wide open airport and you are thinking there is lots of room to pass here. He catches Marco and boom, he loses 2 seconds a lap and that was as close as he could get... he gets up to that same gap as between 2nd or 3rd and Will hit that hole in the air. It's just like when I was running in the desert and the dust when you'd be catching a guy... you'd start closing in as it gets worse and worse... and right at a certain point the dust would be a blackout, a dead zone, a no-man's zone that was difficult to get through. That's what we deal with in the aero. There is this dead zone that can be difficult to get through."

Perhaps if the downforce was reduced along with a corresponding increase in horsepower, then again a driver's car control could return to its rightful place, as a primary factor in determining racing champions. Still, looking back across the various eras of high wings, sucker cars, sliding skirt ground effects, and the almost limitless downforce era of IMSA GTP, one cannot help but remain in awe of those machines. It was a magical era where cars cornered at speeds which bordered upon insanity.

Kendall leads Wayne Taylor with their Intrepids in 1991,
the glory days of GTP
— Photo courtesy of Jerry Howard

CHAPTER NINE

ELECTRONICS

Porsche 911 GT3-R Hybrid steering wheel

A Formula One car of the 1990s is having engine problems while leading in the middle of a Grand Prix. The engine management software modifications needed are quickly sorted by the engineering brain trust at the engine manufacturers' racing division and sent directly to either the car or to the team in the pits, who then upload the revised management program to the car. The car, which could never have made it to the finish line in its original specification, can now limp to a victory.

Gordon Kimball – "Yeah, we could do that. You could send different settings or different mapping… change parameters through telemetry from the pits. I honestly don't remember a time when it really played a part (as in changing the outcome of a race) when I was involved. They could take spark out of it, adjusting spark advance… that sort of thing."

Now, those two-way telemetry systems are no longer legal, seeming at first glance to take away that option. The reality is that now a wide variety of alternative engine management settings are pre-loaded into the car before the race, and require some driver participation in the process. Kimball – "Of course they still do it now, only now they put it on the steering wheel and they tell the driver to change the map. They had to work to put it into the car, the engine guys change things in the maps and the driver has a choice of the maps."

Ammar Bazzaz, formerly with Yoshimura Racing, is one of the electronics gurus for this new era of electronic controls for motorcycle road racing. "From my perspective it began in '97, when the majority of Superbikes were carbureted. The electronics were very simple, a black box where you had to flash and program a chip. Back then there was little or nothing going on, data acquisition was just coming onboard in about '95-'96 here in the US, but World Superbike and US Superbike chased each other pretty closely, there was not that much dissimilarity. It probably took a decade for people to learn how to properly analyze the data, in my opinion. Although I didn't know much about motorcycle setup, my background was such that we could start to process the data in a more useful way that other teams. The big explosion here on the electronics side was in 2003, when it got really serious on the engine management side… the beginning of the traction control era was the first year of the litre-bikes. That was when everybody said 'ok, we need to do something.' That was when things really started to trickle down from MotoGP. At that point it was illegal to run front wheel speed sensors, they started to allow them sometime around '04 or '05. Before that the electronics sensed a change in engine rpm. Once wheel speed sensors came onboard, people started using wheel speed differential, and they found certain limitations with that so they began to use a hybrid using wheel speed differential and engine speed together with inertial measurement units for pitch, roll, and acceleration. At the end of the day, it's all still traction control."

Does the Yamaha team ever get lost in the electronics? Yamaha Moto GP Team Director Massimo Meregalli – "Not now, but back in 2000 when we moved from carburetors to injection systems, we did. I think everybody was lost. I remember in 07 or 08, Corser was complaining about traction control or wheelie control or something. Then we turned it off, and he came back and said that he could not ride the bike any more without it." It didn't take long for Troy Corser to realize that he had become dependent upon the electronics. One thinks back to another highly experienced GP rider telling me in 2009 that he didn't want to hear anything more about electronics (in no uncertain terms), instead wishing to focus upon the mechanical setup of the machine.

We now live in a brave new world where GPS coordinates are being matched up with engine management systems, allowing the engine to be optimized at any point of the track, or any point in a turn… to adjust the engine characteristics to the ideal profile at any given moment. Probably the greatest innovations today occurs in motorcycle racing, where the contact patch is so tiny in comparison to racing cars, that maximizing tire performance becomes hyper-critical. In MotoGP, the tires often have different compounds on the left side vs. the right side vs. the middle of the tread. The sophistication of such tires and their electronic engine management systems now eclipse traditional concepts of traction control. Racing has entered an era where these management systems can be tied into a GPS providing multiple data points at each corner, at entry, middle, and exit. A sophisticated engine management system can then adjust parameters to the optimal for any given moment.

In MotoGP, some of the machines have become so electronically advanced that mechanical setup has become borderline irrelevant. John Hopkins in 2008 had found himself in that situation with the MotoGP Kawasaki. Were the limits in MotoGP now similarly so far ahead of what they would be on a normal motorcycle that you were essentially riding around the telemetry, relying upon the data to show if you can go in or out a little harder? John Hopkins – "It's like that with the motorcycle now; for sure that's exactly where it's going. Instead of working with the mechanics trying to do things manually, now you are strictly working 100% with your computer data acquisition guys, everything is monitored by a little black box on the machine. It's just getting your head around being able at the apex of the corner, at full lean angle, holding the bike wide open... it's all about getting the confidence. If you can get the thing set up where you can actually do that, it's incredible." Ammar sees things differently – "Our electronics were never that sophisticated that I would have total faith in telling somebody to pin it in the middle of a corner."

Not all of the teams have made that same commitment to electronics over all else. A commonly heard criticism of the current state of affairs is how the bikes are all electronic wizardry and have removed the challenge from the rider. In 2008, Stuart Shenton, Technical Director of Rizla Suzuki MotoGP stated his opinion of that perspective – "You have spin control, acceleration control, but it's only the last couple of years that this stuff has really grown. There's a lot written apparently about all this stuff, but it's not the be-all, end-all. The electronics are only so good, and that's why we are still seeing some people get thrown up in the air. Basically, you can still crash a motorcycle, all these people think that with traction control that these guys aren't riding them, that they aren't going to crash... it's just bollocks."

Stuart Shenton formerly with Rizla Suzuki in Moto GP

"There's still a large amount of this that is down to the rider, and you could take it all off and within a year and a half we'd be back up to the same lap times."

Needless to say, the costs of the cutting edge electronic packages have been staggering. All series have struggled with the dilemma of electronics cost vs. "the show", allowing teams with immense budgets to have a huge advantage. In an unlimited electronics scenario, traction control is just a small part of the equation, only triggered if the engine management system does not anticipate the edge of traction properly.

Engine braking is similarly being advanced well beyond some sort of ABS system, to where the electronics can cancel wheel chatter and control the degree of slide allowable. Think of an engine as an air pump with the compression providing resistance. The degree of resistance can be efficiently modulated electronically to assist the braking. Davide Tardozzi was the team manager of the BMW World Superbike team in 2010 – "This is the area where we think we will go more in the future. Engine brake working to automatically operate the butterflies for the brake so there is no chatter on the rear wheel upon entry, the traction on exit, and mid-corner is the suspension working to carry the fastest speed. The lean angle is important, and it (the gyroscopes) recognizes the angle and wheel spin and can adjust more or less power... it is a combination." This sophistication has reached the point to where gyroscope assemblies along with the choice of traction control settings are incorporated into the current BMW S1000RR street bike, allowing certain amounts of power to be accessed depending upon lean angle and other factors.

Troy Corser – "The slipper clutch uses a different spring and ramp mechanism for each rider; we're running different ones from Ruben (teammate Ruben Xaus) for example. A lot of that is not just the clutch, but also the rear shock setting on the bike, and really it comes down the grip at the tire. That's a big influence upon what the clutch "thinks" is happening. Throw in the electronics and that can just confuse it all. We've been trying to get the right combination, to where I feel comfortable on the bike."

The mechanical slipper clutch which helps to eliminate the rear wheel lockup seems that it would be a semi-random acting element creating just one more variable for the electronics to anticipate with the engine braking programming, but it appears to integrate more successfully than one would expect. Add in tire degradation, and the mathematical parameters become truly complex, to say nothing of variations in course conditions, or changes in the weather.

Ammar Bazzaz – "Engine braking is a very important strategy. Everybody focuses upon traction control, but that's one third of the corner. There is the entry, middle and exit of the corner. There are a whole host of parameters that go into that stuff... front and rear wheel speed, engine rpm, gear position, brake pressure At the end of the day all these things are coming in and you have fuel, ignition timing and throttle position to allow the rider to have that confidence to go in there at 300KPH."

Are you finding big gainers doing this vs. with the old slipper clutch? Ammar - "Definitely.... I think you need a combination of both, but today the electronics outweigh the clutch. The mechanical actuation is pretty predictable and there is not a whole lot of back and forth between the two. If the two were dancing on top of each other all the time, it would be very difficult. When you start to look at the data and control strategies it looks seamless."

So, are the rider controls approaching the level of a formula one steering wheel, with 27 buttons and a dozen fine tune knobs? Tardozzi – "No, too many makes for confusion. We have a selected number of maps; there is a button where they can push to bring up map 1, map 2... there are 5 maps they can select from. When the rear tire is new, you can have less traction control...

when increasing the slide, you can step forward to a setting where the traction is more to have less slide. We have buttons to manage launch control, and traction maps, but not too much. I saw once a Ferrari steering wheel (F1) and thought you must be an engineer to drive this car."

There's that term "Launch Control". Obviously if the machine has an embedded software program that can control all the variables to achieve optimum launch, it takes the driver out of the equation other than to engage the process at the correct time. In 1993 such concepts were commonplace in Formula One, but were supposedly removed from the cars for the '94 season, although in one prominent case, Launch Control was still found embedded within the software although the team argued that it had been disabled. One gets a variety of responses when asking about the BMW launch process, with Troy seeing much of that success as his history of being a good starter, his feel for the clutch, rpm, and body position. No doubt those all play a role, but Corser's telemetry engineer Max best sums up BMW's official position on the topic of launch control, by sliding his fingers across his lips, as if sealing a zip lock bag.

One suspects without an enormous amount of seat time, it would be easy to turn the wrong dial and get a one way ticket to the kitty litter. It is far simpler on the World Superbike. Corser – "The buttons are plus and minus on the traction, and plus and minus on the slide... engine brake, and the pit (speed) limiter. We've almost got to build a system that automatically self adjusts as the tire starts to go away." Think of those buttons as fine tuning within the individual maps.

Ammar Bazzaz - "In the big picture, some of the things that have come onboard, I would say individual closed loop controls for air/fuel mixture for individual cylinders has come about in the last 5 years with an air/fuel sensor in each primary pipe, for optimum power as each is different from the others due to the mechanical layout of the outer cylinders in cooling, and also tolerances between injectors and the cylinders… and the dynamics of the airflow. We had it on our superbikes but typically it was from one sensor at the collector which would take an average of all 4 cylinders and apply corrections based upon that. In 2007 individual control of each cylinder really started to become more mainstream. Obviously the traction control systems are in constant evolution, as fly-by-wire has become kind of a big thing in the last 5 years. It's an important component not only in controlling power delivery, but on controlling the bike upon corner entry and the deceleration characteristics. Another item is more integrated GPS positioning. It's been around for a decade but in the last 5 years, it's gone from primarily a tool to show your location on the track, to something that can be tied into the electronics so that the strategies have different values at different points of the circuit."

Of course, the electronic system modeling continues to improve beyond the standard GPS model. In 2012 at Mugello, Jorge Lorenzo completely befuddled his electronic package by taking the back door into the pit lane, leaving the bike confused as to where it was and what parameters to implement. In short, the bike was lost, which meant that their current modeling system does not use GPS coordinates as a reference point, or at the very least that global positioning is not continuously monitored.

Meregalli - "Basically, without the GPS, the bike knows where it is. I do not know how they created this or how it is working, but I know that the bike knows exactly where it is. It is difficult to get technical information from them, but I think everybody has the same. I know when we did GPS, everything was more precise, and we could compare the riders. But now we cannot compare, we cannot do that." Jorge Lorenzo – "To be honest, I do not know." Is it more like a video game every day? "Yeah… sometimes it is, yes."

In 2010 at Laguna Seca, Jorge Lorenzo had an over-the-handlebars highside on the cool off lap in practice. Ammar

Bazzaz – "All of those MotoGP bikes with fly-by-wire, the computer dictates how the throttle opens. With it off, maybe it caught him off-guard. He went for a fist full of throttle and it gave him a fist full of throttle."

Jorge Lorenzo riding the 2013 USGP on the factory Yamaha M1

Jorge Lorenzo - "I was practicing a start and the traction control was deactivated. So when I opened the throttle without traction control and it went away." Having confidence in the electronics package is everything for the rider of a current Moto GP machine. How long does it take before you really trust the machine after getting thrown down the road because of the electronic settings? Jorge - "Oh yeah, to get back the confidence again. There is a light and I have to see the light on the bike." Not turning off the traction control so much these days? "No (laughs) no more turning off the traction control. Always you have to learn from the bad things." No doubt having a teammate as blazingly fast and smooth as Jorge Lorenzo is as stiff a challenge as any in racing. Does each team rider have its own separate development program? Massimo - "Yes, for sure, as every rider has their own style, but everything is open and the data is shared, it is completely open. The bikes are similar; differences are mainly with the tires. First you get the mechanical balance, and then the electronic controls are to help."

Many feel that is no longer possible. Ruben Xaus already took the combination approach with the BMW Superbike in 2010 - "You have only 2 hours to practice and there isn't time for that. You have to do the mechanical and electronics together. There are times where we change from one bike to the other one... different tires in the front or rear, sprockets, suspension, clutch... it is very easy to get confused with it all, but it is what it is. We are professionals and we have to adapt to this." Massimo Meregalli – "We only have so many practice sessions, so we have to do both at the same time. But, the Japanese are very good at this, and when we arrive at the track, the basic setup is working. They know." Massimo is also of the opinion that the younger riders, who perhaps haven't become as set in their ways nor developed old habits, are also more receptive to this ever changing world of electronic aids. It is a brave new world, perhaps mostly meant for brave new riders. As with the highly sophisticated F1 machines of 1993, racers with vast experience struggled to forget everything they knew and simply trust their engineer when he says to do something that every fibre of their being feels is suicidal.

In the ALMS, the 2009 Corvette team was seen chasing the setup with their GT2 car and needed to change rear springs after a session, showing that the art of mechanical setup is still relevant in this world of electronic wizardry. ALMS rules also preclude some complex engine management concepts from being implemented as the air inlet for the engine cannot be adjusted, taking away a vital variable for such management systems. Adjusting the ignition timing alone could have catastrophic results, but in the case of Pratt & Miller, there is a sophisticated ignition timing system that monitors and adjusts those parameters to the limits of clean burn just short of detonation.

The amount of data available from the car is staggering, with sensors that monitor every imaginable parameter in real time. Dan Binks - "This thing is a science project, there are wires going to everything. This thing tells you everything; it sends all the stuff you saw at Le Mans, it sends it to the pit. We can watch rpm to see if they overrev on downshifts, watch the tire pressure, and watch the transmission temperature, clutch temperature... all the things that have caused us problems over the years. It turns red and you can catch it before it is a problem."

Compare that to what the Malibu Grand Prix RX-7 had for data acquisition.

Tom Kendall at Cleveland in 1987
– Photo courtesy of Mark Windecker

Tommy Kendall – "That RX-7 that Clayton kept adding instrumentation to, they wanted me to read 5 of them (gauges) at the end of the longest straightaway, trying to go as deep as you could approaching the braking zone. They wanted you to read engine rpm, exhaust gas temperature, and the airbox pressure magnahelic on the floor. I told Binks that I could get them one every lap, it was a poor man's data acquisition. I own the Malibu car now, and I think Binks said that he found the original airbox pressure magnahelic gauge, as I want to restore it back to original."

Compare that to the task of today's drivers. Binks – "We have temperature paint and infrared that gives us real time us as we are running. I think there are about 200 telemetry points, and I don't know exactly how many data points come back to the pits at any one time, but it's a lot." How much of that information can the driver pull up? "None – The driver just drives."

Other advancements continued into the 2011 season. Binks – "The electronics have changed, and it's got a Bosch 5.1 on it, and we've gone to a new wiring harness that is 10 pounds lighter." Taking 10 pounds out of the wiring of an endurance car that is about to run 12 hours around the pounding that is Sebring seems a debatable concept. Binks – "I think it will hold up fine. We've done a lot of testing with it; the new Cadillac has it on there. It's not 'brand-new' stuff, but it's new to our Corvettes. Is there some risk? There's always a risk, but you have to weigh the benefit of the reduced weight and the interaction with the car. If it makes sense, you do it… and that's where we are right now."

Al Ludington, technical director for AMA Pro Racing has tried to develop some sort of cost containment on electronics issues, based upon his decades of experience in a similar position for American Honda's AMA Superbike program – "Engine management systems have become sophisticated to the point that traction control systems are almost passé. A very expensive, highly developed engine control system will limit the torque output of the motorcycle in various scenarios so that the tire is never overwhelmed and traction control doesn't come into play."

"You either put out a spec ECU or you will have to be prepared to put on a big electronics staff as it's virtually impossible to monitor without a huge cost. There are several ways to do it, a spec ECU, kit ECU, or standard ECUs with piggy back controllers. As the complexity of the class goes up and the needs for more complex engine management increase, we would allow more features that we define."

Bazzaz – "There's a lot of problem that goes with that (spec ecu), because that requires a tremendous amount of technical support. They all have such different platforms, their electro-mechanical actuators. To have one ECU to control all of these bikes, it's a little bit of an undertaking. The manufacturers are constantly innovating, coming up with new actuators... on the BMW it controls the fuel pump, an entirely different technique. The manufacturer now has to drive this particular motor with 'this' amount of current, and using 'this' strategy."

Al Ludington has dealt with this in the AMA rules, as any hardware package of sufficient complexity and features merely opens the door for vast software development. "It is currently possible for a team to incur a pretty large electronics bill. This is not desirable as far as we are concerned. A well funded team could take advantage of the existing rules, "hardware-up", get a good software engineer and really be way ahead of the game. We are just on the very tip of the electronics iceberg."

Ammar Bazzaz – "In 2009 the electronics didn't change, other than having to be on the approved equipment list, but that was just paperwork as all of them made it onto the list. There was no effective change in electronics, the majority of the change was in the forks and engine internals... they really dumbed down the chassis quite a bit but left the electronics wide open. That was the irony of it all... because electronics were THE most expensive elements on the bike. They made the rule changes in all sincerity, but they missed the white elephant. I don't think the manufacturers will stand for that, just sit there and have their bike (electronics) dumbed down."

Is the door wide open for technical wizardry within these hardware limits? Ron Heben of Graves Yamaha, formerly with the Honda AMA Superbike program – It is very difficult to control electronics. There are many variables that can be put into the system, many of these options are dependant on a teams' overall budget. Just as riders use different suspension settings, they also have different electronics settings, and electronics are only as good as the engineer trying to manipulate and configure them to the riders' needs. Sander Donkers, Electronics Engineer agrees – "What makes it work is not the hardware... it is how you set up the software that makes it a good system."

Ludington – "One of the balancing acts is "Do you want to keep up with the technology that is on the street? Are we here to push technology forward, or are we here to put on a good show? One could argue that just about every car in the parking lot at a NASCAR race is more sophisticated than the cars on the race track, unless some guy shows up in his '65 Falcon."

This is the fundamental decision facing the organizing bodies today. In 2013 the American Le Mans series and WEC showcase such advanced machines as the Audi R18, whereas in comparison the Daytona Prototypes of Grand-Am are comparatively low-tech cars that showcase the driver skills more than the technology. MotoGP has felt the economic pinch of manufacturer withdrawal and after two years of mediocre results with a 2 class scenario (Claiming Rule Teams, or CRT), they have adopted a spec ECU from Marelli for the 2014 season. Understanding that the hardware is merely the method by which the software is implemented, there are penalties for those teams who develop their own software vs. accept the software package developed by the organizing body (Dorna). Not only do the factory developed software package teams only allow 20 litres of fuel for a race versus 24 litres (Dorna software spec), they also are limited to five engines for the season compared to the twelve engines

411

allowed the teams running Dorna software. Eventually the lines will cross and a well funded satellite team running the Dorna software will have the advantage of running a more highly stressed engine using more fuel. With ever greater technical advantages granted to the non-factory teams, one can only wonder how that will be received by the "factory" teams when and if the day eventually arrives that the satellite or private team consistently competes for overall wins. Best guess is that an immediate re-calibration of the "spec" software package would ensue.

Where it's going? Ammar – "I don't know, by 2012 the Harley-Davidson Street-Glide was fly-by-wire. It's everywhere. I think in the future we are going to see even shorter gestation periods. It took 6 or 7 years for racing technology to get to the street, now it seems like its 3 years or less. Technology is becoming more readily available. The things we are doing are now becoming more acceptable for somebody that wants to spend a little bit of money and spend some time with it. Whereas 10 years ago it was all kind of prototypical, behind the scenes factory stuff. It was unobtainium. Where this is going is that control strategies obviously are improving, becoming acceptable to a much wider group of people." More than ever before, electronic advances made on the race track will be mainstream in short order.

CHAPTER TEN

DETAILS AND SETUP

*The ability to understand the best adjustment to make from a variety of
options was very much the key to the success of Rick Mears.
— Photo courtesy of Ken Anderson (seated to the left of Mears)*

Sometimes innovation comes in the way of detailed improvements. Sometimes the advances are from an explosion of innovation. 1989 brought such an explosion at Ferrari, with the seven speed paddle shift Ferrari 640. Gordon Kimball – "Before that, Harvey (Postlewaite) had been there, and now John (Barnard) was the technical director at Ferrari. Actually the deal was that we had built the 639, which was supposed to race in 88, but they were doing so well with the turbo that they decided to stay with it for one more year. The idea was to start with the normally aspirated car in 1988, but then they changed their mind. We had built one or two chassis, and did testing, but then did the 640, which was how it raced."

How could the Ferrari 3.5 litre V12 have been competitive with the turbocar competition? Kimball – "They weren't competitive horsepower-wise with the turbo either, so… Most of the problems that we had with that car were called gearbox failures, but they were really alternator failures, or the rectifier that manipulated it. Then they had problems with the drive belt that was driving it off the crank, they kept spinning drive belts. As the alternator failed, the voltage fell and the gearbox was the first thing to fail. It was that way because the old man was really only interested in the engine. The rest of it was only something that was carrying the engine. Everybody was afraid to do anything, but I'd tell them that I'd take the responsibility, and then it was 'Oh, ok', and then we'd go do something. They were just s**t scared because Ferrari would come and crucify somebody. I'd see him go in and out of his office, but not very often in the shop. But the culture of racing was there."

Sometimes those innovative concepts can be revolutionary to the point of being ridiculed. At the Brazilian Grand Prix in 1989, John Barnard's Ferrari 640 F1 debuted with a paddle shift system. This enabled their drivers Berger and Mansell to never take their hands from the wheel. Gian Paolo Dallara – "I was in Brazil for that race when there was the first race for the paddle shifter.

Everyone was wondering why… saying 'you stupid guy, why are you always doing these stupid things.' But he was the person who had the vision, and spent a lot of time, a lot of money… and now, paddle shifters on all the cars." As Thomas Edison famously said – "I have not failed. I've just found 10,000 ways that don't work. Opportunity is missed by most people because it is dressed in overalls and looks like work." Having a vision and the courage to execute or develop new ideas… often, but not always, those details add up.

It goes without saying that without a well funded program of dedicated and talented personnel, success is unlikely. Probably the poster child for how difficult things can get due to a completely ridiculous team environment would be with the early 1950s AJS factory race team, although Perry McCarthy's trials and tribulations with Andrea Moda in F1 come close. 1952 had brought the new AJS factory 350 racer, the 7R3, a 3 valve engine (replacing the 2 valve 7R2 motor). This engine was problematic throughout the following 2 seasons, with the majority of problems centered upon the private fiefdoms of the various departments at AJS, where each department manager distrusted the others. Rod Coleman struggled to develop and campaign their bikes despite these handicaps.

The factory required that the race team run standard production products, however unsuitable they proved to be for racing. Standard production Lucas magneto shafts sheared, although upgraded Lucas racing models were available (being run by Gilera and MV). The team was asked to adjust the clearances in the motors so they could run the standard oils, and the KLG spark plugs were a constant source of failures. When asked how Norton dealt with similar problems, Rod Coleman responds - "No, if Joe Craig got a problem like that… bang, that would be the end of them, he wouldn't use that again." The petty bickering and fiefdom prevalent at AJS stood in stark contrast to Norton's successful combination of experience, innovation and cooperation. Poor assembly also plagued the AJS team in the 52 and 53 seasons as well.

Development was haphazard; some greatly needed improvements were not forthcoming (such as the needed 5 speed replacement for the standard 4 speed Porcupine gearbox). At the 53 TT, there were eight versions of the 7R3 engine at the track, none of which were properly set up. Taking some mechanics with him, testing on private roads after official practice, Rod Coleman eventually was able to get a proper setup on one of the bikes. With properly set up carburetion, he was leading the 53 Junior TT until the engine going off song ended his race. As it turned out, the entire back of the bike was covered in oil due to faulty assembly of the engine. The response of the man in charge was to hurriedly dismantle the engine to eliminate the evidence, and then announce that Rod had stopped for no reason. Despite all the failures and challenges, Rod was often the fastest rider. As a bonus, having the favored Bob McIntyre as his teammate brought other challenges. Rod - "All the mechanics were behind him (McIntyre) because I was a colonial (New Zealand born), I was a foreigner. He had worked in the race shop; they were always trying to work to get him the best equipment. I had to watch out for that."

It wasn't any better riding the AJS Porcupine in the 500cc Grand Prix. The AJS was seriously handicapped running against the streamliners with their dustbin fairings. A mandate had come down from the factory, that customers wanted to see the construction of the racing bikes, not a fairing. This decision proved to be a serious handicap for the AJS team, the only factory team running naked bikes at the time. At Monza, Coleman was forced to retire after being vacuumed along behind 3 of the streamliners and over-revved his engine by 1000 rpm. It had reached the point that riding for the AJS factory was more a handicap than a benefit.

Ferrari in the wake of the death of its founder was another

example of complete and utter frustration with management. Gordon Kimball – "Enzo Ferrari died (summer of 1988), and then we finished 1-2 in the next race at Monza… divine intervention and valve spring failures with the Hondas. Ferrari had died during the August vacation, but soon after the Fiat guys started coming down. It was crap because they had been aching to get in, they wanted into the glory. I had no idea how bad it would get, but they were complete 'doofuses'. They wanted to build a race car like they'd build a production car. They just had no idea what it took to build race cars. You'd try to explain things to them, but they were making management decisions that were useless. They would tell us that the first thing to do was to make a parts list for the car. They didn't care about doing the car right, just build it and test it."

Despite all this turmoil behind the scenes, the Ferraris were to make their mark on the new 3.5 litre normally aspirated Formula One of 1989. Kimball – "The 640s were good cars. John got fed up and Prost was just despondent, you could tell. It didn't get sorted out there until Stepney."

It wasn't long before both Kimball and Barnard left Ferrari for McLaren. At McLaren the issue was one of communication. Kimball - "I left Ferrari because they (the Fiat management) were idiots. At McLaren, Ron asked me to help; we were actually working on putting together an Indycar team. Ayrton was struggling with Neil Oatley as his race engineer, as Neil is not one of the most communicative persons; they used to call him the 'Design Fairy'. After everyone went home at night, he would go around and look at everyone's designs and write post-it notes. So, the design team would arrive in the morning and see what the 'Design Fairy' had left. All day, he would stay in his office. So, Ron asked if I'd help and have a look at the development of the car. So, I did a test at Silverstone, there were a couple of things wrong with it. At the end of the year, Ayrton found out about the Indycar program and put his foot down, and made dropping the project a condition of him staying. Nobody ever told me that exactly, but the Indycar program was the reason I was there…" Perhaps we should all adopt the post-it note method of management as McLaren has certainly had their share of success over the past 20 years as Neil Oatley continues today in his role as Design and Development Director at McLaren Racing.

Barnard was to work his magic on motorcycles as well. Kenny Roberts' KR MotoGP team needed to develop a new 4 stroke MotoGP 990 engine for the upcoming year of 2003. Into this effort, Kenny Roberts was to bring some of the best designers and minds from Formula One to his effort, the crown jewel being the #80 V5 powered machine. Kenny – "The number 80 bike… this is the last one that we built with my 5 cylinder engine. That is the bike that John Barnard designed and that bike is like a watch. That bike made all the Japanese build better motorcycles. When they saw that, they just went f***, that's unbelievable. Hiring Barnard cost a lot of money… for example the swingarm is machined out of solid aluminum, no fabrication or bending. The rear suspension link that connects the shock to the frame, the mechanic told me "I'm not putting that on the bike, it will kill somebody." So I went to Barnard and said "Look Barnard, this thing bends… and he said "It had better bend, otherwise it will break." It's just the little stuff like that we did, and if Barnard had been able to stay in the GP bike game for 3 years, Grand Prix bikes would be different right now."

Regardless of the pedigree of John Barnard, after looking at that suspension link, count me in the doubter camp with the KR mechanic. The width in one plane couldn't exceed 1/32 of an inch and it flexes easily in the opposite axis. The engineering showed it would work, somehow. As with many worthy efforts, the KR team's lack of a long term sponsorship or financing had ended the partnership with Barnard. In this case it wasn't meddling by inept management that spelled doom. It was the inability to secure a long term financial partner. Although there have been recent examples of where vast financial resources did not equal success, typically when it comes to motorsport... money doesn't talk, it screams.

Kenny Roberts with the rear linkage of the John Barnard KR

The John Barnard designed KR

Of course, without the best drivers, all that money and design talent is wasted. There have been few drivers who could consistently dwell on the superspeedway knife edge, and perhaps none have ever had more finesse than Rick Mears. Rick – "At Pocono in the PC-10 year (1982), we had about 5mph on the field going down the front straightaway, probably even on my teammate. Everybody swore up and down that we were running a big turbo, I just let them think what they want. What it was that I had found a little crack in the pavement down next to the grass down in turn 3, right on the edge of the paint line. It was about a ¼" step and I found out that I could put the inside of the left front on that ledge and it would hold the tire in the middle of corner. You had to hit it every time, but it worked great. I could go in 3 cars deeper than anybody, and be on the throttle 3 cars before anybody. Pocono... I loved that place; you had Michigan in 1, Indy in 2, and Milwaukee in 3, three different race tracks to set up for. Any time you made 1 and 2 right, you were pushing in 3. Or, if you made 3 right, you were loose in 1 and 2. It was a hard trade-off. So, when I found that seam, I made the car good in 1 and 2, and used the seam in 3... and then had all 3 corners good. I'd come off that corner like a rocketship, and everybody swore up and down that we were cheating. All it was... was a seam in the pavement."

Derrick Walker – "These guys, the real race drivers... they are out there searching for grip. They are really thinking about it, searching for it. He may have stumbled across that by accident, but it registered with him, he perfected it, and that became the fast way around. They always did think we were cheating, but we never did. Roger is very conscious of his reputation, a respected guy inside and outside of racing." Ken Anderson – "I worked with Rick at Pocono in 1982. The Penske team was running Fox Shox and that is one of the reasons Rick could go for seams or bumps without upsetting the car. I was also his race engineer from 1984 - 1988... an amazing guy."

There are stories that border upon urban legend regarding Mears' ability to sense the stagger in a tire. Could Mears honestly sense differences of 1/100th of an inch in circumference? Rick – "Yeah, sure. I used to change the stagger myself, by how you run it on the racetrack. It didn't take much stagger change to help.

If the car had understeer, I'd run the left front down and hook it onto the apron which would really build up the pressure in the right rear, which would get the car loose building the heat and temp in the right rear, so the air would expand and the tire would grow. You could adjust it by where you placed it on the track, just like going in and saying 'give me a bigger right rear'.

How would the driver know when to make a stagger adjustment vs. an aero adjustment vs. a mechanical adjustment? Rick – "Sometimes any one of them can get the job done, as it can just be a balance problem. But stagger may affect you one place in a corner where aero doesn't. Aero might affect you someplace in a corner where stagger doesn't. So, you look at your biggest problem. An example would be when we had flush wheels one year, it was the first time we ran those wheels all around and we had the front row at Indy (88)."

Front row sweep in 1988 – all 3 Penske team cars equipped with flush wheels – Photo courtesy of Ken Anderson

Rick – "When we put them on in practice, they really cured a problem that we were fighting... mid-turn understeer. Right in the middle of the corner it just sharpened the front end up and they were also better for drag. Well, 10 laps into the race, it's so loose I can't drive it. I knew that if I came into the pits and took a couple of turns of front wing out, it would take the looseness out, but that wouldn't do it where I wanted it. I thought that the open wheels would be a better combination, so I'm screaming on the radio... 'I want open wheels'. Poor Jerry is having a fit because he's got all the wheels mounted sky high, so he has to run them over to Goodyear to break them all down to mount the tires back on the old wheels. He had a set for me by the next stop, and then during the next round he started changing more and got them all swapped out."

"It's that kind of stuff... yeah, I can fix this one way, but there is always more than one way to fix it. How is 'this' going to affect 'this'? By taking wing out, it would bring it into range, but it was better the other way. And that's what you do, the first half of the race you are gearing up to being the best it can ever be, for the shootout... from the last stop on." Mears and his wheel change worked, and he won his 3rd Indy 500.

For Rick Mears, what was the art of the setup, and where does one start? Rick – "I always want to get as much mechanical grip as possible, trying to dial the mechanical in first... trying to work on the bad end. A lot of guys say, 'oh no, it's all about balance.' I can get balance in a car quickly, by hurting the good end to balance out against the bad end. That's easy... it's harder to help the bad end. My whole point was to always work on the bad end until it matched or was better than the good end. Then I'd work on what previously was the good end, which is now the bad end. And that's how I get more total... I want to build a faster car. And I work and work to do that, and when it comes to the end and I've used everything and if I still haven't got the balance right... still can't help the bad end... ok, then you hurt the good end."

Ken Anderson and Rick Mears – 1988 Indianapolis 500 winners
– Photo courtesy of Ken Anderson

Mears continues - "Early-on, when I started, the driver was kind of the engineer. I'd been developing that since I was riding motorcycles or back when I was 12 years old, building my frames in the slot car days. That and working in the desert, trying to build a better mousetrap to get across the ruts and the holes... that taught me to feel equipment, to think about suspension and what changes did what. All of that was a big help to me. Once I had enough experience with Roger and from what I'd learned, and as much as I felt comfortable with the knowledge I had at the time, I enjoyed competing with the engineer. Sometimes the designer would come in and help engineer the car, if he wasn't back designing new cars. Trying to put my finger on the problem before they could, it was a game... it was a race, and we had fun at it, but there was a reason for it. I've seen a lot of drivers over the years come in and say 'it's loose, fix it.' Anybody can do that. In competing with my engineer I always had an advantage because I got to feel it and he didn't. But the main reason was that we have an hour of practice, and we all get to make 10 changes. If I can make 8 of the 10 changes for the good, vs. somebody else who can make 5 of 10, we're ahead. If I could point to the problem we'd have an advantage."

"Of course, back then we didn't have telemetry. We were getting telemetry towards the end (of my career), but we were just learning to read it at that point. Learning how to measure it, and understanding what you are looking at. Then learning how to utilize it was another learning curve in itself. One of the biggest things from an engineer did for me in the early days, was that they opened my eyes that there was more than one way to skin a cat. I enjoyed that era, and it was fun trying to identify if it was wing angle, aero, camber, toe, tire pressure, bump, or rebound that was causing the problem, any of those. And you could change a spring in one corner, and that could be affecting the camber on another wheel. Making a camber change, and understanding what it would do... in the early cars making a camber change would change the cross weights. If it turned out that the camber was in the ballpark anyway, it wasn't the camber change that was making the real difference, it was the cross weight change. When I was out in the car, I was feeling the cross weight change more than the camber change because I'm feeling the left front footprint more on the seam, on the turn-in. The engineer would make his best guess at what would be the most logical thing, the most likely. And it might take 2 or 3 tries, but if I can pinpoint it and get him in the right direction, we are ahead of the game. That was my job, understanding everything that you do on a car and how it affects other things. And always thinking how those pieces went together."

Rick – "If you are talking about the setup on a superspeedway, then I'd put in a lot of aero, unless I felt that one particular portion (of the setup) was way off. But if we were close to a balance, I'd do that. Put downforce in it, until it got pretty solid and then start to trim it off. We worked with whatever we had to work with at the time… it was different in different years. As for the tunnel configurations, not so much in that respect, as that was a pretty solid change. Later on, once you got sorted with where the center of pressure was and what you had to work with tunnel-wise when that was wide open. If the rules changed and they started blocking them down, then you found a tunnel that was working and you didn't end up straying. The chassis manufacturer continues trying to develop a better shape for the envelope, pretty soon you are just filling in the corners. They don't really change that much."

There are no hard and fast rules to this, and as one might suspect it often comes down to experience. Rick - "I just did what the car told me. Where do I start? Well, I do what the car tells me it wants, and that is what I work on. If I felt it needed work on the aero, I'd work on the aero. If I felt it was mechanical, I'd work on the mechanical. It's all from feeling… feeling and experience… and laps. And it's not that aero feels different from the mechanical, it's maybe how the car is responding, loading the wheel vs. loading the tire. If the spring rate is too soft on the tire… if I feel that I'm overloading a corner, am I overloading it because it's too softly sprung, or is the tire too soft? Car spring rate vs. tire spring rate or pressure… if I feel the car is mushy a little bit, with a little bit of wallow or wobble in it vs. just going away… if it just rolls over, sits down and goes away, it could be too softly spring. If just before it loads and goes away, I feel there is movement just as it loads and then goes away, then I'm wallowing around on the sidewall of the tire. The spring isn't going to make it do that, so we can pinpoint the problem to the engineer in one try. Then, where it is doing it on the track, what corner is it? The pavement, is it a crown, is it a dip? You put all those pieces together to determine if it's aero or mechanical.

Geometry, aero... there is no black and white, this is a grey business."

Gordon Kimball was at Benetton when Michael Schumacher came aboard, and it was somewhat different from the sort of involved feedback and participation of Rick Mears. Gordon – "Michael Schumacher wasn't all that interested in the technical side. He'd come in and say, 'here is what the car was doing, fix it', and then go away." Were any of the F1 drivers you worked with, incredibly involved on the technical side? Kimball - "Ayrton was... he wanted to know all about it, and talk all about it. It was Ayrton I was working more with, and technically he was a lot of fun. It was funny when I came there... we'd heard stories about how that everybody on the engineering side at McLaren was afraid of Ayrton. Maybe we just hit it off, but I had a lot of fun with him, because he made my job really easy because he was really good about describing what the car was doing. He would make suggestions, and it was almost like he'd mentally put them on the car, go around the track and say how 'it would help me here, but it does 'this' there in turn 7 and I'm not sure I'll like it.' Maybe we spoke the same language, so we communicated real well. It was easy to set up the car, get a good car and perfect it."

Ayrton's great rival at the time was Alain Prost. Kimball – "Actually, on the setup I think Alain Prost was better. He was very good on the car side...very good at getting the car setup right. Ayrton spent a lot of time on the engine; he worked really well with the Honda guys. Alain did a lot of the car stuff. I think in 1990, Ayrton was missing Alain and his input. I think that when he (Ayrton) came, Alain was already there and was really good on the chassis side. So, it was kind of his way to make his place in the team, to hammer on the engine guys and look at the engine data and talk about things to develop. So, they ended up sharing the responsibility. At Ferrari, when Mansell came on we thought he was going to tear up equipment. Actually, he was good on equipment, very sensitive... really good technically and

427

was better than he got credit for, and better than we expected.

Added to all this, can be the varied effects of different driving techniques. Determining the correct driving technique in the roadster era of Indy car racing was also a grey business for the young Parnelli Jones. Parnelli – "When I first went back to Indy I drove the car that Clint Brawner built, the Dean Van Lines car… that was my first ride. Well, there was this roadster that was built for Bill Cheesebourg. It was a laydown car, the Autolite car… it had the engine laid over to the left, where the Belond car (Salih's 57-58 winner) had the engine laid over to the right. Well, Tony Bettenhausen was doing the Firestone tire tests and they wanted to know if I could just take a ride around the track in this car. They told me "ok, but don't go fast." So, I went out and when I first got on it I didn't go that fast, but it was over 140mph. Well, they started jumping up and down, called me in and chewed my ass out. I told them, 'Fellas, the track record is 149 mph, I think I can go out and break the track record right now.' They told me I had to be kidding, but I told them that the car was fabulous and we asked Tony to take a ride in it. Tony got in the car and almost broke the track record. So, Tony went to Hopkins and said "You either buy me that car, or I'm going to go drive for Agajanian." Needless to say, Tony Bettenhausen was driving the Autolite car at Indy in 1961. Donald Davidson – "They bought it out from under Parnelli."

As a result of this performance, it appeared that the world was Parnelli's oyster. Jones - "Tony had also told Aggie 'If I don't come with you, you'd better get a hold of Parnelli.' Well, Lindsay Hopkins wanted me to come drive his Watson roadster as a second car to Tony." The future was looking bright for the gifted sprint car driver from Southern California, but it went completely wrong as Parnelli tried to push the cars harder in official debut.

Parnelli – "My rookie year was 1961. I'm getting through my 1st, 2nd and 3rd tests, and I told Tony (Bettenhausen) that I didn't think I could find another 5mph. He thought I was kidding, as I had a good reputation in sprint cars, but I told him I was serious. Tony told me 'Fine, I know that there is something wrong, I'm going to have somebody take you out at 6 o'clock and figure out what you are doing wrong.' He got Bob Veith and Johnny Boyd to take me around and ask me where I was backing off, so I showed them where I was using the brakes. They said, 'Brakes? You aren't supposed to be using brakes! That's your problem.' The next day I backed off where they told me to, and gained 5mph so easy that it wasn't funny. It turned out that was why I was running so quick with the other car (the Autolite Special), because I was backing off and running the corner. I was using the right technique, trying to go slow. What happens is that when you hit the brakes it upsets the chassis just enough to feel like you have to back off. If you are trying to see how fast you can go down the following straight, you wouldn't drive it into the corner extremely hard. If you back off and then slowly pick up the throttle early, you are running the corners. By picking up the throttle where I had previously been hitting the brakes, I think I got the 2nd fast time on the next day."

There had been nothing wrong with the car; it had all come down to learning and applying the proper technique. Those lessons learned by Jones at Indy in 1961 remain relevant today. Parnelli's son PJ – "Actually, driving a NASCAR Cup car is much more similar to in his day, driving the roadster. You have to roll out, get back on the gas… don't upset the chassis."

Of course there are times when even the most experienced drivers and engineers are left completely befuddled. One example was the new and supposedly improved F5000 Lola with rising rate suspension for 1975. Brian Redman – "What was the problem? Well, we never really found out. The Lola T-400 was new in 1975, and of course at the end of the previous year Carl Haas always sold that year's cars. For 1975 at the 1st race at Pocono we had the new T-400, I drove it and it was slow. Jim Hall said to me - 'What was the matter? Is it pushing?' Nope. Hall- 'Is it oversteering?' Nope. 'Well, why is it so God damned slow?' So I said - 'you tell me, you're the engineer.' Well, the race was rained out and held again 4 weeks later. In that 4 weeks, Carl Haas, who was the importer... we bought a wrecked T-332 and sent it to him. We raced a month later with that 332." Brian Redman put the rebuilt T-332 to good use, winning the F5000 championship in 1975, along with the first running of the Long Beach Grand Prix. The Lola T-400 was a failed replacement, yet another part of the saga of the legendary T-332/333 that formed the basis for most of the winning F-5000 cars in 1973-76, the single seat Can-Am cars of 1977-79, and then returning in 1981 as the now ancient 332/333 chassis formed the basis of the Frisbee.

Techniques and development methods often remain shades of grey today in GT sports car racing as well. Does one start with a baseline setup? Jan Magnussen – "For the most part, but every year you develop the car from race to race, test to test. If you were to take last years' setup for Road Atlanta, testing through the year might have taken you in a different direction." Are the different setups from year to year mostly driven by tire development? "It's driven by lap time. But with the tires there are always big differences in durability, speed, compounds, construction, things like that. You always try to get the best out of the tire for a stint, or a double stint. And Michelin will try to build a tire to help you for the next year, according to the issues you've had this year. So we stay in good contact with them, the engineers tell them our problems and they can hopefully develop a tire that will suit us better."

Jan continues - "As for setup, Pratt & Miller has a fantastic ability to simulate a lot of stuff back at the shop. So even with a new car that I don't know anything about on the track, they have a really good firm knowledge of the car even before it turns a lap. They can predict pretty well what lap time I would do." Can they simulate the various tire construction as well? "Anything, you name it, they can simulate it.... tires, aero, camber, springs, everything."

Jan Magnussen at ease before a race at Mid-Ohio

Still, there is no substitute for track time. Jan – "When you are developing a car, you tend to go through a bunch of changes that may not in the order of things make sense. Doug Louth and his guys will make out a plan so that today we will go through this… springs, brakes, ride height stuff. Maybe you are moving the car in the complete wrong direction for lap time or balance, but you've got to go through all these changes to get the knowledge. You put that in the bank, and you take it out when you need it. When you have an oversteering car and they are putting less and less rear wing in it… it feels kind of funny, but you have to do this to know what is really happening on the track. It's just super complicated. If you were to go into every little thing, there are not enough engineers in this world, I don't think. I try to come

431

up with my own ideas, but these guys who are sitting up there in the office are probably the best educated engineers you could ever come across, so don't mess with their time. Don't waste their time, just give them the facts, explain every little thing you can think of... is the engine part of the problem, is the downshifting part of the problem, is the way you go onto the throttle part of the problem, is it aero, is it dampers? Give them the specifics then get the hell out and let them earn their money. That's how you get the best out of them. Some drivers are very engineering-driven people, I'm not. I just try to be the best driver I can."

How does one go about throwing different setups onto the car, and what is the awareness of the drivers? Dan Binks – "If we are going to do something that is fairly extreme, and we do some pretty wild geometry changes on the Corvettes... we'll say (to the driver) 'Hey, warm up to this'. We won't tell them what we did exactly, but tell them not to just go out and expect to drive the car like it was the last time. We can change the anti-dive by 4 or 5% and put 5 or 6% more caster in it, so you really need to pay attention. It might turn a lot better, but it might be snappy, so it's better to tell them to pay attention to this. Warm up, don't try to go right out and do a qualifying lap. Sometimes they will come in after ¾ of a lap and say 'I can't drive this.'

When Jean Alesi replaced Michael Schumacher at Benetton in 1996, Jean's assessment of the car was that it was setup like a skateboard. Alesi – Yep, but the engine was an issue, because with the 12 cylinder (Ferrari), I had less power at lower revs and more at the top. This engine was almost more like an electric engine. When I was driving my car, I was always in trouble at the entrance of the corner because I had too much torque. That was my problem that I had straight away."

It was widely reported at the time that the incompatibility was with the stiff oversteering setup preferred by Schumacher, which would have been most surprising, given Jean Alesi's other-worldproficiency with a loose car or with slicks in the wet. Jean –

"Yeah, from outside you would see something quite different thing than from the inside." Maybe some journalists should ask from time to time? Alesi – "Yeah, journalists never ask (laughs)."

Sometimes racers have such unquestioned natural ability that it interferes with their ability to pursue an improved setup. Having unquestioned talent is a wonderful thing. Nobby Clark was a mechanic for Gary Hocking, Mike Hailwood, Giacomo Agostini, and Kenny Roberts during their World Championship motorcycle campaigns in the 1960s thru 80s. Nobby – "Niki Lauda, Ronnie Peterson, and Mike Hailwood and I used to live in the same block of apartments in London. Mike and I had one apartment up on the 9th floor, and Ronnie and Niki were on the 3rd. In front of whole bunch of people, Niki was complaining about the car, when they were both driving for March (1972). Ronnie said to Niki – 'As long as your asshole points to the ground, you are never going to win a Formula One World Championship'. Niki said 'we'll see about that.' Ronnie thought that he was miles better than Niki. Niki Lauda was such a brilliant car developer. But for car control, Ronnie was a genius... like Hailwood was on a bike."

As with Ronnie Peterson, Mike Hailwood's talents were such that he'd just race around all the problems and with the multi-cylinder Hondas of 1966-67, there were many. Stuart Graham - "In my era the guy was Hailwood, he was definitely The Man. In Formula One, if he'd been number 2 and had Denny Hulme as his number 1 setting up the cars properly, Mike could have been just as quick as anyone in the McLaren M23. His lack of commitment to the technical side cost him."

Chris Amon concurs, having been Hailwood's teammate in F1 during 1964 – "Absolutely, Mike had no idea of how to set up a car at all, and I believe that with the bikes as well. I remember Mike talking about the 6 cylinder Honda having a lot of power but was a very difficult bike to ride." In the end development ability trumped sheer talent, as it was Niki Lauda who won 3 World Championships in Formula One, vs. none for Hailwood or Peterson.

Every team knows that if the driver is uncomfortable with the handling of the car, the likelihood of success is diminished. There are no magic answers; dealing with various drivers and their driving styles makes setup an individual art and science. What is the approach to developing a Formula One car? Jan – "That's probably where my F1 career went wrong. I was brand new to F1 and my first job was trying to develop the Stewart-Ford, it was too big of a task for a young driver. That didn't do me any good as it confused me. If you haven't driven a Formula One car, you need to experience a good car to compare against it. I had some experience testing with McLaren, but not a whole lot. When we got into the season about ½ ways, I started to know what I wanted, before that I was trying to guess. The car is so extreme, you can't compare to anything else you've driven. There is so much downforce, so much power, and it brakes so hard. A Formula One car is so fast it is hard to describe for anyone what it is like. For me it was just getting used to all the speed, all the downforce... Formula One is all about downforce."

Jan Magnussen - "In sports car racing there is another side that formula car drivers will never know, and that is the compromise between 2 or 3 driving styles. It may be that one driver loves the car and the other 2 hate it because that one guy likes a car completely different." Sebastian Bourdais – "When you are running with a works team like Peugeot, with the 3 drivers, you can put something on the car but have 2 other drivers thinking the opposite. A compromise can be much harder to find, but in terms of the quality, the environment, the number of people that work with you to make it better, it is no comparison.

For 2011, Pratt & Miller put the ex- F1 alumni Oliver Gavin and Jan Magnussen in the same car, a switch from previous years. Jan - "He and I have a similar wish list, if you can call it that. We still have to compromise but it's a good relationship that we have and seem to want to get the same things out of the car. The compromises are not that big, we're not losing a whole lot of lap time because of it. We spend more time with the seat than anything else. Ollie has the main seat, it is built around him. I have an insert that goes into that so I can reach the pedals."

Lou Gigliotti has a potentially superior setup with his Corvette. "Adjustable pedals… all the way forward is Boris, and all the way back is me, with the touch of a button, and it's only 8 pounds. The seat is firmly mounted and solid, you see some of the other teams and their seats flop all over and their drivers are constantly fighting that." With this design, no seat insert is required which means one less thing to coordinate or fumble at a pit stop.

Of course, then there is seat technology itself. Pratt & Miller have a seat design that others in the paddock have christened an "Air Hockey" seat. The conditioned air is pumped into the seat and cools the entire driver through openings in the surface that is in contact with the driver. Binks - "I would say it is heavier than we'd like, but it is less than 30#. But, the benefits outweigh the weight, because every time a driver gets out of our car they just can't believe how good it is."

Le Mans rules were changed to allow a power offset, allowing a slight increase in performance for those who provided the AC system to keep driver fatigue at a minimum. This spurred the teams into action, as the challenge became to take the power increase, while developing systems that used substantially less power than the adjustment allowed, a gain of approximately 7 horsepower. Is there still a performance adjustment in the rules to provide incentive in giving drivers a higher level of creature comfort and reduced fatigue? Dan - "Nah, they took that away, as everybody is on the same deal now. We deemed that it is worth it for the driver." So, with driving the car creating less fatigue, are they able to go back to 2 drivers at Le Mans, saving countless dollars allowing a greater salary for the Crew Chief? "No, it doesn't work out that way. I think 3 drivers is the right number for 24 hour races. 6 hour races, using 2 is no problem."

Creature comfort is a priority at Pratt & Miller as a comfortable driver is more resistant to fatigue and mistakes. 2009 GT2 car

The system as installed in the car has undergone numerous variations, but the power demand has been continually reduced as a result, to a point where it used far less power than the original rules offset permitted. Elsewhere in the pit lane, the factory Flying Lizard Porsche at one time had trumped the Pratt & Miller team in this regard. However efficient the Corvette low drag AC system might prove to be, it requires some power to run such a system. The Porsche only kicks in the compressor under braking. As a result, there is zero effect upon the engine output when power is being provided, other than the tiny load imposed from the somewhat freewheeling pulley assembly on the compressor.

For 2011, GM came out with its version of a lower penalty AC compressor. Binks – "We have a compressor out of a Hybrid car now, that uses a little less power. It's actually a prototype, working with the guys at General Motors in the AC labs. They know what the heat loads are, so we get the right size parts.

In the old days it was 15 hp when you turned the AC on, you could feel it. This thing is in the neighborhood of 2 hp." It has other features that make the hp penalty even less a factor. Dan – "We can control it to do anything we want. We can shut off the compressor when the engine is wide open or at anything above 70% power… or program it to do whatever we want. You might recall we had the fastest GT car on the straight at Le Mans (2010). We might not talk about everything we do, but we try not to let anything slip through the cracks. We're not shutting the AC system off as much as we used to. In 2010 that stuff was pretty primitive, but it's all the same parts from 2012 to this year (2013). The cockpit rules are such that it needs to stay cool. Here at Laguna Seca, the average speed is way down, and even on a day like today the cockpit temperature in the cockpit will be warm. In France they don't give you any leeway, if it goes above what they say, you are in trouble."

France can be brutally hot in June. "We haven't had one of those lately. But in 2005 it was hotter than hell there." One thinks back to the C–type Jaguars that had aero noses added that cooked all their motors in the early 50s. Binks – "Our guys will do that if you'll let them. There has to be some reason in there. We talk about it, and history says… we've done this. These guys are so smart and they make these cars faster and faster, you can't take any of that away from them. But you need to sneak up on it and say 'This is a long race, and there's a lot of dirt, we might want to take it easy on that."

Nascar's Harry Gant was poisoned from exposure to carbon dioxide. Dan - "We actually did that to Olivier (Beretta) at Le Mans in 2010 at Le Mans under yellow from following everyone around, the fumes got to him really bad. I take that personal, and when I poison one of my drivers, that is unacceptable. We had a carbon dioxide sensor, but it turns out that it wasn't reading correctly. So, we have upped our game to try and get better sensors, using some airplane sensors now. We are getting better information than we had ever gotten before, so we know when it is getting close to being bad news for the driver."

Cockpit control layout can be a blessing or annoyance. The GT cars took a giant leap when extensive state of the art steering wheel mounted controls arrived in the ALMS for 2011. Dan Binks – "The steering wheel is pretty trick. Pratt & Miller designed it and Grant custom makes it for us. It's a video game steering wheel basically, there aren't any switches other than the ones that are on there... adjust the traction control, turn the headlights on, turn the reserve on, the AC on, the wiper, everything that you need, you don't have to take your hands off the steering wheel. The steering wheel went from being a few hundred dollars to who knows?"

Do you still have the little metal rubber collector/hotplate above the exhaust system, to eliminate the issue from when clag off the tires caught fire on the exhaust? Binks - "We still do it. We don't get as much rubber up there as we used to, but it keeps things from smoking when we stop." One would think you could either use that solution or just keep the rubber from getting to the exhaust. "Yeah, but sometimes that is hard, the rubber gets everywhere."

Motor racing often comes down to a chess game between the racers/designers stretching the rules envelope, and those tasked with enforcing technical regulations. Much like the continually raised level of competition between munitions and armor, success or failure is often ensured based upon what you roll off the trailer. The early days of NASCAR offered some of the most obvious examples, between Lorenzen's Banana car or Smokey Yunick's 7/8 scale Chevrolet Chevelle. All this clever manipulation eventually led to the use of car templates to control the deviation allowed from production vehicle shapes, which finally led to the 3 dimensional template cradle with minor adjustments and/or inserts that allow for the slightly different body shapes as used (and previously approved by NASCAR) by the different manufacturers. The tolerance for this body shape variance is measured with a colored tool that allows quick checking for 70 thousandths (red), 1/8" (yellow) or 1/4" (blue). The cars are measured at various times during the weekend to monitor those currently adopted shapes for Cup racing. On occasion one will see mechanics inside the car, furiously pounding upon the rear window braces to push the rear window outward just enough to conform to the template. It is refreshing to know that there is still a place in big dollar racing for using a bigger hammer.

As a result of creative rule bending, the tech inspection process for NASCAR is likely the most thorough in motorsport. After passing all the templates, the car goes up onto a raised area where the wing height is checked to see if within a specified range, checking rear toe (so that the rear axle isn't crabbed sideways within the bodywork) and verifying the wheelbase, as well as the distance from differential to fuel cell. There are a number of radio ID tags on the chassis, which are from parts or assemblies originally certified. Think of that part of the tech process as being like having a bar-code scanner for various assemblies of the car, and if the tag frequency doesn't match the secret frequency of the scanners, you have some explaining to do. The radio ID tags keep the racers from such adventures as cutting off the front clip and making one of slightly different and more favorable spec. As always it is a dance of deception between the teams and the rule enforcers, with an ever escalating contest of electronic verification vs. e-hacking.

Smokey Yunick was the one man perhaps most synonymous with rule-bending for his endless attempts to circumvent the rule book. There were times that it would be within reason to make a comparison between Smokey and Dan Binks. Jack Roush – "At one point in time, I'd encouraged the guys to NOT do something that would get us in trouble with the rules... because our cars were so fast. So, they went without my knowledge to Road America Elkhart Lake, where the car had an illegal extra fuel tank in the car. One of the guys who got beat complained, saying he had prior knowledge that we had an extra fuel tank in the car, and that he'd been told by someone who worked for us… who didn't work for us anymore what Binks had done. They stopped our car at the gate, took the car off the truck and disqualified us."

As always there can be a grey area between rules stretching and creative cheating. This was one of the few times Dan clearly crossed that line. Dan Binks – "Probably in my career, that was the most disappointing thing that I've ever done. Don't get me wrong, we pressed the envelope, but that was over the line on cheating."

Dan had scooped out portions of the foam insert in the fuel cell, so that it would hold fuel in these 'cups' or 'trays' within the foam. Dan – "Think about this… the Trans-Am tech inspector went into the gas tank and couldn't find it. The lid was off, he looked inside and still couldn't understand what was going on. My problem was the first time they filled it up in tech, it held 35 gallons, the second time, 32 gallons. When only 32 gallons came out, I knew this wasn't going to be good. They knew something was up, but they couldn't figure it out. The fuel cell foam was sealed and there were boxes in the foam where you couldn't see it. You could pull the foam out and you couldn't tell, it just looked like fuel cell foam. But, inside the foam there were cups made out of the fuel cell material… you couldn't tell. It just looked like a block of yellow foam."

As the car would go around corners the fuel would slosh out of the foam 'cups' and permit the full 35 gallons to be available. Dan – "They had it in their hand, and couldn't figure it out… it was awesome… unbelievable. Don't get me wrong, I was scared s**tless, and I knew we were in trouble. The problem was that I was greedy but not smart, and I got ratted out. But, if I'd done it the right way, I'd never have been caught. That said, I was horribly disappointed in myself. It was cheatin'."

There is always the ever escalating battle of wits between rule makers, and rule benders. Binks is a master at this game, normally adept at envelope pushing vs. envelope shredding. Dan – "I decided I was no longer going to do something that wasn't at least questionable, something I could make an argument for." Jack Roush – "Danny was one of the most creative... most organized with the hardware."

Of course one of the worst situations for Pratt & Miller in recent years was due to a fuel fire, that left Dale Earnhardt Jr. burned. Dan Binks - "What happened on that car was that it was full of fuel, and it pushed the rear tire into the gas tank. When it pushed the tire into the fuel tank, the fuel neck was out next to the body, and it basically popped it off. When you are a little kid, and you squeeze a drink bottle, you get juice all over you. That's what it did, and it just squeezed the fuel out like a drink bottle, and it got all over him, and all over the car. It was a bad deal. What we did was to move the fuel tank in, and make the fuel probe way longer. That way the fuel connection can't, or is for sure less likely to get knocked off in a wreck. The wheels could still compress the fuel cell, but it wouldn't knock the top off. It's all billet pieces now, whereas before it was like a production car with a rubber hose in there. It is less likely to do that, for sure."

There was also a problem with the frame that had been a contributing factor – "It squeezed the gas tank until it popped the top off. The frame collapsed and allowed the tire to squeeze it. So what we do now is to fill that frame rail with Dow's lightweight foam, which slows down the collapsibility of that part, right by the fuel tank. The foam is only in that 3 or 4 foot long piece (each side). With the flapper down low and the long fuel probe, refueling takes a little bit longer, but it's worthy of being that way just for the safety. There is no worse feeling than hurting somebody on your team, or your driver. With Tommy (Kendall at Watkins Glen), I would have quit that day, but Tommy wanted to keep going. I can't imagine hurting somebody on our team and having to live with that pain."

To win, the car has to start when required every time. Given the sophistication of the starter assembly needed in that GT1 7 litre Pratt & Miller Corvette, one might ask what is required to start the Audi Diesel, especially the later V-10 with its exceedingly tight cold clearances of the steel piston/alloy block design combined with the required high compression for a diesel engine. Ulrich Baretzky – "It is a simple electric starter motor as you know it from road cars, nothing extraordinary. But you have to know, that our race engines are never started from cold. They are always preheated for 30 - 45 minutes to reach a reasonable water temperature."

Sometimes it is the little things that can make all the difference in endurance racing. The tool kit in the Audi R10 racer included a cel phone to call for help, and most drivers are also supplied with some local currency. A little cash goes a long way in getting you out of the kitty litter when the car is buried up to its axles. Headlights also can make a huge difference, perhaps none more effective than those on the Audi R18. Allan McNish – "The LED lighting that we've got is in conjunction with the road car section. It basically turns night into day." It turns night into day to the extent that Ollie Gavin has complained of being temporarily blinded when being followed by an R18 at night. One can surmise that it is only a matter to time before this too is legislated under the rules.

One critical 'detail' that should never be overlooked, is team organization. Sebastian Bourdais was a 4 consecutive time Champ Car titlist when driving for Newman-Haas Racing. He left for Scuderia Toro Rosso to drive Formula One in 2008, becoming teammate to a young rookie named Sebastian Vettel, a daunting task for anyone. Returning to the merged Indycar series in 2011 with Dale Coyne racing, Bourdais shares his insights on the challenge of driving for a small team, having come from the widest possible perspective, with an enormous wealth of personal experience to draw from. Sebastian - "Basically the first four races were a mess. As we were going through the preparations, nothing was said. There was no history, nothing was documented, we had no idea as to what was supposed to be on the car, or what was on the car. At Barber the car was nowhere. It got a little better for the one in Brazil, and later in the season the car wasn't stellar but we could do things with it."

What is there a base mechanical setup for a 2011 Indycar? Sebastian – "There are quite a few things you can do at a pitstop with an Indycar... you have the bars when they are hooked up, which isn't always the case... we didn't run the sway bars very often, actually. This year (2011) we've been super soft, and that's the only way we've been able to find any kind of grip. Sometimes we run a little bit of front bar on a road course. But we never really found something that good for the road circuits, never found something that clicked. I'm also not a big fan of a very forward COP (Center of Pressure). Every time we tried to go above 40% it was not so good for me. It really screwed the stability under braking and in the way the car was putting power down. There are some guys who run a very forward COP and get away with it, but we would start at 39% and then work on the mechanical. I've always been really sensitive to rear stability. We always ran max downforce as the car didn't take it at all when we were trimming it, it would brake horrible. It was very 'draggy' on the road course, as this car was never designed to be taken on a road course with that big ass rear wing and big end plates. They basically had to figure out how to put that thing on a road course that doesn't look too stupid, you know? It was never really meant to be."

There was certainly an obvious downside in taking an "oval only" racing series and trying to adapt those machines to run on road and street courses. For years it had been a crap shoot as to which chassis was better for ovals, but eventually the Dallara proved superior to the competition, and every car on the grid was eventually built by the Italian manufacturer to the point it eventually became the spec chassis. That may not have been the case had the road and street circuits arrived to the series before the G-Force had disappeared from the scene.

Sebastian Bourdais driving the 2011 spec Dallara for Dale Coyne

Despite their limited resources, Bourdais and the Coyne team persevered to find some late-season success. "In Baltimore I think we had a chance for the podium, and that would have been awesome. You don't need to be called Penske or Ganassi to make things right. You just need the right people at the right place. The problem that these little teams have is trying to keep their people. Smaller organizations are hard on people, because with a smaller group it's twice as hard on the guys. At the end of the season, they are worn out... they can't take it anymore. This Indycar thing is much harder than Champ Car was, because of the turnaround on the car from the start of the season to the last race." There is no doubt that for any small team with a limited number of chassis constantly being changed between road race, short oval, street circuit, and superspeedway configurations, would certainly have a long term detrimental effect on a team.

Sebastian – "The smaller team cannot keep its people, the guys want out... they just don't want to hear about it anymore. I knew it was going to be tough... I knew that racing with Dale was going to be difficult and a big challenge, but I enjoyed taking it from where it was, and putting it up there in the mix, where you feel like you could make a difference."

Driver psychology comes into play as well, as the drivers may be made to feel like an integral part of a team, or one may well feel like the flavor of the week, if not flavor of the day. For some drivers, this being constantly at risk of replacement may be a great motivator, or perhaps a great deterrent, depending upon their individual character. Heinz Harold Frentzen was considered an underperformer when in the ever-professional environment of Williams-Renault, yet HHF had previously excelled while at Sauber, and then later did a stellar job, winning two Grand Prix for Jordan in 1999. For his talents to shine, he needed a different team environment. Others such as 7 time AMA Superbike Champion Mat Mladin prefer the opposite, a "cut and dried" approach.

Mladin – "The so called 'family atmosphere'... I'd take a professional race team any day of the year over one where it was like a family atmosphere. That approach doesn't suit me at all. I'm a cut and dried person... if you say that it's black, I take it to be black, if you say it's white, I take it to be white. That's just my personal feeling of what I like as a racer. The longevity of the Yoshimura team has a lot to do with that." Finding that proper fit between racer psyche and team character can be a major factor in eventual success or failure.

Sebastian Bourdais has gained an appreciation for the personal approach. "The thing is that in the States, people are very loyal. They are not going to fire Helio because Bourdais is out there. They aren't going to fire Dario or Scott. It's great, as there is respect for the drivers, and I can only give them credit for that. Formula One is a different planet from that; if you've not won they've got 10 knocking at the door. When I left Newman-Haas, I knew that there may not be the opportunity to come back. If there is not an opening somewhere, they are not going to kick somebody off, or if they do, then it's not the team you want to be in because they could just do the same with you."

In the end, once a hopefully well funded and organized team has done everything it can and has exhausted every avenue it can explore to maximize the performance; it is mostly up to the driver(s) during the race. Racecraft is probably best described as the talent for being consistently in the right place at the right time. Since the retirement of Jackie Stewart, the most prominent master of this art form was Rick Mears. Perhaps his finest example was the 75th running of the Indy 500 in 1991. Rick – "One of the main things that off road racing taught me was that you had to find a pace that was fast enough to win the race, and slow enough to finish. The number one priority is the checkered flag, and I don't care how fast you are… if you can't get to the checkered flag, you can't do anything. In 1991 at Indy, I was struggling. I don't like getting nearly a lap down if I don't have to. But, he (Mike Andretti) wasn't going to lap me. He still thinks he was, but I was running enough to stay ahead of him. I saw him coming, but the car is not where I want it and I don't want to stub my toes. I was just running enough to stay in the hunt without making a mistake. When the car's not right, it's very easy to stub your toe. There were still stops to make, changes to make… and I'm getting the splits on him. I knew where he was at, was just picking it up and he'd have played heck if he'd ever tried to pass me. If I have to bump it up to qualifying, then I'll qualify. He ended up having a puncture, so I didn't have to qualify to stay ahead of him."

Late in the race it came down to a shootout between Michael Andretti and Rick Mears, with the legendary consecutive lap outside passes in turn one. Rick – "We had the apron to run on back then, and he ran on the apron which opened the groove up a little bit in the corner. The lap he passed me, I knew he was going by me. There were 2 cars in front of me, and when I jumped out, John Andretti jumped out, so I had to pedal once to keep from hitting him. That just killed me and Mike had a 3 car hole in the air, and he's quick on restarts anyway. He had such a big run on me going down to one, and we weren't up to speed coming off the yellow. I knew wherever I went, he would go the other so I went to the bottom and let him take the long way around.

The following lap, now it was Mears with the momentum. Rick – "The next lap, I was wide open. I was in the marbles to start with going in, but he hesitated for a moment in the middle which could have caused me big problems... and I chose the outside. As we came into the corner side by side I'm hoping... go down, go down... because I knew I had to get down to at least mid-track to get enough front end in mine. I knew I was going to have a little understeer and hadn't been into the corner that hard all day, period. That was the unknown, with being flat the entire lap before, it was the highest numbers I'd ever seen... that day going into one. I needed to get as much front as I can, if he didn't drop down I was going to have to pedal it. He came down, which was what I was hoping for as he had a little understeer in the car, and it allowed me to go with him. Being mid-track in the middle of the corner gave me just a little bit better front end to where I didn't have to lift." Knowing that Andretti normally ran on the apron, Rick was willing to take that calculated risk which paid off with his 4th Indy 500 win.

Rick Mears had again been the very definition of racecraft... working the setup until the car was at its best for the end of race shootout. In 1991, that combined with his being in a position to exploit detailed observations of the closest competitors. Combine that with a talent for understanding what magical combinations of adjustment will do to the car and winning will often be the result.

Penske Racing & Rick Mears - 1988 Indianapolis 500 Winners
— Photo courtesy of Ken Anderson

CHAPTER ELEVEN

SAFETY

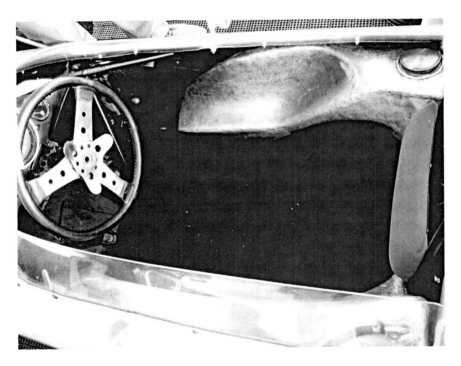

A gasoline tank doubling as a seat. The Porsche 804 F1 car of Dan Gurney, winner of the 1962 French Grand Prix

Race car safety has become an expected part of race car development, but sadly that was not always the case. Formula One drivers of the 1950s and 60s could well be the ultimate definition of optimists. By the end of January 1959, Phil Hill was the only driver still alive from the 1958 Ferrari F1 team. Musso killed in the French GP, Collins killed at German GP, World Champion Mike Hawthorn killed street racing his Jaguar against Rob Walker's 300SL. Stuart Lewis-Evans had also been killed in his Vanwall at the Moroccan Grand Prix that closed out the 1958 season. When shown a Road & Track cover from mid-1959 featuring the Ferrari Formula One team of Tony Brooks, Phil Hill, and Dan Gurney, Gurney's response was "Hey, we all made it."

Phil Hill – "We didn't think about it. We didn't know any better. It was Army syndrome. It's always going to be the other guy; it's the way it is. I have a picture of myself with the whole Ferrari team at the race in Sweden, which was the first European race that I won. There I was with the whole gang, and for most of my racing career, Fangio and myself were the only two left out of the 6 or 8 guys."

Sir Jackie Stewart - "During Phil's (championship) era, there weren't killing as many people as they did later, because it was a 1.5 litre formula then. It became a 3 litre formula on the same racetrack, twice the horsepower and a lot more speed." Chris Amon – "I was talking to some people yesterday. Some of them kept saying, 'how did you do it?' I told them... the first thing was that we didn't know any different, and that's the way it was."

Things weren't much different in American racing. The innovative rear engine Miller designed racers of the late 1930s provide yet another of the sad examples. Donald Davidson – "In '39, two of them burned. With Johnny Seymour's accident in '39, he was quite severely burned. They were gasoline fires, the problem was the pontoon tanks, and in an accident the tank would get punctured. They were underwritten by Gulf Oil, so they had to run on pump gasoline. Then in '40, George Bailey crashed, had a similar accident and he died. When they came back in '41, they didn't have the pontoon tanks anymore."

The open wheel racers of the 50s and early 60s raced in a world without deformable structure and multiple bulkheads. The full force of any accident was transferred directly throughout the chassis, to the driver. Joe Leonard experienced the full wrath of putting a roadster into a concrete wall – "AJ got me a Kurtis roadster to run. Hurtubise had lost an engine and I hit his oil and spun it into the wall, and that was an eye opener. It was in Salt Walther's dad's car, the Dayton Wheels special. Oh boy, they hurt, you were sore for a week."

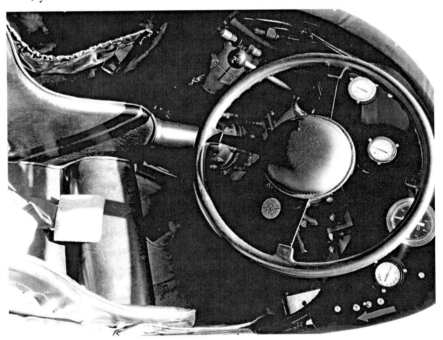

A Dangerous Place. Front engine Indy cars had nothing deformable and transmitted every impact directly to the drivers

As with the timeless line from the movie "Grand Prix", shutting out the potential consequences of an accident, may require a certain lack of imagination. European racers competed in a world of barbed wire fences and stone walls. Almost unbelievably, in Formula One your best odds may have been to be thrown clear of the car, vs. being trapped in a crushed machine full of fuel. The early rear engine F1 cars were far more dangerous in comparison to the previous generation of front engine cars from the late 50s, where the fuel load was typically carried behind the driver.

Few examples were more daunting than Dan Gurney's Porsche 804 F1 car of 1962. The alloy fuel tanks were actually formed around the driver and became the seat for the car. Gurney recalls his early F1 years in the midst of a rear engine revolution – "With the BRM, it (the fuel tank) was more on the sides. Then with the Porsche they had tried to make it smaller, so it had one on each side, and at your back, and the one above your legs… 4 tanks, all just plain aluminum tanks. It was a Molotov cocktail that you drive as fast as you can."

The Belgian Grand Prix winning AAR Eagle of 1967 was no safer, as Gurney's primary car had an exotic magnesium and titanium chassis. It has been said that if the car had a tire go down, the tub scraping along the pavement could trigger a fire from the chassis itself. Dan – "Well, I don't know…. we wanted to win, so as long as you didn't crash it or get a flat, it was good. I was probably half as desperate as some of those motorcycle racers, and that's just the way it was."

As Gurney noted, perhaps no one was more vulnerable than the motorcycle racer of the day. It is important to remember that these were the days when street circuits such as the Isle of Man or Imatra, Finland were part of the World Championship, so it was difficult for any racer to refuse to compete.

Rod Coleman - "As you know, in the 60's and 70's, race circuits were not legislated, as today, to have large run-off areas on each corner and so the thinking then was to put up large barriers to stop cars hitting the spectators. The fact that motorcycles raced on the same circuits with these barriers is unthinkable today but

1967 Eagle F1 car as manufactured and driven by Dan Gurney

not get the thought that it should have back then."

Stuart Graham recalls his experience at Spa following the 1966 Belgian 250cc GP – "We were all visiting at the hospital... the Monday morning routine, the circuits in the 60s were so dangerous... it was only a fortnight before when the Formula One guys had been there in similar conditions, Jackie Stewart ending up trapped in his BRM."

The 1966 Belgian Formula One Grand Prix was the race at Spa-Francorchamps so vividly portrayed in the movie Grand Prix, where an unexpected downpour resulted in Formula One cars flying off into various barns and fields. Jackie Stewart crashed at the Masta Kink and was trapped in his wrecked BRM, soaking in gasoline from the ruptured fuel tanks while Graham Hill and Bob Bondurant tried to rescue him.

Bob Bondurant – "When the race started, we didn't know it was pouring down rain about a mile and a half away from the start line. I was pulling out to pass Mike Spence in the Lotus and all of a sudden he went sideways, it was a torrential downpour. I went a little sideways but caught it. Bonnier lost it, ended up going off and almost went all the way over a wall, off the track and into a barn. As we went down the Masta straight, I slowed down for the Masta Kink, a left right. It was raining so hard you could hardly see, and there was a flood of rain coming across the track. That is where Jackie Stewart hit, he was in a BRM then too, and he aquaplaned on it. I was right behind him and aquaplaned off the track on it too. I went off the road to the left, flipped and cut a tree in half. The roots of the tree kept the car off me. I was stuck inside the car for a little bit, the fuel was running down into my helmet and filling up on top of my head. Some spectators lifted the car off me, and I said "Stewart... Stewart" and pointed across the track. I ran across the track, Graham had slowed way down and pulled off... there was a little house next door where it was all happening. They came out with a little French blue tool box, and got some tools out so that we could get the steering wheel off and get Jackie out of the car. He was sitting in about 6 inches of fuel. From that point on, that was when Stewart decided that he was going to make a difference in racing safety." A three time World Driving Champion, Jackie Stewart's tireless campaigns for safety have become his greatest legacy.

Chris Amon's first Grand Prix with Ferrari was the following year, 1967 at Monaco. His first 2 GPs for Ferrari could hardly have been more traumatic. Chris – "I had a struggle there at Monaco as it was my first proper drive of a Formula One Ferrari. I don't think I even drove the car before, and Monaco isn't the ideal place to start off either. I do remember during practice, since I'd done a lot of tire testing and a lot of suspension setup with McLaren and with Ford, I had them change the front roll bar, and I've got to say that I went the wrong way. I remember Forghieri saying 'I'll set the car up for the race, you just drive it.' I think he probably put the same settings that Bandini had on and the car was significantly better in the race, although I had a pretty lowly starting position and Monaco is not the easiest place to advance. Really I think that was the only struggle I ever had, from there on I felt really at home in a Formula One car."

Bob Bondurant in the BRM finished 4th at the
1966 Monaco Grand Prix
— Photo courtesy of the Bondurant School

On the 82nd lap, Lorenzo Bandini had a horrific accident at the harbor-front chicane. His Ferrari ended up inverted and on fire, with Bandini trapped inside. The efforts to put out the fire and rescue Bandini were pathetic, even by the sorry standards of the day. Chris - "Oh, it was bad... terrible. When I look back on it, I don't know how to describe it... Bandini's accident or Joe Schlesser at Rouen... I mean you can smell the guy cooking lap after lap. It was just horrific. I still have a lasting impression, because I'd gotten a puncture on debris from his (Bandini) accident. I came in, and I can still picture their faces when they changed the tire... they were white as sheets and sort of going through the motions. Unfortunately there are still some very vivid memories of that day. He was such a great guy. I couldn't have found a more helpful, friendly guy than Bandini. I guess the fact that we were teammates in the sports car, helped."

The race after Monaco was the Belgian Grand Prix on the Spa circuit, where again Amon had to deal with another massive accident to his teammate at Ferrari, this time causing catastrophic injuries to Mike Parkes. Amon – "It was on the first lap, caused by Stewart's H-16 BRM getting rid of about 4 litres of oil out of the catch tank in front of Mike. That H-16 and the V-12 Cooper Maserati seemed to have the ability to fill the catch tanks up on the first lap."

You could actually see the oil pouring out of the car? Chris – "Oh yeah, I've got to say that I'd gotten a pretty poor start, and I'd caught up with Mike. Had it not happened to him, it may well have happened to me. Seeing him go off gave me a slight chance to take some evasive action. There were no belts for another year or so. It was like a pulley rolling down the bank. I've got to say that I thought he was dead and I lost concentration for a few laps. At a certain point they hung a board out to me saying 'Parkes OK' which then got me back to concentrating on the race. In fact he was anything but ok, but he was still alive."

Amon - "I was young, and it never deterred me. What it did to me was that it certainly created a sense of responsibility. It was a load on my shoulders, but I was never tempted to stop or anything. It was always going to be someone else. I saw a quote from Jackie Oliver the other day, saying that it was like a flock of birds. The birds in the center will never get taken. You have to think like that."

The air-cooled V8 Honda RA-302 Grand Prix car of 1968 had a magnesium chassis. John Surtees had refused to drive the new car, declaring it unready for competition, but the team went ahead with the car's debut in the French Grand Prix and offered the car to French driver Jo Schlesser. It ended in the worst possible way, with a fiery crash that was unable to be extinguished when the car flew off the road and erupted into flames with a full fuel load early in the race. The magnesium chassis had caught fire and survival was impossible. The RA-302 design never raced again.

Needless to say, at the pre-2000 Corkscrew with minimal runoff this "off" would have been catastrophic. There was no damage.

The 1968 French Grand Prix had been Vic Elford's first Grand Prix. Vic – "It was just nasty, horrible. That magnesium car was a bomb waiting to go off. In those days they didn't stop races for accidents, they didn't even have pace cars. For all of us, in those days when we went out on Sunday morning, we wondered if we'd see the hotel again, literally. This was why none of us were very friendly with each other… we never made real friends, you know. I think we all did that without realizing it, as every Sunday one of us wouldn't be alive at the end of the day."

This was reality for Grand Prix drivers in the late 1960s. David Hobbs, Honda's teammate to Surtees for the last few races of 1968, tells the tale that when they didn't have enough fuel capacity in the F1 Honda they would put another tank in above his knees, held in with bungee cords. That this was the status quo even after the team's horrific loss of Schlesser at Rouen, is mind boggling.

No less unbelievable was Ferrari's return to Monaco in 1969 after giving the '68 race a pass, still disgusted with the circumstances surrounding the horrific loss of Bandini there in 1967. Their solution was similar to Honda's, both teams struggling to carry enough fuel for their thirsty V12 engines in race conditions.

Chris Amon - I always thought with the Ferrari, and it was the same with the Matra, if you could run near the front for the first 1/3 of the race, you were going to be in really good shape once you burned some fuel off. But it was frustrating in a way, because you knew you had a quick car. You had to be careful too, as there was no tire changing and it was very easy to cook the tires or brakes. At Monza in those days, the Ford V8 would have started that race with 50 kilos less fuel onboard. The first 1/3 of a race was always tough. At Monaco in 1969 I was on the front row with Jackie Stewart, who would have started with 180 litres of fuel. We started with 250 litres, the mechanics had spent the night before the race making up an extra tank to put over my knees, to have enough fuel to finish the race." So was the end result a bungee cord special, with tanks hung all around the cockpit similar to the Honda? Chris – "Exactly, that would be right. The Matra was a little bit better, but still we carried 40 kilos more at the start than the V8s did."

It had reached the breaking point for Sir Jackie Stewart, and he became a tireless advocate for circuit safety for most of his F1 career. Jackie - "Obviously it needed to be done... and it needed to be done by somebody who was driven. I happened to be the man to beat in that window of time, and that kept going from about '68 right through my retirement... and after my retirement. So, the media would listen to me and they would print it. Television was beginning to be used heavily, as well as radio. It was very difficult for people to say to me 'if the kitchen is too hot, why don't you get out?' because I was still winning races."

Still, the carnage continued. Another car of magnesium construction claimed Piers Courage when he crashed at Zandvoort mid-race during the Dutch Grand Prix of 1970. The car, once it caught fire, had ignited the chassis and there was no hope of survival. This sort of horrific end was very much a possibility in this era, as Jo Siffert (Brands Hatch '71), and Roger Williamson (Zandvoort '73) similarly died in their burning cars, and it only through sheer luck that Jackie Oliver and Jacky Ickx escaped a similar fate in the 1970 Spanish Grand Prix at Jarama.

Meanwhile, World Championship endurance racing had its own challenges. Races were still being held on the great street circuit of Sicily, the Targa Florio. It was considered relatively safe, due to its very low average speeds, although there was always the ever present potential of falling off a mountain, or driving into a building. Pre-running the course had its own special challenges, as Jerry Grant found out at the 1964 Targa Florio. Dan Gurney recalls an example of the kind of dangers one didn't normally take into account. "We had a Holman & Moody Ford Falcon. It had been modified as a rally car, and we used it as a 'mule'. Everybody was using it for a 42 mile lap around several mountains at the Targa Florio in Sicily, a fabulous track where the first race was held before Indy. Bondurant had been there, driving around the track at race speeds according to our stopwatches. So that meant he was going through 3 or 4 villages in normal day to day traffic, at race speed. We were amazed at how quick he was going. When he finished his stint, the next guy in the car was Jerry Grant. He (Jerry) comes to this village, Campofelice or one of those. He comes around a corner and in front of him a crowd has completely blocked the streets, and on his left walking up is a Sicilian man carrying a double barrel shotgun… and he's pointing it right at Jerry's head. Jerry said that he 'didn't know what to do… how many options did I have?' The guy put the shotgun down and told him to carry on. Well, when he got back to the start and got a hold of Bondurant…"

As if the safety of the cars or the safety of the tracks wasn't enough to give one pause, sometimes the local wildlife even played a role. At Enna in 1964, Mike Hailwood had parked Chris Amon's Lotus into Pergusa Lake. Chris Amon – "Yeah, in that race Mike went flying into the lake, and it was a very quick circuit too, averaging 140mph even in those 1½ litre things. I remember going with the crew to collect it afterward and all you could see was the red noseband under about 4 feet of water. The circuit went right around the lake, but the funny thing was that the lake was full of these water snakes. You'd walk out the back of the pits and see these damn things in the water. 'Ol Mike said that when he ended up in the lake he moved very quickly because all he could think of were those snakes."

As crazy as it sounds, that has often been the primary concern at certain race tracks, such as Shah Alam in Malaysia. Tales from when the World Superbike championship first raced there in 1990 read like something from an Indiana Jones movie. Davide Tardozzi (former Bimota and Ducati factory rider) recalls – "It was a good race track, but I don't like the snakes that were there. Lots of snakes… snakes crossing the race track, snakes during the night, snakes everywhere… you had to be careful even in the pits. I was always checking my suit before putting it on, looking inside."

Other World Superbike legends also took issue with Shah Alam. Carl Fogarty – "Well, there were some (snakes) out there, but the baboons crossing the track at the end of the back straightaway… Jesus Christ, hit one of them and you probably won't be here anymore." Scott Russell – "Snakes and monkeys… pretty gnarly place man. In Kuala Lumpur, coming onto the back straightaway at a test, just off the line was this big 'ol snake just hanging out... and monkeys sitting on the tire wall watching us, 10 or 12 of 'em hanging out in a group. At Shah Alam we started a race and everybody comes onto the front straightaway in a pack. I was in there... 6th or 7th, and somebody in front of me hit a snake that was on the track, and it went flying. It flew off the track in pieces when you hit it."

As for American racing in the 60s, one only needs to think back to the horrific inferno that claimed Eddie Sachs and Dave MacDonald in the 1964 Indianapolis 500 to understand that this was not just an issue with European road racing. At Indianapolis in that era, the racers carried a huge 75 gallon fuel load in alloy tanks, and fire was the common result upon impact. Even having the latest in safety technology wasn't of much benefit. Donald Davidson – "I had once thought the fuel cell was the result of the 64 accident, but Sachs had fuel cells. Ted Halibrand's Shrikes had fuel cells, and apparently the Novi in '48 also had a fuel cell." Halibrand had been a pioneer of the magnesium wheel in Indy racing, his wheels having been on the 500 winner for the previous 15 years. As a result of that experience, the '64 Halibrand Shrike was built almost entirely of magnesium, sadly to prove a catastrophic counterpoint that offset their efforts with fuel cell technology.

Clark, Spence, Rindt, McLaren, Giunti, Cevert, Bianchi, Mitter, Scarfiotti, Rodriguez, Titus, Duman, Savage, Pollard, Revson and many others had also died from racing accidents in the 8 seasons between 1967 and 1974. Jackie Stewart – "Jim Clark went off and died because he went into a forest. There were no barriers to stop him from getting to the forest. I was lucky enough that I was sufficiently determined to change the safety factor, because keep in mind that if you were a Formula One Grand Prix driver at that time, there was a 2 out of 3 chance that you would die, if you were in Formula One between 1968 and 73. We lost so many... as I speak to you now I'm looking out at my garden where

I have 25 benches dedicated to my friends who are dead."

The drivers had begun an organization in 1961 which primarily existed to improve the safety of racing facilities. The Grand Prix Driver's Association would meet to discuss what the most pressing needs were, and push that agenda forward. Their first united stand came when their boycott of the Belgian Grand Prix in 1969 when circuit safety at Spa finally hit a flash point.

The interior of the 1967 Dana Chevrolet 427 that Bondurant and Guldstrand drove in the 24 Hours of Le Mans. This is what passed for a "survival cell" in a 180mph car during the 1960s

Jackie Stewart – "It wasn't acceptable by any means. At that time I hadn't got the whole program in place that we could really have the kind of authority that was necessary. I drove the March in 1970 at Spa, but when I won the Belgian Grand Prix in 1973 it was at Zolder, because we refused to race at Spa." The 1970 race was the final Grand Prix held on the original 8 mile circuit.

1970 also brought one of the biggest fiascos in the history of Grand Prix in Mexico, where the spectators scaled the fences and at along the edge of the circuit, inches from the track. Chris Amon - "I remember before the start, we were all saying 'we just can't do this.' The organizers were very direct, they basically said 'you either drive or you won't get out of here alive.' So we drove. Stewart hit a dog, which I think was the only fatality. I was having a pretty good scrap with 'ol Denny for a portion of the race. Jack (Brabham) came storming past us, kicking up dirt everywhere. It was his last race, actually, and he would have been at times about 2 inches from the spectators. I'd guess for somebody like Jack who'd raced in the '50s in places like Argentina, it was quite common to have the spectators just inches from the cars. Jack was probably used to it. I have to say, that once the race started, you never gave it a thought... you just got on with it. But, I have to say that if you'd ended up in the crowd, you probably wouldn't have gotten out of there either."

There were other driver boycotts, but none so famous at the 1982 drivers strike at the South African Grand Prix, where Teo Fabi (Toleman F1 driver) broke ranks much to the disgust of his fellow drivers. However, now the issue was not over safety, it was over the wording of their Superlicense contracts. Sadly, by the end of the 1982 season, the GPDA had ceased to exist.

During that same era in America, Stewart often dealt with the same resistance to change and pushback that he had encountered in Europe. Jackie - "It happened all over the world for me. I did Can-Am in 1971, and I went to Mid-Ohio driving for Carl Haas, it was the L&M Lola. McLaren were the ones to beat, Denny Hulme and Peter Revson. There was a tree on the exit, directly in-line with the exit of turn one at Mid Ohio. If you had gone off, you would have hit the tree. I told them in practice that they had to cut the tree down, and they didn't want to do it. I said, 'ok, then I don't race.' They thought I was bullshitting, so I said, 'no problem, I withdraw from the race, formally on the basis that you are not prepared to cut the tree down in the interest of driver safety.' I guess their lawyers said it would be too big of a threat if it happened, so they capitulated, cut the tree down and removed the roots and everything. Sure enough, at the very first corner of the first flying lap, Denny Hulme went off and his trajectory was right in line with the tree. I mean the tire marks were there to prove it."

"I went on to win the race, which is also ironic. Of course, the first question coming out of the car was, 'you've just won the race, and you must think the race track is fantastic. Are you disappointed at your earlier remarks?' I said, 'no, they still stand. Had that tree not been brought down, we might have lost another driver.' It was well worth the removal of the tree. When you win a race under these circumstances, you have even more authority, or at least credibility. I was lucky enough to have that, while I was pushing awfully hard, and of course they tore up the Nurburgring and Spa as well. And these were the 2 big race tracks of the world, you know. It had to be done, but it wouldn't have happened if I had been a mid-fielder in Formula One. It wasn't celebrity, it was my position in the sport at that time, because I was either World Champion, defending World Champion, or newly World Champion. When your credentials are right, it is difficult for them."

Mid-Ohio and Spa were not isolated circumstances. Stewart - "At Laguna Seca, I was driving Can-Am there, and they had no barriers and a whole bunch of trees. The barriers were behind the trees, obviously you can't have that. You have to move the trees, or have something... chain link fencing or whatever you want to have in those days. It was a big deal, I was very heavily criticized by a lot of the media on it, but in fact we got the deal done."

Jackie Stewart credits his dyslexia for his singular focus and ability to see his safety crusade through. "If you think about the dyslexia thing it is logic. If something is not right, you don't have to be Einstein... and by the way, Einstein was dyslexic... and if I had not been dyslexic, maybe I wouldn't have gone to the lengths that I did to change safety in motor racing. It just so happened that I was dyslexic, and I was determined, and I knew I was right and somebody had to do it. When you've been called stupid, dumb, or thick for the vast majority of your life, by that time you don't really care what kind of harsh criticisms you might be getting, as long as you know you are right."

The Le Mans start for Endurance racing began with a foot race across the track to the car, which meant nobody took the time to buckle in, as many positions would be lost. This was an era where it was accepted strategy to race without seat belts until you could fumble your way into the harness somewhere along the 3 mile Mulsanne straight. Dan Gurney has mentioned steering at 200mph down that straight with his knees, while trying to get buckled into the car. Bondurant – "Yeah, that's what you do. You tape the over-the-shoulder harness to the roof, with the lap belts off to either side. It takes about 5 laps to get the belts on."

Chris Amon had been teamed with Phil Hill in the new 7 liter Ford GT for Le Mans in 1965. Were there seatbelts in the 1965 7 litre Ford GT? Chris Amon – "Only a lap belt. I think we might have had a 4 point harness in the '66 car. I can remember having that, or at least a 4 point harness, in '69 (Le Mans) with the Ferrari which was a closed car. I can tell you the first time I had belts in a Formula One car was a 6 point harness at the Nurburgring in 1968. We put them on to keep ourselves in the seat, going over the jumps there. I wore them at Oulton Park a couple of weeks later for the Gold Cup race, and when we went to Monza we had decided to leave them in, as they were quite good for support going around the corner."

As it turned out, having the harness in the car saved Chris at Monza when the car flew off into the woods after a rear wing hydraulic failure dumped fluid onto the rear tires at close to 200mph. Amon – "The theory was at the time that you were better to get thrown clear, and I think that probably held up if you were in a 250F or Lancia-Ferrari. As the cars got smaller and tighter, you probably weren't going to get thrown out anyway. The first year I was over there (in Europe) I went off in practice at Monza, in the 2nd Lesmo and went into the trees, breaking all my ribs down one side as I ended up coming out of the car. I had belts at Indy (1967), but Formula One has always been very traditional."

The running start wasn't universally disliked as Bob Bondurant was the master of the technique. Bob – "I had Le Mans starts down so well…. when the arm goes up for the starter, I started running (laughs)." At some point one wonders what might have been running through Bob's mind, as he was already ½ way across the track with everyone else standing there hearing "On your marks" in French. Bob – "I jumped in the car and started, and I was thinking "Holy S##t, did they start the race?" as I was passing the cars that were on the pole. So, we got a nice lead and led our class."

The Le Mans starts were to end after 1969 when Jacky Ickx made his effective protest by waiting for the field to leave, walking to the car, strapped in and then left the pitlane. He was to win the race in the closest Le Mans ever held (the lead changing between Ford and Porsche on the final lap). Ironically it was one race where Chris Amon wished he hadn't had the belts on. Chris – "The problem I had at Le Mans in 1969 was the Le Mans start… the last Le Mans start I ever did. The car wouldn't start, and I got off way in back. I was fastening the harness as I got underway… and found myself a couple of minutes later wishing that I hadn't when I ran into this John Wolfe accident. It was a 917 and it happened right in front of me, like an airplane accident. The thing just disintegrated and I can still remember this fuel tank coming across the road right in front of me and I had nowhere to go. I ran over it, and it jammed under the car, which then set mine off. My car caught fire, and it was getting too hot… I can remember trying to undo the belts so I could get out of the thing. I subsequently jumped out, thinking that I was nearly stopped. I was probably still doing 50 or 60 mph and I bloody nearly got run over by Frank Gardner, who'd had trouble at the start too."

Drastic measures were needed as the dangers were well beyond unacceptable, bordering upon suicidal. The frequency of catastrophic fires prompted the development of much improved fuel cells with internal bladders, with their location eventually moved to directly behind the driver in what would likely be the most protected part of the chassis. These bladders were held in place with internal foam inserts, and were a huge improvement. Later developments with puncture resistant self-sealing bladders, and non-exploding tanks further decreased the odds of fire and/ or spillage in accidents. Despite all these developments, fires continued to occur, such as at the Nurburgring in 1976 where Niki Lauda was scarred in his burning Ferrari.

In 1976, Chris Amon was racing in Morris Nunn's Ensign. "The problem was that it kept losing bits. In Belgium I was having a good scrap in with Hunt and Scheckter when one of the rear wheels came off. In Sweden the steering broke. Once again, they did their best but there was no budget. We had our differences, but he had his heart in the right place. The engines that we were using, I think Bernie had lent them to him, and they were about 3 years old from a 1972 Brabham or something. With a halfway stroke of luck, I could have actually won a race that year."

Amon's comeback to F1 ended at the Nurburgring in 1976, the day that left Niki Lauda fighting for his life after being terribly burned in the wreckage of his Ferrari. It has been said that after the accident a despondent Amon retired from F1 on the spot. Chris Amon - "I've got to say that it wasn't really what happened at the Grand Prix. It was more the fact of getting sick of bits falling off the car. When I saw how long it took for them to get to Niki after his accident... and thinking of what had been happening in the last few races, with suspension failures or something. I don't really want to be stranded in the middle of nowhere with no chance of anybody getting me out of the thing. By that time I'd decided to stop anyway at the end of the year and there was not a lot of incentive to carry on. When you are already planning to stop, the last thing you need is something breaking on you all the time. A lot of people say… 'oh, you are unlucky'. I tell them, 'hang on, I'm still here and a lot of the so-called lucky guys aren't."

Drag racing was also experiencing a safety revolution in the early 1970's. The change to a rear engine layout started to gain popularity at least 6 years after the rear engine revolution had already swept through Indycar racing as well as international sports cars at Le Mans and the Can-Am series. One could argue that it was inevitable, but it surely would not have happened in 1971 were it not for the determined efforts of Don Garlits. Don - "Back in the 1960s, I thought nothing was ever going to happen to 'slingshots'. Of course, I'd seen other rear engine cars. I'd watched them and sat in them… I'd sat in Duane Ong's at the New York National a year before I did mine, and the visibility was unbelievable. I thought it was a damn shame that we couldn't make these damn things work because it would be fun to drive."

It wasn't just 'fun to drive' factor that got Garlits' interest. Don - "The slingshots… we were just young and fearless, and I mean those guys got hurt. They blew the testicles off Jack Chrisman, and another driver, it cut his penis in two. I'll never forget, I went to the hospital that night to see him and they had him under a tent because he'd been burned real bad. He was naked under this thing, and he was crying 'Big Daddy, look what's happened to me.' He raised that tent thing up and looking at him, I tell you what… it turned my blood to ice."

One would think that such first hand knowledge would have been enough inspiration to motivate an immediate redesign for all concerned, but it wasn't. Garlits - "We always thought that the other guy screwed up, and we weren't going to do it. Our s**t was going to be better." In 1970, Don Garlits suffered a terrible accident at the start of a run in his slingshot dragster, Swamp Rat 13. Don – "At Long Beach, I mean I was riding cloud 9. I was a ¼ of a second better than the field when that transmission blew, and every f**king thing went black. I was knocked out, and never knew that until later." The accident had blown half of Don's foot away when the transmission exploded and blew the car completely in half. In the slingshot dragsters of the 1960s, you pretty much sat on/behind the differential with your legs on either side of the driveshaft and transmission. Continued survival had become the motivation for the seriously injured Garlits to find a solution, as with the rear engine top fuel dragster when everything goes wrong it goes wrong behind you instead of in your face or between your legs.

Garlits – "The accident in mine brought all that up in the hospital. I went through a lot of pain in the hospital; I wouldn't accept pain medicine… so I had a lot of time to think about it, a lot of waking moments. I told (Mongoose) McEwen I was going to do it, and he just laughed. He said 'Don, everybody's tried it.' Woody Gilmore was really the pioneer in it, as he built several rear engine cars, one almost killed Pat Foster at Long Beach (Dec 1969). He built Duane Ong's with the rear end turned around to try and get weight on the rear wheels. For traction they had moved the engine way back."

Don was to find inspiration in Scotland's Jim Clark, who had navigated his Lotus Ford through a field of comparatively huge Indy roadsters during the 1963 Indianapolis 500. Don Garlits - "If Clark can handle that car at 200mph in traffic then why in the hell couldn't we get down a quarter mile? That's what kept me going all the time that I was testing and running off the dragstrip, because it wouldn't be under control. I just kept thinking about Jim Clark, and how he was even running in oil coming off of Parnelli Jones. I was right there, I was in Clark's pit… the whole front of the car was just oil, all over him was oil… and he was still able to do it, I was really impressed. They should have black flagged Parnelli, but they knew it was the end of the roadsters, the end of that paradigm."

As it turned out, the challenge of getting a controllable rear engine dragster down ¼ mile strip was huge. Garlits – "We run for 3 months and never got down the dragstrip, if they had dragstrips like now with these barriers, we wouldn't have had a racing car. I was testing at Bitlow, it was 100 feet from the edge of the dragstrip to the stands, 100' of nice mowed grass. It looked like a plowed field after 3 months I'd been out there so much… spun out."

It wasn't looking good for Don's innovative rear engine dragster. "Finally, I gave up. We set the car aside and had our new slingshot… we could turn a car out in a week. We were building the body on it, and my wife came out of the office and said 'What is that?' She knew that nobody had put a deposit up for a car, as nobody was buying any cars because they didn't know what to buy. I said 'Well, Honey that's my new car for 71, you know I can't get down the race track with the rear engine car. This was what I do, and we weren't going to run a transmission anymore, just make it high gear.' She said 'You would get back in one of those monsters after it mutilated you like that? Let me tell you something… you've got a good head on your shoulders, 2 good hands, and all these nice machines in here with 2 guys that will do anything you ask. Now get back in that rear engine car because if there is anybody in the world that can do it, it's you!' We went back to Bitlow the next day and went off the dragstrip again."

"We were messing with the wrong end of the car, working on everything on the back. Different weight, different tire pressure, you name it… anything to make it turn. The rear really had nothing to do with it, as it was the steering was what it was. Coming back I'm riding shotgun, TC's in the middle and Swingel's drivin'. I said 'If I didn't know better I'd think it was the steering. I can't touch the steering to correct it, that it doesn't go too much. But, it can't be that as we put the steering straight out of the slingshot into this car.' Swingel says- 'But Don, this isn't a slingshot, this is a front driver. If you think the steering is too fast, we'll just slow it down.'

The great innovator of drag racing – 'Big Daddy' Don Garlits

"We went back to the shop that night and made long arms for the spindles and a real short arm for the steering box. We went back to the dragstrip the next morning and it ran straight as a string with a 6.86 and the track record was 6.85. 1/100th off the track record and we only had 70% Nitro in it.... and we were just trying to get down the racetrack."Thanks to months of hard work by Tommy (TC) Lemons, Connie Swingel, and Don Garlits, the stars were lining up. Don – "We had this nice slingshot all finished and we didn't know what we were going to do with that. So, when we got back to the shop the phone rang and it was Goodyear. They said 'Do you have any kind of car we can buy from you for show? We got a great big show in Los Angeles, could you deliver it to California?' I said to the guys - 'Get this f**ker in the trailer, we're going to California!"

Crammed into the trailer along with the newly sold slingshot were the various bits and pieces that made up the rear engine dragster, as the trailer would not hold 2 complete cars. Don - "We hung the rear engine chassis from the roof of the trailer, with the engine up in the rack for where we'd put the spare engine. We pulled in to Waterman's shop, everyone was fixing their cars getting ready for the big race at Long Beach. They asked it we had the rear engine car and we opened the door up and there's the slingshot sitting right there. They all just laughed, saying 'we knew you couldn't do it, built yourself a slingshot did ya?' The next morning we drove over to the Los Angeles Convention Center and dropped off the (slingshot) car."

The season opening AHRA National was at Long Beach, the same track where Garlits suffered his accident the previous year. "We pulled into Long Beach, the first guy to meet me at the gate was Jim Tice, the president. He said 'You got the rear engine car?' I said, yes sir... we opened the door of the trailer and there was this chassis, not even painted or anything. He said 'Where is it?' I said... that's it!"

472

"Tice said 'Garlits... you would come out here to a National event and claim this is the race car?' Yes sir, we're going to put it together! He said "I don't want to hear it... this is unreal. Put it together right here by the gate so that the spectators coming in can see that you are actually here.' So... we start assembling it about a ¼ mile away from where the actual pits were, and here comes the Snake. He walks around it shaking his head saying 'Well, I guess that's one way to get publicity. If you can't race anymore, just do something stupid.""

The view up inside a slingshot dragster of the 1960s. Your legs go on either side of the differential, feet alongside the gearbox

Having solved the design problem was one thing, getting anyone who was willing to race alongside a rear engine dragster, quite another. "All the racers got together in the pits, and went to Tice saying 'you remember the last rear engine car here? Pat Foster crossed from one lane to another, and into the stands... it damn near killed him. If there'd been another car in that lane, he'd have run over them. We ain't running him; we don't want to race him.' Tice said 'We don't have any rules against rear engine cars, but what we'll do is to have him make every time trial alone, and if he touches any one of those lines, he's in the trailer and out of here. But, if he gets down the track with every run perfect, then you'll have to race him.' I made every run perfect and went all the way to the final round. I was in the same lane, at the same track; at the same time of day... just as the light went yellow to green I had deja-vu of that explosion from the year before. Coughlin was gone; I ran a better E.T. but couldn't catch him. But that was it, and the rest is history." The following month, Don Garlits won Top Eliminator at the '71 Winternationals, and everything had changed. With his 'Swamp Rat 14', the controllable rear engine dragster had finally arrived, thanks to a combination of misfortune and determination involving one of the great pioneers of drag racing.

In road racing, impact survivability was another key issue which had certainly improved as the cars had become stronger to cope with the massive loads imposed from the ever larger tires at each corner. By the mid- 70s state of the art alloy tubs were being made from honeycomb panels into structures of higher torsional resistance. Crash testing wasn't on the horizon at this time, and the cars became safer mostly as a side effect of the required strength.

By the late 70s/early 80s, the ground effects cars of Formula One with their sliding skirts were the latest development to probe the limits of available track runoff and chassis integrity. Should a sliding skirt stick in the "up" position, the downforce was but a fraction of the previously sealed sidepod. The result could be catastrophic when the expected downforce wasn't there upon turning into a corner flat in 6th gear. Everyone in the sport realized there were corners where the driver would have little or no chance should this occur, and in 1980 at a test session, Patrick Depailler lost his life in the Ost Curve at Hockenheim when a skirt stuck in the up position. It was during this era that Dr. Sid Watkins arrived on the scene, a Neurosurgeon hired to be the first F1 Race Doctor. The usual Italian medical dog and pony show that followed any accident at Monza, in this case Ronnie Peterson's, was to result in Dr. Watkins demanding the formation of a consistent and comprehensive official medical response team, which would follow the cars around on the first lap. Amazingly enough, this concept was resisted at first.

In that same era, the trend in Formula One (and other open wheel series) was to place the driver at the extreme front of the car, to where the driver was pretty much the first part of the car to arrive at the scene of the accident. Eventually legislation required that the driver's extremities/footbox had to be placed behind the centerline of the front wheels, as so many drivers were suffering catastrophic leg injuries. Compounding the issue was the arrival of the early carbon tubs, vs. the previous aluminum skinned honeycomb structures. Eventually the carbon tubs were a massive leap forward in safety, but that was far from the universal case in these early days. Villeneuve's Ferrari shattered upon impact at Zolder, tearing Gilles from the car and throwing him across the track to his death against the barrier. Teammate (and I use the term loosely, as they were bitter rivals to the end) Pironi, had his legs shattered in a massive crash when he ran up the back of a slowing Prost in a rainstorm at Hockenheim. Concepts of adequate cockpit integrity and required hammer tests to verify the strength of the survival cell, were many years from being implemented in that summer of 1982.

However insufficient that some of the early carbon chassis were at providing driver protection, at least the frequency of catastrophic fires had continued to decline across the years. There were exceptions, as Gerhard Berger's Ferrari had a horrific crash at Imola's Tamburello corner in 1989 and was indeed fortunate to survive for over 20 seconds in the resultant inferno before the track marshals arrived with extinguishers.

Geoff Brabham relates some of the dangers that the IMSA GTP drivers of the 1980s faced. The Lola T-810 project was the predecessor to the in-house Electramotive cars. Geoff – "I'd been associated with Trevor Harris through the Gurney Eagle, and a little bit with VDS. I was at home watching an IMSA race at Pocono, and Don Devendorf hit the wall. I remember quite clearly, a picture of him on his hands and knees, next to the car and obviously gasping for air. Not long after that, Trevor rings up and asks 'would you be interested in driving the Nissan?' I wasn't that interested, as that car had a bit of a reputation. I didn't say no, but I made some excuse that I had an Indycar commitment and couldn't do it."

Electramotive was persistent. Geoff – "They rang me back again, and pulled me into coming out and having a look. I could see that even though the car was a bit of a disaster, the team was good and their vision of the future impressed me. I ended up driving the car at Riverside, and I think we were on the front row. Soon after the race started, the car started to handle a bit strange. It was getting to the stage where I was thinking about coming in and getting different tires or getting everything checked out. What happened was that the steering rod was unwinding. We were doing over 200mph down the back straight, and you know the kink before the last turn? When I got to the kink the front steering arm dropped down, and luckily for me it was the left side so I still had steering on the right front. In the kink, I only just made it around the corner, but it was really close. By the time I got it all straight I was going into nine, and there it was only the inside wheel turning. I just touched the wall, I was really lucky. It wasn't a mechanical failure as such. It was just that something came loose." One would suspect that by this point, the Lola T-810 wasn't Geoff's best friend. "No, it wasn't, again it was not one of Lola's best cars."

Following the Nissan GTP car wasn't always a great experience either. Telling Dan Gurney of Amon's oily dilemma in following

Stewart's H-16 BRM, he recalled a similar issue from the GTP days. Dan - "It does remind me of the Nissan GTP car, they used to do that. I remember Juan Fangio won a race in our GTP Toyota powered Eagle up at Portland. After the race I looked through his windscreen and you couldn't see anything at all it was so full of oil and dirt. I said 'Juan, how in the world could you possibly drive when you can't see?' He said very humbly, 'with a windshield like this, it is possible not to enjoy driving."

It was a dangerous era for drivers of the big prototypes, as they were exploring downforce levels and loading never before seen. In the middle of the 1991 season, Tom Kendall's luck ran out, as he suffered a horrific accident turning into the corner at the end of the long straight at Watkins Glen with the Pratt & Miller Intrepid GTP car. Dan Binks – "We pitted early, and we were running 2nd or 3rd when we wrecked. Just as it loaded up it broke the rear spindle at the end of the straight."

Kendall - "We had just made a stop, I was running 2nd and was dicing with Brabham. We made stops on different laps. I got around him going into 1, and he'd passed me on the straight before I passed him back going into 5 the lap before. We were having a real ding-dong. The next lap I passed him into 1 again, and then he passed me back on the straight after the esses, like everything did. There was no chicane, and then he moved over for the next turn so that he was on the inside and I was on the outside. That little difference… if he hadn't done that, I would have been passing him again on the inside when that thing broke It probably would have helped me out… would have been good for me, and worse for him. When I turned in I felt the wheel come off, and I assumed that since we made a pit stop 2 laps before that the wheel nut had come off."

Phil Binks – "It was a 2" axle that broke. 2" diameter high temp steel, I think later they ended up with 2-1/8" or 2-1/4". One of the forensic engineers who did the testing on it said that in ½ of a turn of the wheel, it went from cracked to broke, the crack moved at almost the speed of sound."

Tommy – "My first thought was that I was pissed that I was going to lose 2nd. In the next fraction of a second when the car got backwards I saw how fast the background was going and thought 'oh wow, this thing is really moving'. The car kept rotating and I never saw the wall, it hit right as it got there. Even though it hit pretty much head on, I never saw it coming. It got dark as the car went into the tires and then I remember the car rebounded off, spinning like a top. Then it got bright, as the whole front of the car and the roof was gone, and both feet felt like they were on fire. I looked down and my leg was bent, wrapped up in the steering column, and my left foot was kind of in with the steering rack... it wasn't pointed funny or anything, but it felt like a blowtorch was on it. I got that free and so it was setting on top of the rack. The other one was caught and not straight."

Kendall's Intrepid was crushed against the barriers at Watkins Glen
– Photo courtesy of Jerry Howard

Dan arrived on the scene and was trying to help get Tommy out of what was left of the Intrepid. Dan – "I was just horrified. I'd worked on race cars for a long time up to that point, and you are racing with your buddies. Yeah, it's a professional race team, but Tommy and I had been together at that point for 6 years. It was pretty bad, there was no radio response from Tommy, and Wayne (teammate Wayne Taylor) had called the pits and said that it's big, and we needed to get back there. So, I ran through the fence and Jim Miller's wife was in the van. I jumped in the van and said that I had to go to the back of the track. We went down there and I jumped over the fence, it was literally a minute and a half. The emergency crew was there, but they were so freaked out... there was water everywhere... that water wetter stuff, kind of pink instead of anti-freeze, it helps lube the pump and holds temperature better. This pink fluid was all over Tommy, all over everything, and they were thinking it was fuel, so they were freaked out that the thing was going to blow up."

Dan continues - "First thing when I run up there, I see his legs pointing all the wrong way. I just couldn't believe it. I just couldn't believe that we'd hurt Tom Kendall. I took all the blame and hurt, totally devastated. It was the worst day of my life, probably... just a drag. Here's your buddy laying in the car that you helped build, and it hurt him; the worst thing that could happen. It was one of the points in your career that you are thinking about "Man, should I really do this? I'm thinking that I'm not going to race anymore... I've hurt my best friend. You know this stuff can happen but when it does happen, it is just horrifying." There is an extreme downside to the sport.

Somehow Kendall kept his cool through the extraction. "It's sort of the nature of racing. One of the things I was good at was getting rid of all emotion. One of the reasons I was so good back then was that I was totally analytical and my emotion was tamed. It was all analytical, if this happens, then this happens... I wanted to get away from the car, but I couldn't, so I just tried to control the heart rate, calm down and just breathe. I called on the radio, not knowing the radio wasn't working, and said that my leg is broken and to send medical help. I was thinking of my Mom, so I took off my helmet so everyone would know I was awake and alert, not knowing the way that the car came to rest that they couldn't see that. The doctor, when he first gets there, steps on the side of the car and the car flexed so it was tweaking on the leg that was trapped and I was like 'Owwww...Whoa!'

Kendall continues - "He stepped back, as he couldn't figure out how to get close to me, and I think they started an IV. I had to oversee my own extraction. My knee was jammed up into the bolts that would release the thin steel steering column, so they couldn't get at those. I'm thinking, until they cut that, I'm not getting out of here. They had those jaws, the hydraulic cutters and I said they have to get one of them between my leg and the column. They said, 'no, it's up against your leg'. You know, safety workers are just people too. In your mind you think these safety workers are the experts, but they were all rattled as they don't see crashes like that all the time. I told them to put it in there and cut it, and if I can't stand it, I'll tell ya. I'm thinking that I'm not getting out of here until its cut, and I want to get out of here. I said to do it, and it hurt like a mother..."

Dan – "Tommy said, "I'm alright. Help me get out of this thing." The racer takes over, and it's "Ok, we need to cut this, and God Damn it, it is not going to catch on fire, the fuel cell is fine." The steering column was bent around one leg. A ¾" .060 wall pipe... you can just imagine... to bend it around his leg. So, we've got to cut this thing, as he's drifting in and out of consciousness. We got him out and onto the stretcher, get to the helicopter... his Mom and step-dad are there and she is all freaked out, all she hears is the stuff over the loudspeaker while waiting for him at the track medical center. I'm trying to calm her down and trying to get Tommy into the helicopter. I just thinking that I can't believe it happened."

It is pertinent to note that Watkins Glen did not put a chicane in at that point of the track, until J. D. McDuffie got killed in the same turn at the NASCAR Cup race soon after. The usual sad conclusion is that needed safety improvements aren't triggered when you "almost" kill yourself. Dan – "They discounted that it was a P car, it was a bad rap. It was as close to getting killed as you could come, he was really close to being done."

Dan – "A couple of weeks after Kendall got out of surgery and got going again, he called me up and said "Make sure the next one's ready, man!" So, that was all I needed for my personality, a little motivation and he knew that. He knew he was screwed up and it was going to be a long time, but he knew he wasn't done racing, and that we weren't done racing together. We actually took him out to the car in a wheelchair and lifted him up into it, so he could get the winter testing. The guy is just phenomenal."

Tommy – "That probably wasn't right away because I didn't know what was going to happen. I really didn't think about it as I had a lot of other stuff to worry about. Back then there were a lot of Indycar guys getting hurt and in their first interview from the hospital they are saying 'I just can't wait to get back into the car'. When it was me, that wasn't what I was thinking. I was thinking 'what's my life going to be like now?' But, as time went by, and once I realized the scope of things and started rehabbing and so-forth, eventually then I started thinking about what I wanted to do. The hard part for me was because that wasn't my fault, it was a mechanical. I'd never been hurt, and in 5 years I'd finished almost every race I'd started, with something like 3 DNF's. I crashed the RX-7 at Mid-Ohio on consecutive years but that was just about it. I had convinced myself that if you don't make mistakes you could charge and be fast, and that you wouldn't crash, period. My crash blew that up, that a crash might not have anything to do with you at all, and I had never considered that. That was the hard part for me to wrap my brain around. I wrestled with that a little bit, as how obviously that was part of the deal and I was I ok with that… obviously the answer was that I was. The GTP car made me think about stuff that I hadn't considered before, about how fast we were going, and some of the tracks."

"I have to say that the way that the way my career went and how I ended back in the sedan stuff, I actually liked that. I felt that the next year in the GTP car, I drove the car the same way but I thought about safety more and I'd never thought about that before. But once I got back in the sedans, I never thought about it again, I felt comfortable. The safety/speed/excitement balance was about right."

Thankfully the big prototypes have come a long way in crash worthiness since 1991. Looking at the current Dyson Lola (ALMS prototype) the driver's feet are curiously close to the front wheel centerline of the tub, as in the bad old days of the Porsche 956 (the similar 962 had increased the wheelbase by pushing the front wheels forward, beyond the driver's feet, making the car eligible for IMSA). Being behind the front wheel centerline became a general rule for the improvement in safety for a generation of racers, open wheel and closed. However with the Dyson Lola, there is an extension to the tub, essentially a big additional carbon box that provides additional impact survivability. Also importantly, it allows the damaged sections to be removed in the event of a big impact, hopefully without trashing the tub.

Dyson Lola driver, Guy Smith comments –"That is kind of a big bulkhead within the carbon fibre bodywork, a part of the nose, and that takes pretty much a fair chunk of the impact." Rob Dyson – "It's a huge crash box, a removable piece that is designed to crush sequentially. You've got such an extensive nose on a sports car that you have to strap it on to something." Guy Smith – "This piece right here is really stout, you can ask me how stout as we had a big one at Atlanta. That is as prescribed in the rules; it has to withstand frontal impact, that's basically what they test for. It is the same crash tests as they use in F1, exactly.

In a really bad accident with a side impact it might crack it up, but from a head-on point of view it is very surprising. I like driving a coupe, as it was at Le Mans with McNish going over... it's nice to have a roof, you know. You never expect it, never expect a car to climb over the barrier, but it just shows that you never know what can happen. When you look back at the old cars (from the 80s) it's just horrendous, but at the time that was the state of the art, and they were the latest and greatest. I'm sure we will look back at this in 20 years' time and say Wow. Nothing ages quite like a race car."

In Formula One, there had been a long period of good fortune that many assigned to the improved safety of the cars across the era, but perhaps was luck as much as anything else. No Formula One driver had been lost in during a race weekend since Riccardo Paletti's fatal accident on the start line of the 1982 Canadian Grand Prix when he slammed at speed into the stalled Ferrari of Pironi. There were additional track safety developments over the following years, but some weren't to last long, such as the large Styrofoam blocks placed in the escape roads to absorb energy. At Hockenheim in 1989, Emanuele Pirro tested the Styrofoam barrier system to destruction with his Benetton mid-race. Pirro - "It was a missed opportunity because the car was running real fast and we were catching Mansell who was in P3. It was scary, because I thought it was a wall, and I went head-on into it. I didn't know, I just saw a big thing." Initially unconscious, Pirro was rushed to the hospital. Emanuele was to make a complete recovery, eventually to become a 5 time Le Mans winner, but his accident marked the end of Styrofoam barriers in F1.

Sadly the false veneer of safety was forever lifted from F1 during the nightmare of San Marino Grand Prix weekend at Imola in 1994. First, Rubens Barrichello was gravely injured on Friday when his airborne Jordan cleared the tire wall and impacted the fence posts at speed. The severity of the impact was sickening to see, and with the car virtually stopped upon impact, Barrichello had swallowed his tongue. It was only the immediate arrival and competent attention from the trackside medical staff that saved his life. Then on Saturday, having a front wing failure in the worst possible place, Roland Ratzenberger was killed in a high speed impact at Villeneuve corner, and although the tub itself held up well under the impact, the severity of the crash upon the driver was obvious as the car came to rest in Tosa. His was the first fatality at a F1 event in 12 years. Sadly, the 2nd was to come the following day.

Following a massive start line accident, Senna's Williams had circulated slowly behind the safety car during a long caution period, Senna clearly frustrated with the slow process of the pace car which could result in reduced temperature in the tires. A lap after the restart, Senna went off in the high speed Tamburello corner for a combination of reasons that are still being debated. As was the design fashion of the day, there was little side protection in the cockpit side area, the chassis of most cars literally dropped down to shoulder level or below on either side of the driver. Although the structure of his car remained intact, Ayrton Senna was fatally injured when he was struck by his front wheel/suspension assembly coming over the front of the tub upon impact with the wall.

In the years since, the potential for cockpit intrusion of errant parts has been reduced by increasing the height of sidepods resulting in less of the driver being exposed, and by the use of wheel tethers, to keep the wheels in the general vicinity of the chassis, vs. in the grandstand or cockpit. Perhaps the only good thing to come from Imola 1994 was the recreation of the Grand Prix Drivers Association soon after, and it remains an active voice regarding car and track safety concerns. There will always remain risks with open cockpit, open wheel cars, as wheel to wheel contact can often result in a flying car. And an inverted open cockpit airborne car by definition leaves the driver completely at the mercy of fate, as shown by the death of Dan Wheldon at

The powerful Senna Memorial at Tamburello corner – covered with notes and flowers at the 2005 San Marino Grand Prix

Vegas. That said, the odds continue to improve.

One trend towards improved driver safety comes from designing cars that have sufficient room for the driver and some

485

increased potential for energy absorption. Justin Wilson is one of the few Indycar drivers who are taller than 6', and comments upon the available space in the 2012 Dallara. Justin – "It is good, inside the car I've got a little bit more room with extra padding all around, underneath you, extra behind you. The previous Dallara was really tight, in F1 it depended upon the car. Every car I got into was tight… always. The Jaguar was easier to fit into than the Minardi, the 2003 Jaguar was fine. Minardi had to cut holes in the floor of the car for my heels to fit in. So, they cut it out and put in 2 little cups so my feet could fit. It was a high nose car, fortunately. I didn't fit in the Williams at all. They offered me a test and I couldn't fit in."

No doubt the Minardi lost some underbody downforce because of Justin Wilson's feet. At the other end, one lasting image of Justin racing the Jaguar F1 car was of him leaning his head over on the straight, so as to interfere less with the airflow to the engine intake. These problems are nothing new, as F1 driver meetings could be considered a jockey festival. The 1989 Arrows F1 car featured an incredibly narrow monocoque, which though great in the wind tunnel, had the minor side effect of making Eddie Cheever's tightly packed legs go to sleep in the middle of a Grand Prix. Justin – "Back in the late 80's and up through the mid 90's, I don't think I could have fit."

In their endless quest for ever smaller cross section, sometimes it is the obvious things that designers miss. Joe Leonard – "It was 1972, and they were building the new car (the Maurice Phillippe penned Parnelli Indy car that Leonard dominated the 72 season with). They had Mario (Andretti) down there, and you know… Mario only has size 6 or 6-1/2 shoes. Luckily I came by about 2 weeks later to see my car and set it up. When I climbed in, I couldn't move my feet, they had to re-engineer the bulkheads around my size 12 shoes. It was a good thing I came down there, what if I'd shown up at Phoenix for the first race and I couldn't fit in the car?" One can only assume that Joe Leonard would have experienced heel hole tub modifications similar to Justin Wilson's. Needless to say, these many examples of an undersized cockpit could have safety ramifications, considering how it takes away space that could be used for energy absorbing materials.

It is a testament to how much things have changed when you see something like the uninjured Mark Webber's unbelievable flight into the trees with the factory Mercedes at Le Mans in 1999. However, in endurance racing the closing rates for the fastest prototypes vs. the GT class cars (often being driven by amateurs) create a predictably horrific combination.

Slick looking car, too bad Joe Leonard couldn't fit his feet inside

Last lap Turn 1 battle for the lead between Takuma Sato and Dario Franchitti, at the 2012 Indianapolis 500. The safety of the modern race car has made such moments less fraught with terror

Sebastian Bourdais – "At Road Atlanta (Petit Le Mans) I could not make a lap time that was in any way representative. In the best scenario I hit turn 1 and I've got a car exiting the pits which is screwing my lap time straight away. That's not even counting the next 5 cars in the way. It's like trying to race in a traffic jam, it's wrong. When you have a 4.1 km race track you can not expect to have 53 cars on the track. It's wrong, it's dangerous, it's not fun and there is nothing good about it."

Dr. Ulrich Baretzky (Audi) – "Our car is not a bulletproof car, and GT cars are very solid cars… and the more solid the car, the more idiot the driver. The amateurs aren't looking in the mirror, they see nothing… it's a nightmare, it is really dangerous, a real problem. Sebring, Silverstone, Le Mans… the same. At Le Mans it nearly cost one of our drivers his life, Mike Rockenfeller, when a 55 year old amateur was completely lost on this racetrack. Going racing at 55 is one thing; going to Le Mans at 55 is something else." When the Ferrari GT car came down onto the fast closing Audi in the kink heading to Indianapolis corner,

Rockenfeller speared straight into the barriers head-on at 200mph and the R18 disintegrated, essentially leaving only the survival cell intact. He was indeed fortunate to survive as there have been many whose Le Mans accident was their last.

There appears to be a solution at hand, or at least something that will help avoid such inadvertent contact. Dan Binks – "The one thing that is really cool is that we have a rear view camera with a laser interface that, rain or shine, it predicts how fast the car behind you is coming... if the Audi is coming it tells you its coming super-fast. Even if you get oil on the camera, it still gives you the arrows and tells you how fast it is coming. We will sell it at some time or another. Riley has asked about it, and Falken has asked about it. We have to get it bulletproof before we sell it, but once that happens it will be a huge deal in motorsport. It's a Bosch radar system that Pratt & Miller interfaced with a video. It predicts which way they are going to go by and how fast they are going to catch you. It updates on the screen and the arrow changes colors. It goes to yellow when they are about 200 yards back, and then goes to red when they are about 25 yards back. Those accidents where somebody is coming behind you... the screen has a big red arrow when they get close."

Despite all the proven safety advances with the carbon survival cell, there is a land where it seems that time stands still. Not since Don Garlits' rear engine revolution of 1971 had the cloistered world of the NHRA seen a corresponding revolution in safety. In fact, their safety developments have been positively glacial in comparison to those made in within other sanctioning bodies, such as the carbon safety cell within the DTM series cars raced in Germany. Triggers for safety improvements, as always, come in the wake of driver injury or death. In Funny Car, the tragic death of Eric Medlin in 2007 led to a new 3 rail design frame fabricated by his team, John Force Racing, which they graciously offered to share with any competitor who wanted it for the 2008 season.

There is little doubt that the 3 rail helps reduce cockpit

intrusion by its higher tube placement on either side of the driver, but my voiced initial reaction to being shown the new car at Phoenix in 2008 was that it was an 8000hp Watson Indy roadster with a pair of extra tubes in it. Needless to say, this comment wasn't particularly well received. Since 2010, sheets of carbon fiber have been dzus fastened to steel tubing around the driver, which as one top driver then explained to me, was their 'carbon safety cell'.

Long-time Funny Car driver Ron Capps is considerably more aware of the limitations of this carbon shielding. Ron – "It is nothing structurally that goes into the car. The cover dzus's on, and covers my hands in case of fire. And we have it around the roll cage to protect me around here (the perimeter of his body)." Clearly there is some sort of disconnect between current developments in the NHRA and the lessons learned from other forms of racing worldwide. As might be surmised, much of the field continues to use their older 2 rail funny car chassis with virtually no significant protection to side impact intrusion into the driver.

Gian Paolo Dallara had offered to provide his expertise in carbon safety cell construction to either individual teams or the NHRA itself, after our discussions of the situation at Sears Point Indycar in late summer 2008 in the wake of yet another death in the funny cars. Little has come of this to date. When one considers that we live in a world of multiple carbon bulkheads and deformable energy absorbing safety cells, this attitude is surprising to say the least.

There is some progress, however glacial. Ron Capps – "We are in a good place right now, but it could always be better. We built that capsule, like my teammate Tony Schumacher is using and that is definitely the right direction." This capsule provides a fully enclosed cockpit for their 2012 top fuel car, much like the pioneering "Rat Under Glass" or 'Swamp Rat 30' car from 1986 built by Don Garlits. The car incorporated a transparent lexan cockpit, a first in the class. Capps – "He's the one that did it, and once again was ahead of his time. 20 or 30 years ago he built his canopy car, so once again he was leading the way." Maybe people should start listening to Don Garlits more? Ron – "They should have a long time ago." The reality is that Don Garlits was well ahead of his time (as usual), and the NHRA's current safety standards continue to lag well behind the state of the art.

Ashley Force's Funny Car from 2010

Similarly, Jackie Stewart's commitment to advancing racing safety, continue to this day. In 2001, Jackie was in the broadcast booth at the Rolex 24 Hours of Daytona, and pointed out that Dale Earnhardt, driving a Corvette, was wearing an open face helmet more than 30 years after full face helmets had been standard fare in almost all forms of racing. Jackie Stewart found the use of that helmet absolutely perplexing, and made a point of mentioning it. Less than a month later, Earnhardt died at Daytona, and one of the complicating factors in his death was the injuries that resulted from the lack of protection of that open face helmet. Stewart, as always, had brought to the broadcast booth the attention to detail that most of us overlook. Jackie – "Yeah… well since you are only good at attention to detail, sometimes there is an asset. The other thing is that is you tend to almost over-explain to people. I think that you are as dumb as I am, so therefore I've got to be very sure that you've got the message." There is little doubt about Stewart being an asset to the sport, and countless racers owe their lives to the self-deprecating Scot and his determination to make changes for the better.

CHAPTER TWELVE

THE FUTURE

Gian Paolo Dallara with his racing simulator at the
Dallara works in Parma, Italy
— Photo courtesy of Dallara Automobili

If there is any one aspect of racing that is critical to success, it is a clear vision of the direction where the sport is headed, and your company's part within that future. To Gian Paolo Dallara, a major aspect of that future is with racing simulation. Mr. Dallara - "Where we are engaged a lot is with innovation... in the simulator area. We are working on a simulator that should be able to give to the driver, assuming you are able to organize a very good mathematical model of the car. One that comprises all the responses of the car to different road conditions, to different road profiles... that there are all the characteristics of the tires, the springs, the shock absorbers, of the engine... everything. It would be a mathematical model that can describe completely a car."

"First – you will be able to develop the car, before the car is produced. The development time will be shorter, and you can improve the quality of what you deliver. Second – we help the teams better develop the car. Third – We can help to teach the drivers, at an early stage, if they can become a professional driver, or if they just can become an amateur driver. It is possible you could enlarge the area of recruitment for drivers, when they don't have to wait years and years and spend a lot of money in an early stage, hoping something can develop... for them to realize if they could be a professional driver. There could be a selection... now in some ways, the selection is from young people who have a rich family, or with a family prepared to spend money that maybe they don't have. That is high risk, and very expensive... it is tremendous the cost to become a racing driver."

Another beneficial effect of the simulator testing is a higher quality of field, with the most promising drivers moving on to the feeder series. Dallara - "Maybe it would be easier for the driver to attract many sponsors. Something that shows how the driver has (or hasn't) the characteristics that one needs to grow... and at least then you would realize it, if you were debating to become a driver." One can see the day where a high test result in the simulator might be the equivalent of having a high grade point average at the university, opening doors that otherwise would remain closed. It is also best to keep in mind the success of Lewis Hamilton, who virtually lived in the McLaren simulator, and upon his debut was an immediate factor in the F1 World Championship. This was not a coincidence. Dallara – "Hamilton... there was a person at McLaren who was able to realize that he could be a racing champion... a feeling. In the future with this system, you would have the numbers to see. Maybe you could organize your life to becoming a professional motor racing driver."

Mr. Dallara continues – "So, we have planned well, the Grand Model... where the driver will have the same acceleration he would have in the car. A big system, 6 meters by 6 meters that moves to give the exact same sensation of the car, of a real drive. Then we will make one in Indianapolis, and then with the same software and different mechanical hardware, we can make something at a lower level so the teams can test before going to the track. For a driver they can see how the aerodynamic data changes with another car in front of you... it is very mathematically complex, it takes 10 years of people working full time, for all of the detail of what is going on. These are the problems of the mathematical model." A futurist view of where racing car development is headed, potentially a world of dueling simulators. "Yes, but always there will be the qualifying, someone says start your engines, and at the end the checkered flag is there."

It appears the future is now. Mr. Dallara - "In October 2010, we will have our simulator with the GP2 model for different circuits. You will immediately realize if one (driver) is good or not. Of course, you can grow the talent and maybe after one year you can take the simulator again, but there are plenty of races where you can enjoy yourself. Not everyone is a professional. How many people are in the New York Marathon to win, maybe 60? How many compete... thousands?" In the higher level feeder series such as GP2, there really is not room for amateurs.

The simulator will help make that distinction obvious, between the talented and the truly gifted.

That said, there have been many workmanlike drivers who lacked the amazing skills of their competitors, yet have become World Champions. Former Lotus mechanic Graham Hill, a 2 times World F1 Champion and Indy 500 winner, achieved those same results with nothing like the natural talent of his teammate Jim Clark. Dallara – "I am not a fanatic of the simulator. But if someone does this before me, I may be out of business as it can change the world. It will be a tool, and we will absolutely use it in F3 to improve the performance of the car. Without it you will be lost."

Jean Alesi learning to drive a Dallara Indycar
in the Dallara Simulator at Parma, Italy
– Photo courtesy of Dallara Automobili

Jean Alesi was to become familiar with the 2012 Dallara Indycar, by using that Dallara simulator in Parma, Italy. What was his initial reaction? Jean – "To get sick, immediately. It's amazing, it's a massive machine. The setup I had on my car for the first lap was exactly what I had thought the best on the simulator. They had to compensate for the wing as that was why I had too much pushing, but when they made the aero balance better, I could work with it. I must confess, except for the sickness, and that makes the difference. The motion is not hydraulic, they are magnetic... and the worst thing is when they switch the lights off.

One can certainly understand the getting sick part. At the 1994 Belgian GP, yours truly got to take a lap of Spa with Jean Alesi in the hydraulic V12 Ferrari simulator. There was a slight disconnect of perhaps 3/10ths of a second delay between the visual projection and the actual movement. The term 'Hurl-a-matic' doesn't begin to describe the experience of that simulated lap of Spa.

What was Jean's first reaction upon driving fast laps at the Speedway? Alesi – "I understood why they said to me that I was crazy. But I like it because it is really challenging." There are obviously limitations to the simulation, and one is obviously the start. Jean – "I spoke to Alex Tagliani and asked him what kind of advice he could give me, as last year he was on pole position, and the year before he was 33rd (Alesi was starting 33rd). He said it is crazy, you will see that there is so much draft, that you will have an aeroplane that won't stop, so please be very aware of that."

Indianapolis was the first time Alesi had experienced stagger. Jean – "We did not use it in Formula One because you create problems in a part of the track. They never tried to give us one part of the track; they tried to make it the best everywhere." Is running at Indy more than what you expected? "It is more. The way I have to learn every single detail to be competitive, has been a lot. Of all of the people who talked to me, 90% of them never saw a race here live, or never came here as a driver. At the end of the day, the people… they don't know what they are talking about. It is really different, and in a way, my driving style helped me a lot. The car is not sliding but it is loose, and I like that better. It makes me comfortable. But when I have the pushing, it is a weird sensation because you can't see the end of the corner. In one month here, I learned more than in all my years of Formula One. The passion is a part of my life, and that's the reason that I am here. Since September of last year, I have a trainer with me almost every day."

Jean is probably the only guy at Indy who is more comfortable with a loose car. Jean (laughs) – "I hope it will last for the whole race." Where did this other-worldly ability to drive loose cars or on slicks in the rain come from? Jean - "When I was a kid, I was playing a lot on ice tracks, in the Alps you know… I always had the car control, and I would spend my whole winter driving up there driving on the ice. I am sure that helped me a lot." One suspects that the 'Jean Alesi settings' may find limited use for others in the Dallara simulator.

For the manufacturer of street automobiles, racing will likely increase in relevance as the ultimate proving ground for emerging technologies. What does Audi's Dr. Ulrich Baretzky see for the future of Audi's endurance racing program in this changing world? "I think that until 2013, we will stay basically with our R18. We will do development, that's for sure… engine-wise, car-wise, everywhere. 2011, 12, 13… and then we will have a completely new world, probably. We don't have the rule book, but we are working on it. I think this rule book will be the most important thing in the past 25 years of motorsport, because this is a dramatic change of mindset, going down to efficiency instead of power. It is very difficult to get the rules right, because you are looking at things from a completely different point of view and can make a lot of mistakes."

Sheer performance has it's downside as the speeds increase, the gravel traps get ever larger, and the spectators have to be placed further and further away. Ulrich – "Exactly, this is not the way, and we have to change for a whole bunch of environmental reasons, be socially acceptable. If not, we are going away like Formula One... more and more. That cannot be the target, as they want to have a lot of power as well and the consumption will be very high... or, they restrict the consumption. What I said to Andy Randolph (head of engine development for Earnhardt Childress racing, ECR) if they decide to go for a V6, this is the wrong engine concept, believe me. It is easier for the car maker... that is clear. You get the V8 or V6, bolt in the gearbox and everything is very stiff. That is not the future engine, it has 4 cylinders or less, and you need to develop this in motorsport."

So the ACO rule book of the future will be absolutely focused upon efficiency. It is important to keep in mind that there is a long history of such things at Le Mans. At the 24 hours of Le Mans starting in 1925, the Index of Efficiency prize was given to the car which traveled the furthest with the least piston displacement, the goal being to do the most with the least. In the 1950s, Lotus would bring 750cc special entries in attempts to wrest away the Index of Efficiency from the tiny French Deutsch-Bonnet racers, or similar. In 1967 conventional knowledge was challenged when Porsche and their 2 litre type 907 long tail won the Index, while finishing 5th overall. Small capacity cars were approaching the point where they could challenge for overall victory. A similar category was the Index of Thermal Efficiency, which compared fuel economy to performance. Surprisingly this prize was won by the overall winning 7 litre Mk.4 Ford, proving that large powerful engines in tremendously fast cars are not necessarily inefficient.

In any engine design, friction is the constant enemy, absorbing power from the engine. When probing the wonders of the latest generation of HVAC system chillers, the latest technology uses magnetic bearings (zero drag) vs. roller bearings, ball bearings, or plain shell bearings. This magnetic bearing technology has not yet arrived for smaller applications as it is still 480v commercial building technology for the moment. In the event of power failure, these have a capacitor system to keep the shaft from dropping onto the magnet array. In the event of power failure, these automatically transfer over to something similar to regenerative braking, by becoming a generator which keeps the magnetic bearing sufficiently powered up to avoid catastrophic galling upon what would have formerly been the bearing surface. These concepts of zero friction magnetic bearing application for supercharger and engine technology have not yet reached the level of miniaturization that permits their use in racing. Expect that to change in the quest for ever reduced friction.

Dr. Baretzky - "Gasoline-wise for sure, the next generation of Le Mans cars will be like the A4, the A3… it's all about efficiency. You need a minimum of cylinders, small very efficient engines. To go 220 mph down the Mulsanne, you need great power for that. You won't brake at the last moment like an idiot and waste all that energy, so you will brake with a different style because you will need to get a lot of energy savings through the braking. You will go around the corners in a different style than we do it today, and maybe one of the other guys will overtake you at the beginning of the race. But you will see him later on, when he is running out of fuel."

Allan McNish – "The regulations make you look at all the details to see how you could be more efficient. What it does is that it gives these guys at Audi a reason to be involved. Developing something that can be related to what they are trying to sell, and not just a marketing tool. In terms of performance, if you look at a road car everything is going to small little supercharged engines of 4 cylinders, the world of V-10s and V-12 are kind of history. With really little engines with superchargers or turbochargers, the car is lighter with less weight over the front axle which means the balance of the car is better. That whole shift has happened so quickly in the last 5 years that it surprises me looking back now, to be honest."

In a world where it seems that most petroleum assets are found within the borders of nations who are hostile to many of the beliefs of the western world, there is also a geo-political motivation for efficiency or alternative means of propulsion. As Dr. Baretzky has voiced, motor sport should lead the way in testing and developing these emerging technologies.

The pioneering 2008 Zytek Hybrid with KERS system to power a rear wheel driven electric motor system

Formula 1 and endurance racing have brought KERS (Kinetic Energy Recovery Systems) technology to the grids, where heat energy from the brakes is converted through an inverter into electrical energy and stored to power a supplemental electrical motor. As one might expect, there were numerous issues with learning the new technology, with Red Bull having set the factory on fire being perhaps the most memorable. Of course there is a weight penalty from all the additional equipment and battery storage capacity, and for 2011 the minimum F1 weight was increased so that the KERS equipped cars simply had less ballast to move around the car. The ballast likely could be placed more optimally than the KERS equipment, but the additional hp (legislated at approximately 80hp maximum) more than offset that slight penalty in CG flexibility.

Taken to extremes, one wonders why there would be cooling ducts for brakes or radiators for fluids, as such heat sources could be converted to additional energy for performance… to say nothing of the aerodynamic improvements that could result through elimination of ducts and cooling inlets. If the idea is to create more power through heat, and you have massive heat generators at various points within the conventional race car, why would you want to disperse that heat away into the atmosphere through various heat exchangers that give back nothing? Dr. Baretzky – "That is another philosophy, a completely different story which we have to explore. It is not so easy to understand in the beginning, so we have to learn a lot about that. It is the next step."

While everyone else was going down the KERS path in Formula One, Williams F1 was trying an entirely different concept. If the idea is to create an inertia storage device, then what could be more proven than that of a flywheel? Williams combined their acquired carbon fibre knowledge with massive rpm (as much as 40,000) to store this energy in a vacuum created within a relatively lightweight containment device. As Williams points out, the disadvantage of a mechanically operated flywheel system is that it requires a seal to maintain the vacuum, which can be problematic. Hence, their system uses an electric motor to spin up the flywheel, the electrical energy created from regenerative braking being used to power the flywheel. Regenerative braking is the most common method of electrical energy creation in production hybrid cars vs. the heat generation changed to electrical power through an inverter and stored by batteries, as is common with most KERS racing applications. Williams' success was such that a separate company (Williams Hybrid Power) has been spun off from what began as Williams Grand Prix Engineering so many decades ago.

Porsche decided to use the Williams flywheel technology to power their first generation hybrid racer, the 911 GT-3R Hybrid. In the case of the 911, they use dual electric motors, which also serve as power generators. Marc Lieb has been the development driver most associated with the hybrid program. Marc – "I was also working as an engineer in Weissach, and was with the project since the very beginning doing the test drives, talking to the engineers. Do we need ABS, can we do it without ABS? You want to have a switch, or you want to have a button?"

Wolf Henzler – "I was also involved in the very beginning. When I drove it, even in the earlier days, I was impressed. It was very good to control the car, but it was back when the power did not come on automatically, we had a handle to get the power (to the front wheels). It was a handle behind the steering wheel like a paddle that would turn on the front power, and when I drove the car it was the same power to both front tires. It was just my decision for when I wanted the power. It was really good in the corners; it helped to improve the balance of the car. When you have oversteer, you'd pull the paddle and it would pull the front and improve the balance and helped to get a better exit. It was already very good, but I think the way it is now being automatically is way better. Now the system can charge when necessary and when it should use the power. When I saw the Hybrid for the 24 hour race, so many things have changed this year... all the buttons. It's a huge step from back when I drove it.

The most unique aspect to this later version of Porsche's Hybrid is the ability to split power between the two front wheels as one sees fit. Porsche is not using a torque split device such as a limited slip of fluid or friction type to achieve this, as their dual electric motor solution uses one motor mounted at each front wheel. It is the ultimate refinement in having control over the power application. In practice, it has proven superior to a strong field of GT classification cars in terms of sheer speed across a given race distance.

The Porsche 911 GT-3R Hybrid 2.0 which has individually controlled 75KW electric motors at each front axle. In action, it required 2 or 3 engineers continually monitoring the system

How does one use this RF vs. LF power split in a racing application? Is the Hybrid system active all the time, or is this version still a 'push to pass' system like the earlier system actuated with a handle? Marc – "It is fully automatic system, and you have power in any corner you want to have power in. You want to save the power, it's a lot more complex of a system and a lot more work to do on the race track that requires a lot more thinking from the drivers. Energy management doesn't have to be a hybrid system or an electric car. It is about harnessing the amount of energy you have and making it the most efficient." Timo Bernhard - "Basically, it is a nice tool for the driver, which has an influence on the balance of the car. If it is understeering, you can adjust it by independently adjusting the power. This is something that the engineers put into the mapping which the driver can adjust while driving. You can work with the outer wheel or the inside wheel, it is something that you have to set up too, it's another tool." As the rear of the car is conventional, increasing the power to the front can help to reduce understeer, and there are a variety of pre-programmed maps from which the driver can select, which Timo uses primarily vs. manually adjusting the power split within an individual map. Each map has been programmed and modified by the engineers for an individual track, or series of corners.

In 2011, Peugeot's Simon Pagenaud had a photo of the Porsche GT3R Hybrid steering wheel on his computer desktop, to give an indication of the appreciation of the system's complexity within the paddock. Lieb – "They are trying to do so many things… so many switches on the steering wheel, you have engine map, engine map for the hybrid system, you have the torque vectoring which means you can add a little more power to the outside wheel than on the inside, which helps you on the turn-in." So, increased power to the outside front wheel is the setting for reduced understeer, reduced power to the outside front wheel can help induce it? Marc – "Yes, but it is more complicated than that. We have mapping for the 2 engines where the outside wheel runs a little bit quicker, so you move the moment a little bit so that when you turn into the corner you have less moment to one wheel."

As with most engine management systems, the car knows where it is on-track, and each selected map is programmed with a slightly different engineered solution based upon that information. Marc Lieb – "If we want a little more oversteer on turn-in, we can adjust that vectoring on the steering wheel. When you can adjust the steering wheel so that the 2 front motors respond differently, you can induce a little more moment, or make the car more stable." It can also make the car significantly faster as the hybrid system at maximum power can add as much as 200hp to the total power output of the car.

How is the reliability of the system, and what are the advantages of using the carbon flywheel vs. a deep cycle battery inertia storage system? Lieb – "The first year we had some reliability issues, but they are now sorted out. The problem with batteries is that their life cycle is not as good as with the flywheel. With a battery if you heat it up quickly, and discharge it quickly, it's gone after 2 hours... especially for races where you need the energy quickly, storing it under braking and using it on corner exit. With a battery it is much more difficult to get the energy out, and to get this amount of power the battery has to be very big and you'd still probably have to change it at 12 hours in a 24 hour race."

One downside might be sitting alongside a carbon flywheel that is spinning madly. Wolf Henzler – "Yeah, you think about it." Marc – "It spins up to 36,000 rpm, but they are following all kinds of safety stuff. The flywheel is in a carbon box, and inside of that is steel... quite heavy really. We really have to be clear that we are 100% sure you can go next to it. In the beginning, another thing was electrocution, as you had some failures. At the beginning when we first tested the system... it's electric and you don't know what it's doing sometimes, we had some failures so you have to be careful. When the car is braking, and it doesn't recoup (direct an electric charge to the flywheel) and accelerates under braking, then you have problems. When we first ran the car we had some problems and we had the Williams engineers from the hybrid company to help us a little bit, but all the software is developed by Porsche. Williams provides the flywheel hardware, but all the components and systems other than the flywheel... the engines, cables, they are all made by Porsche."

The computer decides how much of the braking is to be directed to the flywheel from the regenerative braking generators, or how much is directed to the conventional front brake system. Marc – "We had a white sheet of paper in the beginning and started talking about how we were going to do it. Should we change the brake pressure to be less severe, of make it feel like other cars? You want a consistent feeling at every corner, for example when you go down the straight and brake, you want to always brake at the same point. We wanted the perfect hybrid system. Should the system charge 80% instead of 100%? It has the standard brakes, and you have millions... billions of compromises where you can change that. It's just ridiculous really, how many you have. You have 2 or 3 engineers just looking after the hybrid system while the car is actually running."

In ALMS, early hybrid systems were focused upon KERS systems that converted the heat to energy from the rear wheels only. Marc Lieb – "You are now also allowed to have it in the front, but are only allowed to use it when the car is over 120kph... with the LMP cars they want to avoid the torque vectoring and complexity, they want to ban that. I think it's quite a good idea because it is so complex and it is getting more and more like an active suspension kind of deal and is very expensive. There will be some interesting projects coming up, especially with the new regulations for Le Mans." How much heavier is the Porsche 911 hybrid vs. the standard race car? "It is between 170 and 200 pounds."

The successor to the 911 GT3R Hybrid is the mid-engine Porsche 918, again using the system of dual electric motors (one per front wheel) similarly coupled with the cockpit mounted Williams flywheel storage device, although this flywheel system of hybrid drive did not last much beyond the 2011 Porsche 918 debut, likely due to that system making the 918 a single seat car, a hard sell to even the most fanatical of enthusiasts.

Peugeot was experimenting with the Hybrid concept for their LMP1 prototype, but that effort was shelved with the closure of their racing program in early 2012. However, there was an Audi R18 based effort similarly under development, first tested in November 2011, officially known as the R18 e-tron Quattro.

Dr. Wolfgang Ulrich described the concept at Sebring in 2012. "The idea of the e-tron is to recuperate the energy used for

The original Porsche 918 from 2011 took up the passenger area with the Williams flywheel system. Fine for racing applications, but effectively made this car a single seater, and it was revised.

braking, store it in the car, and use it for additional acceleration. In addition to the standard V6 engine that we had last year in the rear of the car, which drives the rear axle, we have an electric front axle which makes it at least a part-time Quattro. The idea is an electric engine generator at the front axle, and we use that generator when we want to brake. The energy from reducing the speed is converted into electric energy which goes into a energy storage system, with a motor that spins a rotor to a very high speed level. We then can bring that electric power back to the motor to power the front axle. Then it becomes a Quattro, but the rule makers found out immediately what we wanted to do. They said, 'ok, then we have to eliminate the advantages of the Quattro.' So, they limited us to boost from the Quattro only at speeds higher than 120 kph, so we cannot use the traction advantage. But, we can add this power that we had recuperated before, but as the rule book says 'we don't want to have too much of that'. But it is an interesting way, and it's a way that shows us how they are going in the future. With these 2 electric motors we can, for a short period of time, put out an additional 200 horsepower. The R18 Ultra is 85 kg lighter because we needed to do that to bring the weight down to adjust for the hybrid system in the car. It was a big achievement from our engineers."

In other words, the energy storage is a flywheel device, using the concept as designed by Williams, and then incorporated at Porsche, except for Audi using an inboard vs. outboard generator/motor system. The Audi engineers had managed to achieve the integration of this system without a weight penalty vs. the previous years' Le Mans winning R18. Perhaps most importantly, the system is now incorporated into the standard class structure, vs. running as an exhibition or science project. An energy storage Hybrid car could now win Le Mans overall, and did in 2012/13.

The 2012 Audi R-18 e-tron Quattro that was to win the 24 Hours of Le Mans overall in both 2012 and 2013

Is the e-tron Quattro similarly controlled by either the driver, or by the pit lane engineering brain trust who map the ideal independent usage of the motors through GPS? The answer is neither. Allan McNish – "It is automatic."

Dr. Martin Muehlmeier is the head of Technology for Audi Sport – "It has added less than 100 kilos. The 2 motors are symmetrical (the electric motors at the front of the e-tron R18), as individual control is not permitted under the rules. One motor would also have been possible, but then that would have required differentials, so we decided to go for two." Is the flywheel placement similar to the Porsche with the cockpit mounted system alongside the driver? Dr. Muehlmeier – "The same, just on the other side (the Audi R18 has the driver on the right side of the car, the opposite of the LHD 911 GT-3 Hybrid)."

Was the reasoning behind using the inboard motors and driveshafts to reduce the unsprung weight at the front suspension? "No, not really, it was for packaging purposes. There was no reason for the motors to be mounted in the hub or something." Mass centralization was the goal? "Yes."

Is there a reason that there is no driver input for the engagement of the hybrid drive? Dr. Muehlmeier – "It is mandatory in the regulations… a push-to-pass button is forbidden, it has to operate automatically, it must be controlled by the ECU in the car." With these latest rules, active control from the pitlane with real-time programming of the system is similarly not allowed. "It is also forbidden. You can send data from the car to the pits, but not the other way around."

Dr. Muehlmeier also confirms that per the rules, the motors have to engage at the same time, so there is no adjusting the power delivery between left and right front wheels. Also, there is no GPS control over the implementation based upon the car 'knowing' where it is on track and when to feed in the power. "It is triggered by the speed, not by a GPS, per the regulations. And when the storage (flywheel) is empty, it goes off… which the

the driver also feels. The time of operation depends upon the braking before, but maybe for 5 or 6 seconds. We are talking about seconds, in any case." Dan Binks - "It's awesome when you can get that kind of power for a 5 or 6 second burst, that's cool stuff. For me it is much better for it to turn itself on and off by itself. I'm sure the Audi guys have got this s##t figured out to where it is going to rock. Everything they do, they do it right."

It is almost as if Marc Lieb's concerns over the present complexity of the Porsche system were taken into account with these latest rulings from the ACO. The goal is to make the energy storage technology achievable to the teams that operate without a NASA budget. Thoughts of course go to the early KERS systems in F1 that lit up a BMW Sauber mechanic, or the more recent KERS explosion in Senna's Williams garage, right after the team had won their first Grand Prix in 8 years. As for ALMS, there was the Corsa car with a KERS system for a while, and of course the Hybrid 911 previously discussed. Binks – "It's scary to me because it's all big voltage... 600v, 1000v stuff. I don't want to work on a race car that can kill me, you know what I mean? If somebody runs over me, that's a different story. With big voltage it's only going to take one mistake and somebody gets hurt."

Into this mix of AWD hybrid power application arrived Toyota with their TS030 prototype for the 2012 season. In a similar application to the earlier Corsa Hybrid or current F1 car, the Toyota uses a 300hp electric motor that drives the rear wheels, powered by a supercapacitor energy storage system. Hisatake Murata, Hybrid Project Leader at Toyota Racing and General Manager at Motor Sport Division provided some insight into the unique Toyota version of P1 Hybrid.

When did the supercapacitor become Toyota's energy storage system of choice? Mr. Murata – "At the beginning of this project, six years ago when Mr Kinoshita asked me to develop a hybrid system exclusively for motorsport, we looked at the options for energy storage: battery, flywheel and supercapacitor. During this evaluation, we discovered that the charge/discharge properties of supercapacitors made this technology the most appropriate for motorsport. Along with our technical partners, we began developing in this direction."

It is said a supercapacitor's energy storage is not as good as batteries for the same weight. Is that true with the TS030? Murata – "The important characteristic in motorsport hybrid development is speed of charge/discharge and this is where the different systems need to be judged. Braking times are so short in motorsport that we need a specific solution. To have maximum benefit from the hybrid boost, the system must fully charge during two or three seconds of braking. This is where supercapacitors have an advantage over other systems." Is the supercapacitor a custom development for the TS030? "Yes. Together with our technical partner Nisshinbo we have created a supercapacitor specifically for endurance racing, as part of the motorsport-specific Toyota Hybrid System - Racing." Is the supercapacitor a hybrid lithium ion capacitor, or is it something else? "It is not a hybrid lithium ion capacitor but to protect our technical developments we cannot explain further."

Is there any measurable degradation of the capacitor from the continuous charge and discharge cycles? Mr. Murata – "No, the supercapacitors function without noticeable degradation." Was a front wheel hybrid system considered? "Yes, we wanted to use hybrid systems on the front and rear, as we did with the hybrid Supra which won the Tokachi 24 Hours race in 2007. We even designed the TS030 to accommodate this. However the technical regulations do not allow front and rear systems so we were forced to make a choice.

Why did you choose the RWD? Murata – "The regulation limiting front hybrids to use only above 120km/h was a major factor in this decision. Quite simply, the hybrid system delivers more performance when you can deploy at all speeds. But this was not the only reason for the choice: packaging and integrating the system was also a consideration and in this sense a rear system also gave benefits."

The Toyota TS030 HYBRID racer brought real competition to Audi by winning 3 of the last 4 races of the 2012 season, and Fuji in 2013

Has the hybrid boost made rear tyre wear a challenge? "Of course this is something we were very interested to find out, but we have suffered no unexpected effects on tyre wear through using the hybrid system. The Michelin tyres we used in 2012 are not specific to our car - they were originally developed for the diesel LMP1 cars. The diesels have higher low-end torque compared to petrol cars, meaning the forces experienced by the tyres under hybrid boost are not massively different." Is there a different pit cycle for front vs. rear tyres? "No, in 2012 we changed all four tyres together."

Are there any heat sensitivity issues with the motor in the gearbox casing?

Murata – "We have already installed many kinds of cooling countermeasures before racing to avoid this becoming an issue. So we had no heat sensitivity issues with the motor in the gearbox casing throughout 2012, even in the very hot temperatures of Bahrain." Can the hybrid system be disabled from the cockpit if there are problems?

"Naturally there are safety switches to shut down the system in case of an extreme problem. But our hybrid system is an integral part of the powertrain - we do not have, and we do not want, the option to simply turn off the hybrid system and continue the race."

Is there potential for supercapacitors to replace batteries for production car hybrids in the near future? Mr. Murata offers his personal view. "It is difficult to talk in too much detail about road car hybrid technology as my job is purely in the field of motorsport. My personal belief is that supercapacitors are unlikely to replace batteries in the short term; however they have potential to compliment batteries. Supercapacitors are suitable for big deceleration situations and journeys with many stops and little distance in between. The quick charge/discharge of a supercapacitor could be used to give extra performance in sports-type road cars or for delivery trucks and buses in a city. We are now evaluating many possibilities for the future."

For their production sedan, in 2013 Mazda has introduced a system using energy recovery to charge a supercapacitor that runs the engine accessories, eliminating the engine drag of the alternator. It is only a matter of time before such production car systems are of sufficient capacity to operate an electric supercharger, allowing the use of ever smaller and more efficient engines.

Battery storage systems, while combining electric drive with internal combustion engines have become accepted technology for production cars, such as the Toyota Prius or Chevrolet Volt. The all-electric Nissan Leaf is perhaps the most widely available current example of a usable all-electric vehicle, which makes the most economic sense if one is generating their own electricity through PV technology (ie: roof mounted solar) or has access to an inexpensive power grid. As one might expect, this has led to the emergence of all-electric vehicles in motorsport.

The Toyota TS030 took center stage at the 2013 Los Angeles Auto Show

There have been numerous all-electric races, with sports car races at the Grand Prix de Pau in 2011, and the TTXGP single lap (of 27 miles) concept being well received at the Isle of Man since 2009, having now spread to a series with a support race at the United States MotoGP at Laguna Seca in 2011.

Future generations of these bikes may include pit stops for quick battery changes as needed. Or perhaps not, if the electric version of an oversized fuel tank strategy is used to stretch out the number of laps between stops. This could be accomplished either with larger or more efficient batteries, an onboard KERS, a flywheel energy storage design, compressed air energy recovery systems, or a new as-yet undeveloped approach. As always, the trade off is weight/performance vs. range. Azhar Hussain, founder of the TTXGP - "What we have done is to allow a number of other innovations to happen. We are allowing you to reclaim energy from the bikes, streamlining, front wheel drive, rear wheel drive, and dual drive systems. We aren't just dealing with the technology of running the machines, but also with the technology of running a race that doesn't use carbon. That requires a level of infrastructure that currently doesn't exist. We are looking at pit lane configurations that fit the purpose, so that we can expand it to 3 laps. There are a lot of things we have to develop."

Jeremy Burgess sees the concept of the all-electric motorcycle becoming common, especially for competition, as being far in the future – "I would think it would be rather different on an electric powered motorcycle, in the way that the power would arrive. That's something that the big companies are going to get involved at some time, but not until the fuel is gone, or the fuel is going to go. I treat it as a bit of an amusement really, interesting from an engineering exercise aspect, but I can't see for the life of me, trying to make a competitive one." Time will tell, but if there is a firm at the forefront of this industry, it is MotoCzysz.

Portland, Oregon is about as far from the traditional vehicle manufacturing and design centers of America as one can get, and perhaps this environment helps to nurture those who choose to follow a different path. Years ago, the MotoCzysz twin crank four cylinder GP machine was innovative to the extent that it was given exhibition laps before the US MotoGP at Laguna Seca. It was hardly surprising that this company would also be attracted by the wide-open rule book for the Isle of Man's inaugural carbon free TTXGP with its encouragement of innovation. Company founder Michael Czysz – "All the focus has been on these, and that's the kind of re-tool we've been painfully going through the last couple of years. We wanted to be the same kind of innovative company, but we re-tooled from internal combustion. The conclusion that many people have come to is that this is more pure prototype racing, than MotoGP."

We've all seen the alternative to pure prototype racing, which ends up being a spec series with spec engine, chassis, and tire, which Michael Czysz finds of little interest, while he laments the lack of design freedom. "You would have more interesting racing. The problem with spec racing is that it's hard to have more passing when they are all alike. They all accelerate the same, they all brake the same. I'd like to see them open up the rules in racing, and in Moto GP, have NO rules. You want to run a turbo, or 8 cylinders? Ok. You'd see better racing and that's not what is being done."

The innovative zero carbon racers of MotoCzysz

Innovators such as Czysz hark back to an earlier era, such as the 750kg maximum weight formula of 1934 for Grand Prix, or the Can-Am series of the 60s-70s. Solutions to liven up spec racing in recent years have been such gimmicks as 'Push to Pass' or 'DRS', wings that open up to reduce drag... when within a specified distance of the racer in front, and within a designated DRS "zone". All of these are to make up for the similarities in specification across the field, to try and bring excitement to the 'show'. Thankfully this is NOT a concern in zero carbon racing, as the solutions differ wildly.

The first version of the MotoCzysz for that initial TT race in 2009 had an interesting modular triple battery design, anticipating that pit stops would soon be a part of the TTXGP (which so far has not happened), to accommodate quick changes for the energy source... which in all examples to race so far, has been a battery. The 09 bike featured triple aftermarket Agni motors, arranged fore-aft with all 3 in-line at the extreme bottom of the fairing below the battery modules. Motor failure proved the Achilles heel of that initial effort, losing a motor in practice and then rider Mark Miller had to retire the bike in the race. Michael Czysz – "Agni won, but we should have won that first year if we'd gotten our s**t somewhat right. Our inexperience in combination with their motor was not good." It had been one of the few aspects of the bike that was sourced from outside the company, and for 2010 MotoCzysz would return with an extensively reworked single motor of their own design. This new motor had the equivalent of 200hp.

Michael Czysz – "The following year, Agni knew we were coming for them hard, and they pulled out a dustbin." Dustbin fairing designs had been outlawed in GP racing since 1958 due to their sensitivity to cross winds, although their aero drag is greatly reduced in comparison to a conventional fairing. Czysz – "Well, there were some winds. We had decided from day 1 not to go with the dustbin. I think the dustbin is the wrong part of the motorcycle to make aerodynamic. We are going... I hope... to come out with something more aerodynamic." So, is there is going to be a new-age Kneeler Norton coming soon from Oregon? Czysz – "It probably would work, but we can't afford to build a bike just for the Isle of Man. We build a bike that can go to Laguna, all the tracks that we run, and the Isle of Man. So, the Kneeler wouldn't work. We are working on trying to reduce the overall cross-sectional area."

With this new motor, MotoCzysz were far more in control of their destiny. General Manager Ray Crepeau - "Exactly... the power (of the triple motor version) was way down, on the new one everything was designed here. Some of the internal components are outsourced, but the overall packaging and cooling are done here. We did the frame, the swingarm, the bodywork... everything you see on this bike was built here, except for the wheels, the rotors, Brembo brakes, and maybe the clip-on bars."

The 2010 final version of the modular battery concept, designed for pit stop battery swaps and a rule change that never occurred

The 2010 bike maintained the modular battery layout of the E1pc-09 machine; however there were now 5 modules vs. the previous 3. Michael - In fact, with this bike, we can have that top battery out in a couple of minutes if we really hustle." Ray - "This was the bike where you can really see the hot-swap batteries, it was done really well and they come out really fast with one bolt to hold them on. The energy growth was phenomenal between the first bike and this bike... and from this bike to the 2011 bike, both in energy density and overall power." Michael – "They've gone up quite a bit, every year it's gone up in the 20% range while at the same time going down at least that much in size. Across the 3 generations we have seen something like a 40% improvement. We've been saying since day one that it was 2X energy density, and now this is at a good 3X. And there are people who feel that 10X energy density is coming. Get on it, there is no warm up, no clutch, just get on it and ride all day. At 4X energy density, you would have a really good alternative track bike, a racer. 10 seconds is a lifetime in racing, but this is a bike that's handmade, that didn't exist 3 years ago, and vs. a factory Yamaha or factory Ducati, how can you compare? You can't build a formula one car that can lap within 10 seconds. At 10X energy density coming down the line, we can lose 150 lbs, and before you know it we'd be under their (Moto GP) lap times with more horsepower than they do. Will that happen within our lifetimes? I have no idea, but there are people focusing upon that being forthcoming." Their 2011 machine had lapped Laguna within 10 seconds of the Moto GP pole time.

The primary key to success at this level is staying current with latest developments in energy density for the battery pack, and as one might expect they avoid giving specific information on recent developments. The obvious weak link in electric vehicle development is energy density for a given capacity, which translates into a highly limited range for street use. At the moment, the range of most production EVs have rarely exceeded 100 miles on a single charge (when operated in electric-only mode), often substantially less.

Part of the MotoCzysz success is that they use regenerative braking to restore some charge into the battery upon using the rear brakes. Energy preservation being a priority, expect front wheel regenerative braking to be eventually adopted as well. This can all be a delicate proposition as excessive regenerative braking upon lifting the throttle can upset the balance of the machine, or require a great deal of rider adjustment and anticipation. Michael Czysz – "That is one of the very powerful options of having the electric motor. You should be looking at regenerative braking like you look at throttle control. Like throttle control, it can be quite tricky." There isn't much in the way of a heat source for any KERS options to generate power, nothing close to justifying the additional complications. Michael Czysz – "The motor is 95% efficient, the heat is about 7500 watts and you need to cool it for sure. But we don't have anything like the heat source a piston engine would."

Needless to say, aerodynamic efficiency becomes a huge concern with such limits on propulsion energy. Surprisingly there have been few dustbin fairings (banned in 1958) or laydown attempts making a comeback since the typical road racing motorcycle is, as Stuart Shenton insists… "not an aerodynamic device". In a series devoid of aerodynamic limitations, it certainly could be. Aero lower fork sliders were used along with the conventional round tubes for both the '09 and '10 machines; however the 2011 machine has both lower sliders and tubes made from aero tubing. However the largest single recent aero difference for the 2011 version may be the abandonment of the hot-swap battery concept, allowing a much more condensed packaging for the battery pack. Ray - "You can save space by packaging much tighter, without the cracks and crevices that obviously take up space." The result is many inches narrower as a result of this repackaging of the battery system and the battery is no longer a prominent and celebrated design element as it was with the 2 earlier efforts. Although one assumes the battery location results in a higher CG than conventional gasoline powered 4 cylinder race machines, it is getting closer with each generation.

The carbon frame is exceedingly stout in depth and one presumes it would be massively strong, although as always with carbon assemblies looks can deceive as it's all in the weave, material, direction, and resins. Ray - "We have some help from Swift with this." Swift rapidly progressed from the initial David Bruns designed F Ford in 1983, to become a Champ Car winning manufacturer with one of the first rolling floor wind tunnels in the business.

An engineering tour-de-force, the 2011 MotoCzysz with carbon pushrod suspension, carbon frame, and a repackaged single battery concept that reduced the bulk of the machine

In 2011, Michael Rutter was to win with this new machine, with the 2010 winner was again ridden by Mark Miller, this time coming home in second place... a sweep by Motoczysz. "For 2012, again we're looking to take 2 bikes." Will these both be new generation bikes? "We are not going to do that at this time;

we will take this existing package and make some modifications to it." Their Isle of Man success along with a strong second place in the carbon-free race at the 2011 US Moto GP, shows that the sportbike developed at Motoczysz is capable of maintaining a significant race-pace for a significant length of time. In fact, their 2011 machine only narrowly missed breaking "the ton", the highly significant 100 mph average speed over a lap of the TT Mountain course. Michael Czysz – "This is probably the most significant thing to happen to motorcycles in the last 50 years. This 3rd generation bike is the most fun motorcycle I've ever ridden, and one of the fastest. People don't realize it, but this bike was a bigger departure than it was in the previous year. The first 2 years were a similar concept with the backbone chassis but this year we made the jump to get the rigidity with the backbone out of it. It was as much a clean sheet as the first one was." Rutter was also to win the TT Zero in 2012 and 2013, proving that MotoCzysz remains the class of the field.

In a race like the TT Zero event, reduced battery life from continually cycling up and down isn't really an issue compared to what hybrid racers competing at Le Mans in a 24 hour race would face. Hence, the Williams flywheel system as the kinetic storage device contained within a vacuum chamber isn't currently an option. Perhaps someday when zero-carbon motorcycle races become endurance affairs, we will see such technology adapted to suit. As for now, the drivers have to contend with a 36,000 rpm carbon buzz saw running alongside the driver seat, which one assumes would be more reassuring than having it spinning away between a rider's legs.

Michael Czysz - "We started out with the GP, which was combustion focused before our switch to electric. It's come a long way in just the handful of years that we've been doing it. The achievement from year to year has been unbelievable compared to the combustion (engine) as a whole. There is only so much we can get out of a combustion motor. As for the future plans, they have the potential for being on the cutting edge of an innovation explosion. Ray – "With the transformation to electric, Segway came on board as a title sponsor, but it has grown into a larger relationship and we are now doing projects with them. We've been hired by them to do some design work." One can only imagine the potential synergy from the sophisticated technology that has been applied to their 2 wheeled devices in providing electronically controlled stability, or using in Segway-speak "Dynamic Stabilization" being applied to a new generation of motorcycles. This and the drive-by-wire technologies in machines that Segway has under development such as the EN-V (something visually akin to a 2 wheeled Smart car) could revolutionize vehicular transportation much as it has with its trademark personal transportation device.

Michael Czysz – "We have a pipeline of unlimited things to do for a very small private company. That was the plan; we set out to build that kind of company." Expect this partnership between MotoCzysz and Segway to bear both strange and highly innovative fruit.

Segway founder Dean Kamen had previously developed such wonders as the iBot Mobility system, best described as using his later Segway technology to balance a wheelchair atop 2 wheels. Later developments include his "Luke Arm" which is essentially what one would assume, similar to Luke Skywalker's prosthetic arm from the closing minutes of George Lucas' The Empire Strikes Back.

As one might expect, the advances of the future would not be limited to improving the performance of the machines, but could similarly improve human performance. Advances in creating functional replacement limbs makes one wonder if the concept of an Avatar is not as far-fetched as it first seems. However in the past, racers have often had to invent lo-tech solutions to cope with disabilities brought on by racing injury. Mel Kenyon had but a stub for a left hand after he lost his fingers in a horrendous

Indy car fire at Langhorne. He and his family modified a glove that would hook onto the steering wheel, and he went on to race in 8 Indianapolis 500s, four of which resulted in top 5 finishes. He also was to win seven national USAC Midget championships. Only one of those USAC championships was won before his accident.

Clay Regazzoni, a F1 winner for Ferrari and Williams, had a horrendous career ending accident at the Long Beach Grand Prix in 1980 when the brake pedal broke off his Ensign F1 car at the end of the Shoreline straight. The combination of a short escape road, with broken F1 cars left on either side of it, left him little choice but to drive directly into the back of a parked Brabham in a desperate attempt to slow the car. A paraplegic as a result of the accident, Regazzoni's great drive to compete again eventually saw him return to racing with hand control systems, competing in major Rally events and in the Firehawk series 12 hour race at Sebring, teamed with similarly injured MX racer and team owner Mitch Payton.

Perhaps the most prominent amongst those currently racing with disabilities is the Italian CART champion, Alex Zanardi. Alex was in a horrific accident on the oval at Eurospeedway Lausitz in Germany when the front of the tub was torn away along with both his legs. It was only due to the extraordinary efforts of the CART safety team, that Alex survived at all. Zanardi, still having use of his remaining upper legs, has been able to use carbon prosthetic legs to operate the brake pedal. The large ring on the back of the steering wheel operates the throttle through a wide range of positions, vs. the earliest versions he had experienced using, which were essentially a thumb switch for a throttle. Alex has developed this through a number of variations to the point that he has as much or perhaps more throttle control than he had pre-accident, assuming fingers and hands are more sensitive to precise control than are feet.

One driver who is entirely using hand controls, is Michael Johnson, FF2000 racer. In Michael's case, he lost the use of his legs due to spinal injury, versus the partial amputation issues of Alex Zanardi. Michael - "It really only took me a few test sessions to get comfortable. With my background in motorcycle racing (primarily road racing, & some flat track/MX), and with all the controls on the handlebars, my responses were there. So, it was pretty simple to get used to it, it was just doing it on four wheels instead of two."

If there is a more inspirational person than Alex Zanardi, I've yet to meet them. Alex has returned to a successful racing career and developed his own refined set of hand controls for racing the car

Some motorcycle racers struggle with this transition, as they may have had little interest in the cars previously. Michael is not one of those. "I'm a car guy now. I wanted to get into something big, and Skip Barber was our options for the hand controls, and he was the one who set it up to see if I liked it. I did, and last year I was 3rd in the Championship in the Skip Barber regional series, where I ran against the national guys. It was working really well." In the case of Michael's current setup, there is a thumb throttle on the side of the wheel, and one pushes away on the steering wheel to actuate the brakes. The clutch is left hand lever operated, and the right hand operates a traditional shift lever. And an engineer who has worked with Michael is the same engineer who has worked with Zanardi on his controls.

Michael Johnson is finding success racing on 4 wheels. He has come up through karts, the Skip Barber series (3 wins), and USF2000... the first paralyzed racer to be licensed by Indycar

Yet another route has been taken by Wayne Rainey, the former 3 times 500cc World Champion, injured in 1993. In Wayne's case, he races a Superkart with motorcycle handlebars and standard motorcycle controls. There is a pneumatic operated shifter that is controlled by buttons on the steering wheel.

Another racer who could not let his injuries keep him away from the cockpit is Darrell Gwynn. A massive accident in his top fuel dragster during the 1990 season left Darrell with a broken neck, a quadriplegic. He eventually retained some limited use of his right arm. Mike Gerry is one of those who worked to create a dragster which could be controlled given this highly limited range of physical function. Mike – "Darrell, he is an amputee, his left arm was amputated. It takes us 20 minutes to get him into the car… unbolt the cage and take both side panels and cowling off. It takes 4 guys to lift him up, 2 guys to get him strapped in and into position. His right hand is tied into the controller, we Velcro him in, and then we duct tape it in because the torque of the motor will jerk your hand out. It's a throttle pedal for a hand, basically. Push forward to go, left or right to turn, and pull back for the brakes. We just put a steering wheel in the car, because it's too hard for somebody who isn't a 'joystick person' to drive. Going about 35 mph, one click to the side turns the front wheels about a quarter of an inch… which is a lot. Single speed, so there is no transmission, with direct drive through a spool." There are a number of switches and buttons on the control box. Mike – "It's for the steering, you can speed it up, or slow it down, and he's competitive." If Darrell finds the controls too sensitive, it's a quick fix and the steering can be electronically slowed down to whatever ratio is preferred. Darrell Gwynn and Don Garlits have recently been holding a series of match races in their electric dragsters, to benefit The Darrell Gwynn Foundation. "Match Races For A Cause" not only raises funds for a worthy charity, but just the fact that such races are possible gives additional hope to seriously injured racers everywhere.

Mert Lawwill, the Harley-Davidson racing legend, has developed a prosthetic arm, only in this case it was for motorcycle riding and racing applications for those who lost an arm or hand. Chris Draayer was a member of the Harley-Davidson racing team when he lost his left arm in a horrible crash at Sedalia in the 60s. Mert – "In 1990 I made him the first hand. Chris was paranoid that he would lose the hand in transport because he travelled a lot. In 2000 he approached me saying 'you've got to make me a backup one.' I figured if I'm going to make one, I'll do a CNC program and make a bunch of them. So I called several prosthetic companies and they told me 'don't waste your time, don't bother. First of all, 90% of the amputees, life is over and they don't go any further. And those who are left wouldn't want a sporting device to hang on to a motorcycle, bicycle, or snowmobile. You wouldn't sell one, so don't bother.' It took me about 2 years to sell about 10 of them, now I do them in batches of 40. If you could see what it does for people, you just can't believe it. Just because you are an amputee, life is not over."

Wayne Rainey, 3 time 500cc World Champion in motorcycle Grand Prix racing, has a kart heavily modified by his father Sandy Rainey. It incorporates motorcycle-style controls.

"I've done the hand for the last 10 years, so I'm moving on up the arm now to develop a prosthetic suspension elbow. The reason for the suspension part is that for an amputee with a missing arm to ride correctly on a motorcycle, he has to lock out his elbow. And once you lock out that elbow and go around a corner, you're body has to shift because your elbow doesn't move and it really causes uncomfortable riding. So, I've developed a shock that goes in the elbow that moves when a guy goes around a corner, so that it simulates a normal condition. I'm also addressing on other issue with this. For an amputee, when he goes to stop going downhill, he only has one arm to slow himself down... it's an off-balance thing, that can make it really hard to handle. So, I have an energizer system with electronics that energize the shock when you put the brakes on. It changes the fluid viscosity in the shock, becoming more rigid, so when you put the brakes on it stops more evenly."

"I just did the first human test on this device and it was overwhelmingly successful. The most positive rider I've ever met, is the guy who tests my elbow. He started out with a tumor on his lower arm, and ended up losing his entire right arm from cancer. He knows that the kind of cancer he has is terminal, but in the meantime he's doing all he can to help amputees, and is just the most positive person to be around. Being around somebody like that really pushes you to do something."

Does it use an accelerometer (deccelerometer?) to sense the brakes being applied? Mert – "Not at the moment, but it might be as we are looking at that and we'll see where it goes. It's a 'walk before you run' kind of deal. Right now, it uses the hydraulic pressure in the brake lines to change the shock. Think of it as instead of doing the rear brake light, it changes the shock."

One runner, Oscar Pistorius 'the blade runner', has carbon fibre blades for legs, and raced for the South African Olympic team in 2012. At one time there were concerns that he should not be allowed to qualify for the Olympics due to the technology nearing the point that the officials are unsure if the prosthesis has reached a point where it could be an advantage. Mert- "Greta Neimanas (bicycle road racer) has run into that, there are some Paralympic events where they won't allow her to run the hand I made, they say it's an unfair advantage... that's it's a race for the disabled, that she's potentially "normal". It's very satisfying to change somebody's life that much." Mert Lawwill has made a difference. To say that an amputee is no longer considered to be disabled must be the ultimate compliment.

Inventor and former AMA Grand National Champion, Mert Lawwill developed a mechanical wrist, which has allowed amputees to compete in a variety of sports with great success

Of course, disability isn't limited to missing or non-functioning limbs. There are a number of diseases that have often precluded racers from competition. That is no longer always the case, and currently the highest profile racer in this category would be Charlie Kimball of Indycar. Charlie has Diabetes, and he is the first driver in the series to compete while knowingly having the disease. Charlie – "I am proving as a living example, if you will pardon the pun… that Diabetes doesn't have to slow you down. You can still live your dreams, chase your passions, and do what you want in life. For someone who is part of the Diabetes community, who lost a friend or has a family member… they come up and share their stories with me. It means a lot to me that I'm having an impact by doing what I love, driving race cars…. and at the same time being fulfilled by those relationships and connections."

Mid-Ohio winner Charlie Kimball is the first to knowingly compete in Indycar with Diabetes. His blood sugar monitor is the small white dashboard to the upper right of the steering wheel

The son of Gordon Kimball carries with him homage to both his team owner and his father's long career in racecar engineering and design. Charlie - "When we were picking out car numbers the team said we got numbers 38 and 83. I asked my Dad if there was any significance that he knew of, and he said, 'yeah, Chip drove my car in 83.' A lot of people don't realize the reason my car is number 83, is that 1983 was Chip Ganassi's best finish in the 500, in a car my father designed." By mid-season 2013, Charlie had joined the ranks of Indycar race winners, with a convincing victory at Mid-Ohio.

In closing this vision of the future of racing, one cannot ignore the Delta Wing concept racer pioneered by Ben Bowlby. Narrow front track does not begin to describe the car, which resembles the Goldenrod LSR car of the early 1960s when viewed from the front, and an early 80's BLAT Eagle when viewed from the side or rear. Originally designed for the Indycar series as a single seat replacement for the now retired Dallara chassis, the reactions to the car spanned the entire spectrum. Only one thing was agreed upon by everyone, and that was the recognition of the Delta Wing as a bold statement of design innovation. Dan Gurney's All American Racers has taken up the challenge of turning this design concept into AAR's first entry at Le Mans, a race that Gurney won in 1967 with the Mk. 4 Ford.

Is the car as much of a next generation BLAT (Boundary Layer Adhesive Technology) Eagle as it appears to be? Ben Bowlby – "It is. When you look at it… that is what the car really is. I think it's one of the reasons that Dan is so motivated. We've developed the car with CFD, and so what we did was to take the geometry of that car, applied it, and made it work. From the very first year zero, it exceeded the performance. We continued to develop it, and the aero is extremely powerful. It is bringing back some of the best technology, and I'm proud that it's got part of Dan Gurney's thinking. It is an absolute BLAT underbody."

What part of that similarity to the early 80's BLAT Eagle had brought Dan Gurney and AAR into the Delta Wing program? Dan – "There was absolutely none, I talked to Ben a lot and he is a terrific guy. I felt that somebody should try and step up to help if they can. He can't do it by 'chin music' alone."

Gurney continues – "We thought we were marginally close to the edge so we wanted to see if we could improve it. Ben, the designer of the Delta Wing…we showed him some footage of our car that ran in 1981 with Mike Mosley and Geoffrey Brabham. He said 'Dan, would it be ok if we were to jack the car up?' We have an 81 Eagle in our little museum… the Pepsi Challenger. I aid, 'Sure, let's do it' so we digitized the thing. Once we put the digitized information into the CFD, all of a sudden it was terrific… a big improvement. So, we went ahead with it and that's what we are running now. The BLAT side of it was a definite help. Ben got all excited; it actually made a huge difference in the car. It's got a lot of 1981 DNA in it."

The Delta Wing at its public exhibition debut at the 12 Hours of Sebring in 2012, driven by Marino Franchitti.

It is obvious that Dan has a great deal of respect for Bowbly and his abilities. Gurney – "Ben was the one that asked the question, he knew that there might be something there. His curiosity was very important in making it happen. And he doesn't think any of it would be here without us, which is awfully nice. In addition to being a thinker who is out there... outside the envelope, he's also a very good leader. I think it is going to turn out very good for him and everybody involved."

Simon Marshall - "I worked with Ben Bowbly for 10 years at Lola from 92 to 2002, and that how I know him. He phoned me up mid-2011, and we rocked up to Dan Gurney's place and then we rented a house, me and Zach, and Ben, Zach's wife, my wife, our dogs... John Ward lived nearby, it was like we were in this little club where all we did was work, go home, drink beer, work."

"It was only good because it was interesting to work with the guys we were working with... at Dan Gurney's place and in California. It took it out of the regular and made it into this mission."

So how does the BLAT system work? Simon – "This tunnel coming through here was inspired by the '81 Eagle, and it has a little sort of aluminum tunnels extending ahead of the big old diffuser which comes out of the sidepod. Allied with our delta wing shape, we trip a vortex off this delta shape here which wraps underneath, grows bigger and bigger and is super-low pressure. Which is how a Delta Wing works, and that's the same as what sticks out the front of the Eagle sidepods. John Ward was on the design team, and they dug up the drawings of the original shape of the BLAT Eagle. I definitely remember them in the showroom under the Pepsi Challenger car. John & Ben together worked it up into a series using an expansion ratio to scale it to this car. Then Ben took the idea and put it into cad on this car and sent it for CFD testing. We did around 100 runs with CFD through the entire project, which turns out to be about 100,000 dollars, 1000 dollars every time you pressed 'go' on the program. We worked with a group in England called Total Sim. Ben knows them, they have a good reputation and they came in absolutely spot on. When we got the car back in Moseville and put the car in the full size tunnel it was really close."

Note the leading edge of the delta wing shape that is shared with a
1983 Eagle (above) and the 2013 Delta Wing.
It was the secret to success for both designs.
— Top photo courtesy of Dennis Firestone

Trevor Harris was a team engineer at AAR during that 1981 season - "Dan was the one who coined the term BLAT. I recall once upon a time that Dan and I were sitting on a trailer, trying to come up with a name for what we had going with that Eagle aerodynamically. I credit Dan for coming up with BLAT, and he and I laughed at great lengths about that name when it started appearing in print with several articles in 1981. We had this miraculous aerodynamic system on the car, which until the past year had not been really identified for what it was. They discovered that what we had going on under that early Eagle was something that was more interesting that what we were aware of at the time. The term BLAT was actually pretty appropriate. It requires a sharp lip at the lead-in of the leading edge of the underwing, where the air went into it. There wasn't a radius on that corner, it was a very sharp corner. It turns out that the sharp corner causes a rotating vortex to form, the length of the diagonal sharp edge leading in to the underwing."

Note the Delta Wing shape in plan, and the sharp edge to it

Trevor - "That vortex actually helps keep the air attached on the surface behind the leading edge. It is a vital thing, if you put a radius on that corner, it doesn't do that. They verified this at the Eagle works in the past year with the development of the Delta Wing. It was a modification that was developed very late.

Something like a month before they ran the car, they made that change and it really improved it. We really did have Boundary Layer Adhesion Technology from the vortex, something that we were unaware of back in that era. CFD didn't exist in those days. It took all those years to find out that Boundary Layer Adhesion Technology was real... it wasn't a figment of Dan's and my imagination."

The rest of the Delta Wing / Eagle underbody is conventional

The BLAT Eagles ran for years in CART, crowd favorites everywhere they raced with their booming exhaust and staggering grunt coming off the corners. Ironic indeed that the big booming V8 Eagles from 30 years in the past would form so much of the basis for an experiment in efficiency.

Were there a great number of compromises that had to be made, to convert the original Delta Wing chassis into a wider 2 seat Le Mans prototype? Ben Bowlby – "Yeah, there were a lot of compromises; it hurt us a lot, but we got it together. Aero is always about making all the parts work together."

In 1976, the Project 34 Tyrrell 6 wheeler had a narrow front track design, with reduced frontal area and a large actual footprint due to the doubling of the number of tires. For 1977, the team went to a wide-track 6 wheeler design, as they mentioned that they had learned that track was a function of handling.

Ben Bowlby – "It is very difficult to say, as there could have been a huge aerodynamic difference from just a few inches of track width. There were a number of different reasons as to why the wider front track could have been an advantage. In our case, if we were to widen the front track right now, we would actually pick up a lot of understeer." The Delta Wing has a short front suspension, and looks highly conventional under the skin, with short double a-arm suspension with outboard coil-over shocks, the advantages of not having to funnel airflow through the front suspension compared to most contemporary designs with aero-driven pushrod, pullrod, or rocker types of suspension. Where it looks odd is that the a-arms from each side nearly touch at the center of the car. Ben – "Yes, independent front suspension with about 8" arms. With the amount of travel that we are talking about, there is very little camber change. We are basically running zero camber, and we use the high caster angle in the geometry at the front for a camber gain."

Another radical experiment in narrow front track was the 1976 Tyrrell Project 34, that was the technological shock of the season

The lightness and efficiency of the car mean spring rates that one never hears in modern road racing. Ben – "The front of the car has 400# springs at a ratio of 1.3, so when you take the square of the motion ratio, there is only about 250# on the front for a wheel rate. At the rear we are running 750# springs at 1:1." It seems that in the front, the effective spring rate for the tire could exceed the spring rate in the suspension. Ben – "Absolutely, it could be more." Adding to the uniqueness, there is no anti-roll bar in front, which is likely done because that sway bar could compromise front tire grip, and begs the question… how much body roll could there be in a 24" wide car?

Does the car get its front grip from a high degree of underbody downforce on the front? Ben – "No, there is about a 25% aero balance on the front, and the low pressure area is directly under the driver. Everything is in harmony, a bit like an airplane where you have to have the mass distribution and the air distribution in harmony."

The aero has been extensively tested, even backwards in the wind tunnel at speeds up to 200mph, to alleviate concerns with the Le Mans organizers that the car would lift off the ground if it were to spin at speed. There has been a recent history of blow-overs at the circuit, like with Webber's Mercedes in 1999 which took off into the sky and did backward cartwheels like an Unlimited Hydroplane off into the trees. Bowlby – "We have tested it 360 degrees at 200mph, and it has no propensity to get airborne. We have half the underbody area of an LMP1, but look at the distribution of the weight… it's like a triangle and you can imagine how much less over-turning moment that there is, so we are in great shape. We have taken extremely seriously the requirements to keep a super-lightweight car on the ground, outside of normal operating conditions. We are so out there on the ragged edge, and we are trying to do everything we can." As a result there are flaps that deploy when the car is backwards to the wind, with Gurney flaps at the end to create what Ben refers to as a 'High Pressure Puddle" in an area that would otherwise create lift.

The Delta Wing was the most unique car of the 2012 racing season

How does this all work from the driver's perspective? One would think most of the concerns would be from the narrow track front, and the turn-in response. Marino Franchitti has been driving the car in testing, and offers these observations. "My understanding is that most of the weight is on the rear, and you aren't trying to turn the weight like with a normal car. I can only tell you how it feels, and it feels good. Within 2 laps, you know if a car feels good or not, and this car feels good, it turns in very well. The track we ran at Buttonwillow had no hairpins, so Sebring was the first time we've had it through a hairpin. We've got a long way to go, but so far it works in all areas, braking, turn-in... the base we are building from is very good. We're not sure exactly where we are going to be in performance compared to the regular LMP cars, but we're a class of one. We want to be ahead of the LMP2s, and behind the LMP1's... that's what we're aiming for. I think that Indycar did us a favor by not using the

concept. As a fan, I think the worst thing it could have been was to become a spec racer. Here, it can be completely cutting edge, with petrol cars, diesel cars, and the great melting pot of technology that is these sports cars. That's what I love about sports car racing, I love the innovation. The history of the sport... to try something that nobody in my generation will get... not just driving a new version of something, but truly like nothing before... it's very important for me to be involved."

Of course, looking back at the similarly radical six wheeled P34 Tyrrell, its Achilles Heel proved to be the limited available compounds for the tires, vs. those available for the 4 wheel competition. In the end, by 1978 Tyrrell had reverted to a traditional 4 wheeled design. Bowlby has gotten assurances from Michelin that there will be tires that suit the needs of this unique design. Ben – "That was one of the things from the first round of talks... without that, the car would never have rolled." The following season of 2013, this issue again became of primary concern. Simon Marshall - "Because of the loss of Michelin and Nissan we've gone backwards, so now it's been up to us to go forward again. Bridgestone were keen to get involved with us as they had molds for this crazy tire from the Delta Wing Indycar proposal with Chip Ganassi. So we got them to make us some tires really quick."

Trevor Harris had similarly grappled with the sensibilities of running smaller tire sizes with his early Can-Am Shadow. Trevor - "I was pretty familiar with the original Corvair engine, and by mid-1968 I was looking at making a very small Can-Am car, and my original concept was to use a Corvair engine. Don Nichols had a Lola that needed a Chevrolet installed in it, to be driven in Japan by Pedro Rodriguez, so I installed it and they ran it at Fuji. That was a few months before the Shadow project actually started. I showed him what I was up to with my Can-Am project."

One could certainly see where the ultra-low Shadow would have been a packaging ideal for installing a boxer engine like a

Corvair in the rear. Trevor – "Potentially, there were a number of things about it that looked good to me. The car was interesting in a lot of ways, as there were some good things about it, but also some very bad things about it. The project technically was kicked off when Firestone agreed to build the tires. Well, Don Nichols asked if there was any possibility that I might put a Chevrolet V8 in it. So, the original design then had a Corvette radiator on either side of the car behind the rear wheels. That didn't work, it did not cool properly. So, I ended up personally cutting off the back end of the car, and we mounted a wing on it. The neatest aerodynamic configuration that ever ran on that car was the wing we ran with the radiators inside it. I had the air coming in the nose of the wing, through the radiators, and then the air went out the back... it was a very special and cool wing. That ran at only one race, St. Jovite, but unfortunately we didn't have enough money to pay for our spare engine from Al Bartz. So, we had an engine that only ran on 7 cylinders and that's how we ran the race. Then the car was crashed into when we had a trailer accident. I thought there was no hope for it, so I left the project at that point. Within the next year they got UOP (for a sponsor) and the rest is history. They were very well funded after that, and won the '74 Can-Am. In retrospect, if I hadn't left when I did and stuck it out, I would have done the next car which would have made use of the good things, shed a lot of the bad things, and could have done a very legitimate second car, quite possibly without the super tiny tires."

As it often seems to go, when a radical design appears using different tires from the balance of the field, there are fewer tire compounds and options available. Trevor – "That's what happened with my Shadow. The wheels on the front were 10"x 11" wide, and the rear wheels were 12"x 18" wide. The tires tended to run very hot, hotter than they ever expected. So, the tire compounding was several steps behind what the regular people (with conventional Can-Am cars) could run. So, even if the car was 100% as good in every respect as everybody else, which it wasn't, it would have been seconds off the pace just because of tire compounding. We never had engines that were the equal of what McLaren ran, as we never ran anything bigger than a 427 engine in the car, when all the good guys were running 494s."

How much of the driving force behind the design was for an extremely lowered CG, or was it mostly aero and frontal area? Trevor – "The driving forces were all of the above." So, for Delta Wing in 2013, is it back to the old Shadow/P34 Tyrrell dilemma? Simon Marshall - "I think we got our first tires in mid-March and we are now waiting for some experimental tires, as they have their production going to serve the Indycar series. They have to work around their Indy car commitments and so we are testing in June. I think they'll have about 5 testing tires and we'll try to get through them and work on from there."

The car is really strong on the straights, faster than the competition. Simon – "Especially because we have low drag and since drag goes up by a square of the speed, we look a lot better at the end of the straight than the prototypes, because by regulation they have to run a ton of drag. That's just the way the regs are."

It is clear that Ulrich Baretzky's vision at Audi, of an ever smaller and more efficient powerplant would dovetail well with Bowlby's vision of the Delta Wing, which is similarly pushing the concept of smaller, lighter, less powerful, but of equivalent performance. For now, it is the groundbreaking "Less is More" concept in racing. Ben – "Ulrich was the one who told me that to have a global race engine like that in LMP1 you would need a car like this. We were sitting in this paddock 3 years ago, discussing this program. He (Ulrich Baretzky) was another founding influence." Baretzky – "It is a very smart approach, a very good project." Both of these creative forces in racing have come to the same conclusion at the same time. Ulrich Baretzky – "Yes, it's called efficiency."

Jay Leno is another believer in such advances. He has an incredible wide ranging collection of rare and exotic vehicles across every era and means of propulsion. Yet, one stands out... and that is The Rocket, designed by Gordon Murray. That Jay considers his Murray Rocket to be the (low speed) performance equivalent of Murray's later McLaren F1 is high praise indeed. The McLaren F1, a design that won the 24 hours of Le Mans overall, is still unsurpassed. The Rocket is another elegant predecessor sharing that same concept being pursued with the Delta Wing, in this case by 20 years vs. the 30 years for the BLAT Eagle.

The Gordon Murray section of Jay Leno's Garage. On the left is the light and nimble Rocket, pure joy and efficiency.

As always, radical change has its detractors. Simon Marshall – "There were press releases as we were going, and people were saying 'it's never going to turn.' So, we would find quotes from experts about 'how they knew race cars and this isn't going to work.' We would find a photo of them and put them on the wall. So, we had like this s**t list of the 'experts' who said it wasn't going to work."

It all reminds one of Gary Anderson who had written before the 2013 season about the obvious aero deficiencies of the 2013 Mercedes GP car, which had been on the pole for 4 consecutive

Grand Prix, prior to winning at Monaco. Simon - "He was on our s**t list, because he talks a lot. He gets his face in Autosport every week, but normally he doesn't have to prove anything."

Ben Bowlby – "My take on it is that the naysayers are the same naysayers who say they hate spec racing and yet they don't like it when you want to see what you can do. I don't get that at all. We resist change like no other species, and yet we adapt faster than any others. We are the ultimate weed aren't we? We can proliferate in any conditions, we do adapt to change. So, we don't want change, but we adapt. It's all a bit of a paradox, really. The American Institute of Architects invited me to come and give them a speech, because I was talking about 'Form Follows Function'. Louis Sullivan said that, and then said 'Ornament is a Crime', and that you should only do what is real. They mentioned that with every landmark building, initially people say how they hate it. Once it is built, then they become fans of it, they love it. 100 years after the Architect is dead, it's held up as one of the great architectural examples of its time. There you go."

Radical innovation can either reward or take a heavy toll upon the visionaries, but fortunately they are a determined lot. In years to come, the technological gains that result will filter down to the benefit of us all.

CPSIA information can be obtained at www.ICGtesting.com
Printed in the USA
LVOW10s1628150614

390125LV00025B/1245/P